Food for Thought

D1807398

frei
9.9. 10
JF

Julia Bernstein is a lecturer at the Institute for comparative educational studies and social sciences of Cologne University.

Julia Bernstein

Food for Thought

Transnational Contested Identities and
Food Practices of Russian-Speaking Jewish Migrants
in Israel and Germany

Campus Verlag
Frankfurt/New York

Published with the support of "Stiftung Irène Bollag-Herzheimer", "Fazit-Stiftung" and "Hans-Böckler-Stiftung".

Bibliographic Information published by the Deutsche Nationalbibliothek:
The Deutsche Nationalbibliothek lists this publication in the Deutsche Nationalbibliografie.
Detailed bibliographic data are available in the Internet at http://dnb.d-nb.de.
ISBN 978-3-593-39252-3

Printed on acid free paper.
Printed in Germany

For further information:
www.campus.de
www.press.uchicago.edu

I would like to dedicate this book to my beloved grandfather,
Max Segal

Table of Contents

Acknowledgments

I am grateful to the Hans Böckler Stiftung for awarding me a doctoral fellowship grant as well as for partially financing the linguistic corrections of this manuscript and the publication of this book.

I would also like to thank the Stiftung Irène Bollag-Herzheimer and the Fazit Stiftung for their support in financing the proof-reading fees and the printing costs of this book.

Special thanks to Georg and Franziska Speyer'schen Hochschulstiftung for awarding me a one year fellowship grant for the last stage of my work including revisions for publishing.

And, I am also grateful for the financial support received from the Bucerius Center for Research of German Contemporary History and Society. This grant supported the first stage of the German fieldwork.

I would like to express my heartfelt gratitude to my supervisors of this research project—Professor Gisela Welz and Professor Lena Inowlocki. Both gave me endless support and their ongoing advice guided me throughout all stages of this work. Since becoming acquainted with Professor Lena Inowlocki in Israel, I have been inspired by her reflective and professional work, her deep understanding of various key aspects of migration research and Jewish identity, as well as by her openness, humane character, and interest in my work. All played a crucial role in my decision to engage in doctoral studies in Germany. The readiness of Professor Gisela Welz to serve as my adviser during the second stage of the German fieldwork enabled me to advance this study within the cultural anthropology framework. Her ongoing and strong support, thoughtful comments, and her deep understanding of cultural anthropology and transnational research were of inestimable help throughout the entire research process, and in preparing this text. Her excitement about the topics investigated and consistently constructive suggestions encouraged me throughout the entire process. Both Professors Welz and Inowlocki enabled me to present parts of my work in different academic frameworks and assisted me in establishing important academic contacts. I am indebted to both for their emotional support, belief in me and in this project, and thoughtful suggestions to improve this work.

I would like to express my gratitude to the Institute for Cultural Anthropology and European Ethnology for placing at my disposal the office in which I wrote and prepared this manuscript.

I am very appreciative of Professor Karlheinz Schneider who gave generously of his time in our numerous and very interesting informal discussions of different aspects of this work, as well for his emotional support and belief in me. All of which motivated me throughout all stages of this work. I am also grateful to him for important academic contacts that facilitated the process of my own academic socialization in Germany as well as for his enthusiastic support for the idea of engaging in a comparative research project in the contexts of Israel and Germany.

I would like to thank Dr. Peter Lemish for his excellent, detailed, and very patient work on language issues in the preparation of this manuscript, as well as for his valuable, sensitive, and constructive remarks and suggestions. His critical and direct comments as well as notation—"NC" [not clear]—helped me be precise and to reflect on taken for granted concepts. I am grateful to Tina Delavre for the last linguistic corrections of this work as well as for her emotional support. I would also like to express my gratitude to Rebecca Schaarschmidt and Julia Flechtner of Campus Verlag for their help in the lay-out of this book.

My special thanks and gratitude to Dr. Deborah Golden for her initial idea (14 years ago) that I combine migration research, material culture studies, and my strong involvement and interest in the visual arts. This integration enabled me to develop the unique analytic approach to the study of the visual presentation of artefacts and everyday life of migrants presented in this manuscript. Her very interesting academic work influenced my thinking and approach to both research and preparation of this manuscript. And, our very pleasant exchanges motivated me throughout this project. In particular, I want to thank her for her remarks on an early draft of the second chapter that presents my analysis of the participants' perceptions of capitalism.

Also, I am very appreciative of the always highly interesting and productive discussions with Professor Alex Demirović and for his thought provoking questions and sensitive proposal of various arguments. His comments to the topics of racism, anti-Semitism, "being Jewish" in the SU and participants' perceptions of capitalism were especially meaningful and important in improving this work.

I owe a considerable debt to Professor Yifaat Weiss for supporting my desire to engage in comparative research as well as for initiating very important academic contacts on my behalf, including the introduction to Professor Lena Inowlocki. Her invitations to participate in different academic conferences enabled me to present different parts of my study that stimulated and enriched my work. And, her helpful feedback and critiques, too, were important in improving this study. I also would like to thank Lea Dror for our conversations, as well as for her support and comments.

I would also like to express my gratitude to Professor Yoram Carmeli who supervised my master's degree thesis that served as the basis for the Israeli case study in this comparative research project. Professor Carmeli played a crucial role in my decision to choose qualitative research and cultural anthropology in combination with sociology as my professional interests. His professional and emotional support and valuable comments in the initial stages of this research helped me further my thinking and development of new directions for the analysis.

Also, I want to thank Professor Nurit Bird David, Professor Michael Soltman, Professor Ilan Talmud, and Professor Esther Levinger, all of Haifa University for sharing with me their academic knowledge and for their support, investment of time, and inspiration that I received from their lectures and seminars.

Thanks to Professor Ursula Apitzsch, Professor Andreas Gotzmann, Professor Doron Kiesel, Dr. Volker Harms, Dr. Julia Lerner, and Dr. Ulrike Schrader for inviting me to present parts of my work on several occasions in different academic frameworks and for their willingness to share valuable comments and thoughts with me.

And, special acknowledgment to Agnieszka Satola and Andrea Neugebauer for their important contributions during our work group in which we regularly presented empirical materials and parts of our doctoral research works for common analysis and discussion. I want especially to thank Dr. Ramona Lenz and Agnieszka Satola for their emotional support during the last stages of preparing the manuscript.

Thanks, in particular, to Alexii Eremenko for his important remarks on the chapter about the perception of Russian-speakers abroad about WWII and the Holocaust.

This study and manuscript would not have been possible without my partnership with participants in Israel and Germany. I am deeply grateful to them for the generous time they invested in speaking with me, their cooperation, and willingness to share their insights and thoughts. My special thanks to Veronika and Yuri Mostoslavski for their emotional support and for collecting artifacts at the first stage of the fieldwork in Israel.

My extended family accompanied me throughout all the various stages of the research process and I am especially grateful to them all. In particular, I want to thank my parents Anna and Boris Simonov, for their contributions of different visual artefacts for analysis, for assisting me contacting participants, for our many discussions of different topics related to this research project and for their support and belief in me. Nor, do I want to neglect thanking them, in particular, for their time and energies in taking care of my children and for their delicious meals—all of which enabled me to invest the time needed to dedicate myself to this work. I am very grateful to my grandfather, Max Segal, for his efforts, patience, critical questions, and very valuable analytic contributions during our discussions of different chapters. In particular, I want to thank him for his analytical ability to question and to reflect on the things I have come to take for granted. I am also very appreciative of the help of my mother-in-law Natella Fedorischsheva who provided me with multiple contacts to participants and, as well, shared with me her thoughtful insights and constructive comments of my analyses. I am also grateful to her for taking care of my children, which enabled me to work on the preparation of this manuscript and for the tasty meals she prepared for us.

And, my very warm thanks also to Isana Leiderman for her strong emotional support during the all stages of the process and our inspiring friendship.

Finally, I want to express my heartfelt gratitude to my husband, Costa Bernstein, who has supported me—always—both emotionally and practically—throughout this process. I benefited inestimably from our discussions about my doubts, his critical comments about my interpretation of findings, his deep understanding of various situations I was confronted with, and for his unlimited investment of time in our children while I wrote this work. I am also very grateful and appreciative of his professional design of the visual material presented in this manuscript.

May, 2010 Julia Bernstein

1 Migration collages: Studying Russian-speaking Jews in Israel and Germany

The study focuses on migrants who are involved, by necessity, in reconstructing their cultural perceptions as well as finding and confirming their place in a new reality. The comparative investigation presented here was conducted in two different contexts—Germany and Israel—among Jewish immigrants who came from the former Soviet Union (SU) after the initiation of *Perestroika*. The study's principal aim is to examine the multiple affiliations of immigrants that were shaped and modified in these two different cultural and social contexts. This analysis highlights and illuminates the cosmological perceptions and self-definitions of migrants transported from the SU along with their own meaningful experiences and interpretation of key concepts and symbols (Golden 2002; Stonequist 1935, 1937). Undertaken as a project in cultural anthropology, this study aspires to highlight the sites of conjunction and contradictions between, on the one hand, the ideas and perceptions that evolved while living in the SU; and, on the other hand, the expectations of receiving societies, normative thinking, and everyday knowledge of dominant host society.

1.1 Migration and socio-cultural affiliations

One of the basic, central premises of the study is that the perceptions as well as the physical conditions of the individual are dynamic and subject to change. Therefore, identities of individual and collective affiliations also undergo changes. As, for example, in the foods selected and prepared by immigrants on their dining table. Hence, we will find that these food products symbolize being—Russian, Jewish, Israeli, German, educated, European and/or that they signal transnational practices of belonging to a certain social stratum.

In investigating the migrant experience, I assume that people do not *bear* or transport with them a self-contained completed culture, but rather there is fluid nature to cultural affiliations as they select and employ cultural elements that are integrated through involvement in special situations, states, or conditions of their existence (Bloch 1963; Boyarin 1994; Gudeman and Rivera 1990; Kalekin-Fishman 2000; Welz 1996, 1997, 1998). Hence, I assume that culture is created through dynamic dialogues as well as permanent changes and modifications, rather than being limited to preserving of stable habits and practices. Therefore, based on these assumptions, this study sought to understand how different affiliations of migrants—be they cultural Russian, European, ex-Soviet, Jewish and different Others—are constructed, modified, co-exist, and presented/performed in particular situations in response to needs within specific situations. Bodnar (1985) referred to this process of identity redefinition as *transplantation.*

Accordingly, analyses advanced in this study do not perceive participants through insulated categories, such as Jewish, Soviet, Russian or German, but rather as "doing being Jewish" (Inowlocki 2000, 175) or doing being—ex-Soviet, Russian, Israeli, or German—through their dynamic practices and everyday interactions. The findings demonstrate that multiple identities co-exist and often contradict one another in various ways: Interviewees speak Russian and act according to Russian cultural practices, but are offended if referred to as Russians; or, they consume pork and simultaneously feel themselves to be Jews, accept support by the social welfare system but perform elitist cultural *habitus,* invest significant energies and time over three days to prepare meals for a birthday celebration, but claim that food "has actually no meaning for spiritual life." In addition, participants in both contexts articulated affiliation with different collective and "imaginary communities" (Anderson 1991), often expressed through linguistic forms of "we" and "they." These uses were created, changed in situ, presented, confirmed, and performed in various manners. For example, self-referential terms *nashi*[1] and *svoi* [lit. ours, ourselves, our own,[2] Rus. approximated meaning as "people of our kind" or those who

---

1 See Caldwell (2005) for analyses of the centrality of the concept "nashi" and its instrumentalization in Russian advertisements.

2 Whereas only objects can be literally possessed in languages such as Hebrew, German, or English, in Russian the linguistic construction "nash or svoi person" and "nashi or svoi people" [lit. "my person" meaning "person of my kind," and "our people" meaning "people of our kind"] is constructed with the same word of possession and can have a symbolic meaning of common belonging, as in this case.

represent a unified "us"] were involved in a very dynamic and fluid process of *doing being nashi* that could be called *nashi-zation*. The meanings evolving in this process are presented throughout different chapters of this work.

Thus, the numerous examples of empirical evidence presented throughout this monograph demonstrate different uses and modified meanings of key cultural symbols in the Russian language.

1.2 The research approach

The theoretical background integrated throughout these discussions involves two principal domains: First, sociological and anthropological literatures in the area of "migration research." Particular emphasis is placed on research involved in developing the transnational theoretical perspective, in general, and involvement of groups investigated, in particular. Second, domains within the sociology and anthropology of food that study the importance of food in persons' lives and the establishment of collective cultural, social, national affiliations, and hierarchies of power. In particular, the study focused on the literature that analyzes migrants' food consumption and food entrepreneurship in different countries as compared with patterns constructed by the groups investigated in this research.

Migration and material culture research continue to be treated with disdain by scholars. Indeed, Jackson and Holbrook observed that in the case of consumption there is a "patronizing view of apparently undifferentiated members of an anonymous mass society" (Jackson and Holbrook 1995, 1913). Similarly, I found in my review of the migration literature that migrants are often presented as a passive marginal group—deprived of a voice, of any understanding of events in the new society, and of their own opinions and rights. According to this view, all migrants' transported resources represent deficits rather than contributions to the receiving-host society. Therefore, the assumption seems to be that these transported views are "frozen," permanently; that is, kept from learning and adaptation (Morawska 2003; Schiller, Basch and Blanc-Szanton 1997).

In contrast, the basic assumption underlying the investigation reported here is that consumption and migration processes[3] are acts of personal and collective agency. Accordingly, migrants are perceived as "knowledgeable consumers" (Jackson and Holbrook 1995) and knowledgeable, responsible, and mature agents who are sensitized through migration experiences as they confront and cope with different *social worlds,* make decisions that affect their lives, and change their social and local environment (Bodnar 1985; Kivisto 1990). Hence, migrants as the subject of this study are not viewed as persons who need to be reshaped, resocialized, and treated like children (Golden 1996, 2002), nor are they considered to be socially incompetent or immature (and consequently unauthorized) members of society.

Given the intent to investigate everyday practices of Russian-speaking Jews, as well as, their patterns of consumption/procurement in the Russian food stores in Israel and Germany, the transnational theoretical perspective initiated by the American anthropologists Schiller, Basch, and Blanc-Szanton (1997) and developed since by many different researchers was selected as potentially very applicable to this study (e.g., Appadurai 1991; Gold 2001; Hannerz 1998; Levitt and Glick Schiller 2004; Levitt and Sorensen 2004; Morawska 2004; Olwig and Sorensen 2002; Pessar and Mahler 2001; Pries 1997; Römhild 2002; Vertovec 2004). The primary rationale underlying this decision is that this approach to migration does not assume it is an exceptional or static state, but rather a continuous, dynamic process to be investigated in terms of how social actors participate in multiple social environments. Furthermore, migration processes and the establishing of enclaves need to be examined in light of the dynamics of globalization in which the physical barriers between societies have become porous due to the media and modern means of transport. In this new reality, immigrants have continuous access to information about their society of origin and so refresh, renew, and modify old models and practices.

This approach stands in contrast to previously dominant "host society–centered" (Morawska 2003) theoretical models of adaptation and assimilation based on envisioning societal space as a "closed container" (Schroer 2004) within a definitive closed territory and border. Rather, in the approach adopted in this study, the theoretical constructs of *transmigration* and

---

3 *Migration process,* as used in this monograph, refers to the years spent in preparing for emigration, the act of emigration, the transition into the new society that may take place over many years.

transnationalism were deemed to be especially appropriate and fruitful for this investigation, because they help to develop of a new perspective on immigrants' lifestyles. Furthermore, this pair of concepts has the potential to shift the analytical focus of research from viewing the "place of origin" and the "place of destination" as "binary opposites" (Levi-Strauss 1970) to understanding the moves involved in sustaining cross-border livelihoods (Olwig and Sorensen 2002, as cited by Levitt and Sorensen 2004, 2). According to this perspective, migrants are involved in managing a transnational social field composed of multistranded social relations in different countries. This is what Levitt and Sorensen defined as "a set of multiple interlocking networks of social relationship through which ideas, practices, and resources are unequally exchanged, organized, and transformed" (Levitt and Sorensen 2004, 3).

The creation and modification of constructed identities of immigrants in transnational space, without closed national borders, fits the currently observable situation. Immigrants living in Israel or Germany have access to live Russian TV broadcasts transmitted from the former Soviet Union [44 channels in Israel and 19 in Germany] and different world channels translated into Russian in the receiving society.[4] These media outlets enable them to engage in a variety of activities: follow news from their society of origin; read Russian newspapers[5] and books regularly; enjoy broadcasts of performances by visiting Russian theatre companies and musical groups; purchase "their" groceries in Russian shops; fly to their society of origin for holidays; and invite friends and relatives from former Soviet republics (or those who have already emigrated elsewhere) to visit them in Israel or Germany. One can even observe [especially in Germany] the development of organized material support for relatives and friends who remained in the state of origin (e.g., monetary payments as well as packages containing clothing, food, electronic equipment, kitchen appliances, and toys).

Finally, in looking beyond this study, the findings from the fieldwork in Israel and Germany reported in this monograph are consistent with the trend in contemporary anthropological and sociological research to investi-

---

4 Media in Israel consist of: (a) six Israeli channels broadcasting with translated Russian subtitles, one Russian Israeli channel; (b) approximately 22 channels transmitted from the CIS in Russian; and (c) approximately 15 channels from different other countries translated into Russian (or with subtitles).

5 As of 2005, there were nearly 100 newspapers and magazines published in the Russian language in Israel (Yelenewskaya 2005, 267).

gate transnational actions, activities, and phenomena in a particular society (or more in comparative research) as a case study for engaging in holistic macro-analysis in the future (e.g., Appadurai 1991; Guarnizo 2003; Guarnizo et al. 2003; Portes et al. 2002; Smith 2003). Furthermore, in terms of my own interests, I intend to report on, to demonstrate, and to analyze the domains of the participants' transnational praxis as initial insights into the nature of their contradictory and dynamic involvement and as causes of conflicts between different narratives and personal affiliations.

1.3 Research questions

General questions

1. How do migrants create, re-define, and perform their affiliations in their everyday lives and transnational practices through food consumption (e.g. in selection of food products and sharing of meals around the dining room table)? Do these affiliations differ in the two contexts (Israel and Germany) and, if so, how can we explain these differences?

2. How do immigrants in Germany and Israel construct the image of *home* or fill the vacant sense of *homeland* in their everyday lives, transnational practices, and food consumption? Are there any differences between the two contexts in this regard and, if so, how can they be explained?

3. In this study immigrants are involved in a transition from a socialist society to two different capitalistic societies. What are the meanings, significance, and consequences of this transition for them? Are there any differences between experiences in the two receiving societies and, if so, how can they be explained?

4. What do Jewish, ex-Soviet, Russian, European, Israeli, and German affiliations mean for participants in both contexts? How are these affiliations performed?

5. How do people interact in a situation in which different bodies of knowledge, different political narratives, and different constructions of social worlds, usually taken for granted, meet, and clash in the inner phenomenological domain as well as in the transnational biographic experiences of migrants? What happens, when through migration and intercultural interactions the same events are remembered, understood,

and interpreted in completely different manners not only by different groups in the CIS, Israel, and Germany, but also by different Jewish groups in these countries? How do migrants cope with the situation, when there is pressure to demonstrate loyalty to narratives that contradict one another in many significant ways?

6. How do patterns of interpretation and remembrance change during the migration process? What new meanings of the past appear in the new environments with their local discourse contexts?

7. How do the different contexts of Israel and Germany impact on individual coping strategies? How do they shape historical memories and affect the process of collective identity construction?

Special questions with reference to investigating Russian food stores

1. What products do Russian food stores offer? What different kinds of food appear on the dining room table in the two contexts?

2. What images are desired and why? Are images different in Russian food stores in Germany and in Israel and, if so, how can this be explained? How and according to what criteria is special food chosen?

3. What memories of taste, smell, outward appearance, and content of products consumed are articulated in everyday practices of participants in the new contexts?

4. What, if any, modifications are observable in food products available in Russian food stores in Israel and Germany? How do key symbols of different national cuisines and foods meet and co-exist within the framework of Russian food stores in both contexts?

5. How do social skills of consumption change after migration to either of the two contexts?

6. How can we conceptualize Russian food stores?

7. What role and significance does the Russian food store play in creating a personal identity among the immigrants? What roles and meanings do cultural and economic enclaves play in Israel and Germany in recent years, for both groups? Are their differences in the two contexts and, if so, how can they be explained?

1.4 Research methods

This comparative study applied qualitative methods of polyfocal or *mobile ethnographic* research (Marcus 1995). In doing so it compared two different domains: First, the *physical places* in which Russian speakers live and act in a certain area of two chosen cities in Israel and Germany; and, second, *imaginary transnational spaces* as they are created modified and performed in migrants' everyday praxis—both verbal and non-verbal (through material culture)—in both contexts. Whereas physical places remain fixed, their conceptualization as *imaginary transnational spaces* is constantly changing. Given the de-territorialized nature of affiliations and cultural processes (i.e. mobile research subject), comparisons between two fieldworks are considered to be "moving targets" (Welz 1998). In this process, different transnational spaces are created simultaneously and interact with one another. Thus, on the one hand, the complex societal contexts of Israel and Germany have physical localities and, on the other hand, they are cross-bordered imaginary transnational networks involved in dynamic de-territorialized cultural processes. Hence, we are dealing with a complex subject composed of dynamic, multi-sited or polyfocal fieldwork settings in Israel and Germany inter-connected and developing through pendulum-like dynamic processes swinging between them (Marcus 1995).

Given this understanding of the complexity of the phenomena under study, I determined that the most appropriate methodologies for collecting materials were extended periods of participant observation and open narrative interviews. Accordingly, I conducted long-term participant observation in Russian food stores[6] that also included multiple, open narrative interviews with clerks and owners of shops selling Russian food products, in both locations. In addition, I visited the homes of the participants in Israel and in Germany over a two year period. The methodologies employed during these visits in the field consisted of participant observations and multiple, open narrative interviews (n.b., most of the interactions took place within the close circle of research participants as well as with salespersons and owners of shops selling Russian food products in both locations).

---

6 Several additional observations were conducted at the end of the fieldwork in Russian food stores in other cities in Israel and Germany, in order to assess if the same tendencies exist there.

The Israel case study benefitted in significant ways from materials and findings developed from previous research undertaken by this researcher between 1998—2000 on food consumption and the creation of identity among immigrants from the USSR (Bernstein 2000). This research served as the basis for the present set of investigations. Three short periods of fieldwork in 2006, 2007, and 2008 enriched and validated these materials and findings. Fieldwork in the German context, conducted in parallel periods between 2002 and 2004 substantiated earlier findings. The Israeli case study was conducted in 2006—2008. The researcher and participants had extensive and intensive contact in both contexts.

Three additional frameworks for data-gathering proved to be informative in the German context. First, I participated in and observed the activities of the Jewish community in Germany that plays an active role in the lives of the Jewish immigrants. Second, I conducted regular participant observations in different centers and churches where several participants received free food rations. Third, I visited official agencies with participants on a regular basis and observed their interactions with public servants. Indeed, I served as their translator [from Russian to German] on a number of occasions and in doing so helped to meet a need that many participants had in communicating with representatives of official organizations. This way, I tried to reduce the inequality of relations between participants who generously shared information about their lives with me and researcher who makes use of this information for the research but had a relatively limited number of opportunities to compensate contributors for their time and efforts.

In addition, I collected, catalogued, and categorized numerous artifacts of the packaging of food products sold in the Russian food stores over the last ten years in Israel and the last six years in Germany. Indeed, many of these exemplars were actually given to me by participants in both contexts who concluded that this was my own unusual hobby. The assembled collection consists of thousands of artifacts organized in four thick binders, representing a multitude of images and product affiliations. This collection proved to be very rich, interesting, and useful in two ways: First, the artifacts provided relevant topics for discussion during the observations and interviews. In particular, tendencies and cultural messages on the packaging were discussed with participants in both settings. This enabled me to understand the participants' perceptions of these products and especially the contradictory, often politically-laden messages found on the packaging.

Second, the collection was a rich resource for conducting the content analyses.

While this extensive collection proved to be very useful and insightful, I concluded that it was necessary to go beyond a semiotic analysis that involves decoding of these visual materials in order to discover their implied different cultural meanings (Barthes 1957, 1964). My rationale in extending the analysis was that it would assist me to understand the dynamics and multiple layers of meanings observable in the field. Indeed, the inclusion of extended periods of participant observation sessions and the interviews proved to be very important components of this study. Thus, collectively, these visual materials as well as the participant observations of food practices developed into a rich resource that complemented the verbal articulations of participants in both contexts.

Framing/bracketing researcher involvement

Due diligence requires that the author reveals that the phenomena investigated were and remain closely related to her own autobiography. I was born in the Ukraine and experienced life in the Soviet system prior to as well as during the Perestroika period. Following emigration to Israel at the age of 18, I lived and studied there for eleven years before coming to Germany, where I have been living for the last six years while undertaking graduate studies. Consequently, all three physical spaces (SU, Israel, and Germany) are very familiar and I drew upon my personal experiences and understandings as additional resources in this research project.

I believe that our socialisation, personality and biography also play an important role in the *work alliance* with interview partners as well as regarding the quality of information we receive during the fieldwork. During the research I was able to develop a kind of *inner compass*, which helped me to position myself optimally in the work alliance, in order to remain as loyal as possible to the research object.

More specifically, my multi-sited background was utilized in a number of distinct ways. First, as documented in the monograph, I am well aware that I was perceived to be a person who had undergone similar emigration experiences and, presumably, shared a common knowledge of different Soviet-Russian symbols, norms, and customs.

Because of my socialisation in the SU my interview partners assumed that I shared the same common knowledge with them, which also contributed to my *inner compass* as my interview partners felt that their experiences were understood—which seems to me a very important communication basis in the migration situation, when reactions and self-evident thinking categories of migrants are often perceived as incomprehensive, strange or even absurd to the outsider and many migrants have a feeling of being perceived inadequately related to their expectations.

Second, my reflections on relevant categories for analysis undoubtedly involved my own perspectives as well as insights. A part of my *inner compass* as researcher was my own experience when coping with different bodies of knowledge through multiple migration (first to Israel and then to Germany) as well as through my socialisation in the Israeli and in the German academic world. This contributed to my reflection on multiple pressures of dominant discourses towards migrants and expectations towards their "integration" and, secondly, on emotional reactions of my interview partners to such delicate topics as the Holocaust, being Jewish or conceiving capitalism. I presume that similar socialisation and common affiliations assumed by participants played an especially important role in trying to discuss such traumatic topics as their experience with anti-Semitism or painful biographical aspects of their Jewish identity and coping with the Holocaust history. Aside from continuous reflection and bracketing of the nature of my own involvement in the research, I was also an active participant in the academic discourse in migration research in Israel and Germany. The latter participation enabled me to attain a certain degree of distance from the subject of my study. Indeed, self-dialogue and these reflections were extremely helpful in enabling me to deal with the very difficult task of reflecting on such questions as: What does it means to be Jewish? What is it like to live in a capitalist society? What is the nature of reflection on the nature and meaning of the Soviet winners' narrative for Jews? Moreover, I discovered that the challenge of writing this monograph, in a foreign language, has had the advantage of enabling me to reflect on habitual concepts and to gain greater precision in their use.

An additional aspect of the *inner compass* refers to the sensibility for the used linguistic categories in Russian as well as to the formulation of investigated topics in a sensitive way which enabled me to create a positive atmosphere and to avoid potentially unpleasant questions (such as "Why did you emigrate to Germany and not to Israel?"). This was helpful in finding a way to build trust and to develop rapport between me and my interview partners.

All interviews were conducted in the Russian language, my mother tongue, and later transcribed by myself. The use of Russian was crucial for the success achieved in the fieldwork, as it enabled participants to articulate their thoughts and feelings in ways they chose to be appropriate as educated intellectuals who have great difficulty expressing themselves at the same level in either Hebrew or German. Moreover, on a number of occasions during the fieldwork, nuances or brief remarks were made that later, during analysis of the transcripts, emerged as very important and influenced directions adopted in the analysis. Such remarks might not have been heard or understood in a foreign language, as they require a certain social experience in the SU and cultural knowledge. More precisely, I wish to note that I had to invest great efforts in both fieldwork settings to speak in the form of Russian spoken by the Soviet intelligentsia to which participants belonged and according to which many participants perceived and measured speaking partners.

In order to preserve the authenticity of the study, I have attempted to remain as faithful as possible in all translations and descriptions to the original Russian meaning and context. In this spirit, original Russian words are retained and reproduced in numerous places throughout the monograph; for example, product names and key symbols of the participants' social reality are preserved in their original form followed by translation into English that appears in brackets along with citation of the original language—Russian, Hebrew or German. Hopefully, this will enable the reader to gain some insight into the "social worlds" of the subjects of this research (Schütze 2002).

Recommendations from personal contacts and acquaintances in both field settings as well as from participants themselves were the primary resources for introductions and gaining access (entry) to participants. Entry obtained through personal contacts assisted me to arrange the initial meetings and contributed to the feeling of informal communication, which I believe helped participants to feel open and willing to share their views. However, even when I was presented by informants in the German fieldwork setting in Russian, language itself was not always sufficient for achieving acceptance. Many participants were suspicious of the fact that I came from Israel, thinking, perhaps, that I might be judgmental about their decision to emigrate to Germany or, even, would try to convince them to re-immigrate to Israel.[7] Furthermore, while most participants wanted to remain in contact with me and were very curious about life in Israel, they tried continually to reveal only the best sides of their life in Germany.

Indeed, fear of judgment and the perception of me as representative of the State of Israel were especially evident in one insightful case. This occurred at the very beginning of the fieldwork when I was interviewing a number of persons living in one house. Immediately upon my entrance into the house, even before I was introduced by the informant and without any prompting from me, Fira, whom I had never met, stated the following:

[Speaking aloud in a slow, pathetic tone] "Well, *we did make a mistake!* [meaning: when we came to Germany]."

Her husband, followed: "But we are proud of *you!*" [meaning: me, as person who made the *right* choice to emigrate and to live in Israel].

While this is an extreme example, this first sentence of our meeting is representative of the fear and mistrust I sensed in some migrants upon meeting me, initially, as a researcher. On the other hand, such a perception can also be seen as indicative of pre-existing ideas and *imaginary relationships* (or inner dialogue) between personal migration stories and ideas about what should be shared with different Others (i.e. Germans, local Jews in Germany, Israelis, Russian-speaking Israelis). Interpretations of these perceptions are discussed in the final chapter of this manuscript. Yet, after three-four months of meeting, participants started to open up, exhibit trust, and see in me as more than someone categorized under one certain category (e.g., as Israeli or researcher).

In this regard, it was interesting to follow how most participants created their own version of why I resided in Germany and the nature of my work. One of the most certain signs of having established rapport and gaining acceptance by participants—not only as a researcher but on a personal level with all of my family members—was a new question that replaced previous self-justifications when I was asked on numerous occasions: "So, have you decided to remain in Germany?" Through developing mutual respect and a sensitive researcher and participant "work alliance," our discussions became informal friendships and productive dialogues

---

7 At least two families thought that I was an agent of the Sochnut (The Jewish Agency) or the Mosad (Israeli Secret Service) charged with learning about the life of ex-Soviet Jews in Germany.

during which we discussed different aspects of life in Germany (Inowlocki and Bernstein 2006, Resch and Steinert 2003).

In general, I was amazed by the openness and intensity of the cooperation I received throughout the entire period of fieldwork in both contexts. Participants expressed their willingness, even desire, to speak for as long and in as detailed a manner as possible about different aspects of their new lives. One indicator of such interest, indeed commitment, was the atmosphere within which our meetings were conducted. On nearly every occasion, our discussions took place around a richly laid-out dining table, always followed by dessert, even if the interview was prolonged and lasted from three and half to five hours. A second indicator was that people gave me clean wrapping papers of food products and Russian food stores advertisements. They also informed me about different Russian forums and activities in the city, invited me to celebrations of their birthdays, presented me to other participants, recommended literature in Russian that might be applicable to this research project, even if not scientific in nature.

In my opinion, one of reasons for the participants' interest and active involvement in this project was the fact that these are highly educated people who are not employed in jobs for which they were trained or which challenge them intellectually. Hence, they lack a sense of professional and social fulfillment in the new society. Moreover, because of language difficulties and rare informal contacts with members of the dominant resident groups in both contexts, many seemed to be motivated by a sense that it was very important that the *outside world* [i.e., non-Russian speakers] understand their *real educated status*, cultural capital, views, thoughts, and problems they were confronting in the new society. That is, above all, there seems to be a need for them to be recognized and understood by persons in their new environment.

The topics discussed in this research touch upon some of the most strongly felt needs of persons involved in the migration process (e.g., Schiffauer 2003). This was especially true in the German case study, as many interview partners, women in particular, often were in tears when recalling special situations encountered upon arrival and in the transition to living in a new land. Further, in retrospective reflection, they seemed to consider these past events as quite different from their current situation. This affirmed the false nature of claims made about the "irreversible nature of historic times" when "the past can be modified by the present" (Moses 1989, 39 quoting Boyarin 1994, 11). Moreover, many descriptions and reflections shared about experiences were closely linked to their ideas about new positioning and desire for future scenarios. As Breckner stated: "The construction of a biography functions as a way out of past experiences in order to find direction for the present and future" (Breckner 2000, 92).

Of course, an evolving work alliance can involve very sensitive questions and unresolved problems, especially when the researcher receives especially rich and sensitive empirical data. Two such issues involve the nature of the participants' authority in the research and *ownership* of thoughts shared with the researcher. One insightful situation in which the work alliance with a participant was negotiated involved potentially contested ownership of material shared. This occurred at the very beginning of the fieldwork in Germany in 2002 when near the beginning of the first meeting with Sergei he stated:

Sergei: "I can also interview you."

JB: "Sure, why not [pause]."

Sergei: "I will tell you everything, in detail, and you can then hire me as your assistant in the university [this could be] something technical. [After all,] I need a job."

JB:(confused): "You know I don't have any position myself at the university, but [smiling] as soon as I become a professor I will appoint you immediately as a professor, too (Sergei's laugh seems to be indicative that he understands the absurdity of my sentence, then we both laugh]. "

JB: (seriously): "Is working a problem here?"

Sergei: "Actually I don't know German very well, but you know it really is THE problem [the interview begins]."

Sergei presented himself as an educated person and hinted at the onset that he was unwilling to function in a hierarchical relationship between researcher and investigated person. My reaction to this well-known problem in social research was a spontaneous attempt to dismantle the tension and to reveal that I did not intend to establish or function through such a relationship.

My *inner compass* helped me to understand that to a certain degree I and my interview partners pursue a similar goal, i. e. to describe social reality and ways of self-definition and self-positioning of participants loyal to their own concepts and thinking categories as my contribution to the academic concepts and theories developed before. Conscious of the "valuable gift" of information received from the participants as researchers, I attempted to preserve, respect, give voice to, if not empower their views and contributions to this study by setting them in the foreground of this entire research report. I do this by means of numerous and extensive citations of the participants' views. Additionally, during the course of this research, I sought to advance a holistic approach that, among other things, did not detach, for example, personal collective affiliations through the food consumption from the participants' other life experiences living in Germany or in Israel, nor from experiences in their former life.

Generally, I acted throughout the fieldwork through what Bertaux referred to as "the saturation process" (Bertaux 1981, 186-189): wherein the content of stories, behaviors, and activities repeated themselves to the point of researcher anticipation and repeated confirmation of responses. Thus, it was this saturation process that defined the temporal parameters of the research.

Selecting the research population

The following characteristics of the population studied required special consideration in selecting interviewees: The large number of migrants who emigrated to Israel and to Germany; the variegated structure of immigration (a factor noted by immigrants themselves); and varied demographics, such as: age, education, family composition, cultural perceptions, and original place of residence. Therefore, it was necessary to define and to apply uniform criteria in selection of participants from such a varied population. This process started in Israel and was then applied in Germany in the following manner:

Israel

In order to solicit the study's research population, I began my search in my immediate surroundings - among relatives, friends, and acquaintances. As a result, data-gathering was conducted among a group of immigrants from the Ukraine and Russia who lived in Haifa at the time of the investigations were conducted. Haifa is a city that absorbed a large proportion of the immigration from the CIS over the past decade. In fact, among Israel's three largest cities—Tel Aviv, Haifa, and Jerusalem, Haifa has become the symbol of the latest wave if immigration and is presented as a Russian city in the Russian language press.

The research population selected consisted of 30 families, comprised of 55 persons,[8] all of whom were 48-65 years of age or older, though most were above 50 years of age.[9] This allows us to associate them with one generation and to assume that they share common memories. Their children were between 15-38 years of age at the time of the study. For the most part, most of the research population knew one another in their locations of origin or became acquainted in Israel through participation in institutions such as the Ulpan [Hebrew language school].

All the participants in this case study had earned a higher education degree in the fields of technology or humanities. Most of the interviewees were not employed in their original profession, made their living in jobs that do not require extensive education, and, consequently, were overqualified for these jobs. For instance, an engineer and former specialist in thermomechanics, formerly employed in the SU in a heat engineering factory (employing 500 employees), assembles batteries in a company developing a new kind of electric motor to be used in environmentally friendly automobiles; a construction engineer is employed as a liaison in a nursing home for the elderly; and, a mathematician works as a typesetter in a printing shop.

The population studied in Israel arrived between 1990 and 1995. During this period, there was a disintegration of the larger states of the SU and development of a new constituency, the CIS, which bears the entire economic, social, and cultural burden of the former SU.

There are three social circles among the Israeli research population, each of which shared and preserved similar characteristics. While friendly relationships existed between members, I do not claim this to be a consolidated network. Accordingly, the research study undertook an independent investigation of each social circle as a separate case study.

---

8 There were 26 couples and three unmarried women.

9 One of the spouses was a little bit older or younger than this age in several cases.

Germany

The town of Standstadt[10] in North Rheine/Westphalia selected for this project absorbed many immigrants from the CIS over the past decade. The entire Jewish community of Standstadt numbers almost 2000 members and it is an active Jewish community. One important reason for the choice of this city is that nearly all of the Jews in Standstadt are from the former Soviet Union, except for a few German families who converted to Judaism. This stands in contrast to other cities, such as Berlin or Frankfurt, where there are Jews from a variety of backgrounds and longevity in the location.

One very active resident facilitated my entry into the Standstadt community. We met during the fieldwork in Israel when she came to visit relatives and friends. Access to her network of friends and acquaintances in Germany facilitated greatly my entry into the field—the first, perhaps most important, as well as difficult stage in anthropological fieldwork. Introductions by this well-connected informant to potential participants established a good basis for development of the necessary condition for qualitative research—attaining mutual trust and rapport with participants. Through information obtained through a few key persons, I was able to complete preliminary work over a two-month period (prior to coming to Germany for an extended stay) during which time I conducted initial observations in the community and participated in several social meetings in the homes of informants where I endeavored to meet other participants.

In order to establish some resemblance between the two groups, I decided to choose participants in Germany according to the same criteria applied in Israel, noted above. Therefore, I selected 30 families, consisting of 57 individuals[11] within the 46-65 year old age group, who had earned a higher education in the technology or humanities fields. All interviewees emigrated from large cities of Russia and the Ukraine over the last ten years. It is important to remember that whereas in Israel the large immigration wave arrived in 1990-95, emigration to Germany began in 1995.

---

10 A fictitious name for the city in Germany has been created for ethical reasons.
11 There were three single women in addition to 27 couples.

1.5 Comparative view of the two populations

The following comparison of the characteristics of these two populations is ground in the professional literature that served as the basis for this comparative study:

1) Jewish affiliation was the main criterion applied by both receiving societies for decisions made to accept immigrants and for their gaining immigrant status. Yet, when living in their original setting, Jews from the SU saw themselves first and foremost as part of a specific social class (the intelligentsia) and only after that as Jews (Oswald and Voronkov 2000, 343). Yet, ironically, while immigrants in both contexts sought to actively preserve the Soviet-Russian cultural habitus, for the most part they were perceived by the resident population of the host-receiving society and presented in the media first and foremost as "Russians," not as Jews (Becker and Körber 2001; Elias and Bernstein 2007; Golden 1996; Oswald and Voronkov 2000).

2) An assumed moral basis was present for the immigration of Jews to Germany and to Israel. In Israel, according to the Zionist ideology that underpins the Jewish state, immigrants are defined to be persons returning to their national ancestral homeland (Golden 1996, 2). In Germany, in the aftermath of the Holocaust, claims are made for the historical obligation to rebuild the German Jewish community (Shutze and Rapoport 2000, 351).

3) While Russian-speaking Jews were granted formal legal "invitations" in both cases to immigrate, in practice they reported feeling unwanted, in both cases (Golden 1996; Oswald and Voronkov 2000).

4) The main reason given by immigrants for emigration from the former SU was, in both instances, the perception that the economic and social structures in their land of origin were crumbling (Lewin-Epstein, Roi, and Ritterband 1997; Oswald and Voronkov 2000, 338-9).

5) In both cases, immigrants moved from a socialist or post-socialist society to a society proclaiming to be capitalistic, pluralistic, democratic, and multi-cultural. And, in both cases, immigrants' standard of living rose considerably; they were exposed to new phenomenon—abundance; and were able to express themselves in a new way in a dynamic culture of material consumption.

6) Most of the participants (of the age-group studied) in both contexts were highly qualified but no longer employed in their original profession trade or profession, and their income was low in comparison with resident

populations with similar background (Carmon 1996; Cohen and Kogan 2005; Oswald and Voronkov 2000; Parkes 2000). In both cases, immigrants from the CIS of the age group investigated reported experiencing a certain degree of "social marginalization" and felt unable to realize their professional potential (Oswald and Voronkov 2000). Finally, after 15 years of residence, in both contexts, most immigrants still experienced language difficulties.

7) In both cases, immigrants participate in developing and thus influence the Russian-speaking enclave. Such participation includes intensive and ongoing interaction, via transnational networks, with compatriots, relatives, and friends in the CIS, Israel, Germany, or USA.

1.6 General characteristics of the investigated groups

More than 1,700,000 Jews emigrated from the SU since 1989 (Remennick 2006, 69). Today, this group represents "the single most educated community on the global migration map" (ibid., 71). Israel accepted an influx of immigrants that has significantly increased its population. Today, out of five million Jewish Israelis, one million speak Russian (c- 20 percent of the Jewish population of the state). Most of the newcomers completed an academic education, are of employable age (48-65), and are not employed in their original professional field (Cohan and Kogan 2005; Levin Epstein 1997; Lissak 1996; Ritterband 1997). They tend to live in large cities where, due to financial constraints, they reside in the less attractive areas of cities; for example, the Hadar neighborhood in Haifa where most of the participants in this study lived (Carmon 1996; Levin Epstein 1997; Lissak 1996; Ritterband 1997).

Germany has accepted about 200,000 Russian-speaking Jewish immigrants to date and more than one million ethnic Germans from the former SU (Cohen and Kogen 2005; Schoeps 2001). The total number of Jews represents 0.25 per cent of the entire population of Germany today, which numbers about 80 million persons. However, of the number of Jews who arrived, only c-50 percent became members of Jewish community.[12] Today

---

12 Matrilineal Jewish affiliation was deemed necessary for acceptance in the Jewish community. Thus, the father's Jewish affiliation was sufficient to acquire the status of Kontin-

there are approximately 108,000 Russian-speaking Jewish community members and they are a majority of the members of the Jewish community in Germany.

Previous research found that immigrants left the Russian Federation for a number of negative reasons, including limitations on civil liberties, discrimination and anti-Semitism, concern over the children's and the family's future due to increasing uncertainty accompanying the disintegration of the SU, and socio-economic difficulties (Levin- Epstein, Roi and Ritterband 1997; Rivkina 1996, 162). Other reasons that participants mentioned include the growing number of relatives in Israel and impressions after having visited there, as well as the reaction to the "open door" policy adopted as part of the Perestroika process (Gitelman 1997, 32).

Russian-speaking cultural enclaves thrive in Israeli and German societies for a variety of reasons: the size of the Russian-speaking population; the arrival of Russian tourists—including artists, actors, poets, and musicians; accessibility of Russian broadcasts (Russian cable channels) and newspapers; and the understanding exhibited by Israeli as well as German society and their authorities of the immigrants' need to have their own means of cultural expression. All of this reflects the engagement, indeed struggle, both within the community-enclave as well as with the receiving society to formulate the immigrants' unique identity (Lissak 1996).

As we shall see throughout this research report, the foods displayed on immigrants' dining tables reflect these processes. Enclaves involve interaction with fellow immigrant neighbors, including strong evidence of a high degree of self-sufficiency achieved in provision of different kinds of services and businesses that serve this particular ethnic group (Gold 1997, 261—284). In fact, these cultural enclaves include every kind of institution necessary for individual and community life.

The main circumstances that influenced the character of the settlement process of the last immigration wave to Israel and Germany can be summarized as follows:

First, the *Perestroika* process, the opening of the borders, and technological developments made it possible for Jewish immigrants to remain in contact, post-migration, with their social connections and networks in their land of origin. This is a strikingly different situation from the fate of immigrants in the 1970s and even with the 1989-1991 wave, when people emi-

---

gentflüchtlinge for many immigrants, but not for acceptance by the German Jewish community.

grated "forever" without knowing, if they would ever see their friends and relatives again. In contrast, late in the first half of the 1990s and even more so after 1995, intensive efforts were invested by migrants to maintain the stability of social networks so that they could remain in contact with people who remained in the CIS as well as to keep up with current events in the CIS through the media. In addition, a significant decrease in travel costs and increase in post-migration standard of living made it possible for immigrants to visit, often frequently, as well as to manage properties they owned in their country of origin.

The second factor that assisted the settlement process was the legitimization of the multicultural character of the society and lifestyles that emerged in the latter portion of the 20th century worldwide as well as in the host societies. This facilitated the emergence, rapid establishment, and growth of minority groups' infrastructures in the public sphere, such as ethnic enclaves.

Third, as noted by Portes, Haller and Guarnizo (2001), the role of transport technology and electronic communications made the exposure to "near-instantaneous" normative economic, cultural, and political exchanges possible and facilitated as well an intense level of contacts when distances are not great and can be easily, cheaply, and rapidly bridged. Some of the exemplars of how these developments integrated into migrants' lives include translations of advertising, inexpensive telephone services, rapid import of goods from the CIS, and even participation in CIS elections – as evident from lines of migrants waiting at Russian consulates in Israel and Germany.

Finally, one should also take into consideration the *negative* motive that drove some forms of transnational immigrant entrepreneurship. The limited if not non-existent opportunities for immigrants to be employed in their original professions in the local market also influenced the mobilization of all their available social and cultural resources as an economic success strategy. To a certain degree, these seem to be creative and "worthy" alternatives for migrants' experience that assisted them resist being disqualified or humiliated, which they experienced all too frequently (Kapphan 2000; Razin and Schlinberg 2001).

All these factors enabled the establishment, steady evolution, and success of economic and cultural enclaves, in general, and immigrants' food enterprises, in particular. These efforts were reinforced by Russian-speaking immigrants who emigrated during the 1970s and 1980s who, too, (for the first time since their arrival) joined, participated in enclave activities, and in doing so strengthened the enclave, in general.

As a new phenomenon, we should note the scale and meaning of the Russian-speaking communities and enclaves in Israel and Germany. In the case of Israel, Russian-speakers now make up 20 percent of the Jewish-Israeli population. Common terms of reference used in the media—*Russim* [Russians, Heb.] or "Russian Ghetto"—might seem to be unusual in a country that has an official policy of unification and integration of Diaspora communities into (the myth of) the Israeli "melting pot." That is, presentation via retention of diaspora-ethnic affiliation is so unusual as to suggest that the Russian-speaking migrant enclave in Israel is presented as Other, perhaps because they are perceived to be a demographic and axiological threat to collective Jewish identity (Elias and Bernstein 2007). This may be due to the fact that Russian-speaking Jews in Israel continue to practice non-kosher food practices and cultivate Russian culture. In doing so, they "break" with the expectation that they will integrate through certain prescribed terms of modification to be the "right" type of Israeli Jew (Golden 2002). Indeed, concerns are frequently expressed about the fact that Russian is heard everywhere and pork is eaten by Russians, a behaviour that penetrates and threatens to destroy the society built by Israel's pioneering generation.

Numerous and very interesting studies were conducted in Israel about this community since the last wave of immigration from the SU/CIS (e.g., Al-Haj and Leshem 2000; Elias 2005 2008; Elias and Lemish 2008, 2008a; Fialkova and Yelenevskaya 2003; Gitelman 1997; Horowitz 1998; Lerner 2003; Lissak and Leshem 1995; Lomsky and Rapoport 2000; Markowitz 1998; Mittelberg and Borschevsky 2004; Rapoport, Lomsky-Feder and Heider 2006; Yelenevskaya and Fialkova 2005, Zilberg 2002). These innovative and sensitive investigations have produced important insights into this group as well as exposed contradictions and conflicts between cultural perceptions and political narratives of different groups within Israeli society and Russian-speakers (Erdreich, Lerner and Rapoport 2005; Golden 1996, 2001, 2001a, 2002; Lerner, Rapoport and Lomsky-Feder 2007; Roberman 2007; Yelenevskaya and Fialkova 2004; Yelenevskaya 2005).

To date no cultural anthropological studies have been undertaken that focus on the lived experiences of *being Jewish* in the SU as compared with post-migration transformations after the emigration to Israel. Moreover, there are few anthropological works that reveal the fluid, changing, and contradictory nature of the personal-collective affiliations of the investigated group by means of the authentic voices of participants (ibid). This also serves to complement macro—and all too often frozen theoretical categories, such as—integration, assimilation, enculturation, and adaptation. Furthermore, none of the qualitative studies known to the author have verified and illuminated the problematic nature of the theoretical approaches applied in the sense of their capacity to explain different aspects of Russian speakers' life in Israel and Germany through "thick description" and findings about participants' own worldviews. And, when such analyses have been applied in studies of the investigated group,[13] in general, none have revealed the contradictions involved in transnational action.

In Germany, Russian-speaking Jews are assigned "Kontingent-flüchtlinge" status [contingent refugees, Ger.].[14] Accordingly, they are granted permission to live in Germany due to moral obligations encumbered following the Holocaust and other WWII-related events (Gilman 1995; Joppke 1998; Shutze and Rapoport 2000). The expectation is that the immigrants will become part of German society in order to contribute to the rejuvenation, enrichment, and reinforcement of local Jewish minority communities (Dietz 2003; Schütze and Rapoport 2000).

As in Israel, the Russian enclave in Germany raised serious concerns among the resident Jewish German community. This is because local Jewish residents define themselves in predominately-religious terms and cannot accept the non-kosher Russian food practices of Russian-speaking immigrants or treat mixed couples as recognized members of this community. Yet, the Russian-speaking population is now the majority of persons associated with the Jewish community in Germany. In some German cities (such as Potsdam, Mönchengladbach or Wuppertal) there are Jewish communities comprised entirely of Russian speakers. It remains to be seen how the resident and Russian-speaking sectors of the German Jewish community will negotiate and reconcile differences in their perceptions of the cultural, religious, historical, and ethnic Jewishness.

No ethnographic studies had been published about the "lived Jewish culture" of Jewish communities in Germany prior to 2005 (Hegner 2008, 13). However, since the beginning of the 1990's numerous studies had

---

13 This was the case primarily in regard to Russian-speakers in Germany, but not in Israel.
14 Paragraph 16 of the Basic Law, known as "Kontingentflüchtlingsgesetz" states: "The politically persecuted enjoy the right of asylum" (Parkes 2000, 301).

been conducted about Russian-speaking Jews in Germany that highlight diverse and interesting aspects about their life in the new society (e.g., Bade and Troen 1993; Becker and Körber 2001; Cohen and Kogan 2005; Doomernik 1997; Grüber and Rüßler 2000; Kessler 1996; Oswald and Voronkov 2000; Schoeps, Jasper and Vogt 1996, 1999; Schütze 2000; Schütze and Rapoport 2000). Yet, among these publications, there are very few qualitative studies that provide "thick descriptions" (Geertz 1973) or ethnographic analyses and insights into "doing being Jewish" (Inowlocki 2000) by different of social actors, namely ex-Soviet Jews as compared to so-called residential Jews (e.g., Becker 2001; Darieva 2003, 2004; Elias 2004; Yelenevskaya 2005). Both these groups have differing perceptions of their Jewishness, embody different *social worlds*, as well as, continue to be influenced by socialization to and life in two significantly different historical contexts; namely, the SU with a long history of prohibitions on the practice of Jewish religion, culture, and traditions, and Germany with its history as the perpetrators of WWII and the Holocaust. Thus, in order to understand what often appear to be conflicts as well as questions and reflections on the nature of mutually stressful, seemingly unbridgeable cultural differences (between newcomers and resident Jews), it is especially important to understand what it means for Russian-speaking Jews in Germany to be Jewish. Prior to doing so, in the remainder of this monograph, the following is a brief summary of the elements that composed the Soviet Jews' pre-emigration identity as seen both by Jews and dominant groups in the SU.

1.7 Transporting Jewish identity from the SU

There is a common impression, mistaken in my view, that Jews from the CIS lack any sense of Jewish identity, cultivate exclusively Russian culture, and instrumentalized their Jewishness in order to emigrate for economic reasons to Israel or Germany. Gitelman who studied this group's Jewish identity claimed that it, like any other kind of identity, is neither universal nor permanent, rather it has a changing nature (Gitelman 1995, 35). He and other researchers are convinced that Jews in the SU identified themselves as Jews in a singular and specific manner (Chervyakov, Gitelman and Shapiro 1997; Gitelman 1997; Lewin-Epstein, Roi, and Ritterband

1997; Rivkina Shapiro Chervyakov 1996). Deprived of its cultural and religious content, "being Jewish was something they were constantly reminded by their neighbors and co-workers and the authorities; it was not necessarily a consequence of their own choosing" (Lewin-Epstein, Roi, and Ritterband 1997, 12).

According to Gitelman's survey of immigrants from the last wave of immigration, some three-fourths of the immigrants reported that they had felt at home in the SU all or almost all of their lives (Gitelman 1995, 26). Although they were classified in the SU as "domestic foreigners" (Levinson 1997, 12; Slezkine 2005), Gilman (1995, 19) suggested that this status was similar to the classification assigned Jews in Germany as "integrierte Fremdkörper" [integrated foreign bodies, Ger.]), when Jews were perceived to be members of the SU "intelligentsia." Indeed, despite different forms of discrimination, Jews were overrepresented in almost all spheres of cultural life in the SU/CIS (Slezkine 2005). Indeed, according to an interview published in the magazine *Humanite*, Michael Gorbachov claimed the following:

"While Jews account for 0.69 percent of the USSR population, they were represented in its political and cultural life on a scale of at least 10—20 percent" (Weinerman 1997, 215).

In this regard, one may claim that the vacuum left by cultural or religious Jewishness was filled with the claim of *cultural Russianness*, as discussed in Chapter Six. A survey conducted among Russians that included the question—what is Jewish identity?—produced the following conclusions: Most Russians do not see Jews as being particularly different from themselves in regard to language or other cultural aspects, but maintain that Jews differ in their interpretation of norms and general values. Jews are perceived to be persons who possess talent, are educated, cultured (in reference to Russian education and culture), avoid physical work, and are above average in economic status (Levinson 1997, 223). According to these common perceptions, being Jewish can be easily reduced to the familiar, rigid stereotype of *clever and rich Jews*.

By means of comparison, very few ethnographic or qualitative studies have investigated the Jews' own perceptions and responses to complex questions about what it meant to be Jewish in the SU, as well as, post-emigration transformations of such perceptions (Gitelman 1996; Gold 1996; Hegner 2008; Slezkine 2005; Sternshis 2006). Thus, in implementing multiple interviews as a research methodology, one of the goals of this study was to understand what Jewishness meant for concrete social actors, the participants in this study, and how their sense/understanding of Jewishness has been transformed after emigration to Israel and Germany?

1.8 Overview of the book

Chapter Two deals with one of the main topics of this research project, namely, the participants' responses to the transition from a socialist society, with its deficit food supply system, to two capitalistic societies characterized by, for our purposes, abundant, stable, accessible food supply systems. It is true that as citizens of a formerly closed society, the Soviet Union, Jewish migrants were not very well acquainted with the characteristics of Western abundance, consumer culture, and mass consumption that seem to be "the dominant context, through which people in modern societies relate to the material world" (Miller 1984, 4). This chapter presents analyses of their everyday consumption practices within the Russian-speaking milieu, and in particular procurement/consumption conducted in Russian food stores. This is especially the case with migrants in Germany who actively relate to "life in the capitalist world," experiment with its components, and presumably, undergo behavioral changes after living in the socialistic system.

Participants' adjustment to life in a consumption-centered society is the focus of Chapter Three. The analysis begins with a reconstruction of Soviet consumption patterns as *living memories* on the basis of the participants' retrospective views of their past ways of living in the SU. This discussion is grounded in relevant research literature and includes documentation of the different ways participants responded to the question: How were consumption ideas, patterns, and skills acquired by immigrants in the SU adjusted and modified in their post-migration surroundings in Israel and Germany? Serving as a basis for discussions in Chapters Four and Five, this chapter highlights dreams of material prosperity transported by the migrants from the SU. Finally, this chapter analyses how Soviet terminology, developed during periods of economic shortages in the SU, is reactivated and instrumentalized in the new contexts.

Chapter Four presents analyses of the participants' perceptions of multiple and sometimes contested use of images in marketing food products found in Russian food stores in both contexts. Special attention is devoted to the analysis of food product images that mediate multiple narratives, cultural and social affiliations, *imaginary home* and *homeland's scenarios* in real praxis, and their "place-making practices" (Ray 2004, 5). This discussion relates to such concepts as *home* and *homelands, proletarian food, food as a Soviet communist paradise, food as powerful political icon of the Soviet empire* and, in the Israeli case, food consumption as embodying a new political icon of Jewish Zionist *homeland*. New and borrowed food images of the *contemporary nationalized Russian homeland* are presented and contradictions with Jewish history and affiliation analyzed. The chapter concludes with discussion of the multiple meanings of Russian food stores.

Based on the previous chapter's discussion of multiple imageries within Russian food stores in Israel and Germany, Chapter Five analyzes Russian food stores as a contradictory transnational framework. This analysis will demonstrate how different national narratives co-exist within this framework and often struggle for their role, place, and significance in regard to notions of the collective identities of migrants in Israel and Germany. The key symbols of pork and caviar consumption are focused on as special national foods as they cross borders and manifest identities in different societal contexts. The rapid growth of a broad range of non-kosher food stores is discussed in terms of their contribution to the struggle of the ethnic Russian-speaking Jewish transnational enclave. This struggle involves attempts to gain recognition for pork as a legitimate practice of the Jewish national collective. This analysis will demonstrate how changes in political participation influence local hierarchies of power in relation to food habits of resident populations. Finally, the generalized labeling reference to "Russian" is deconstructed into the different components of Russian food stores within the transnational framework. This enables us to proceed to a critical discussion of two theoretical concepts—*transnational entrepreneurship* and *ethnic entrepreneurial niches* as a part of an enclave; and proposal of an alternative concept—*virtual transnational enclave*—that seems to be most appropriate for the phenomena investigated here, and beyond.

Chapter Six examines the different contents of Soviet Jewishness as transported, reconstructed, and performed by the participants. Four central elements applied in construction of Jewishness transported and developed in the new context are identified and analyzed. First, Soviet ideas of *innate Jewishness* and *visible Otherness*, including their construction and contradiction in comparison with local Israeli and German ideas about ethnicity that the migrants confronted post-migration. Second, the construction and stigmatization of *significant Jewish Otherness* or *engraved Jewish identity* that utilize different anti-Semitic strategies and complimentary coping strategies developed by Jews while living in the SU and after migration to Israel and Germany. Third, the *emotional attachment to the State of Israel* of Russian-speaking Jewish identity, which functioned as an exclusion mechanism during the participants' lives in the SU, assumed different dimensions and directions following migration to Germany. The final component of Russian-speaking Jewishness—the paradoxical ways of *being Jewish* through affiliation with the Soviet Russian cultural elite—was transformed following migration to Israel and Germany. The summary discussion of these four components, as they developed in two different contexts—in Israel and Germany—focuses on the concept of *triple trans-Jewish affiliation* as lived by Russian-speaking Jews in the two receiving contexts.

Chapter Seven deals with the meaning of WWII and the Holocaust in everyday life as well as the transnational practices of Russian-speaking Jews living in Germany. This discussion examines the co-existence, integration, and contradictions between three contested narratives involved in construction of the collective and personal identities of ex-Soviet Jews living primarily in Germany, as compared to those in Israel: The Soviet victory narrative, the Holocaust narrative, and the German narrative about the country's Nazi past. The analyses presented in this chapter compare the contextualization, re-actualization, and amendment of the perception of the Holocaust and WWII by Russian-speaking Jews in Germany with that constructed by Jews in Israel. The goal in this chapter is to demonstrate how participants interact in a situation in which different bodies of knowledge, different official versions of remembrance of the past events, different political narratives, and different constructions of social worlds, usually taken for granted, meet and clash in the inner phenomenological domain as well as in the transnational biographic experiences of migrants.

Chapter Eight, the final chapter of the monograph, presents and discusses the multiple contradictions as well as paradoxes of the simultaneously existent and contested *social worlds* in which Russian-speaking Jews live in both new contexts. The analysis identifies and discusses the following ways of self-positioning and individual strategies of coping with paradoxes: First, multiple affiliations and images that had a supportive function in developing the individual's positive sense of belonging in the SU that evolved into a contested and painful terrain post-migration. Second, migrants' perceptions of the dominant normative thinking and hierarchical structures learned in both contexts; for example, conflicts between what they are expected to learn from host residents about life and the *right* forms of agency in the new society and the humiliations of being perceived by host-residents as *semi-adults* in contrast to their self-perception as educated people who are mature social agents. Particular situations and different coping strategies applied by the migrants in Israel and Germany illuminate the existential challenges faced in their daily lives. The third topic discussed is the especially delicate issue of the emigration of Russian-speaking Jews to Germany, the land of the Holocaust, rather than to Israel. The affiliation with participants in Israel, too, is analyzed on the basis of the participants' views, as articulated in the interviews. And, finally, the chapter concludes with a proposal of the contributions of the research as well as potential directions for further development of the research in the future.

2 Transnationalism and capitalism: Migrants from the former Soviet Union and their experiences in Germany and Israel

This chapter explores the participants' perceptions and cultural constructions of *capitalism* or the *capitalistic West* after their emigration to Germany and to Israel. Not only is their migration accompanied by significant transformations in all spheres of the migrants' everyday life, it offered them a unique opportunity to reflect on knowledge as well as behavioral schemes and values normally taken for granted and to act on the basis of these reflections. The special circumstances of the population investigated are that this is a case of emigration across the previously tightly closed borders of the Iron Curtain from what Markowitz (1991, 638) referred to as a "total system" to capitalist societies characterized by abundance and consumption-oriented cultures.

As former citizens of a closed society, the SU, participants lacked experience in the actual realities of living everyday amidst Western abundance, in a consumer culture, and with mass consumption. According to Miller this "is now the dominant context through which people in modern societies relate to the material world" (Appadurai 1996; Miller 1987, 4). Thus, emigration to a Western society led this group to encounter an absolutely new phenomenon and required that they develop strategies to cope with it on a permanent basis.

Moreover, throughout their life in the SU, they were exposed to the powerful Soviet political machine's propagandizing about life in the West. Thus, migrants were socialized to view the Western society through negative deconstructions in which the West was the symbol, *par excellence*, of evil social regimes and the wrong way of life. The "decaying capitalist West," as it was called in the Soviet media, was permanently juxtaposed to such frequent appellations as the "positive," "right," "humane," "just," "equal," "spiritual Soviet socialist system." For example, a poster purchased by a participant in a Russian bookstore in Israel is a reprint of a 1948 poster that displays two pictures (picture 2:1). On the left side is a black-white picture of a violinist, in a capitalist country, destined to play on the streets while being completely ignored by passers-by who are portrayed as men in coats and bowlers (recalling an old image of capitalists). The violinist looks very depressed. Depicted above this scene are many lights and advertisements, such as White Horse Whisky. The caption at the bottom of the *capitalist* side of the poster states "The fate of talent…"

The fate of the violinist in socialist countries is presented on the poster's right hand side in red letters. There the violinist is depicted appearing on stage in a big concert hall together with a huge organ, an orchestra, composed of hundreds of male and female musicians. The national emblem of the SU is depicted on this *socialist* side of the poster in approximately the same place as the advertisement for whisky is displayed on the *capitalist side*. The title for socialist depiction is positive—"The route of the talented!"

Even if certain educated Soviet people from dominant groups or discriminated minorities (such as Soviet Jews) doubted the absolute nature of such statements, nobody had a clear idea, pre-migration, about life abroad. The extent to which Soviet Jews internalized official knowledge could also be seen through differences in post-migration practices. Accordingly, the main purpose of this chapter is to trace how ideas transported by immigrants about capitalism are (re-)created, practiced, transformed, performed by them in practicing and living knowledge. Especially interesting are contradictions in the practice that occur when presumed capitalist knowledge is applied, as well as, the demarcation of affiliations that sharpens during the post-migration transition. Thus, this chapter will compare perceptions, practices, and living knowledge of capitalism in two significantly different contexts, Israel and Germany. The overall aim in doing so is to reveal transformations in transported ideas about capitalism.

It is important in this discussion to keep in mind the special SU migration context, since it concerns the unprecedented period of *Perestroika* and the so called "wild nineties," during which the country belonged to nobody (Gustafson 1999).[15] During the 1990s, participants in both the Israel and German case studies experienced and had to cope with the difficult SU economic crisis that included:

---

15 For transformations of ex-socialist societies, see Balcerowicz 1995; Verdery 1995; Humphrey 2002.

Pic. 2:1 Soviet poster "Talent route in capitalist countries" and "Talent route in socialist countries!" (I)

Pic. 2:2 Processed Finnish cheese "Viola" in Russian food stores in Israel

Pic. 2:5 "Hermitage Chocolate" (I)

Pic. 2:3 Soviet chocolate "Inspiration" (I and G)

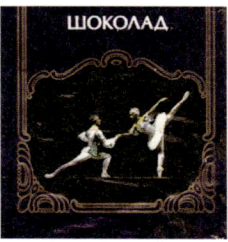

Pic. 2:4 "Theater Chocolate" (I)

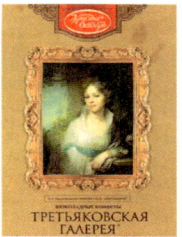

Pic. 2:6 One of the series of chocolate boxes "Tretyakov Gallery" (I)

"[…] rapid inflation, increasing social polarization, political and economic instability […] breakdowns of work collectives, changes in professional identity and prestige of one's occupation, and reconfiguration of opportunity structures. [These processes led to] dismantling, both physical and conceptual, of many structures and legacies" (Shevchenko 2002, 843).

Such were the conditions of life during the first stage of capitalism in the CIS, in general; and these same processes influenced migrants' ideas about the free market system, in particular.

The comparative analysis undertaken in this chapter recognizes that there were two sets of differences between the Israeli and German contexts that influenced migrants' post-migration ideas of *coping with capitalism*. First, since most of the participants in the Israeli case study emigrated at the beginning of 1990's, during the SU collapse, the reality of the participants' lives pre-migration lives was characterized by having to cope with strong economic deficits. In contrast, most of the participants in the German case study left the CIS after 1995—1996, as part of a mass emigration movement to Germany that included many non-Jews. Thus, these *later* migrants experienced life in the CIS when there was greater stability, as seen for example by the different foods supplies available, continuously, on store shelves. Second, whereas participants in Israel emigrated, at least theoretically, according to Israel's official policy to "their" land, the Jewish Homeland, participants in Germany immigrated to the land that embodied the West and stable capitalism. Ironically, contrary to what was purported, in the sense of material wealth, it was Germany rather than Israel that literally epitomized, in economic terms, "the promised land of milk and honey."

My own perspective on the phenomena of "capitalism" follows Herzfeld, who based himself primarily on Bird-David's view of Western capitalism as a "cultural system:"

"[Western economies] do not follow a universal or supra-cultural logic. They do […] cover their social and cultural traces" (Herzfeld 2001, 94).

Furthermore, both scholars noted that ideas about economic aspects of capitalism should not be decontextualized and detached from "Western morality, epistemology, and cosmology" (ibid., 95).

Emigration from a socialist society and economic system, characterized by permanent deficits, to a capitalist society flowing with material abundance gave participants' a sense that their aspirations and hopes for achieving a better material life could be realized in their post-migration lives. Methodologically, given the "embeddedness of material life in culture or [the] cultural constitution of material life" (ibid., 93) in a certain value system, it is important to examine transformations of "cultural capital" (Bourdieu 1984) and "social worlds" (Schütze 2002) in the transition to the capitalist societies. Accordingly, these transformations are one focus of this chapter.

Following the assumption that guided Demirović's analysis, knowledge unlike other consumer goods is not expended through practice and usage; rather, it is reproduced and crystallized (Demirović 2004, 259). This leads us to inquire into the fate of migrant knowledge during the migratory transition: Is it permanently devalued and rendered superfluous? How do participants change and use their transported knowledge about *life in capitalist world*? What are the components of their idea of capitalism as cultural capital, and how did they change and apply it in everyday life after emigration to Israel and Germany? What differences are there between the Israeli and German case studies? More specifically, how does a participant choose one product from among seemingly endless exemplars, particularly when the consumer does not have access to the product's *story* or *biography*, no personal history of purchase or any manner of association suggested by a shared body of knowledge? That is, how do participants' assess material goods available in the West after a lifetime in the SU? How do they decipher meaning? What happens when the old dream to taste living abroad is realized?

There are very few studies published that provide us with ethnographic insights of emigrants' perceptions of the transition process from the closed socialist system to the capitalist society as well as transformations of ideas about capitalism (e.g., Yelenevskaya 2005). Thus, although millions of former Soviet citizens moved to the West after Perestroika, the fundamental question yet to be investigated systematically by researchers remains: How do ex-Soviet migrants understand capitalism and make sense of their experiences?

Investigation of immigrants' views of capitalism must take into account the influence of their Soviet experience as well as the influences of their present context in terms of unemployment, economic difficulties, physical state of residential areas, the frequent indifference of the receiving society, and so forth (Golden 1996, 2002). Furthermore, we can posit that migrants see the concept of capitalism through at least two prisms: First, as highly educated former Soviet citizens; and, second, as migrants who are located at the lowest level of the social and economic pyramid in their new society.

In summary, this chapter focuses on the participants' articulations of life in capitalism, their experiences with material culture and food consumption in both contexts, and engages in comparative analyses and explanations of differences in immigrants' working knowledge in Israel and Germany.

2.1 The Soviet kind of capitalism: Soviet *spirituality* vs. Western *materialism*

Immigrants' ideas about the social world are rooted, predominantly, in the political context of their earlier lives. In that context, everything described as capitalist was rejected immediately on ideological grounds. Portrayals of capitalists and of capitalism's features included: inhuman features and particularly "excessive rationality" (Yelenevskaya 2005, 269), as well as, "the orderliness and regimented lifestyle" (ibid., 275) in the capitalist system in which people "function" like mechanized robots. This last theme is contrasted by what was perceived to be an "antithesis to impulsiveness and spontaneity identified as primary features of the Russian soul" (ibid) and "life after the heart" (ibid., 269) of the Soviet people. Similar dichotomies of Western capitalistic and East European socialistic images were also found in Daphne Berdahl's analysis of social transformations in the former GDR citing Robert Darnon: "the two Germanys: one super-modern, hard-driving, serious, and fast; the other archaic, inefficient, absurd, and slow, but with a lot of heart" (Darton 1991, 155 by Berdahl 2002, 479). In one of the few studies conducted about ex-Soviet migrants coping with capitalism, Yelenevskaya (2005) found these perceptions were retained by migrants in their post-migration lives in Israel and Germany.

The ideals and features of the socialist life were introduced, nourished, and maintained by the Soviet political propaganda machine and internalized by the citizens. Among the key ideals cultivated and stressed were societal equality and mutual support, state provision of free education and medical care, and the absolute necessity of collective wealth, inclusive of all private interests and wealth. In the Soviet collective culture, free education for all Soviet citizens and strength of *spirit* were portrayed in opposition to material values or the "useless and senseless 'meshanskii' [petit bourgeois, Rus.] preservation of [domestic] stuff" (Boym 2003, 55 [Rus.]). Capitalist comfort was referred to as an "obsessive retreat into the shelter of bourgeois comfort" (Boym 2002, 54 [Rus.]). Wealth was frowned upon, assumed unique political significance, and stigmatized through the Russian concept of *vesh'ism* [lit. thing-ism Rus.] and *potrebitel'* [consumer Rus. derived in Russian from the word "required" and connoted as an individualistic person living only for his interests].

The alternative to material wealth was *intellectual nourishment*. This ideal functioned in the minds of the intellectual strata through an assumption that the supposed schism existing between the spiritual and the material was reinforced, as a sort of surrogate, in a period of economic restrictions and permanent shortages, or was a "forced asceticism" (Roesler 2005). In particular, "love for decorative things" was interpreted as "profanation of ideas" (Boym 2002, 84). The historian Musya Glants, who analyzed the significance of food in the SU, argued that the culture of "intellectual nourishment" in this context served as a means of defense and symbolic flight from the difficulties of reality (Glants 1997, 223—4). Such a system strengthened the idea that the Soviet intelligentsia "inherited [the] aristocratic principle of selectivity and goal to achieve spiritual superiority" (Boym 2002, 82 [Rus.]).

Yet, hidden but present was a deep wonder about the West. Indeed, the myths fostered suggest that it was projected as an enchanted, secretly desired paradise. There was a glamour connected with Western goods such that consuming them was framed as a "goal in and of themselves" (Humphrey 2002, 55). The portrayals of the capitalistic life in foreign countries presented to Soviet citizens, living on the other side of the tightly closed Iron Curtain, was of a "world beyond the grave," the "hereafter," or of an unknown, distant planet.[16] Indeed, these very references to life in the West were repeated several times by participants in both fieldwork settings when recalling memories of images of the West held when living in the SU. For example, Alex (Israel) stated:

"You know, at that time, the capitalist West seemed to us to be "the world beyond the grave," the "hereafter"—from which nobody came back."

---

16 Examples of post-emigration formulations by such well-known Russian-speaking Jewish authors as Dovlatov (1995) and Genis and Vail (2003).

This glamorous, albeit nebulous and unrealistic image of an essentially unattainable life in the West was enriched and composed bit by bit like a jigsaw puzzle with the help of stories transmitted by word of mouth and carefully edited television programs. The latter included programs about journeys to various places or peoples throughout the world, reports on foreign delegations visiting the Soviet Union, and films with short scenes of Soviet citizens abroad. Interestingly, this particular form of knowledge about and understanding of the social world produced in the capitalist system was constructed through Soviet mythology about the West developed by Russian writers who emigrated to the West after the revolution of 1917 and whose work became popular in the SU (Yelenevskaya 2005).

Furthermore, multiple and often contradictory layers of this view of the West was exemplified by the high demand for Western commodities that accelerated growth of the Soviet Black Market in the 1970s (Boym 2002). Previously known as *Westernized* food,[17] the newly introduced commodities included Coca-Cola, jeans, bubblegum, coffee, whisky, martini mix, gin, rum, truffles, oysters, cognac, and cigars. Among these products were the processed Finnish cheese Viola (picture 2:2) and salami, both of which are very popular in Russian food stores in Israel and Germany today. The demand for these products preserved their status as the embodiment of *capitalist life* in the minds of migrants.

The use of negative connotations in official statements related to material goods contributed to shaping the population's idea of capitalism. The following two examples from interviews with participants demonstrate the deep antagonism for the capitalist Western world advanced by and among Soviet citizens, epitomized by its key symbols, for example, jeans and bubblegum.

Felix (Israel) remembered that in the mid-1980s his daughter returned home from school and recounted an incident at school. A boy who came to school dressed in jeans was standing in front of the class, as the teacher addressed all the pupils: "Today he is wearing jeans, tomorrow he will sell his motherland."

Katia (Germany) spoke at length about a similar situation: "Once, he [her son] came from school—he was in the second or third grade—and was obviously confused and fearful. It turns out that the class went to the museum where they happened upon a foreign delegation. The guests gave them bonbons and bubble gum.

---

17 See, for example, LeBlank (1999) for discussion of the symbolic meaning of oysters, truffles, and pineapples as Westernised food in 19th century Russian literature.

But, when the children started to open the gifts, the teacher took them directly to the nearest garbage bin and ordered them to throw them away immediately because it was certain that they contained needles and poison. Later she devoted an hour of class time to this incident and looked into the eyes of each child to make sure that they had thrown it away. However, Andrei [her son] tasted one and was very fearful that something would happen to him. He did not tell me anything, but later told his older brother because he thought he did something dangerous and terrible."

Another very important key symbol of capitalism was formulated in well-known lines written by Vladimir Mayakovsky: "Eat your pineapple, chew your hazel grouse, your final day has arrived, bourgeois" (Glants and Toomre 1997, 19 [Rus.]). This set of images led to the pineapple becoming one of the most well-known symbols of the abundance present in capitalist society, in the eyes of residents of the Soviet Union. Later, I found the pineapple featured during festive meals in immigrants' homes in Israel and Germany. Here it seemed to serve both as a symbol of their active capitalist practice as well as of economic opportunities not available to friends and relatives who remained in the CIS.

The dichotomization of the *spiritual* and the *materialistic*, too, was strongly preserved, post-migration, by these former members of the Soviet Jewish intelligentsia, in both contexts. Indeed, during the interviews, immigrants always distinguished between "food" and "culture," seemingly considering them to be two opposite domains. And although they spent a great amount of time preparing meals and meeting friends around the dining table, they constantly stressed that food had no significance for them, as they would say: "After all, it's only food." Described as typical for the middle-aged the tensions between "gluttony and orgiastic excesses of upper class members" is no new phenomenon (Verdon 2002 by Kaufmann 2005, 21)

Analyzed at a deeper level, these dichotomies seem to juxtapose, on the one hand, a disembodied, superior, preferred masculine philosophy including intellectual and spiritual activities; and, on the other hand, inferior, embodied practices typical in other Western contexts associated with the feminine and food (Lupton 1996, 2).

This dichotomy was treated and nourished politically in the Soviet context though not directly in the sense of gender hierarchy and differences, but rather as cultivating the idea of antagonist societal regimes. Thus, as demonstrated in this research study, the "triviality or guilt" often ascribed to the subject of food proves to be deceptive (Barthes 1997, 21).

This reflects tension between action, on the one hand, and self-vision and strong internalized ideas about hedonistic festivities and banquets as a perverse bourgeois attribute, on the other hand.

For example, Boris (Israel) whispered that he thinks my attempt to direct the conversation to food is inappropriate: "You talk about food too much!"

Slava (Israel): "In Israel, food is just not important any more. I can spend the whole day reading and completely forget about eating. For me, food is not the least bit important in life."

This comment seemed to be an especially obvious contradiction, as it was stated at a birthday celebration as we sat around a table filled with dishes that had taken two days to prepare.

Similarly, participants frequently stressed (cultic) spirituality by means of reading through the metaphor of the book as opposed to projected illegitimate materialist interests:

Nikolai (Israel): "Israelis think we come from a barbaric state, but over there [in the SU] we read books while standing in line. And, here, there is only one Steimatzky [bookshop] in the whole of Haifa."[18]

Igor (Israel) and his wife, Polina, repeated the following sentence at least four times during the fieldwork: "We brought 500 kilos of books with us to Israel!"

And, Arkadii (Germany) shared this comment while standing in line for free food distributed at a local church:

"Yesterday, at the second-hand market, I bought so many books that I couldn't carry them all. I had to sort them out and leave half of them there, because there was no more room in my backpack or bag."

It is difficult to reconcile this rejection of the importance of food on the part of the immigrants with their practice of serving lavish, indeed luxurious meals at every opportunity, in amounts far beyond what is consumable in one sitting. It seems to me that these two, very different practices reveal the conjunction between contradictory interests and aspirations: On the one hand, to experience capitalist abundance and achieve material wealth; and, on the other hand, to remain loyal and to live according to deeply internalized principles of the Soviet intelligentsia. Doing so means that one

---

18 The last sentence is factually inaccurate [JB].

is not a "consumer but rather an inventor and innovator who wanders through life with light baggage" (Boym 2002, 108 [Rus.]).

Furthermore, though I documented in my field notes numerous occasions when material prosperity did seem to play a very important role in migrants' lives, most participants in both contexts did not acknowledge, directly, that a desire for material prosperity, frowned upon in the SU, as a value was one of the main reasons why they decided to leave the SU. Indeed, striving for material prosperity was mentioned infrequently in verbal interaction. Furthermore, in interviews, participants referred to the constant preoccupation with obtaining basic material necessities (especially foodstuffs) in the SU/CIS as a humiliating experience for highly qualified intellectuals. As Ira (Germany) described it (in a syntax repeated in other interviews): "I was fed up with reading books while standing in the queue for soap powder."

There is, though, another reason why immigrants in Israel reject the Russian-language Israeli press' use of the term "sausage immigration" to describe the last wave of arrivals from the former SU [n. b., term refers to economic rather than Zionist motivation]. This attitude seems to reflect the politically distinctive and widespread dichotomization of the cultural and the material that was ideologically important in the socialist context that is also expressed in conversations with immigrants conducted in their new homes. Moreover, it emphasizes the importance of "nourishing intellectual food" carried forward from the past that has an additional function in the new contexts. It was extremely important for the participants to present themselves as a highly-educated intellectual group. In doing so, they employed a familiar, politically loaded dichotomy between the *spiritual* (Soviet) and the *materialistic* (decadent capitalist) in order to preserve and to revive a previous social status and dignity lost with migration.

Packaging of food products has proven to be a very useful resource for tracing the tendencies presented above. For example, similar to the analysis of food symbols in France by Roland Barthes, sweets symbolize "romance, luxury, decadence, indulgence, reward, and sensuousness" in the Soviet tradition (Barthes 1989, 38). Accordingly, given this spiritual-material dichotomy, special efforts were needed to refer consumers to the spiritual dimension of such products. Products found in Russian food stores in Israel and Germany demonstrated how advertisers understood and dealt with this dilemma. The classic claim of Lévi-Strauss "to achieve that food can be consumed well, it has to be imagined well[19] (Lévi-Strauss 1965, 116) can be demonstrated by these examples perfectly well. For example, the very prestigious Soviet chocolate called "Inspiration" displays an image of the Russian Ballet and the Bolshoi Theatre (I and G) (picture 2:3); the Theater Chocolate displays the picture of ballet dancers (I) (picture 2:4); bonbons were named—Theater, Première, and Ballet. Different art museums or well-known cultural venues in Moscow and St. Petersburg were referred to on packages of Hermitage Chocolate (I) (picture 2:5), the Russian restaurant—Hermitage (G), a series of chocolate boxes named Tretyakov Gallery that displayed well-known paintings from the Russian cultural heritage (I) (picture 2:6), chocolate named Vernissage, Russian Museum (G) (picture 2:7), the box of the Russian Museum Chocolate (G) (picture 2:8); *Petrodvorez* Caramel [Peter's Palace, Rus; well-known symbol of Russian culture and tourist attraction near St. Petersburg] (I) (picture 2:9); *Letniy Sad* chocolate [lit. Summer Garden, Rus., well-known symbol of Russian culture and tourist attraction in St. Petersburg] (G) (picture 2:10); St. Petersburg Chocolate (with sculptures and fountains of Petrodvorez) (G) (picture 2:11); and a box of Petersburg's Nights Chocolate with a painting of the Neva River (I) (picture 2:12). In addition, there are numerous chocolates with different images from stories by Pushkin, the world renown Russian writer and one of the key iconic symbols of Russian culture: for example, Fairytales of Pushkin Chocolate with the image of a golden cock (I) (picture 2:13) or Yevgenii Onegin Chocolate with a self-portrait by Pushkin marking the bicentennial celebration of the poet's birth (I) (picture 2:14).

2.2 Post-Soviet capitalism on food commodities

I suspected that the move to a capitalist society might influence migrants' ideas about material values, as well as, their intellectual, cultural, and social life. Since such influence might be expressed overtly and implicitly, two domains were analyzed: First, the visual versions of post-Soviet Russian-speaking capitalism evident on food commodities in Israel and Germany; and, second, immigrants' own descriptions. The following is a brief

---

19 "Damit ein Nahrungsmittel gut zu essen ist, muss es gut zu denken sein"

Pic. 2:7 "Vernissage—Russian Museum Chocolate" (G)

Pic. 2:8 Chocolate box "Russian Museum" (G)

Pic. 2:9 "Petrodvorez Caramel" [lit. Palace of Peter, Rus.] (I)

Pic. 2:10 "Letniy Sad Chocolate" [lit. Summer Garden, Rus.; in St. Petersburg] (G)

Pic. 2:11 Chocolate box "St. Petersburg" (with sculptures and fountains of Petrodvorez) (G)

Pic. 2:12 Chocolate box "Petersburg's nights" with old picture of the Neva river (I)

Pic. 2:13 "Fairytales of Pushkin Chocolate" with the image of the "Golden Cock" (I)

Pic. 2:14 "Yevgenii Onegin Chocolate" with self-drawing by Pushkin (I)

presentation of the key findings arrived at through analysis of these two domains.

Since many visual images of food commodities will be presented and discussed in future chapters, the discussion here will focus on six indicators of *capitalist commodity* design and images directly linked to migrants' *capitalist* views and practices. It is fair to say that all six indicators are firmly ground in previous, negatively-laden Soviet ideas about capitalism. However, these six indicators, which I submit, developed since the Perestroika, strongly reflect both general processes connected with re-formulations of the concept *capitalism*, as they appear in contemporary Russia (because many products found in Germany and Israel are imported from there), and as they are reconsidered by Russian-speaking producers of food commodities in Israel and Germany. While the following presentation focuses on delineating each of the indicators, the participants' statements presented later in this chapter elaborate on them, as well.

The *first* indicator—the ideal of endless richness and luxuriousness—is visible and legitimized as a standard feature of individual praxis in several ways: First, allusions are made in products to the pre-revolutionary stratum of merchants via imitations of commercial emblems and old drawings of rich Tsarist Russia; for example, on Korkunov Chocolate (G) (pictures 2:15—16). Furthermore, symbols are employed to make the connection with the richness of sweets through use of pre-revolutionary writing style, such as the letter "ъ" in Русский холодъ ice cream [Russian frost, Rus.], also adorned with a gold crown (I). Another example is the use of pre-revolutionary units of measure, as in Unziya Chocolate [unziya—ounce, or 28.3 grams] (G).

In addition, many Russian words connected with capitalism were known to exist but were used infrequently in earlier generations of the Russian language. Yet, since the establishment of the CIS and for post-emigration participants, these words have been restored and associated with practicing the newly legitimate *capitalist life*; for example: Lux Chocolate (I), Royal Chocolate, (G) and Magnate Beer (G) (picture 2:17); Governor Salami (G) (picture 2:18); Prestige chocolate waffle tart, (I) Prestige Pigeons Milk Bonbons (G); confectionary Azart [adrenalin excitement, Rus.; word used in relation to risk taken in card or casino play]; Casino Chocolate (G); Casino Success Bonbons (G); Elite Chocolate (G); Cream of Society as name of a dish—"shrimps mixed with fresh vegetables and bread"— served in the Israeli Russian restaurant Nest (I); *Svetskoe* champagne

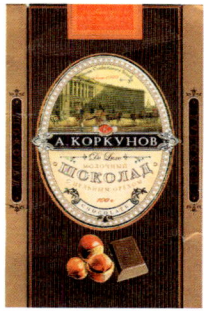

Pic. 2:15 "Korkunov Chocolate" (G)

Pic. 2:16 Chocolate box "Korkunov" (G)

Pic. 2:17 "Magnate Beer" (G)

Pic. 2:18 "Governor Salami" (G)

Pic. 2:19 "Svetskoe Champagne" [secular, high society, Rus.] (G)

Pic. 2:20 "Bourgeois Salami" (G)

Pic. 2:21 "Chocolate-lux Lights of Paris" and logo "Sweet Fairytale for all Times" (G)

Pic. 2:22 "Yemelia Croutons" (G)

Pic. 2:23 "Chocolate with Cognac" (I)

[secular, high society, Rus.] (G) (picture 2:19). The last example is especially interesting because it represents an almost exact replicate of the previously very well-known champagne Sovetskoe [Soviet, Rus.]. Thus, by
removing one letter from the Russian word for Soviet, advertisers shifted
the meaning to entice consumers to purchase a capitalist version of the
"champagne of high society."

As discussed more fully in Chapter Four, the symbol of gold remains a
primary signifier of richness used in design of Russian food products; for
example: White Gold Vodka (I); Ideal Chocolate, whose packaging displays
numerous gold medals and the sentence "give a present, the best!"; Gold
Nut Chocolate (G); Golden Rain bonbons (G); Golden Barrel croutons
[snacks to accompany drinking alcohol]; truffle chocolates— Golden
Dome Bowls (G) and Golden Corn Field (G).

The word "bourgeois" was used in marketing, presumably since it is a
word that attracts consumers; for example: a dish on the menu of the Nest
restaurant is named Modest Bourgeoisie Charm (baked liver in red wine,
soya, honey, and pine nut sauce); and, another product is referred to as
Bourgeois Salami (G) (picture 2:20).

Finally, by way of observation, one wonders if advertisers realize that
symbols of richness may have special appeal for migrants located at the
bottom of the economic pyramid in the new societies—perhaps as a compensatory role or as a dream.

Capitalism, according to the *second* indicator, appears in association with
dreams of paradise and an easy life; for example: Paradise Chocolate
Cream (G); Dream Caramel (I); Russian restaurant—Myth (I); chocolates—Beautiful Life, Bacardi (I) and Southern Night (I); bonbons—Am-
bar Cloud (I), Rivera (G); Chocolate-lux Lights of Paris accompanied by
logo—"sweet fairytale for all times"—and a firework display (I) (picture
2:21).

In the closed context of the SU, Paris represented a special symbol of
the "beautiful life abroad." For example, a very popular Soviet joke goes as
follows:

"I want to go to Paris once again!
Have you already been in Paris?
No, but I wanted to go already once before."

In fact, it was only after the fall of the Iron Curtain and the initial wave of
emigration that participants began to sense that there was the possibility of
realizing an old dream—to travel to different countries. And, accordingly,

the dream of discovering the world by means of different tastes began to be employed widely in the names of food products, food advertisements, as well as so called "ethnic" restaurants (e.g., Bell and Valentine 2001). This is the context for such products as Bon Voyage chocolate (I), Scotland's Breakfast tea (G), and Spring of Prague tart (I); among other examples discussed in Chapter Five.

Similar to fantasizing about visits to the capitalist world, dreams of enjoying a relaxing life in paradise, too, appeared in food marketing. For example, Yemelia pickled gherkins or croutons (G) (picture 2:22) were named for a very well known Russian fairytale character: Yemelia is a lazy peasant who lingers all the time around a stove until forced to go to the river to bring water. Upon doing so, he finds a magic fish in his pail, which promises to fulfill all his desires. By the end of the fairytale, he has married a princess. Yemelia embodies the idea of *successful laziness*, or more precisely *becoming rich through magic*, and symbolizes the realization of any desire without investing any work or time. Interestingly, advertisers chose the image of Yemelia for a product within a new food category—sneki [snacks][20]— that have became very popular in recent years in Russia, as part of another new Western-oriented category of activity—*leisure time*.

The *third* indicator is consumption of foods that symbolize a common dream of foreign *capitalist life*. Different from the second indicator in which the dream of enjoying a relaxing life in capitalism is projected onto the desire for a rare holiday vacation in Europe and similar to the first, the third indicator realizes dreams of capitalism through consumption, at the dining table. Here, various products provide consumers with tastes of foreign foods, for example: The packaging of Truffle with Brandy (I) includes the statement—"Classic consumption of chocolate with brandy;" Whisky chocolate (I), Chocolates with Cherries (I), Chocolate with Cognac (I) portrays a picture of a small Cupid offering a glass of cognac (picture 2:23), Punch chocolate (G).

The design of box of Komilfo Chocolate is especially interesting. The origins of the product's name are the French phrase—"comme il faut" [correct, as in the "correct" or appropriate way of doing things, French], written here in Russian letters and accompanied by portrayals of Caribbean melon, mango, orange with cognac, and pineapples with champagne—all exotic foreign foods. Indeed, the last three products are used repeatedly in

---

20 In the Russian version, *sneki* are usually packages of dried fish or flavored croutons eaten with beer.

the SU to signify capitalism (G) (picture 2:24). Their association with "comme il faut"—implying "our tradition" or "the proper life"—seems to be both a realization of dreams and "indigenization" (Mintz 2003, 21), of "invented traditions" (Hobsbawm, 1983), or "naturalization process" (Kaufmann 2005, 47) applied with the availability of new food commodities.

The *fourth* indicator projects new relations with capitalism and appears in product names and packaging design, where many new and foreign—mostly English—words are Russified by appearing in Russian letters; for example: Top Ice Cream (G), Einem Lux Chocolates (G), Airish Krem Chocolate [for Irish cream]; croutons—Sneki s bekonom [snacks with bacon] (G); waffle-chocolate tart—Sharman [charmant, Fr.], chocolate—Kappuchino [Cappuccino]; chocolate—Pralinetka [pralines], chocolate—Bon-bon [previously unknown in Russian]; jelly with chocolate—Frutty [fruits]; chocolates—Potobello (G), Monty Pina Colada" (G), jelly—Speis [space]; Jorge [obvious foreign name in Russian], Ddzhemmi Lait [for jam/marmalade light (probably diet)]; mayonnaise Provansal [Provencal, Fr.] (G).

A *fifth* indicator highlights physical and psychological pleasures obtained from eating previously taboo foods that due to the Perestroika were released from social sanctions; for example, the name of a Russian food store in Jerusalem—Mountains of Food (see store advertisements in picture 2:25) or a product name such as Doctor Sausage XXL—employs one of the key characteristics of capitalism—abundance—as its signifier. While this may seem to be attractive, it is also a significant challenge given the socialization of Russian-speaking consumers (see quotes of different interviews and comments, below).

In addition, emphasizing physical enjoyment is based on the previously noted idea of food as a form of bourgeois decadency. Here we see that attempts were made—through product design—to change the emotional association with this idea by constructing meaning that is diametrically opposed to the previous cultural position; that is, to make it positive. For example, Russian food stores in both settings displayed products with names such as: Delight for the Taste-buds Chocolates (I); Delicious—zucchini salad (G); Choose me, Sweet Pleasure Cookies; Delicates Salami

Pic. 2:25 Russian food store in Jerusalem "Mountains of Food"

Pic. 2:24 Chocolate box "Komilfo" [written in Russian letters for Comme il faut, Fr.] (G)

Pic. 2:26 "Liqueur Caramel" (I)

Pic. 2:27 Sprat "Fat Boatswain" (I)

Pic. 2:28 Marinated pickles and tomatoes (I)

Pic. 2:29 "Gluttony Cookies" (I and G)

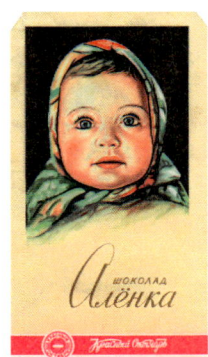

Pic. 2:30 "Alyonka Chocolate" (I and G)

Pic. 2:31 New version of "Alyonka Chocolate" (I)

Pic. 2:32 "Malvina Chocolate" (G)

(I); Doctor Sausage XXL (G); Tasty life Tart! Victory of the taste Chocolate, with the logo "Even more chocolate" (I and G); sweet condensed
milk—Chocolate Paradise. Sweet Moment (I); Rye croutons slogan—
"Take the tastiest from the life!" (G); chocolates—Explosion of
the Taste (G); Passion Fruit Jelly (I); caramel—Delight (G); chocolates—
Crunch with Appetite! (G); cookies—Russian Delicacies (G); pickled tomatoes—Tomato Temptation (I).

There are also obvious names that use an oxymoron to achieve a similar
effect, such as Gourmet Meals—canned pigfish in tomato sauce (known as
proletarian food) (I) or semi-prepared *chebureki* [meat paste, fried in oil]—a
traditional, simple food named Gourmet (I). In some cases gluttony is
stressed explicitly, as in the example caramel—Liqueur, accompanied by a
picture of a fat, drunken, sleeping cat (I) (picture 2:26); sprats—Fat Boatswain (I) (picture 2:27), marinated pickles and tomatoes with image of a fat
peasant (I) (picture 2:28); or Glutton Cookies (G) (picture 2:29) showing a
caricature of a person waking up at night and coming with a lighted candle
in the darkness to eat a snack of cookies. In the accentuation of the gastronomic physical enjoyment combined with passion connected with food
these images recall (even in a different sense) Frank Chin's term of „food
pornography" (1981).[21] Here we can also pursuit the post-socialistic kind
of what Kaufmann calls the "formation process of enjoyment and taste"[22]
(Kaufmann 2005, 42), which is expressed on the etiquettes as different
versions of "living for eating" (see also chapter five and the picture 5:3).

And, finally, a *sixth* indicator highlights probably the strongest of the
transformations of food commodities—images of women and girls. For
example, one of the most well-known Soviet chocolates—Alyonka (I and
G) (picture 2:30)—is represented by a blue eyed, rosy cheeked full bodied
girl with a headscarf depicted against a black background. This is a direct
reference to Russian fairytales and peasant life. Yet, this image can also be
seen as an antithesis of the Barbie image.

It is interesting to follow the image's transformation. It first appeared
on packaging of a new chocolate Alyonka (I) (picture 2:31) with the image
of a traditionally dressed young girl. This was replaced by the image of new
girl on chocolate—Malvina (G) (picture 2:32). In comparing these three

---

21 "a form of cultural self-commodification through which Asian Americans earn a living by
   capitalizing on the so-called exotocism embedded in one's foodways" (Mannur 2005,
   59).
22 "eine Formierung des Genusses und des Geschmacks."

pictures, one can see how the naïve image of a peasant child with headscarf was modified to a girl with make-up and then to a sexual young female in pink colors.

In general, the use of images of women as a means of advertising on packages of food products was a rare sight during the Soviet period. One was more likely to find such images on Soviet politically-laden posters with images of emancipated Soviet women embodying communist ideals. Exemplars of these posters were hung by participants in the new contexts. For example, a 1941 popular poster presents an androgynous-framed female worker (I) (picture 2:33); a 1948 poster of a waitress states—"We will serve every guest in a civilized manner!" (I) (picture 2:34); and a 1963 Soviet poster captioned—"To the fields, to the building sites! The party said: 'You must!' The Komsomol replied: 'Yes!'" (I) (picture 2:35). However, following Perestroika, new images of females appeared. As cited previously, some of these images preserved the idea of sweets as "romance, symbolizing luxury, decadence, indulgence, reward, and sensuousness" (Barthes 1989, 38).

Indeed, many packages portrayed a new image of a *lady* not applied to women in the Russian language or culture during the Soviet period in either word or concept. For example, this image was linked to chocolates via a mysterious, romantic atmosphere along with references to passion and sexuality, also topics articulated in the public sphere as features of *capitalist life*.[23] Some sweet food commodities refer the consumer back to pre-revolutionary time by employing portraits of elite noble ladies. Others emphasize women in poses that stress sexuality and women's sensuality, for example: Ladies Happiness Chocolate" (I) (picture 2:36); box of Emmi Chocolate employs the image of a 19th century lady (I) (picture 2:37); chocolates—Birthday of the Heart (I), Intrigue (I), Lady's Caprice (G), Musa (I), Coquette Lady (G); Queen of Spades Ice Cream, (I and G); Mask Chocolate, accompanied by the portrayal of an enigmatic lady (G); Visit chocolate whose packaging displays a noble lady lounging on a big pillow

---

23 By way of example, we recall a statement made by the actress on one of the first so called "TV bridges" made between Russia and the USA at the beginning of the Perestroika, viewed by millions of people in the SU. She expressed a common understanding of what is allowed to be said publicly: "For us [in opposition to the capitalist world] there is no sex!" This sentence immediately became a very popular joke and rudiment of Soviet times and official rhetoric.

Pic. 2:33 Soviet poster (1941) posted in Russian book store: "Don't gossip!" (I)

Pic. 2:34 Soviet poster (1948) posted in Russian book store with image of Soviet waitress and slogan: "We will serve every guest in a civilized manner!" (I)

Pic. 2:35 Soviet poster (1963) posted in Russian book store: "To the fields, to the building sites!" The party said: 'You must!' The Komsomol replied: 'Yes!'" (I)

Pic. 2:36 'Ladies' Happiness Chocolate" (I)

Pic. 2:37 Chocolate box "Emmi" (I)

Pic. 2:38 Chocolate "Visit" (G)

Pic. 2:39 "Parisian Lady" Chocolate sweets (I and G)

Pic. 2:40 Chocolate "Carmen" (G)

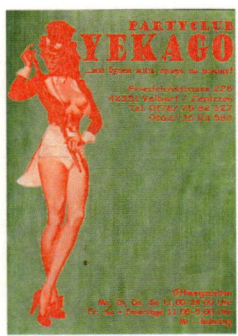

Pic. 2:41 Postcard with Russian party club "Yekago" and statement "Now we will live in a new way!" (G)

surrounded by roses (G) (picture 2:38); chocolate sweets—Parisian Lady (I and G), with an alluring dame in a black dress (picture 2:39); chocolates—Cabaret (I) and Carmen (G) (picture 2:40), along with for Moulin Rouge. Also, a postcard portrayed a Russian party club—Yeager—along with the image of a sensually dressed cabaret women accompanied by the statement—"Now we will live the new way!" (G) (picture 2:41). In my experience, such images do not reflect actual female migrant behavior.

Collectively, these indicators help us deconstruct and understand the visual changes observable in the Russian-speaking commodities culture. Certain elements of these changes—particularly the first, third, and fourth indicators—were also articulated by migrants in both contexts. This material contradicts other aspects of the participants' lives, for example: the image of *exaggerated richness* and an *easy life in the capitalist paradise* contradicts the low economic and social status of the participants in both contexts; the physical enjoyment of abundance with reference to being *spoiled* stands in direct opposition to earlier strongly held and internalized ideas about the necessity of *spiritual asceticism.* Yet, whisky and pineapples (may) have a *bitter* aftertaste and may as well serve as compensation for professional ambitions unrealized in new contexts. Paradoxically, the propaganda poster about "lost talents in a capitalist world," mentioned above (picture 2:1) was confirmed as self-fulfilling prophecy in many of the participants' personal biographies in Israel and Germany.

The following sections of this chapter focus on the divergent views and actions of participants as they experimented with and tried to invent their own manifestations of the concept *comme il faut* of *capitalist life* in Israel and in Germany.

2.3 "Arrival on a new planet"

> "In order to get from A to B,
> it is not enough to board the tram.
> You must change in such a way that
> your fellow passengers no longer
> recognize you."
>
> *Veil and Genies* (2003, 87)

The following extended selections from interviews with two participants—
one from Israel and the other from Germany—enable us to understand
transformations in ideas about intellectual, cultural, and social life after
transition to capitalist societies. These reflections serve as the basis for
further discussion about migrants' modes of coping with the new capitalist
society.

The case of Misha (Germany)

Misha (58) is a mechanical engineer and scientist who emigrated with his
wife and daughter from Odessa (Ukraine) to Germany in 1991. Since then
he divorced his first wife and married a German woman, with whom he
has a 13-year-old son. Misha worked for seven years in Germany as a scientist with a grant from a national science foundation. He lost his job in
2004 because of budget cuts, was unemployed, but volunteered to continue
in the same position for two years. At that time, he was rehired again on
soft money through another grant that was to expire soon after the interview. Authorities of the firm informed him that they may not be able to
employ him in the future.

"Germany was my first experience in a foreign country. It was a shock to me, as
someone who had not experienced anything similar before this in his life. Our
arrival was like coming to a new planet [...]. It was also an economic shock and, in
particular, for me it was a food shock. In this crazy Rewe store [means regular
German supermarket; he used a Russian phrase unusual in such contexts, as an
adjective meaning 'crazy'], in Unna-Massen [the first place where ex-Soviet Jews in
Germany live after arrival before distribution to different cities], there [were all
these] yoghurts. [I mean] we left a state where there was nothing there [means
especially difficult times in 1990—1 with literally empty shelves in food stores].
And, here, no fewer than a hundred containers of yoghurt! This is coming from a
person who knows only one kind, namely, yoghurt [in Russian 'Kefir'], sour cream,
or sausage.

I was stunned and confused by the variety of cheeses and different packaging.
Of course, my jaw dropped in bewilderment [pause]. It's not surprising that I
gained 10 kilos. Because you don't know how many calories things contain. For
example, yoghurt—you think it is not a meal and you eat immense quantities
[pause].

Once when I entered a supermarket, I immediately remembered the story of a
friend of mine: She was a mathematician from Moscow and visited Boston for the
first time. This was in the 1960's. And it is important to say that she was a very
sensible, reasonable, thoughtful person, for whom material stuff and food did not

define the meaning of life. As she entered a supermarket for the first time, she went literally into hysteria. When she calmed down, she only said: 'We were lied to our entire life, infinite lies!' [pause]

I was reminded of this story upon entering the shop [pause]. The shop window is flooded with light, having a system of mirrors so that everything is seen double. As a friend of mine said: 'I got tired of sausage and now one must cope with life' [laughs]. Today, I try to walk away from them, walk around the shops, not enter, or go through them quickly.

I am furious that one must search and search, and I start to get annoyed. I still haven't and I probably never will get used to it. I get tired very quickly from all the options. [pause] I wouldn't oppose there being ten times less. I have no need for all these seasonings [pause]. One must be relaxed about it, but it takes so much time away from you!"

In this passage, Misha shares with us his initial impressions after his arrival at the "new planet" with all of its material abundance. On the one hand, like all the other participants in both contexts, he is thankful that he no longer has to put up with product shortages, a main deficiency of the socialist system. Even though they continue to experience economic difficulties in their new context, for the first time they can eat whatever they want at mealtimes. This freedom of choice is a new social existential situation for them.

The burst of initial enthusiasm for limitless and accessible supply of goods ("they are there;" "you can see them on the shelf!") is repeated in many narratives. At the same time, abundance comes as a shock. For example, Misha mentioned that he felt paralyzed by the hundreds of containers of yoghurt, sour cream, and sausages. This is a gastronomic shock for a person who would not mind, if there was only one tenth of the commodities on display. Where do you start? How do you choose one thing out of so many, when individual products have no obvious history for immigrants and are not associated with anything? Adopting the terminology of the cultural anthropologist Igor Kopytoff (1986), one could say the product has had its bography withdrawn.

The unknown, anonymous array of goods on the shelves and the absence of anything immigrants could associate with these products is a reminder of the fact that they are strangers in this new country. The differences are so great and this world is so new and unknown to Misha that he calls the new environment a "new planet." The products he sees contradict, obviously, everything he knew about the West and Germany before his arrival. His most powerful impression of the "new planet" is described through strong descriptive expressions, such as "my jaw dropped in bewilderment;" the "crazy Rewe supermarket." Becoming annoyed at first, then furious, and quickly tiring in search of pepper at the supermarket, Misha even reports about feeling physically ill at ease because of the variety and choices that had to be made.

This experience of being unable, physically, to cope with the phenomenon of abundance is repeated in many other interviews, in both contexts. Participants describe dizziness, fatigue, and feeling nauseous upon being confronted with endless commodities. Also characteristic of others' experiences of the *capitalist life* is his realization of the false Soviet promises about abundance and quality of living standards when he shops in the German supermarket through the eyes of life in the socialist system.

Particularly interesting and unusual is Misha's quotation of a friend—"I got tired of sausage and now one must cope with life." This statement follows his long, detailed description of his impressions of the capitalist world with its abundance of commodities. He recalls the impressions of his mathematician friend, whom he stressed was a rational, intellectual person "for whom material stuff and food did not define the meaning of life." Then, when Misha juxtaposes life to "sausage," we see the Soviet dichotomy between "spiritual" and "material," mentioned above. However, this sentence cannot be developed further as he feels that material commodities and abundance remain an important topic. With "on the other hand," it becomes clear that he cannot switch the direction of his description and he returns to the same topic, stating that "abundance" continues to occupy and disturb him until today.

Misha also reflected on different expressions of *capitalist life* in the West. In the next selection, he refers to fundamental and essential Western concepts like citizenship:

Misha: "I think I am, so to speak, an average person among those who came here [...] And, what did we know before [we came]? Nothing. It is only here in Germany that I discovered that it is an expressive picturesque country. What did I understand when I said 'German lyric' before? I have heard it mentioned since childhood—'sweet' lyrics. The word *Bürger* [citizen, Ger.] had no connection to the word *grazhdanin* [citizen Rus.]. If somebody was called a '*dobroporyadochnyi nemezkii grazhdanin*' [conscientious and neat German citizen, Rus.], it was always understood arrogantly, always said negatively, and it was clear that this human being is a piece of shit."

JB: "Why then?"

Misha: "He is too good, he is not human. Such a robot lives only according to laws and written rules. At the same time, he has pink cheeks, is fat, and lives in Munich. He eats and drinks sumptuously and these are his only interests. But nobody ever mentioned that he lives as a free human being in a dynamically developed society and knows his duties and rights. It is very convenient in politics to present a one-sided view of reality. But, then, it turns out that the lyric is sweet and the German citizen is a 'conscientious and neat citizen.' These were linguistic and conceptual difficulties. All the initial difficulties are also the last [to go away]. The difficulties of life on a new planet—where should we go? How should you select the city? Actually, Gabochka—our dog made the selection for us. We ended up in the only hostel in X-town that allowed us to bring our dog."

Especially interesting is how Misha related to the stereotypic nature of everyday Soviet knowledge about capitalist "Germans." He recalled common Soviet ideas about "German capitalists" as materialistically oriented people—"inhuman, robot[s] who live only according to laws and written rules." This statement is amazing similar to Yelenevskaya description in her research of "the orderliness and regimented lifestyle" of capitalists (mentioned above) retained by the Russian-speaking migrants in Germany (Yelenevskaya 2005). Moreover, Misha realized that the same words for citizen (in Russian and German) have completely different meaning in Soviet and German realities, and hence lead to different experiences in socialization and knowledge. Here, as well as in the last part of the citation, Misha reflected about the "conceptual difficulties" that have arisen in his transition to the West. Thus, these politically loaded social concepts transported from his former life in the SU are not only past difficulties, they are incorporated in behavior he takes for granted, in perceptual patterns, and become consciously evident in "collision" with his new life, namely through the example of the Other society and its everyday life.

Pointing out the immutable nature of these "conceptual difficulties," which in his view remain unchanged after 17 years of living in Germany, implies a certain degree of alienation from this new Other society that accompanies him in his current life. He related that sometimes, at moments when decisions had to be made, he lacked the "tools"—the social competences—needed. He stressed, through irony, the absurdity of this state-of-affairs when he recalled that the decision of where to live was made because he had a dog. Nevertheless, as we will see later, he tries continually to find his way, to reflect on concepts, and to act as a mature social agent rather than be a victim of circumstances. Not only does he continue to confront the necessity for change, he also tries to do so actively, by transforming everyday experience into new understandings of the German environment. And, he thematizes this as a learning process. This point distinguishes him from many other participants who often refused to speak about their learning process, because it contradicted their framing and positioning of themselves as mature social agents and highly qualified persons. They preferred to stress their resources, professionalism, and the social knowledge they hope to apply in the new society.

"There was a question about everything. One had to be learning the entire time. To know one's way around, exactly like a child with little knowledge or psychological ability in Bochum [one German city] at the university.

[For example,] I showed my paper to a professor: I held up the paper and asked: 'Do you read English?' He looked at me over his glasses and was silent. And, I turned red [pause].

So one learns. In order to learn the rules on the new planet, one needs a map. This map is called language. This is the key element. At the beginning, you feel like an idiot. This helplessness suppressed me; although objectively my language [possession] has developed [...] You also study other things simultaneously: In regard to capitalism, I heard many references to 'sharks' [the Soviet propaganda word for capitalists]. One must not give one's soul away, rather patent your idea quickly, as long as it has not yet been stolen...

[There are] many conceptual difficulties. For example, the word 'shares.' Of course I knew the word, but I didn't know how it functions concretely, because there was no comparison with it in my former life. And, there is no chance to find your way around, even though I have devoted much time to math and chess [...] Or, for example, you want to buy shoes in this new system. You find some that cost 10 DM and look great. You know the statement: 'I am not rich enough to buy cheap things,' but one buys them nevertheless. After two weeks, they fall apart, and you are strongly dissatisfied.

Then, you understand that not only are there quality products that are produced in capitalism, but there are also many that intentionally have only a short lifetime, in order to increase the profit. One also has to say that for this person 10 DM was a lot of money at that time, because he constantly converted the money into rubles and realized that for this sum he could buy very good Italian shoes in Russia. He doesn't understand why good shoes should cost $100 here, and how such shoes cost there only the equivalent of 10 DM. The prices to which he was accustomed were fixed and obscenely inexpensive, in relation to the labor exerted. But, now, they preoccupy my thinking and I am often offended by capitalism.

Immigration brings eternal stress to people who are mature in age; maybe not at the beginning, but it prevails nonetheless permanently. They will never feel at home. A human being is shaped so strongly by his childhood, education, and surroundings; and is so defined by it that one cannot accuse him... [Here I ask: 'Who accuses him?'] Well, yes, or cannot expect that he should change. The residue from our Soviet life is in everything. For example, a concrete example—I must change my job now. There, in Odessa, [...] [living according to] capitalism was unthinkable. You never had to change your job. Everyone went to their same job their entire life. Here, I needed great mental effort to understand that I was fired from the research project after seven years of work not because people do not like me or because I am not suitable, but because a permanent position in my department is no longer economically feasible. It is difficult for me not to take it personally and to understand that economic circumstances also decide this."

Following his *capitalist life*, Misha's initial reaction changes from enthusiasm to helplessness and psychological lability. But he tries in a number of active ways to manage his situation. He undertakes important changes in his life, at his own initiative: Misha learned German and improved his English, when he realized that both were necessary for academics in Germany; he divorced his wife and married a German woman; and found a research job where he was employed for seven years.

Misha also reflected upon and used new economic ways of thinking, as for example his conceptual coping with terms such as "shares," "stock exchange," the dynamic processes of the Western market system, the defining of prices in the capitalist system, the production of artifacts with an intentional "short shelf life" and the "right" presentation (self marketing/promotion) and marketing of your own ideas. He tried not to be "offended by capitalism" and "not to take personally" his being laid off, by attempting to explain it in the context of general economic circumstances. At the same time, he is aware that since his worldview was shaped by his life in the Soviet Union, he often misunderstands local social, cultural, and economic codes. His feeling that the receiving society expects immigrants to undergo crucial inner transformations ("one cannot accuse him") in order to be integrated, contradicts his own everyday experience, through which he finds out that "residues from his Soviet life are in everything."

Misha's very personal and candid account of his experiences is laced with cynical comments, accounts of absurd situations, descriptions of associations, discoveries about different forms of Soviet political manipulation, everyday observations, comparisons between what they were taught by earlier immigrants and their own experiences. All of these point to an active confrontation with the concept of capitalism and Misha's self-reflections about his position in the new system of the free economy. In his conscious approach to dealing with his situation, we see that he dealt not only with linguistic but also conceptual difficulties connected with the transition to a capitalist system. In this sense, Misha's account is typical of many other interviews with people from the group under investigation.

Despite Misha's unemployment at the time of the interview (2004), he was an active, energetic, and contemplative person who sought—with great effort—to defend his dignity and worldview and was not ashamed of what he referred to as the "Soviet residue" that shaped his whole being. This effort to retain his understanding of the social world is combined with confusion about intuitively noted challenges that migrants confront in the host society that require them to become completely different persons, of course, under terms established by the host society that remain unclear to Misha, or, as Golden stated, that require them to be (like children) re-reared and "schooled" (Golden 2001, 70).

In spite of internal changes and transformations, many Soviet experiences remained active in his consciousness and Misha referred to them in order to justify his actions to himself and to avoid the accusations made by the (invisible) host society.

Overall, we see that Misha is engaged in an inner dialogue involving reflections on his previous experiences and attempts to retain and interweave them in his immediate situation. He also wants to counteract images like the labile child who does not know his way around, as migrants are often perceived, in favor of presenting himself as a mature, responsible, and socially active agent (Golden 2001, 2002).

"Capitalism can be demoralizing for people:" The case of Ella (Israel)

Ella, now in her early 60s, is a construction engineer who immigrated to Israel from the Ukraine in 1992. She arrived with her husband Felix (63), an electrical engineer, and two daughters (then eight and 15) and has resided in Haifa the entire time. Neither Ella nor Felix are employed in their original occupations: Ella worked for the first year after their arrival as a building engineer and then decided to establish her own business. She had her own real estate agency for eight years and since closing her business has been employed as a caretaker in an old age-home. This is her story and views:

"In the beginning, when we arrived, it was horrible. So many lines and bureaucratic officials. And, anger, because you have no idea where you should go? What you need to find out? Whom to turn to [for help]?

And, so, what happens is that you learn by idiocy. A friend arrived a year before us. She told us: 'The most you can withdraw from an ATM is 50 shekels at a time, not 1000 all at one time.' But, we were not accustomed to such a banking system. I wanted to have a large sum at home, on hand, so I could be sure not to run out of cash and have to go to the ATM all the time [...] But he was insistent and we listened to him. I was always anxious, worried that we did not have money [pause]

And, the overflowing supermarkets and huge stores. When I entered the Mashbir [at the time of the interview this was one of the biggest chains of department shops in Israel], I wandered around and felt bad for a quarter of an hour. I mean, really, physically. It was from being overwhelmed by it all, from so much stuff, all at once. I became nauseous and had to leave. My friend told me that she also became ill from being in the stores in the beginning."

Three themes evident here that are characteristic of many other interviews. First, Ella's disorientation upon arrival, as she reacts with difficulty, psychologically, to situations in which she did not know the right way to act. Second, Ella consulted with veteran immigrants, only to be disappointed by their advice. Here she admits that there were many concrete things she did not know how to manage, such as withdrawing money from an ATM. Thus, a small thing that a person socialized in Israel would not consider to be a problem caused Ella ongoing existential anxiety during the initial period of her adjustment to life in a new society. Third, Ella became nauseous from the abundance that surrounded her. In the next section, Ella continues to reflect on her adjustment to the capitalist system.

"We economized the entire time. We wrote down all of our expenses—bread, milk, and the bus fares. We economized on the bus. Then, we thought—let's play the stock exchange. We borrowed money from a relative who had lived in Israel for 17 years and invested it somewhere. We thought—'now we will earn something quickly.' But we lost everything. We had to use what little money we had to pay him back [pause] Acch! [bends her hand down]. . .

It was terribly cold in the apartments. We were used to it being cold outside, but not inside the flat. We economized on electric heating, because we had been told [pathetically]: 'This is [the nature of] electricity!' They said: 'Ze mamash yakar b'aretz!' [It is very expensive here, stated in Hebrew] I don't think I stopped trembling that entire first winter. I was cold the entire time. We did not turn on the heater at all.

Another friendly couple, who immigrated earlier, explained to us that they cannot afford local meat prices and that we should be content with chicken wings and offals. So I bought chicken offals that we never ate in Russia [thought to be cheap and tasteless], and prepared a soup. No one in the family ate this dreck [crap, Yiddish].

Another time, we visited friends who also immigrated before us. I asked if I could make a phone call. The woman replied: 'You know, this costs money in Israel!' I wanted to go back [to Russia]."

Ella articulated, in a dramatic fashion, the many challenges and extreme changes in her life as well as experimental actions undertaken in the new conditions, some of which seem to her to be absurd to her on hindsight. She is very explicit and expressive about these changes. Her ironic account of always feeling cold in Israel is a good example, as this is the last thing expected upon emigrating from the cold Ukraine to the heat of the Middle East in Israel. However, Ella was accustomed to state subsidized Soviet flats where heat was cheap and therefore constantly available—an aspect of her life in the SU that she had taken for granted. Now she had to pay for something that according to her habitus was nearly free in the SU, since it was a primary necessity of life. This exemplar is representative of the need she felt for continuous reappraisal of expenses and money. This, too, recalls Misha's reflections on what he referred to as "obscene prices." Both Ella and Misha expressed openly how much they had changed since their emigration. In their new reality, many of their monthly expenditures were directed to needs that were free in the SU (e.g., education, medicine, and organized activities for children), required a low monthly payment (e.g., rent for state flats, telephone, gas, electricity), or had been strongly subsidized (e.g., postal prices, transportation, books).

Ella related to mistakes and inadequate actions taken in the past through a perspective rich with experience—from their experiment with one of the key symbols of *capitalist life* through which one can become rich quickly—"easy money from the stocks"—to reflections on statements on food packaging. In addition, she noted that in the beginning she did not realize that those who gave her advice were immigrants, who were themselves experimenting with new conditions in their lives. Thus, she failed to realize that this move involved her in a hierarchical relationship of "veterans" and "newcomers."

"However, I did believe that we would find a place for ourselves here. My husband found work as a technician. I began to work for a company as an engineer and was paid a minimum wage for one year. The work I did there was what I did 20 years ago in Russia. Also, I didn't like the atmosphere. Dependence as an employee always weighed me down.

When we started to look into buying an apartment I observed how the real estate agents acted with *alimi* [newcomers: Russified Hebrew word for immigrants, olim] in an unprofessional manner. And, I thought, I could do it better. The word 'self-employed' seemed attractive to me. After all, [in the SU] we had been dependent on someone throughout our life there. I wanted to be independent. I did well for six years, but then the business was no longer profitable, since there was a decline in the number of Russians coming to Israel. So I had to look for another job. I became a caregiver, and from time to time a real estate agent in order to supplement my minimal income. I work many night shifts because the pay is better.

One thinks constantly about money in capitalism. Never in my life have I thought so much about money as I do here. But, I must say honestly, this way of economics suits me better. It was always difficult there [in the SU] for creative professionals—'each initiative was strangled' [well-known Soviet idiom]. One had either to adapt to the regime, drink, or leave. You were not allowed to be free."

This passage shows Ella's flexibility and her attempts to experiment with new directions in her post-emigration life. Even though she found work in her profession (following completion of a program that prepared academics for work in the local job market), she felt that the work she was assigned did not match her qualifications. Then she dared to experiment with the idea of self-employment—another key symbol of capitalism—for which she had neither knowledge nor any practical experience during her life in the SU. Later, in discussing her successes being self-employed (e.g., she repaid her mortgage), she stressed that these actions were just the opposite of what she had experienced in her life in the SU, where "each initiative was strangled." Even if she had to change jobs later—to one more difficult to less pay—and realized that her preoccupation with money haunts her, she still claimed that she preferred life in the capitalist system in comparison to what she knew before.

"There are so many enticements and temptations, so many things around you. You want to have everything and, with some people, moral values are pushed aside. They have enjoyed so little in their life and now it is difficult to see all the richness around them and to be unable to afford it for themselves. It shatters people.

In order to get something good, one must often set aside one's principles. I often discuss this with my friend—it is really exciting. But, how can one avoid losing oneself here? You must accommodate yourself, fight for your place under the sun. Your true self emerges here. Many fight at all costs and act meanly. It is not only education, but upbringing plays a role.

It is difficult for us to enter capitalism—it is too late [in life]. And, for many educated in socialism, capitalism is pernicious. They are educated to make their future secure. But there are also people, especially women who, no matter what job they have, don't lose their self respect. I see it in their eyes when I go on the bus. They dress with style—green blouse, green jewelry. You know, attentive to their appearance—orange sweater and amber necklace. They are well-groomed, even though they do physical work and have many severe problems. She has a 50 agorot notebook [inexpensive] and is reading something from it. I look inside—something about cosmetics. She is probably studying to become a cosmetician. Maybe she will earn nothing from this preparation course and it's idiotic. But, she keeps trying, wants to develop herself further, not just to ask for charity. And, sometimes they go to a café or buy books or attend concerts. Others are grabbing for things all the time, trying to 'to make a deal' quickly. They would rather be supported by welfare than go to work. Capitalism can be really pernicious for people."

Ella focused on the challenges and difficulties involved in coping with material temptations and the potential of losing face in the new system. Intuitively, she realized that capitalism is much more than an economic system. Ella referred to it as an upbringing and is disturbed because she realized that this is what she lacked. Stressing the importance of initiative and action in the new system, she concluded by sharing observations about the lives of migrants who fail to cope because they are trapped in the contradictions, claiming that capitalism can be pernicious. This claim remains a metaphor for "adapting to life" [...] "so that we don't burn ourselves out," as Yugoslav writer Ugresić (1999) described her experience of exile (cited by Shevchenko 2002, 859).

In summary, the revealing stories of Misha and Ella are very personal, candid accounts of their experiences. They also shared cynical comments, absurd situations, associations, discoveries of Soviet political manipulations, everyday observations, as well as comparisons between what they were taught by earlier immigrants and their own experiences. All of this points to an active engagement and confrontation with the concept of capitalism and their reflections about their position in the new system of a free economy. Misha and Ella's reflections are oriented as well to their new environment (e.g., coping conceptually with terms such as—citizen, shares, and stock exchange). They interpret the place of immigrants and their personal position "on another planet." Misha's initial enthusiasm changed quickly after his first "collision with the life" in Germany to helplessness and "psychological lability," which is very similar to Ella's dramatic presentation of her experiences in Israel.

Both Misha and Ella realized that "life in the capitalist world" requires knowledge beyond the economic system. Both admitted that their conceptual as well as psychological difficulties of "life on the new planet" were the result of certain deficiencies in their "upbringing" [meaning socialization] or "Soviet residue." Indeed, like many other participants in both contexts, Misha and Ella's experiences correspond with the findings of Keller and Vihalemm's 2005 study of how elderly urban people in post-Soviet Estonia coped with consumer culture when the "profusion of goods and free choice …foreshow new scarcities that have to be coped with on an individual level" (Keller and Vihalemm 2005, 69). It seems that participation in the abundant consumer culture compensated for professional frustrations and their expectations of the receiving society, as well as, loss of what was previously important and taken for granted in the sense of social participation and values in the SU. Moreover, coping with capitalism and its new concepts, in general, and with abundance, in particular, represented their new participation in the capitalist Western society, one that extends beyond the consumption process.

However, in contrast to Keller and Vihalemm's study, this investigation revealed the creative agency of participants in Israel and Germany. Shortly after the arrival, both Misha and Ella undertook initiatives to change their lives: Both speak the local language fluently.[24] Misha divorced, married a German woman, and found a job as researcher. Ella tried her hand in the stock market and then became an independent real estate agent. All of this was undertaken in spite of the fact that participation in the local market economy required commercial knowledge and independence completely new to them. Despite Misha's unemployment and Ella's being overqualified for her work as a caretaker, both presented themselves as active, innovative, thinking persons who have succeeded with uncanny effort to protect their dignity and personality and who are not ashamed of what Misha referred to as his being shaped by "Soviet residue." Indeed, Ella seems to have resisted being in the difficult position of an immigrant and sought, as did many other participants in both contexts, to lead a spiritual life with dignity by reading books, attending concerts, without letting herself be humiliated, despite the economic difficulties and loss of her previous social status.

---

24 Their level of language acquisition was especially high in comparison with other participants in both contexts.

2.4 Reviving Soviet knowledge about the social reality of life in the capitalist system

What is the nature of the symbiosis of transported politically loaded Soviet ideas and perceptions of capitalism shaped through migrants' everyday experiences in the new context? This study found that immigrants disparaged much of what had appeared to them in the SU as normative, right, and appropriate. Now many of them act often through categories defined in the previous context as "capitalist" and interpreted as immoral. Thus, without the benefit of precise ideas or knowledge about behavior codes, unspoken norms, and implicit values characteristic of the new society, many immigrants oriented themselves toward the opposite of what was considered to be morally proper in their society of origin.

This finding is evident time and time again in stereotypical opinions about capitalism expressed repeatedly by immigrants in the interviews. Furthermore, it is interesting that the use of stereotypes about capitalism was significantly more frequent and widespread in Germany than was the case in Israel. In fact, it was during the initial German fieldwork that I noted the strange ways in which capitalism was interpreted on numerous occasions and began to realize that it was necessary to analyze this topic.

Several explanations can be offered for why there were significantly more exemplars of this phenomenon in the German fieldwork than in Israel. First, the concept of *capitalism* is only one of a number of equally important features with which immigrants in Germany characterize Israel, along with *Mediterranean, Jewish, Zionist, oriental and determined by Aliya politics.* In contrast, capitalism was one of the key symbolic constructions and most significant characteristics of life in Germany cited by participants prior to emigration.[25] Many participants repeated references to Germany as "European, capitalist, and developed country." In what can be referred to as multiple senses of collective affiliation, participants in the German case study felt more alienated than did those in the Israeli case study. Such views may have made it easier for an economic interest to come to the fore.

---

25 Sometimes the images of "wild capitalism," and the USA as its embodiment, were partially transferred by immigrants to Germany, as in the case of another stereotype: *"Under capitalism, people sue each other all the time."* In this case, we should remember that at the time of the mass immigration to Germany, it was no longer possible to go to the USA, where absorption policies changed in 1991.

Second, since participants in the Israeli case were forced, due to local infrastructures, to accept any available work in order to survive, they interacted significantly more with non-Russian speakers outside the enclave than did participants in Germany. In contrast, German participants were supported by social welfare and interacted almost exclusively within the Russian-speaking enclave of their compatriots. This may have contributed to repeated observations of situations in which stereotypical Soviet ideas about capitalists and *capitalist life* were evident and applied with other Russian speakers (see below).

Third, as different examples presented throughout this work demonstrate, transnational actions—such as being in close touch and enjoying intensive interactions with relatives and friends in the CIS (significantly more than their compatriots in Israel)—led participants in the German case to refer more often to old Soviet ideas about capitalism and to present themselves as "capitalists from the West" to those who shared the same cultural terms.

Finally, whereas immigrants in Israel are granted Israeli citizenship upon arrival in the country, immigrants in Germany must wait for seven years before becoming German citizens. And, in order to do so, they must pass different German language and history teststhat are difficult for the age group investigated. Thus, even after this seven-year period, most retain their CIS passports and, hence, remain Russian citizens living abroad. In turn, in extension of the first explanation, this may be related to the participants' feelings of alienation in Germany and support use of dichotomized categories of life in capitalism juxtaposed to the life in socialism.

"We always thought capitalists (the bourgeoisie) were rich…"

The original, socialized Soviet idea of presumed richness of all capitalists collapses for most migrants as soon as they become part of the free market society, even though most suffer from a low economic status. However, rather than disappearing, this view takes on new forms. First, it is retained, symbolically, on the packaging of products found in Russian food stores in Israel and Germany. Second, friends and relatives, who "stayed behind" in the CIS and continue to be part of their intensive social networks, express their view of the immigrants giving them a new symbolic status as "bourgeois" immediately after their departure to the West. Accordingly, migrants are expected to accept this role and to act in accordance with it. In doing so, a significant and powerful misunderstanding emerges between friends. On the one hand, migrants seek support from their best friends during the first period of migration disorientation and its continuation as they navigate the settling process many years after arrival. On the other hand, they live in the *rich capitalist West*, desired by many of those still living in the CIS. Participants frequently complained and expressed frustration about this situation in the interviews, as we see in the following statements by Natasha and Olga (Germany):

Natasha: "All our relatives and friends, who are still there, think we must be unbelievably rich. If you live in the West, you *are* rich. The moment we crossed the border, we became inostranzy [capitalists] instantly in their eyes. [The Russian word for foreigner is often a synonym for capitalist.] No one wants to hear anything about your problems. Your only duty is to send presents to all your friends there."

Olga (Germany): "When I was there on a visit [in St. Petersburg], no one asked me about how I was *really* getting on here. They all think that because I live in Germany everything must be fine and, at any rate, better than in Russia. They don't want to hear about our problems. They find all our difficulties ridiculous. For example, here you can't fulfill your social aspirations; while there they can't buy enough food and have to sell their possessions to survive. They also don't want to hear details about how good your life has become there [abroad], because it can be a painful comparison for them. So it is better not to know. One of my best friends didn't want to see me at all, because she was afraid that I look like a 'Western well-groomed lady' and she is an old grandma. We talk for a long time on the phone. [pause] Yeeees [says to herself, obviously offended], in general, all *you* have to do is listen to everything from everybody, to sympathize, and to help."

This having been noted, there is evidence of partial acceptance of this troublesome *capitalist* role, for it is only among friends and members of their social network, who remained in the CIS, that they retain and seek to revive their lost respect and social status. Doing so enables them to compensate for their low economic position due to being employed in jobs for which they are overqualified in Israel or as social welfare recipients in Germany, who subsist at the bottom of the pyramid. Playing such a *capitalist* role is only possible within a group that understands and shares the same symbolic system and social capital. In this sense, they have a unique opportunity as transmigrants to fight against their low status in the new society by *activating the status of rich capitalists* or *bourgeois* at least for the short period time when they visit the CIS, through the gifts they distribute among friends and relatives. In addition, transmigrants are capable of purchasing Russian food products in Russian food stores in Israel or Germany that their friends in the CIS cannot afford. As we will see in Chapter Five, these products are advertised over Russian broadcast channels in the new country as well as in the CIS. This is an act that symbolically raises their economic status in the context of the reference group of their friends in the CIS.

A number of transnational cross-border activities developed around this *capitalist* role which can be described as *helping the poor*. Transmigrants do extend capitalism to their land of origin. They support friends and relatives by sending them money or parcels usually with clothing bought at flea-markets, received from veteran immigrants or residents, and/or by taking with them and leaving as much clothing as possible when they visit Russia. There were frequent and detailed discussions observed among immigrants in both contexts about the dozens of kilos of clothes that have been or needed to be sent, if possible, to all one's acquaintances "there." Participants discussed a long list of issues associated with this practice: What was purchased and where? The costs involved? How thoroughly and carefully was the clothing washed and ironed? How nicely it was wrapped in the parcel? And, how deeply recipients were moved and grateful for the presents? One often heard an additional comment that people "there" (in Russia or Ukraine) have no idea how expensive it is to buy all these things as well as how difficult it was to *dostat'* [procure with difficulty; Rus; key Soviet term discussed more broadly in the next chapter], and then find someone prepared to take the parcel to Russia or Ukraine.

Participants, especially in Germany, also demonstrated a partial yet paradoxical revival of old, internalized Soviet political images about *rich capitalists* in the manner with which they referred to local "Germans," in general. The residual nature of these stereotypes was dominant since the immigrants had few direct experiences of informal interaction with members of local groups. The following examples from Germany demonstrate such a practice:

Olesia: "Germans are happy to give you the old clothing off their rich backs. They think this is better than throwing them away. How virtuous of them. [...] Here everyone fights for themselves. We *plopped down* [unusual verb for this context even in Russian] and found ourselves in advanced capitalism."

Rita: "The main difference between the Germans and us is the level of material prosperity. They can afford to sit in a cafe from eight o'clock every morning, and we can't. That's why we will never be able to understand one another."

Both Olesia and Rita mentioned material prosperity as the main difference between "them" (constructed Germans) as juxtaposed to "us" (ex-Soviets). Furthermore, in using the unusual expression—"we plopped down and found ourselves in developed capitalism," Olesia seemed to claim that she did not consciously immigrate, but rather plopped down and found herself there "heteronomously" (Schütze 2007), in the middle of a foreign world. This suggests a claim that it was difficult for her to assume responsibility for this as a conscious act.

From these examples and other comments cited, it can be concluded that we are not dealing only with stereotypes, as internal conflicts and contradictions also occupy transmigrants and involve them in serious inner dialogues. Participants were ashamed that, even though they were highly qualified professionals, they occupied the bottom of the economic pyramid, accepted used clothing, and could not afford to visit cafés. As highly educated professionals, they had dedicated the best part of their lives and their capabilities to their work in the SU. However, through their retrospective interpretation of their post-*Perestroika* lives, they are convinced that "the state cheated them." This was due to the fact that the Russian state only allocated them a monthly pension 60 Euros, at the most.[26] As a result, they concluded that the *social world* in the totalitarian socialist system, to which they had been socialized, was false and manipulative.

"Under capitalism, everything costs money…" and, "everyone cares selfishly only for himself"

Immigrant discussions and the issues they confronted reveal that there is some confusion, even bewilderment, about *money* and the necessity to undergo internal moral transformations in dealing with it. Overall, the moral values and views of their relations with friends shared by the immigrants revealed a stereotype that refers to changes in the meaning of money and the consequences connected with this change.

Olga (Germany): "You have to pay for everything here. We are living in capitalism, you know. You begin to place a high value on your own work and what happens is that suddenly everyone remembers how highly qualified they are. This means that

---

26 Only Russian (not Ukrainian) citizens in Germany (and not in Israel) received a Russian pension, most of which was deducted from their social welfare allocation by German authorities.

even if one helps someone redecorate their flat, even their own good friends, they spend time on it and so they think they should be paid…None of nashi [lit. Our, people of our kind, meaning Russian speaking milieu in Germany] wants to do anything for nothing anymore."

Yet, the interviews revealed that the common symbolic meaning of money remained strongly tainted by meanings about their lives in the previous context, in their land of origin. Even after their personal experiences with capitalism, Soviet like clichés continued to be used; such as: "in capitalism you have to pay for everything" or "everything is valued in terms of money." Some immigrants accept this transformation as an inevitable fact of their new life, while others are afraid of assuming undesirable changes; that is, they seemed to be anxious that after living in the West for a while they will turn into new people, behave differently, even inappropriately.

Ira (Germany) explained: "You have to pay for everything here. Our television did not work, so we invited a technician, a nashi [Russian speaking immigrant], to come to our home and to repair it. It took him five minutes to replace a part, but he stayed for another three hours, had lunch, had a drink, taught us all about life here, and then charged us 25 Euros and went home. We were completely shocked. [pause] *25 Euros* for five minutes' work! And he wasn't ashamed to sit here as if we were great friends, chatting and eating [pause]. It's terrible to think we might turn out like that, if we stay here long enough."

Yet misinterpretations or clichés about alleged normative behavior in capitalism can also serve as motives for action or have an educative value that in this form would be unthinkable for local Germans. Such misinterpretations led participants to act intuitively and to experiment, according to their understanding of supposed but actually imagined local norms. Such behavior might well have been disapproved of or even considered to be immoral in the SU. For example, it seemed that some participants living on social welfare "practiced" imagined scenarios about the capitalist agency of businessmen communicating with their compatriots.

Katia (Germany): "We were walking along the street and passed a bakery. They were selling jam-filled *Berliner* [doughnuts, Ger.]. He said: 'I've spent four months experimenting and I've worked on a technology that works. Now I can make doughnuts just like those.' So, I said to him: 'Tell me how you do it!' He laughed and replied: 'Are you joking, do you think I would tell you? Go inside and ask them. Will they give away the secret?' So I asked: 'Do you mean you would sell the technology?' He said: 'You haven't got enough money…' and laughed. And he's 65, so it's obvious he isn't going to open his own bakery… I don't know. Here [in Germany] everybody cares only selfishly about themselves."

Obviously Katia was disturbed by the behavior of her good friend who *transgressed* her understanding of friendship codes. However, this and many similar situations that she shared with me caused her to reflect on new, presumably capitalist norms for such relationships. In most of these efforts, she seemed to be attempting to convince herself while speaking aloud with me.

In general, and especially in the German case, the findings from analyses of the participant observations and interviews confirmed the findings of Markowitz (1991) in her study of Russian-speaking migrants in the USA. There, too, many participants complained about loss of relationships, of the *real* friendship type, and the formation of a new type of relation, one less trustworthy than in the SU that emerged under the conditions of their new life.

This having been noted, it would be a mistake to claim that the greater stress placed on the importance of individualism is a unique Soviet invention about capitalists. Rather, it represents one of the most broadly ascribed features of the concept of capitalism. As elaborated by Herzfeld:

"Pursuit of private ends…has been central to 'native Western cosmology'…and fits with larger and still older notion of 'European possessive individualist'" (Herzfeld 2001, 95; based on Macpherson 1962).

Also, in reflecting on neoclassical economic theory, Bird-David claimed that it is based on Western ideas "of selfish parts, each instructed by the same instrumental rationality and making up a providential whole" (Bird-David cited by Herzfeld 2001, 95).

Brief respite for researcher reflexivity

The experimental behavior of migrants, conducted according to what many thought capitalists would do, also involved confrontation with a methodological issue. Some of the situations observed—as in the cases of Olga or Ludmila (German) (below)—were so unexpected that they tested my own anthropological limits. Since to a certain degree, I—as the researcher—belong to the investigated group, these situations caused me to confront the following dilemma: On the one hand, as a researcher I sought to act within the constraints required of me, for example, to practice neutrality as events transpire and to aspire to minimal influence during participant observations. Yet, on the other hand, I did have a strong desire to express my own opinions about what was happening. For example, the following exchange occurred when I was assisting Katia (Germany) re-decorating her flat. Katia remembered that the husband of a friend of hers (the friend was an immigrant, her husband was German) had a table that could be used for wallpapering. The following exchange developed following her idea:

Katia: "We can borrow it from him and pay something for it, but I'm not sure how much…"

JB: "Why should you pay?"

Katia (aggressively): "But you *don't* understand [German rules]! He's *German!* Perhaps I could just ask [to borrow it] if this only involved her, but not with him. He has to be paid for everything [means not his personal features or character but him as German]. You can't just borrow, you have to pay him. Maybe in Israel it is different but *here* it is *like that!*"

In another situation, I came with my son to interview a woman, who had a son the same age (six years old). I conducted the interview with her while our sons played together. In the middle of the interview, Ludmila proudly told me about a new innovation they had adopted in her family concerning her son. This situation created a similar unresolved dilemma for me as a researcher:

Ludmila (Germany): "We pay our son wages."

JB: "Wages?"

Ludmila: "Yes, ten Euros a month. You know, all parents pay their children wages here."

JB: "You mean pocket money?"

Ludmila: "Yes, these are wages, but he doesn't have to do anything to earn them. We worked out a system. We made a daily plan for him. If he fails to do something, we deduct one Euro from his wages—one Euro for every point. I don't know yet how it will work, we only introduced it a couple of days ago."

"Under capitalism, people sue each other all the time…"

Continuing reflection of my own subjective sense of social agency, I observed many situations—especially in Germany—that seemed to me to be absurd, at first glance, and that, I submit, need to be explained. These cases involved what I consider to be helplessness as well as misunderstandings and misinterpretations of various aspects of a still unfamiliar capitalist system. In my view these misinformed interpretations of supposed behavior patterns, norms, or values of the local dominant group are due to superficial interactions with the non-Russian speaking world (mostly official interactions with institutions and government agencies), as well as, insufficient knowledge of the language and understanding of social codes that are part of commonly known social worlds and socio-cultural capital in situ. An example of such misinterpretation-in-action is this statement by Tania (Germany):

"The Germans take each other to court all the time! Even their relatives, their friends. It's viewed appropriate here. People don't see anything wrong with it."

Tania seems to be coping in her own way with something that obviously contradicted her previous experience in the SU. There, in the SU, seeking assistance from the courts in regard to private issues involving friends and relatives was extremely rare, indeed considered to be amoral. In coming to learn about such process in Germany, Tania polarized and presented this phenomenon as if it was an appropriate and *normal* everyday practice, of which everyone availed themselves, with anyone. Beyond being an implied attempt to make significant Otherness habitual and usual behavior, Tania interpreted such action as a form of power, possessed by every member of the dominant group that enables him or her to control the social order.

Although participants never experienced the process of actually suing someone or being in court, they often referred to court cases. They seemed to think that the courts would be a site where they could seek protection of their rights. This view reflected their general "belief in the ineffectiveness of official channels and infrastructures" (Shevchenko 2002, 859) after the collapse of the Soviet system, as well as, their mistrust of the new environs and dominant resident groups (in both contexts).

The following quote from an interview is an example of the special meaning and significance that the courts had for migrants. This account can be interpreted against the background of their experiences with government agencies in Germany, when frequently they felt themselves to be powerless, deprived, and in need of protection. On the other hand, as a group, the participants did not seem to have a clear idea about their actual rights and the social structures of the receiving societies.

Roman (Germany): "You have to take the Social Security office to court. They are in breach of fundamental human rights. They force me to go there every time to collect my welfare payments, and I'm an old man. [pause] In the first three years it should have been enough just to have to come once a month to get the money [As it turned out what was really making him angry was the fact that his welfare payments were stopped for a month because he went to Russia].

And, another thing, there's a regulation that says you get money every two years for new bed linen. I go [uses present tense] to them and ask for new *Bettwäsche* [he uses the German word for bed linen], and they ask me: 'What about *your old* bed linen? Is it..? [does not find a right word] Is it...? Eh, what's the word? The same as [happened] to Hitler. What is it, mm?'"

JB: "Kaputt?"

Roman (excited, aloud): "Yes! Exactly! I say [speaks in present] my bed linen is old, but the woman [official] asks: 'Is it kaputt or not?' [pause] I just walked out [angry, aloud]. They should give us the money without asking if it's kaputt or not. How mean! They [German officials] don't allow us to go to Russia to visit our relatives' graves. They say that if we can afford to go there, that must mean we have enough money, and they won't pay us anything for that period."

Olga (friend) who is listening intervenes: "But you know that a lot of nashi [ex-Soviets] who get welfare here [in Germany] live in Russia for most of the year. Why should the Social Security office support them? Are we any use to Germany? We worked all of our lives in Russia and what sort of a pension do we get there today? And here, in Germany, they pay us for doing nothing! We haven't given them anything!"

Roman interrupts her [angry]: "No, they mock us here. You have to take them to court!"

2.5 "The Russia we had always dreamed of"—some conclusions

The concept of capitalism appeared in the new migrant contexts in a variety of interactions between immigrants and in the ways they dealt with different situations in Israel and Germany. On one hand, there was initial excitement about abundance and new possibilities after emigration.

Faina (Israel): "It [life in capitalism] opened up so many possibilities: to make trips abroad, to buy clothes, electric things, to design your flat, to cook delicious meals

without investing a lot of time, and to treat your feet with cream. Who had a time
to do that there [in the SU]?"

Excitement about new possibilities was usually mixed with and included
allusions to Soviet lies, political manipulations as well as significantly different post-migration socialization at different stages after arrival.

Tamara (Germany): "When we first arrived, we went into the shops and said to
each other: 'Look how beautifully they are rotting here.' [A popular cliché in the
SU stated that Western capitalist society was rotting.] There were special clips for
Kohlroulade [stuffed cabbages, Ger.] so that it doesn't unroll! Now that's capitalism!
But people *are* different [in Germany]. Some time ago I said to my German boy-
friend: 'You are an exploiter!' And he replied: 'Who, me? How?' 'You really don't
know? Didn't you read thw *Kapital?*' None of them [Germans] ever read the
Manifesto."

Given participants' everyday life experiences abroad, stuffed cabbages can
become a symbol of *capitalist civilized life* that disproves Soviet propaganda
and caused Tamara's amusement. Taken for granted Soviet myths, transported with participants to Israel and Germany, were questioned, reactivated, and changed while others were strongly criticized and even abandoned. Tempted by hopes of an easily attainable better life and a better
future in the West (Golden 2002), immigrants in Israel and Germany were
exposed to and grappled with the different consequences of the transition.
This included the fate of certain ideas and images about the West acquired
in the past that turned out to be no longer valid or effective in their post-
migration lives.

In both cases, participants realized that term *capitalism* implied much
more than an economic concept about certain market relationships and
rationality. Participants arrived at this understanding when confronted with
a need, aroused in encounters with members of the new, anonymous, receiving society to reassess their positions, ideas, interpretative schemes,
norms, and values as well as to meet expectations about "moral regulations" (Corrigan and Sayer 1985 cited by Golden 2002, 7) and "moral
transformations" (Golden 2002, 6). They tried, actively, to identify the
newly valid *body of knowledge*[27] as well as to reconsider and to objectify values that would *fit* the local context. *Fresh baked* stories about failed socialism that confirmed rights of the Western system were welcomed in both
new contexts. Participants tried to define it for themselves and to put these

---

27 As in the German sense of *Wissen.*

definitions into practice and action. Sometimes they did so in ways that may have seemed strange to the local population. Furthermore, interviews in both contexts found that many participants believed there is a system of monolithic capitalist knowledge that when learned would orient them to action.

Placed in the existential context of their lives, the participants had to confront, intensively, a wide variety of new topics for the first time, such as: the importance of individual interests, perceptions of freedom and democracy, attitudes to money and material culture, bringing up children in a democratic system, and decision-making processes in the capitalist system. The participants were not always conscious of or reflexive about these experiences, as well as, the implicit and explicit forms of socialization and learning. And, in some cases, participants responded by reproducing stereotypes, while others—such as Misha or Ella—consciously tried to understand the dissonances and contents of conceptual differences. However, the analysis of the interviews revealed that there are traces of understanding achieved by all participants in both contexts that demonstrate an intuitive appreciation of numerous cosmological differences with their transported common sense knowledge and views of cultural capital and social worlds. As Boym observed about contemporary Russia, concepts such as

"'private life,' 'public sphere,' 'civil society,' and so forth, which are neutral in the European context [..], sound in the Russian context artificial, histrionic/factitious, theatrical, insincere/ dishonest/false" (Boym 2002, 47 [Rus.]).

In applying this interpretation to participants in both fieldwork settings, I can confirm and extend this list to include additional concepts that were— at least at the time of the fieldwork—foreign to Russian speakers. For example, concepts such as *identity* or *material culture* are key symbols of postmodern Western societies that remain barely comprehensible in Russian. This became immediately obvious when I tried to present the topic of my research—focusing on identities and material culture—to participants in Israel and Germany. After multiple and seemingly interminable explanations about what I am actually studying, these topics remained unclear to participants. Therefore, I was forced to generalize this research project through the sentence:

"I am studying the settling-in process of Russian-speaking Jews in Israel and Germany, and contradictions between self-perceptions and different bodies of everyday knowledge in CIS, Israel, and Germany."

Thus, many years after their emigration from the SU to Israel and Germany, traces are observable of what Shevchenko called "bridging post social holes" (Shevchenko 2002, 859); meaning "the narratives of deceit, decline, and infrastructural collapse" (ibid., 262). However, individualization or "autonomization" (ibid) processes that characterized lives of participants in both settings were strongly influenced by societal contexts, mediated by an individual sense of collective belonging. Thus, the approach "no one [else] cares" (ibid., 260), which was a source of complaint by Moscow respondents after the collapse of the SU, was typical for participants in the German case study. Indeed, in the German context, participants seemed to be alienated in four ways, both within settled Jewish communities and generally in German society: as Jews, ex-Soviets, immigrants, and as receivers of social welfare who live and act for the most part within the Russian-speaking enclave.

In the Israeli case study, participants also stressed the importance of individualism as well as the selfish indifference of non-Russian speaking Others among the main characteristics of the *capitalist life*. However, the idea of *capitalist selfishness* was regularly blurred by inclusion of the myth about the "common goals of Israeli Jewish people" to which they felt a strong sense of belonging. Moreover, in the Israeli case, I noted several ways in which participants maintained regular involvement in acts of voluntarism that were directed beyond the Russian-speaking community; such as distributing food in Israeli hospitals, assisting families injured in terrorist acts, performing free concerts in old age homes, volunteering their services to the army (e.g., organizing first-aid packets, preparing sets of things for *kitbacks* [military rucksacks, Heb.] for new soldiers, and repairing uniforms), volunteering at Yad Sara [organization that lends medical equipment for no fee to the infirm, elderly, and handicapped] in repair and distribution of equipment, and sharing free food rations. Some participants hosted young soldiers who were in Israel without their family (Russian-speakers) for the visits on weekends and holidays. And, in 2006, during the second war in Lebanon, some participants helped to organize food parcels for residents who were the target of missile attacks in the city of Nahariya [northern most city in Israel on the sea coast].

No similar acts of volunteerism were found in the German case, in spite of the fact that participants were unemployed and had plenty of free time. This may be due to the participants experiencing multiple forms of alienation, and their status at the bottom of social and economic pyramid.

Hence, they perceived themselves to be those who receive charitable donations. The idea of giving charitable donations in German society was neither raised nor was evidence of such actions provided.

It seems that in the German case one has to consider irritating situations and frequent verbal statements about "how to actually live as a capitalist" (with "limited liability") in a specific context in which professional self-realization was absent and in which they practiced *imagined scenarios or held dreams about capitalist agency* and *being successful as businessmen* with compatriots.

Overall, a high degree of mutual support was found within Russian-speaking enclaves during crises in the German case study, even if it did not correspond with multiple verbal expressions of participants about *capitalist way of life*. This demonstrated very well the fragmentary, situated nature of reactions and action in coping with contradictions as well as fluctuations of concepts and their legitimization. Furthermore, long term socialization to the *spiritual* as opposed to *materialist* culture of the Soviet intelligentsia stratum imposed additional difficulties on participants as their cherished values were contradicted by their desire to aspire to material prosperity. This situation made it appear as if it was illegitimate or improper, given their self-vision as intellectuals, to enjoy material wealth or to aspire to material prosperity as life's value (not "comme il faut"). In fact, for many participants in both contexts, the Russian word *potrebiteli* [consumers] retained its negative connotations and was accompanied by the Soviet presumptions of selfish and materialistic individuals living only for their own interests. In coping with conceptual contradictions and fear of becoming an *individualistic materialistic capitalist*, participants tried to adapt certain concepts to their new life. This was accompanied by a parallel desire to be free thinking, self-employed, to decide about one's own destiny, and to live in material prosperity.

Furthermore, it seemed that participants in both contexts continued to be strongly affected by painful experiences of the collapse of the Soviet *social worlds*. On the one hand, this seemed to make them suspicious about every form of regime or system. On the other hand, as Shevchenko found in her study of Moscow residents, here, too, they demonstrated flexibility and "[were] always ready for anything" (2002, 844). Experimentation by trying out different aspects of *being a capitalist* took place for the most part in transnational practice among those with whom they shared a common understanding of symbolic coding, that is, with Russian speakers.

Trying to be a *capitalist* with other migrants in everyday practice or with friends in the CIS by means of financial gifts has been part of Soviet narratives over an extended period of time. In addition, according to the Soviet understanding, the concept of *capitalism* was frequently replaced by a myth of Soviet prosperity and material abundance among members of the Russian-speaking enclave and especially in Russian grocery stores in the form of a *symbolic or mythical transnationality*. For example, at one group meeting, Vladik (Germany) passed around a picture of himself picturegraphed against a background displaying a Soviet slogan and said laughingly:

"We built communism there. And [aloud] *where* is it? We've brought it with us, *here*. Look round this flat! [pointing to different objects around the room, including different electronic equipment and our dining table filled generously with plenty of food]. *Everything* is just as they *promised* us it would be! [laughs]"

Sometimes even the idea of an *ideal Russia in a new environment* becomes a subject for discussion. Ira (Germany) explained how she sees this:

"You can get almost everything in Russian here: TV, newspapers, visitors from Russia all the time, contacts. And, we can travel there. It's as if this was the Russia we always dreamed of. A Russian-speaking Germany is a Russia where everything is fine. If only it was possible to live like this in Russia, nobody would leave."

The dream of the *ideal Russia in a new environment* that can be partially realized within the Russian-speaking enclave, in general, and in Russian food stores, in particular, provides a system of symbolic coding that everyone (among members of this group) can understand. The migrants perceive their situation in a competent manner in these contexts. Here they can speak, feel, and be respected as persons. However, this situation is often misperceived in interactions with the "outside."

The characteristics of life in Russian food stores, as well as, participants' skills and dispositions in consumption practices during their life in the SU and the post-migration changes to Israel and Germany are presented and discussed in the next three chapters.

3 "Chocolates without history are meaningless:" Pre- and post-migration consumption

Consumption as a social skill as well as the logic of consumption, may have different meanings not only for different people within a group but also in different societal contexts. Accordingly, the ethnographic investigation of consumption reported here followed the assumptions of Miller (1989), as well as Jackson and Holbrook (1995), who stressed the active, creative role of consumers as social agents and consumption as a "socially situated activity"(ibid., 1913). Such a situated approach rejects the "common reduction of consumption to an isolated and momentary act of purchase" (ibid., 1914). Accordingly, the approach adopted assumed that "the meanings that goods and artifacts acquire are not free-floating but linked in identifiable ways to the social relations of production and consumption."(ibid)

Furthermore, given that the Soviet Union was a totalitarian society, the meanings assigned to goods and artifacts were derivative of a political regime that infused all societal infrastructures.[28] Indeed, following Pierre Bourdieu, we understand that objects play an important role in the "naturalization of ideology" (Miller 1995, 142). Hence, objects taken for granted have "great significance in making ideological assumptions second nature" (ibid). Hence, analyses of the interviews and artifacts of post-Soviet material culture presented in Chapters Four and Five demonstrate that Soviet consumption was so highly politicized as to be a strong influence in immigrants' post-Soviet consumption practices. By changing their living context, ex-Soviet Jewish participants immigrated to the capitalist consumer culture in which "mass consumption is the dominant context through which people relate to the material world" (Jackson and Holbrook 1995,

---

28 About consumption as top-down phenomenon through state-sponsored consumption programs as well as about the state as actively engaged in shaping consumers and consumer regimes in Eastern Europe, the former Soviet Union, China and Cuba see Klumbytė 2010 who mentions such researcher as Berdahl 1999, Merkel 2006, Patico 2008.

1913; Miller 1989, 4). Thus, an aim of the investigations reported here, was to trace the fate of the immigrants' consumption patterns and ideas in the new contexts of Israel and Germany, or what Miller referred to as tracing the active role of migrant consumers in "resocializing commodities" (Miller 1995, 143). To do so, the present chapter presents findings that portray how immigrants' consumption ideas, patterns, and skills acquired in the SU were adapted to their post-migration surroundings.

The general information about the Soviet economic system presented in Chapter One served as the basis for analyzing the part of the interviews that inquired about the participants' *living memories* about consumption in the SU. Interestingly, participants in both settings used an expression key to understanding their views. "*V toi zhisni*"[29] [lit. in that life; meaning in their former life in the SU, Rus.] refers to a belief in the connection between reincarnation and rebirth. This concept includes a clear separation between past and present lives as well as an understanding of significant differences involved in two very different contexts in which they managed their home and provided the family with desired goods.

As mentioned in the first chapter, everyday life for people living in the SU was organized around limited availability of resources, food scarcities in state stores, and inflated prices of the products on the market. Katia (Germany) recalled those days as follows:

"We [meaning her ex-husband and friends] shared common difficulties. You had to solve problems, struggle to survive, break your neck [solve certain problems], run, achieve [...] be constantly involved in the process of *dostavaniya* [procuring with difficulty; Katia uses Russian verb to attain as a noun to emphasize that this is a constant state of affairs]."

These constant economic difficulties included having to wait in long lines only to find out that many basic foods were unavailable and that cash was the only form of payment accepted. Hence, personal preferences were deferred except when by occasional luck one was able to *dostat'* [procure with difficulty, Rus.] a desired article. As a result of this situation, social norms and practices evolved that enabled people in the SU to cope and manage the difficulties involved in surviving in such a system.

---

29 Using of this expression stresses the division between pre- and post-migration life. But, it has another cultural connotation; namely, association with the hereafter, the other world, afterlife, reincarnation. See discussion in Chapter Two.

In contrast to strategies that enabled persons living in Western societies to function amidst unlimited possibilities and to manage their consumer-oriented lives with abundant material resources, socialization to life in the SU required learning a sophisticated form of agency that facilitated living within numerous limits. In a system grounded in constant scarcity, procuring food for the family was much more important than living according to a healthy, nutritious diet, as stated picturesquely by Larisa (Israel):

"Purchasing products was experienced as a kind of *food expedition*: You do not buy what you need, rather what is available at the moment and can be used later."

As Jochnowitz (2008) found in her study of Russian Jews in New York, the necessity to procure enough food to sustain a family explains in good part the relatively high proportion of fat products consumed in the SU (and partially after emigration), as they were regarded as filling and nourishing. Pasha (medical doctor, 45 years old, Germany):

"I just don't understand. The best sour cream has 29 percent fat, is tasty, and hard but it is cheaper here [in Germany] than 1.5 percent fat sour cream that has 1.5 percent fat, which is actually not sour cream at all. It is liquid and tasteless as if it was mixed with water, like [you find] in a Russian Gastronom [Supermarket in the SU]. If you want to buy normal smetana [sour cream, Rus.] buy *Schmand* [fat sour cream, Ger.] and not *saure Sahne* [sour cream, Ger.]."

Nearly all efforts of everyday Soviet consumption practice were related to the *procurement* process. Personal success in this process required possession of economic resources as well as development of competent social skills. Such social skills included the capability to act cooperatively and to share products, to economize on expenses, to save money and to preserve products, the fortitude to stand for hours in the long lines while waiting for highly desired products (e.g., mayonnaise, canned peas, sausage or sweet concentrated milk) in one's free time after work, and to be prepared to engage in the adventure of spontaneous procurement at any moment. Since waiting in line characterized Soviet life in general, according to numerous participant accounts, people lined up before they actually knew what was to be sold.

In reflecting on his pre-migration consumption experiences, Felix (Israel) started with a popular Soviet joke that captures the *adventure of hunting* for products:

"A person stops to look in a store window. Immediately a long line starts to form in hope that something worthwhile is going to be sold. When after awhile it turns out that he stood by the show-window, someone asked him why he didn't leave? He answered: 'Are you crazy? For the first time in my life I am the first in the line. Why should I go now?' [we both laugh; pause].

We were all involved in seeking to attain something, anything. Don't you remember? When you see that *chto-to dayut* [something was offered; meaning in Soviet jargon that something was for sale] it was something worthwhile, that would not spoil, you purchased the maximum number, thinking you would store it. Or, if only one was distributed [lit. placed in one's hands; meaning distribution of one article per person], you lined up twice and waited and waited. But in the end, you obtained more. Everyone was involved in scouring, managing, finding solutions."

According to the participants' descriptions, even during a business trip to the city [mostly Moscow was mentioned], where there was a better supply of food, participants invested more of their time searching for products they desired. As Nikolai (Israel) put it to other participants sitting around an evening meal:

"Well, everyone wanted to be sent on an Institute business trip [where he was employed as an engineer] to a prosperous city with a perspective [Nikolai means a prosperous city where there is a better supply and where one could be more successful in procurement]. It is crazy when you think about it now. It was 600 km [from his city in the Ukraine to Moscow] and people bought back bags filled with products—sausages, spaghetti, chocolate, hard cheese, coffee, even fresh meat. Do you remember the cold boxes under the train where one preserved it during the trip? It is hard to believe now how much energy and time all this took."

3.1 Soviet "hunting and gathering"

Frugality, creativity, energy, endurance, cooperativeness, and reciprocity are all needed in coping with the given economic difficulties every day. However, probably the most important social skill needed to perform the procurement of desired goods was to belong to and to know how to activate social networks. Indeed, this skill embodies the concept of the competent social agent. This finding can be seen in Toma's (Israel) recalling a familiar Soviet mantra needed for survival:

"You take [buy] everything given [sold] and help everyone in your circle."

Through social networks one could:

— learn about rare goods currently being sold in a certain store in the city;

- reserve a place in the line for a friend when you heard rare goods were available;
- register on a *spisok* [list, Rus.; meaning list of those waiting in line for goods that is managed and renewed periodically (like every hour) by some people in the line];
- assure, reconfirm, and strengthen reciprocity as well as purchase rare goods from acquaintances or friends who bought them for you and for whom in turn one would perform the same act;
- purchase *tovary is-pod poly* [under-the-counter goods, Rus.; rare goods reserved by salespersons for special customers]
- support and assist those in need.

Overall, given the constraints of the Soviet system, the development and extent of participation in social networks seems to have been a crucial requirement for success in the procurement-consumption process. Indeed, competency in *dostat'* [lit. to get, to procure with difficulty, Rus.] was a measure of a family provider's success.

In the Soviet context, conventionally gendered division of roles in Western society, with men as provider and breadwinners and women as nurturer and homemaker, is partially applicable to the investigated group, as both women and men assumed responsibility for the role of *dobytchik* [provider, Rus.] (Baxter and Paterson 1983; Beagan, Chapman, D'Sylva and Raewyn 2008; Beardsworth and Keil 1997; Bell and Valentine 1997; Lupton 1996; Murcott 1982, 1986; Starr-Sered 1988; Williams 1985). Yet, similar to findings in other studies regarding the division of family roles, women were primarily responsible for domestic part of family life, primarily seen as nurturer and homemaker, and referred to as *"chranitel'nizy ochaga"* [keepers of hearth and home, Rus.]. Consequently, as the *domestic sacrarium*, the kitchen was associated more often with women than men, and they were identified with and played a central role in producing the image of the "Russian" or "Jewish" kitchen as the symbolic marker of cultural ethnicity.

Limited economic circumstances not only required mature, competent social agency but creativity which also played a very important role in the Soviet procurement-consumption process. In contrast to Beardsworth and Keil's formulation as something that "could not be enjoyed but only ensured" (Beardsworth and Keil 1997, 95), consumption was far more than being a burdensome, boring part of everyday life required in order to cope with difficulties and constraints. Indeed, on the basis of the data collected from investigated groups in Israel and in Germany, the meanings associated with it were quite the opposite: The *procurement process* was emotionally laden and culturally managed. Thus, it cannot be reduced to an economic activity of bare survival. Igor (Israel) captured an essence of this *Lebenswelt*:

"So much worrying, arguing, and shouting went on in the lines. You stand there and wonder—Will it be worth it? Who will make it first? The salesperson or the people in line decided on a certain quantity that everyone would receive [in order to insure that the people at the end of the line obtain the article as well] [...] After spending hours in line, you don't get to choose. You take whatever you get and feel great! *You got* it! That was *sufficient*! You bring *home* something unexpected and *everyone* is thrilled!. "

And, when Larisa (Israel) described her memories of participation in this process, she used the present tense (sometimes mixed with the past) as if she was returning to the past and experiencing the situation anew:

"It's not boring. I prepare jam, winter dressings, marinade, paprika, sauerkraut, and so on. All of this is humorous. I invite my husband's older sister, my friends, and my mother-in-law to come over after work. Sometimes they stay until morning. We share all the cans *fairly*.
    At home we made a wine called 'to greet Gorbachev' [laughs and looks at me, waiting for my reaction to the funny name; she is referring to the ironic reaction of citizens to the dry law introduced by Gorbachev]: [We mixed] Three liters in a jar—two liters of red grape juice and one bottle of beer; place a surgical glove over it, shake it, and when the glove explodes like a cock—that is the greeting to Gorbachev. You wait another couple of days and then one can drink it. Life is funny…"

In ways similar to descriptions provided by Igor and Larisa, participants mentioned repeatedly not only the time invested and courage required for successful participation in Soviet consumption, but also their joy and pride in being able to procure certain food goods and to manage these difficulties, with humor. These are all important indicators of mature and competent social agency.

Kolkhoz

Qualified workers (e.g., teachers, doctors or engineers) were required to complete "dobrovolno-prinuditelnoi" ["voluntary-forced" labor, Soviet-Russian jargon] in harvesting crops in Soviet *kolkhozes* [collective farms, Rus.]. These trips were an additional resource for procuring products. In return for one day of harvesting, workers were entitled to take as many products as they could carry from among the harvested crops and they also received one additional vacation day from work.[30] Hence, given constraints of the economic conditions, food products brought from a *kolkhoz* played an important role for many families.

It is important to note that people worked in the field*s* of the *kolkhozes* with colleagues from their regular work places. At home, the fruits or vegetables collected in the fields were prepared as marinades or jams and samples shared at work among members of the same team. Sharing sessions were opportunities to exchange recipes and to remember the common experience they shared at the *kolkhozes*. Faina (Israel) related her memories of such an experience:

"I remember how all my colleagues laughed as I collected the smallest gherkins at the kolkhoz [to take home]—none bigger than 5 cm, [shows me their size]. When I brought a jar [to share] with pickled gherkins made from them, everyone was amazed at their special taste."

And, in one of the cooking books brought to Israel, Faina showed me the names of colleagues from work written by every recipe:

"Sveta's pickled tomatoes; Oksana's sauerkraut; Inna's chamomile jam; Nina's raspberry jelly."

Apart from noting the importance of the Faina's performance at work as well as the social recognition and reconfirmation she received, participants' noted that cooperativeness among colleagues was an inextricable part of the procurement-consumption process in the Soviet Union (Markowitch 1998). Caldwell summarized several studies about these phenomena by noting that "friendship, mutual trust, and mutual responsibility are the idioms through which Russians frame their social and economic interactions with each other" (Caldwell, 2003, 255; also, Patico 2001; Pesmen 2000).

---

30 The quantity of the products procured was limited to the individual's physical capability to carry the food home by hand, since they did not have cars. Participants reported that until the 1980s these products could be taken without any payment, and later were obtained very low prices in comparison to state stores.

Zakazy system

"Zakazy" [orders, *zakaz*—singular, as in placing an "order," Rus.] was a unique, well-known system practiced in the SU recalled by participants. *Zakazy* were rations distributed at work places at the nominal value of state stores. In the Soviet situation of permanent food scarcity, such practices embodied not only political power but also served as an important control mechanism through which certain people or groups (i.e., the "right" citizens; meaning active supporters of a given political system) were rewarded with food rations while others (the disobedient, less loyal) were deprived of them (Breadsworth and Keil 1997; Glants and Toomre 1997; Munro 1997). As Toma (Israel) observed:

"It was a clever way to feed the labor bees of the Revolution, those who were active in the system."

The *zakazy* products allocated were dependent on the kind of work, position, and function performed. In practice, the highest or best level of *zakazy* was distributed among those considered to be exceptionally important for the functioning of the social system (referred to in the Soviet system as *nomenklatura*[31] groups; e.g., KGB workers, party leaders, local or regional party committee members). However, while this highest level of *zakazy* was only known to participants from stories, it served another purpose—as a dream; that is, the products included in the highest level of *zakazy* embodied the most desired diet, which in reality was unachievable in everyday Soviet life.

The actual composition of *zakazy* varied by location, in particular from periphery to the major cities where there was a better supply of products. In addition, *zakazy* were not available for sale at all work places. Only certain, usually large factories or institutes contracted with a particular store for supply of *zakazy*. Consequently, working for an organization with *zakazy* was perceived to be an attractive additional privilege or benefit.

Zakazy usually consisted of prestigious products unavailable in stores. Analyzing the participants' descriptions of the desired *zakazy* products

---

31 *Nomenklatura* refers to the lists of trusted officials who were placed in positions of responsibility in Soviet times.[...] According to Eyal, Szelenyi, and Townsley (1997) the *nomenklatura* retains power in Russia; this is unlike the situation in Central Europe where a skilled, managerial, business elite is dominant. In Russia, power is used to amass personal wealth, especially in real estate, to a much greater extent than in Central Europe" (Humphrey 2002, 242).

revealed that a can of red caviar was the most desired product followed by salami, a can of sprat fish, a package of buckwheat, a box of condensed sweetened milk or condensed milk with sweet cocoa, a kilo of hard yellow cheese, a kilo of ham, a box of chocolates, a smoked salmon, a jar of instant coffee, a package of Indian tea, a frozen chicken, a can of green peas, and a jar of mayonnaise. These preferred products match Heller and Nerkin's description of meals offered to those regarded as the most important Soviet state workers (*nomenklatura* workers):

> "[It] abounded in tasty dishes, as everything in Russia is rich. Breakfast at eight consisted of eggs, ham, cheese, cocoa, tea, and milk. Yoghurt, at eleven, was followed a few hours later by a midday meal that consisted of soup, fish, meat, dessert, and fruit; tea and pastries were shared in the afternoon; followed by a light two-course dinner in the evening" (Heller and Nerkin 1986, 61).

In fact, this was an ideal list, as in practice participants reported that they received lower "levels" of *zakazy* that consisted of more modest products, only some of which were desired. Products distributed in these lower levels *zakazy* included basic articles normally available that had to be purchased as a part of entire *zakaz* package; for example: one kilo of sugar, rice (or millet, groats, or oatmeal), flour, salt, or 300 grams of butter. This package was embellished with some desired, generally unavailable, and prestigious products such as one kilo of buckwheat, a smoked fish, a can of sprat, one jar of canned herring, one box of canned sweet condensed milk, and so forth.[32]

Allocation of *zakazy* was the only way most participants could obtain products unaffordable on the black market. Aspiration for products of the ideal *nomenklatura zakazy* (i.e. the highest level distributed nominally to high-ranking party leaders) created a symbolic hierarchical system in which caviar, canned sprats, buckwheat, and sweet condensed milk were perceived to be especially delicious. As Falk (1991) explained, all were prestigious, limited, and hard to obtain products.

Aspirations for such foods accompanied participants to Israel and Germany. On the basis of the fieldwork in both contexts, it became clear that it was not only a general aspiration for abundance for which interviewees longed. Participants also shared definitive, substantive ideas about

---

32 While participants from the biggest cities—Moscow, Leningrad, Kiev—reported that they could enjoy *zakazy* regularly, participants from smaller cities reported that *zakazy* were rarely supplied.

the abundance they desired in the West. These statements seemed to embody the promises of communism enjoyed only by privileged Soviet leaders; that is, people close to the *"kormushka"* [cratch, Rus.; Soviet jargon for
state welfare and material resources that could be obtained though connections with a certain political position].

Women's role in advancing consumption

Apart from social skills connected with the procurement process of consumption, other social skills were required related to hospitality. According
to descriptions provided by Russian-speaking female Jewish participants in
Israel and Germany, such skills were expected to be the result of women's
socialization. Collectively, the image of the good *khozyaika* [mistress, hostess, housewife Rus.] was the person responsible for feeding the family at
home. Hence, she needed to know how to cook, as at this time eating out
was not a well developed practice in the SU.

Specifically, she needed to know how to prepare white cheese from
milk, homemade sausage, fruit liquor, and compote; to pickle and store
vegetables (often collected in the *kolkhoz*) and different sorts of mushrooms (collected by family members in nearby forests during the weekend); to marinade meat as well as to dry or preserve fish in brine; to make
sauerkraut [pickled cabbage], home-made jams and fruit jellies; to prepare
different pies, pastries, home-made *vareniki* [sweet dumplings filled with
meat, potatoes, cheese, curd or fruit, Russ.] or *pel'meni* [dish similar to ravi-
oli; small round dough pockets filled with meat and cooked in water].

In this regard, it is important to remember that participants interviewed
were neither peasants nor women from rural areas, rather they grew up and
lived in large Soviet metropolitan areas and had attained a high level of
academic education. Yet, under the circumstances of Soviet economic
constraints, they developed skills strongly associated with peasant life.
Additionally, according to these women's descriptions, a proper *khozyaika*
also had to know how to improvise with available, inexpensive products
while preparing a tasty dish. On many occasion, this skill was tested when
she was called upon to feed to a guest who appeared without prior notice
and who was to be fed generously, in accordance with the norms of Soviet
hospitality. This ability was an important, gendered social skill that was
assessed within the closed social environment such that a woman could be
proclaimed to be a master in regard to culinary matters.

Katia (Germany) described culinary performance and assessment as follows:

"There is no trick to make a table groan under the weight of food, when all necessary components are there [referring to her impression about the life of a female German hostess in a society blessed with abundance]! [...] [Our challenge was to] make something delicious from nothing [meaning the Soviet situation when products were not necessarily available].

Once we [she and another Russian-speaking female friend of her] were invited by an older German lady for a meal. The hostess spoke at length, several times, about an old salad recipe that she received from her grandmother that she wanted to make for us. She made a *Termin* [German word for appointment that seems to be key cultural word, she uses in the middle of her Russian speech] for several weeks in advance. We were excited to see this salad and then, you wouldn't believe it, we came and she served us simple, cold potato salad, worse than *nashe Olivier* [our Olivier salad, Rus., a popular Soviet potato salad including pieces of meat]. And it was the only one on the table [pause]. They [Germans] just don't know what it is like to live your entire life amidst difficulties."

As noted previously in citing Jochnovitz's research (2008), Katia not only stressed the sophisticated skill required to "conjure up" something delicious with limited products, she also referred to the tradition that large quantities of food were expected to be served to a guest. Katia's ideas are concretized by juxtaposing different norms of hospitality. Katia revealed her discovery that Germans did not share the normative expectation for nearly instantaneous preparation of plentiful amounts of food with the appearance of a guest and the pressures involved in the necessity of creating something "from nothing." As a result, German women are perceived by Katia to be like an infant who "doesn't know about real life." Such an assessment reaffirms her valuing her own skills.

Studies of normative gendered skills in Western society found that male family members do not perceive housework to be a form of work, it is rather understood to be a taken for granted activity performed as an expression of love for the family and, at the same time, a social duty (Kunow 2003; Lupton 1996; Murcott 1982). The present study confirms these conclusions.

In addition, economic difficulties and scarcities in the SU had a significant impact on the life of Soviet women as this work required a greater amount of their time than is needed in societies where basic raw products are not seasonal and hence available throughout the entire year. In fact, according to the descriptions of female and male participants in both field contexts, the daily *procurement-consumption project* (including the nearly daily need to search for food, standing in lines, cooking in order to preserve seasonal products, and preparing for celebrations as well as daily and festive meals) consumed most of their non-work related time. All of this work made it practically impossible to plan whatever, if any, remaining leisure time; if we can speak of leisure time in relation to the SU.

Finally, among the unique features of the Soviet consumption process that influenced the participants' post-migration activities in both Germany and Israel was a core set of social skills and competences that they developed and that defined mature and competent social agency and consumerism. Such competencies include an interesting mixture of the rural farmers' way of life and their affiliation to a highly qualified stratum of urban intelligentsia. Thus, although the investigated group belongs to the educated highly-qualified strata from of large Soviet cities, the way of life in the SU they described is similar in some respects to that of rural farmers: regular participation in *kolkhoz*-related work as a form of self-sufficiency in collecting of vegetables and fruits; dependence on seasonal products; as well as gathering and preparing stocks of raw vegetables as winter foods (e.g., preparing dozens of pickled vegetables and mushrooms, compotes, jams, jellies).

Furthermore, participants reported that the worsening economic conditions of the 1980's and beginning of the 1990's forced many to search for additional sources of food supply. As a result many started to grow fruit and vegetables on land around the large apartment complexes (nine-twelve stories) where they lived. Additionally, some participants purchased small plots of land in rural areas, where they spent most of their free time growing food products. Thus, a mixed *cultural habitus* was possessed by highly qualified people from the intelligentsia stratum who through regular visits to the *kolkhoz*, working in their own *dacha,* preparing hundreds of canned vegetables and marmalades, and familiarity with the world of nature (e.g. with mushrooms) practiced a kind of peasant way of life while living in large metropolises like Moscow, Kiev, St. Petersburg, or Kharkov. Thus, if it is possible to use separate categories, as does Lupton (1996) in her research, each family was a "consumption" and a "production" unit.

3.2 The classic Soviet recipe book: *On the Tasty and Healthy Food Book*

One of the most important, historic resources necessary for understanding Soviet consumption practices and Russian food stores in Israel and Germany is *On the Tasty and Healthy Food Book* first published by Sivolap in 1952 during Stalin's regime and republished many times during the Soviet period and after Perestroika. Indeed, this book remains the richest source of self-evident, collective symbols and ideas about food and food consumption in the Russian language. However, we would be mistaken to limit viewing what is sometimes referred to as "Soviet food bible" to matters of food alone or to limit it to the category of an authoritative recipe book for homemakers. Rather, this book is highly political in nature, as ideals about present and future Soviet life are interwoven throughout this textbook for national cuisine. 400 pages in length, this book was written and edited by a huge team and hence authorship is ascribed to the Soviet collective. In addition to the 19 names mentioned at the beginning of the book, the introduction claims that "*many* nurses, scientists, engineers, master chefs, and homemakers" participated in the book's creation (Sivolap 1952, 1). Thus, it claims to present professional, scientific, as well as, folk thought about food consumption.

The Tasty and Healthy Food Book delineated the ideal, future communist life. One of the book's aims was to declare different ideas about appropriate lifestyles in the socialist society in its transition to communism; to legitimate the existing regime; to extol the beauty, bounty, and richness of the life of people living in the regime; and to present readers with the vision of the communist paradise soon-to-arrive (Glants 1997). Hence this book served as: "An encyclopedia of the Soviet way of life, where the process of preparing food became the symbol of a world transformed according to a recipe-plan. Each dish described in the book is a metaphor of the plenitude and variety of the socialist life, expressed in a tightly considered menu" (ibid., 219).

As "an encyclopedia of the Soviet way of life," this book is not only an "embodied memory" (Sivolap 1952, 1) that legitimated the regime current at the time, it also embodied the politically constructed, collective Soviet memory.

The book begins with a citation from Stalin who personally supported Mikoyan's idea to publish it:

"The characteristic feature of our revolution is that it gives our people not only freedom, but also material wealth and the possibility of a prosperous and cultured life" [Tr. Sivolap 1952, 1].

Published after World War II, during a period in which the Soviet winners suffered from poverty and economic deprivation, this book was a kind of "cultural tale" (Appadurai 1988) that presented the dream of abundance, a dream that was never realized during the life of the participants in the SU. While this book was well-known to all participants and *emigrated* with some of them to Israel and Germany, it was above all a dream that participants brought with them abroad where, ironically, we will see it could be realized for the first time.

Four main components of the dream are presented in the *On the Tasty and Healthy Food Book*, each of which was evident in the lives of participants outside of the SU: Appropriate setting of the table; abundance; pre-eminence of the Russian kitchen among the international Soviet kitchen; and public kitchens.

The appropriate setting of the table and kitchen organization

The cover page of *On the Tasty and Healthy Food Book* portrays a richly set table: Crystal glasses, numerous decanters of alcoholic beverages (*Khvanchkara* and *Kinzmarauli*, Georgian wine favorites of Stalin are featured), dishes of red and black caviar, olives, big vases of flowers and fruits, sophisticated and aesthetically served dishes filled with fish and meat, cupboards stocked with plates and glasses to be supplied to each person during the three course main meal (picture 3:1—2). The last page of the book displays a luscious dessert table displaying liqueurs, chocolates, bowls filled with bonbons, cakes, as well as, plates and tea cups made from thin porcelain embellished with flowers (picture 3:3). All these well-chosen components of the ideal banquet setting illustrate Stalin's *prosperous and cultured life,* cited above.

Aside from chapters containing an enormous variety of recipes, the book includes detailed information about setting the table, managing the kitchen, manners to be used during a meal, use of new food-related technologies, rules for cutting and dressing meat and fish, information about different factories producing milk products and sausage brands, and tips for the daily management of the household (e.g., how to clean old cups, to mend broken clay dishes, to attend to burns, and so forth).

Pic. 3:1 Cover page of On the Tasty and Healthy Food Book

Pic. 3:3 Last page of On the Tasty and Healthy Food Book

Pic. 3:2 Khvanchkara and Kinzmarauli-Georgian wine, favorites of Stalin, popular in Russian food stores in Israel and Germany

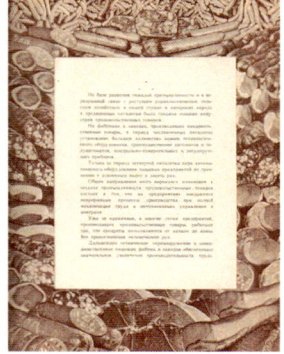

Pic. 3:4 Mountains of bread stocked in a Soviet grocery store, The Tasty and Healthy Food Book

Pic. 3:5 Abundance of meat and sausage, The Tasty and Healthy Food Book

Abundance

The book starts with a bold title proclaiming a Soviet aim—"Towards Abundance!" As will be discussed later, the introduction does not only deal with nutritional chemistry,[33] it is rather a political text that praises the flourishing Soviet motherland, the political course chosen, as well as, the tremendous achievements and accomplishments of the food industry and its modernized technology. It stresses the endeavors of the Central Committee in caring for Soviet citizens, juxtaposes the justice of the socialist Soviet approach to amoral capitalist regimes, projects an ideal image of the newly liberated Soviet female homemaker, and delineates the historical changes that have taken place since pre-Revolutionary Tsarist times that have continued the drive to achieve the socialist dream. A latent, very important theme interwoven throughout the highly politicized introduction of this book bridges the current realities of living conditions in the SU to the promised, imagined ones. This is accomplished through three arguments.

First, the authors assert that the problem of inadequate food supply is universal, making it an absolute, not a Soviet problem.

Second, they claim that the decrease in food supply is much worse in capitalist societies and as a result "workers are doomed to a fate of permanent malnutrition, insufficient rations, hunger and death from starvation" (Sivolap 1952, 4 [Rus.]). This claim is supported by information that could be considered to be quite dramatic at the time it was first published in 1952. Presumably taken from an American scientific source, the claim presented is that 80 percent of the Americans earn a salary that is beneath the poverty line; that in England as well as other capitalist European societies ration cards have been introduced for the most important food products; and, in general, consumption of basic products has decreased significantly in comparison with the prewar period (e.g., 39 percent decrease in beef, 88 percent less pork, 50 percent less butter, 68 percent less rice) (ibid). Overall, it would appear that this claim seeks to convince the Soviet citizen that the government has chosen the correct policy.

Third, the gap between real and ideal life conditions was blurred by presenting actions needed to improve the food supply of the Soviet people in the future. These actions were asserted to be among the goals of the

---

33 Six of the book's editors mentioned are professors of medicine.

Communist Party for the coming years and would require even harder work by citizens in order to be realized.

The book's introduction is printed against the background of pictures that demonstrate the richness and abundance of the SU. Important national symbols also appear from the most important on the title page to least important at the end of the text. Appearing at the beginning of the text, alongside the proclamation "Towards Abundance!" is one of the most important, key Soviet symbols of abundance—ripe wheat growing in vast fields being harvested by Soviet combines (the symbol that we will meet in discussion of post-migration Russian food stores). This is followed by the portrayal on the following page of mountains of bread stocked in a grocery store (picture 3:4).

Other key symbols—meat and sausage (picture 3:5)—are portrayed on the third page, followed by a picture of a Soviet fisherman on the next page hauling in a big net full of fish awash in a stormy sea along with overflowing barrels of herrings in the background (picture 3:6). The pages of texts that follow are set against backgrounds that portray pyramids of tinned goods—fish, meat, and fruit (picture 3:7); massive numbers of foul being raised for food production (i.e. chicken, ducks and geese); milk products on shelves including cylinders of cheese and eggs; cans of sweet concentrated milk and concentrated milk with cocoa and coffee, and bottles with fresh milk. The last three pages of the introduction portray mountains of different vegetables and fruits including big ripe watermelons and trees bowing down under the weight of hundreds of apples.

Many of the recipes included in the book require ingredients that were too expensive or unavailable in regular Soviet stores (e.g., sturgeon, rabbit, salmon, caviar, or crabmeat). Hence, their inclusion suggests that the authors sought to tell a mythic "cultural tale" (Appadurai 1988) exemplary of a futuristic prosperous life. Moreover, some products mentioned in the book—for example, artichoke, capers, marjoram, marzipan or asparagus—could not have a concrete meaning for participants before they emigrated since they had never tasted them while living in the SU. Rather, they served to signify a composite lifestyle composed of the former lifestyle of the rich during Tsarist Russia and the Western world, with products such as oysters, bananas, pineapples, lemon, or coffee that were perceived at that time to be foreign or exotic significations of the capitalist West. The use of such symbols is not accidental as the book's publication during the apogee of optimism following the Soviet victory in WWII included recalling and re-

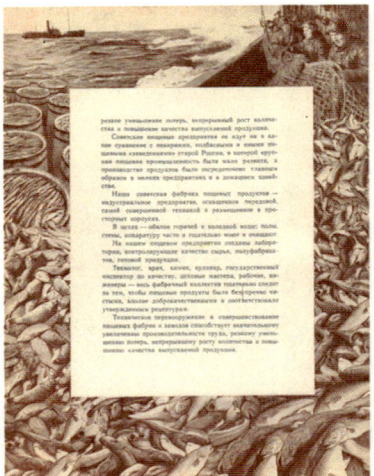

Pic. 3:6 Abundance of barrels of herrings,
On the Tasty and Healthy Food Book

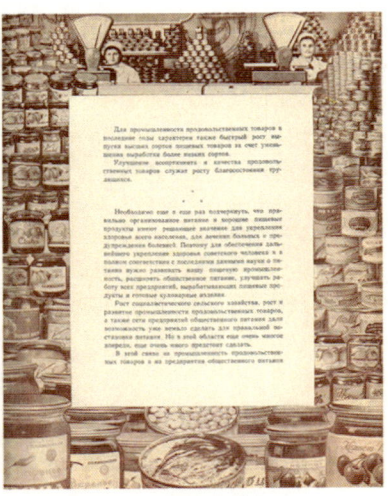

Pic. 3:7 Pyramids of tinned goods, On
the Tasty and Healthy Food Book

Pic. 3:9 Kniga zhalob [so called
Soviet "book of complaints", Rus.]
in Russian food store in Israel

Pic. 3:8 Dehydrated soup, buckwheat, jelly all
made by mixing water with dry powder, On the
Tasty and Healthy Food Book

using bourgeois concepts from the turn of the century in public and private Soviet life (Glants 1997).

In summary, the food products imagined to exist in the highest rank of *zakazy* as well as the pictures of dishes and food products portrayed in this primary Soviet recipe book are among the sources of the participants' ideals about abundance. That is, they represent the form of material objectification of the life promised in the communist era that emigrated with the participants to the capitalistic West.

Pre-eminence of the Russian kitchen amidst the greater Soviet kitchen

On the Tasty and Healthy Food Book projects images of both the aspirations of communist life and a unified, powerful, victorious post-war early Soviet empire composed of 15 republics. The latter are represented through recipes selected from different nations within the SU. However, such representations are only symbolic as most of the book's recipes stress their Russian nature. This is not accidental. Indeed, Glants claimed that this book reflects the chauvinism of the Soviet national policy, when after WWII the Russians announced that they were the "big brothers" of other Soviet nations or the "most equal among the equals" (Glants 1997, 22). This policy was not latent, as immediately after the WWII victory Stalin declared in an official speech:

"I drink to the health of the Russian people, because Russia is the most outstanding nation among all nations of the Soviet Union" (ibid).

This statement embodies the essence of the Russified socialization process advanced in regard, as well, to cultural food habits that were predominantly Soviet-Russian in nature, including the Jewish population investigated in this study.

The public kitchen

The complex, nearly scientific presentation of recipes in the *On the Tasty and Healthy Food Book* is constructed through a sophisticated integration of the traditional Russian kitchen with the political and technological innovations of the new Soviet kitchen. In doing so, the book advances two contradictory aims: On the one hand, a pretension that the homemaker can prepare complicated traditional recipes and, on the other hand, an attempt to motivate Soviet women to introduce new technologies, tinned food products, and semi-prepared dishes into the private household in order to liberate them from extensive meal preparations so that they could attend to more important social matters.[34] Thus, on some pages there are complex explanations for preparation of certain dishes of Russian *haut cuisine* and on the other pages colorful advertisements for semi-prepared dishes for a three-course meal; for example, dehydrated soup, buckwheat, jelly—all made by mixing water with the dry ingredients shown on the picture (picture 3:8).

Interestingly, the book assumes and implicitly supports the development of the residential, home kitchen. This stands in contrast to the project posed by Lenin in the 1920s that called for Soviet women to support the establishment of communal kitchens. And, indeed, mention is made in the book's introduction that, in the future, communal kitchens should completely replace the home kitchen. However, the communal kitchen project failed due to the poor economic conditions of Soviet citizens as well as prolonged food scarcities in stores (Borrero 1997, 167). As a result, managing the home kitchen, including cooking and preparing foods for long-term storage, were tasks performed by Soviet women, even by the most educated, successful career women.

In conclusion, *On the Tasty and Healthy Food Book* encapsulates collected aspirations and images with positive connotations and mimetic power as well as ideals of mythic abundance. As I will show later in this and the next chapter, strong traces of all four main themes of this book were evident in the fieldwork in Russian food stores. Thus, on the one hand, these stores and the participants' home kitchens represent a historical continuation and connection to these aims; on the other hand, nearly all four themes were only realized for the first time *after* emigration to Israel and Germany.

3.3 Social skills of post-migration consumption

Following migration, the realities of everyday food consumption changed drastically: Food deficits and scarcity disappeared and consumption was not as dependent on the availability of seasonal foods. Accordingly, there

---

34 See explicit statements in the book's introduction.

was no need to purchase food products during the summer in order to prepare stocks of homemade jams, marinades, and pickled vegetables for the winter, as was the case in the SU. Nor was there need to forage for and to store hundreds of kilos of potatoes for the winter or to stock up on canned products needed for preparing upcoming birthday celebrations; to transport meat, spaghetti, or canned beans from a city 600 kilometers away; to line up for mayonnaise or canned sweet condensed milk after eight-nine hours of work; to stock up on food provisions in self-built niches in hall-ways of flats throughout the year, and to preserve vegetables in self-made warming boxes on the balcony during the winter. Furthermore, migrants left behind such habitual SU procurement processes as: hunting for desired products; spending early all one's monthly income on food leaving little for clothing; working in the *kolkhoz*; procurement of *zakazy*; the need to grow vegetables on bits of land in the middle of the city; or the need to share produce gathered in an outing of monthly food gathering. And, of course, migrants left behind their work places and immediate environment in-cluding co-workers and friends (i.e. those who recognized their compe-tences and provided support for difficult tasks of procuring foods).

Generally speaking, almost all participants in Israel and Germany ex-pressed great appreciation for the fact that post-emigration consumption processes did not involve any of these difficulties. Larisa (Israel) captured the essence of the changes in this aspect of their lives:

"Thank God this madness is over. Here no one has to buy three cartons of eggs. [pause] Do you remember those huge niches to store provisions? Buckwheat, boxes of chocolates bought by chance as future presents, mayonnaise, and [canned] peas for the salad in an upcoming feast…[turns to her old friend Alla with whom she worked in the SU, sitting at the table]: Do you remember when we traveled together on business to Minsk? [she means from the Ukraine when they lived to Belarus]. Suddenly we saw boxes of concentrated [sweet, canned] milk. It seems unbelievable now that each of us was transporting twenty boxes on the nighttrain back home [one night trip away from Minsk]."

Alla continued: "Yaaa [yes], our hands were "breaking apart" [Russian expression for it was too heavy] And, milk was nothing. Remember the rest? It was so heavy! And now it seems so ridiculous."

Inna (also sitting at the table) concluded: "It's unbelievable how much time we spent on *kollekzionirovanie*—[collecting, collection; Rus.]."

Ironically, Inna used the Russian word for "collecting" in recalling the complicated process of procuring food in the SU, when food articles were purchased by chance and reserved for feasts and celebrations. Such usage is unusual for the discussion of food, as it usually used in the context of collecting cultural artifacts, such as pictures or coins. By combining "collection," which implies retaining products over an extended period of time, with food usually assumed to have a limited "shelf-life," she stressed retrospectively the senselessness of a process in which she participated throughout most of her life in the SU.

However, this research study sought to determine whether all aspects of Soviet consumption patterns were retained, adapted, or abandoned in contemporary practices in the new contexts of their lives? This aspect was addressed by asking participants: Did the skilled nature of shopping change with migration? Did consumption become an exclusive, pleasant form of entertainment? Using the analysis presented so far as a basis of comparison, the following presentation focuses on continuity and change of post-migration consumption practices in Israel and Germany.[35]

Socialized into a context in which there was a permanent necessity to cope with difficulties of living in a system built upon scarcity, participants developed requisite skills to manage their lives; skills that reflected competency as mature creative social agents. In contrast, none had ever had to deal with or find their way around a system in which there was an abundance of food products. Furthermore, given that while living in the SU participants had learned to keep a distant from propaganda, and along the way developed a certain degree of "immunity" to communist slogans, the study sought to determine the following: How did the participants cope with the new phenomena of abundance given their own limited economic resources upon migration? What new skills did emigrants need to develop and which SU-skills were retained post-migration? The overall conclusion of this study is that they did not resist abundance nor were they immune to the influence of commercial advertisements surrounding them in the new context of their post-migration lives.

---

35 Discussions of realization of the Communist paradise dream presented in *On the Tasty and Healthy Food* Book are presented in Chapters Five and Six.

Frugality reciprocity and social networks in the new contexts

The general standard of living for Russian speaking migrants is significantly lower than that of the average resident population in Israel and in Germany (Cohan and Kogan 2005). According to the research conducted by the Neilson Institute (Israel), 10,824 shekels was the yearly expenditure by a Russian-speaking family for food consumption. This is 37 percent less than the average yearly level of food expenditures by veteran Israeli families, estimated to be 14,874 shekels.[36] The gap between the average income of Russian-speaking immigrants and the German resident population is even wider. This is because, first, the percent of unemployed migrants (c-50 percent) is significantly higher than in Israel (12.3 percent); and, second because the average income of employed migrants is significantly lower than that of German residents (they make 60 percent of the wages of German residents) (Cohan and Kogan 2005). Given a situation in which Russian migrants in the two contexts have generally limited economic resources, most of the consumption patterns and social skills acquired in the SU proved to be very useful in managing their lives in the post-migration period, in the following key ways.

First, their long experience in frugality and efficient management of limited resources facilitated in significant ways coping daily with the circumstances in the new reality of life in Israel and Germany, where their material income remained very limited for the most part. Kolia (Israel) captured the essence of such a challenge:

"*Sovetskaya sakalka* [lit. training, developing toughness and endurance, reference to Soviet socialization, Rus.] is hardly comparable with indulgent, spoiled, coddled Israelis. For example, when their car breaks down they grasp their head, swear for a long time, and then call the masach [garage, uses Hebrew word] where their friend works. In contrast, Russians [meaning ex-Soviets] also swear, but quietly. Then they try to fix the car by themselves or clean it by flashlight. If you purchased a car in the SU, you would lay under it frequently [meaning, you would have to fix it]. We [ex-Soviets] always first attempt to do something by ourselves, even if [pause] nobody showed or taught us how to do it before, and even if we are not sure it will work. The more you try, the more you learn. There are a lot of '*samodelkiny*' [lit. 'do-it-yourself', Rus., he means a category of people who can be called like that]. You don't meet such persons among Israelis. I can do a lot of things at home and I am proud of it. I don't have to hire a master [craftsman] for

---

36 Online publication: http://www.newsru.co.il/finance/21feb2008/rus_pokupki308.html, 21.06.2010.

every small problem. I fixed all the plumbing in my flat and the electricity. You are supposed to know how to fix things."

When Katia (Germany) spoke about the same topic she also noted the difference between Russian speakers and members of residential groups:

"*Nashi* [Our, we; meaning Soviet people, Rus.] can get along with any amount of money, anywhere, you know [pause]. They [Germans] think that they know how to save. Everywhere you hear *sparen, sparen* [be frugal, Ger., uses German word along with Russian], but it is nothing in comparison. They never had to get along under the constraints we lived with throughout our entire life. When Germans have a problem they invite a serviceman to fix it; for example, to fix a sewing machine, to replace a light switch, or to repair a blender. But when I could not open a locked door, because I forgot the key [recalling a situation related earlier in interview], a friend of mine came and opened it with bank card. So I saved the Euro190 it would have cost if I had to call a locksmith. And, another friend of mine fixed my TV. Or, you have to know how to fix a zipper in a jacket and to shorten trousers. My two sons repaired our flat: They pasted the wallpaper, laid 62 cubic meters of parquet floor, and painted the doors. My German teacher paid Euro1800 to have six doors painted in her flat. Russians [meaning Soviets] are *mastera na vse ruki* [craftsmen; handymen, Rus.]. [pause] Even for such simple things as dyeing one's hair, German *damy* [ladies; uses word usually not applied to Soviet women; Katia stresses the bourgeois life style of local women] go to the hairdressing salon [elongated pronunciation] to have their hair styled and cut. [pause]
    Sometimes one person has all of these skills [hinting at herself]. I remember that I tried to fix my iron and I surprised myself when I succeeded. [In the SU] it was normal to have such skills—to say nothing about food preparation and preservation, and to try to do it all by oneself.
    And if not [if you did not succeed], you ask a friend to come [speaks in present]. It is *vsaimovyruchka* [mutual aid, assistance, Rus.], one of the main signs of friendship."

The inclusive "we" (ex-Soviet people) is used in these citations in juxtaposition to "they" (referring to local Israeli or German residents). Among components of the constructed category "we," used frequently throughout the entire research, Kolia and Katia discuss two important social skills: frugality and self-reliance. Both skills were acquired through SU socialization and were used daily both in the SU and in the new context, in coping with damaged appliances, faulty car brakes, or when anything goes out of order in everyday life. Whereas Kolia spoke about male skills (e.g., plumbing, electricity, and car problems), Katia spoke mostly about female skills, but also recalled being proud of how she fixed a broken iron (i.e., she succeeded in male activity). She also mentioned other associated male skills all of which were very useful in the new reality (e.g., repairing a flat tire, opening the door with a bank card, repairing a blender, or a light switch). Moreover, Katia referred to mutual assistance and cooperation that were carried over from her former life in the SU applicable in managing her life in Germany.

This having been noted, participants in both contexts pointed out that it is much more difficult for them to manage on their limited income amidst abundance than it was in former contexts where scarcity was a permanent fact of life. Larisa (Israel), for example, explained why this was the case:

"Because, if you don't see all this [abundance], you don't think about it and don't imagine the whole variety so vividly. There is not comparison. Here you want so many things and cannot afford them and you have to justify yourself to your children and explain that you cannot buy this or that; that this is expensive and that unaffordable. It makes you feel bad. It is humiliating."

And, Katia (Germany): "It is terrible knowing that you invested your entire life and succeeded in your work. And you were as good a teacher as they are here [in Germany], but they [retired German teachers] can purchase so many things. Yet, your *Sozialhilfe* [social welfare, Ger.] is just Euro340 per month, not even enough to cover expenses or to realize all you desire. I just don't go into expensive supermarkets or shops at all. I don't want to feel upset and frustrated."

Thus, in order to manage with generally very limited material resources, all participants in both contexts tried to save and to search for and purchase cheap items, just as they did in the SU.

Interestingly, in an early study of Russian speaking Jews in the US and Israel, Markowitz found that there was a shift in the character of friendship among ex-Soviet people after migration. In the SU, friendship was inextricable—"a central part of daily life" (Markowitz 1991, 637)—and "by no means [a] luxury" (ibid) in the SU. In contrast, post-migration "friendships become more a matter of voluntary and convenient association than of mutual need" (ibid., 641) [such that the] "intensity and urgency of trust and mutual dependence seems to have dissipated from [migrants'] friendship" (ibid., 640).

However, the research findings from this investigation demonstrate that social networks among Russian speakers in Israel and Germany proved to be highly necessary and worthwhile. Indeed, they were a new form of a social capital and seemed to be useful for functioning in the consumption process in the new context, particularly for persons older than 50 years of age. Indeed, these relationship networks of Russian speakers in Israel and in Germany were highly valued, intensively maintained, and characterized by reciprocity, exchange, mutual support, trust, and cooperation.

As discussed in Chapter Two, these networks enabled immigrants to manage the procurement of material goods through use of Soviet-based skills, while experimenting with the new capitalist system. For example, during the fieldwork in both contexts, I found that participants informed one another when they discovered special sales. Here is how Faina (Israel) formulated this practice:

"Friends call to say—'Did you know that there are *dayut* vegetables at so-and-so a shop on Thursdays [lit. are given, Rus.; uses Soviet terminology meaning sold at a low price] and there is cheap sausage *po mivze* [uses Russified form of Hebrew word *miv'tza* meaning 'at a good price'] at Tiv Ta'am [biggest non-kosher supermarket chain in Israel]."[37]

Participants shared information about cheaper stores in the city, the hours they were open, directions how to get there, where better quality products can be purchased for less money, and interesting advertisements. Those who owned cars transported friends without cars to the less expensive supermarkets ("saving them from having to carry heavy bags"). Russian-speaking residents who emigrated a couple of years earlier shared information with newcomers about special offers available in certain shopping areas or stores. Migrants advised one another about the best ways to bargain in the local market or flea market. Clothing obtained from non-Russian-speaking Israelis or Germans was shared among friends. Furniture was obtained as well as transported through contacts with other migrants and people (usually Israelis or Germans) who wanted to give it away. Some migrants organized themselves in groups in order to order food from other cities in order to reduce costs for everyone and to save transportation expense.[38] They exchanged new recipes and new experiences about preparing their favorite dishes using local products (Bernstein and Carmeli 2004; Jochnowitz 2008).

In Germany, they exchanged information about where different supplies could be obtained, such as churches that provided free food. Then, when they visited these places, they shared foods collected with other mi-

---

37 See Chapter Five for detailed discussion of Tiv Ta'am.
38 See discussion about caviar in Chapter Four.

grants who did not participate in a "collection" outing. Last, but by no means least, participants shared information about job possibilities—official as well as informal [moonlighting]—and often provided recommendations for one another in order to assist other migrants obtain work. They also helped in writing letters in Hebrew or German and put fellow immigrants in contact with organizations that informed them about their rights in the new context.

Similar to the findings of Markowitz (1991), participants in both contexts also noted that the quality of their friendships changed; that they missed old friends who did not emigrate with them; and pointed out their compatriots' selfish behavior. However, in contrast to Markowitz's findings, the current study found parallel coexistence of two contradictory tendencies among these skills of social agency. First, the old ideals of friendship and social networking brought from the SU functioned to provide practical solutions in the very different new contexts of immigrants' lives. Second, there were different individual responses and forms of experimentation in reacting to their perception of social pressure to change their behavior and personality as they adjusted to the new capitalist society.

In this regard, we can temper the views shared by noting that personal ideals and perceptions were not necessarily realized or implemented in everyday practice or they were applied in a fragmentary manner in certain but not all social constellations. This was the case in both field settings. Indeed, except for younger migrants, the very fact of migration to the new foreign society as well as the urgent need to manage their lives, which required utilizing nearly all their limited material resources, determined to a certain degree their capacity to retain old cooperative patterns of every day management.

Post-migration stocking of provisions

Though it declined, the practice of stocking up on provisions did not completely disappear post-migration. Large amounts of canned fish, boxes of canned peas, corn or tuna, buckwheat and different grains, as well as packages of chocolates for presents were observable on kitchen shelves. Reuven (Israeli spouse of Lora, daughter of the participants Nikolai and Lena)[39] remarked:

---

39 Lora is 34 years old and immigrated to Israel with her parents at 1992, at the age of 17.

"Lora is not comfortable, if she looks the the kitchen shelf and does not find some cans with peas, tuna, condensed milk, and if the refrigerator is not stuffed with meat."

And, Bella (Israel) commented: "I love it when there *are* things at home. It is depressing for me to see empty shelves."

Tamara (Germany): "Unlike the Germans, I cannot just buy 300 grams of meat and three slices of cheese. Rationally, I realize that I can go to the supermarket and buy everything, and that there is no need to stock up. But my feeling is—Who knows, it is better when there are some products *at home* [smiles, pauses, looks at me. I nod]. I always have some jars with canned peas, tuna, mayonnaise, marinated gherkins, grits, and buckwheat. You know, like we are always used to doing…"

The feeling of being uncomfortable when there are empty shelves can be traced to the Soviet practice of acting to secure the future: A significant quantity of desired products available on the shelf at home was perceived as being a much more secure situation in comparison to products being available on the shelf of the store which you do not control, as they may disappear at any moment.

Deeply internalized anxiety about scarcity is often used instrumentally by clerks in Russian food stores in Germany and in Israel to persuade customers to purchase products. Indeed, the argument for stocking appears to be among the most convincing for Russian-speaking consumers. For example, a clerk in a Russian food store in Haifa (Israel) stated:

"This smoked salami is really good. People buy several whole ones and stock up on them."

Evidence of the importance of stocking up food can be found in the numerous stacks of canned fish and meat as well as jars with other preserved food articles imported from the CIS found in Russian food stores in Israel and Germany. Hence, it appears that habitual consumption practices continue post-migration, even if in the new society these products are not necessary, as there is no problem of scarcity or expensive fresh meat or fish, as was the case in the SU.

3.4 Alternative ways of procurement and free consumption

Evidence was found in the fieldwork of two alternative practices of procuring supplies for free that continued post-migration in the new contexts—collecting foods grown in nature as well as visiting food and clothing distribution centers. Both activities were performed as social events since participants did not engage in them solely as a means of coping with difficulties as a result of limited economic resources. They also performed and reconstructed their personal identities through different social interactions.

Collecting foods from nature was especially evident during the fieldwork in Israel, as I witnessed numerous conversations about collecting mushrooms. As in the SU, this is a leisure time activity undertaken during the weekend; and, as well, it served as a kind of alternative means to procure food for the family for free. The focus during conversations about mushrooms was about how a beloved cultural tradition was being adapted to life in the new society, to new local nature settings, and to the climatic conditions. This involved discussion about the types of mushrooms available, new ways to prepare them, and their different forest locations. The following citation is an excerpt of a conversation that took place at the dining table during a birthday celebration. It was evident that there was an excitement and passion involved in this discussion that was unrelated to the "basic" search for rational economic solutions to help ease their poor financial situation. Felix speaks to Faina, the hostess, and says:

"In Haifa one searches [for mushrooms] not by the pine trees [as it was in Russia] in the forest but in grassy clearings and by low bushes. I don't know their names, you know, those with needles. [pauses and then continues to share his thoughts aloud] Nooo, collecting mushrooms is a hard work in Israel. It is not as much fun as it used to be. Well, in Jerusalem, it is different, because there are a lot of pine forests [he means the mushrooms grow near the trees]. But here [in Haifa], you are going to be pricked and scratched while you collect the amount you need."

Igor pointed to the marinated mushrooms on the table: "Are those from this year? [Faina nods] Did the season already start? [seems emotional and confused] I didn't know that…"

Ella: "Sure, last week. You will not believe it. We filled our trunk with *maslyata* [yellow boletus, Rus.]."

Vladimir: "I also collected them near the Technion [Haifa] yesterday—new, fresh small [shows with two fingers], strong ones, better than the others."

Larisa turns to Faina: "How do you prepare them here [in Israel]?"

Lena answers first: "Don't add much water when you cook them. This kind here [means yellow boletus in Israel] is very watery but still cook them before you fry them."

Felix: "I make two sorts, either marinate or cook them first. Then I put small portions in bags and put them in the freezer. When I want to prepare them, I defrost them, roast them with onion, and mix them in with cooked potatoes. You know they can stay there [in the freezer as well as marinated] *the whole winter.*"

In such conversations, people exchanged information about the best ways to find and to prepare mushrooms in the new context, as well as, shared past experiences and identified common cultural interests that can enrich this free time activity. Additionally, this "in"-group often engaged in comparisons with "Israelis" who were presented as incompetent in regard to mushroom gathering; that is, they were perceived to be uninterested in collecting them, viewed them as poison, and (consequently) neither shared in this group's enjoyable activity nor appreciated the use of accessible environmental resources.

Furthermore, similar to Katia's comments cited above about German consumption patterns, Israelis (in the sense of non-Russian-speakers or people who have not had the Soviet experience of dealing with scarcity) were often depicted as impractical, naïve, and wasteful. Here, for example, is what Bella (Israel) had to say about Israelis in regard to mushrooms:

"They [Israelis] would buy the same sort of mushrooms in the supermarket but don't realize they can find it in the forest. You know, they have certain fixed ideas and don't budge from them left or right [looks at me, JB: "mmmm"]. For example, why do you need to buy plastic bags for garbage when you can use those received for free in the market. Or, they waste a lot of money on nuts, chips, *pitz'uchim*, *pitzputzim vekola* [snacks, nibbles, and Coke Heb.] or ready made products [pauses] Such expensive things that we [probably Russian speakers] never buy. And, we [probably Bella's circle of friend's from which she generalizes to a category ex-Soviet migrants] still make sauerkraut, white cheese, marinated mushrooms, and strawberry marmalade at home. Its much more tasty and sure is significantly cheaper."

An alternative way to obtain free goods for consumption [referred to by participants as *satovarit'sa*—overstocked goods, Rus.] was found in Germany in the form of free food rations distributed regularly (usually once a week) at churches (or Christian organizations such as "Caritas Germany") to needy citizens. Thus, in answer to a friend's question whether he picks mushrooms in Germany, Sergei replied: "I collect up everything in dining rooms" [meaning, free food rations]. Whereas distribution centers for obtaining free material goods were used for only a short period of time upon arrival by Israeli participants (usually in the first settlement phase), they remained popular and were visited frequently by German participants, sometimes as long as eight to ten years post-immigration.

German charitable food distribution centers were popular and controversial points of discussion among participants, particularly in regard to the ethics and dignity of those who visited them regularly. Some were proud of investing their time there and being courageous in order to "obtain" food products for free and to provide security for their family in the new environment. Others saw such places as humiliating and reproached compatriots who visited them, as we see in the following informal exchange between two friends, Luba and Dima (Germany), both of whom were living on social welfare:

Luba: "And you, don't you feel poor and depressed coming to *otovarki* [lit. places with surpluses, Rus.; she means places where free food rations are distributed, using special Russian word, see below]. I can't go there. Its' humiliating. I would not respect myself anymore if I did so."

Dima (offended as he visits these places regularly): "If I obtain social welfare support meant for poor people here, does it mean that I agreed to (accept) being poor?"

Luba (who rarely visits such places and when doing so is ashamed to admit it): "And were we not poor there [in the SU]?"

Dima (face lights up with pride and declares in a loud tone): "There [in the SU], I made a living and the pension I received was for my work. Here [in Germany] they just give us alms [meaning welfare] and *we all take* it. So why should I feel ashamed to go to *otovarki*? On the contrary, I am glad I can get something there and help my children [both PhD students at the university, living away from home]."

This citation reveals the machinations of the inner self-image involved as each participant deals with the question—"should or should I not take material goods from public resources?" Luba and Dima are two highly educated, intelligent persons who are coping, psychologically, with their low status as social welfare recipients. Luba considers the churches that provide help as places for "really" needy people in the local societal context. In her view, such persons are located at the bottom of economic and social pyramid. She feels that she is being forced to belong to a group with whom she does not want or need to be associated, even if she receives social welfare. In response, she draws on her former social status, so that an *imaginary space* (her former high societal Soviet position) is projected onto the real and current one. Trying to dissociate her social from her economic status (as social welfare recipient), she recalls the parallel where these two statuses could be dissociated: they had respected social positions in their original [Soviet] society and, though their economic resources were very limited, they did not accept social support. Dima, in contrast, is humiliated by dependence on the German social welfare, calling it "alms," and has the same view of free food rations. Consequently, he tries to make the best of the current situation and to find positive aspects by demonstrating his social competence in "procuring" food that will be useful for his children. Even though Dima recalls the Soviet terminology of "hunting and gathering," and Luba does not, both speak through the same sense of a painful loss of societal respect and dignity.

Interestedly enough, *otovarki* the Russian name given to distribution centers in Germany, is derived from *otovarivat'sa*, which can be translated as something akin to a place overstocked with goods, a merchant center, or site where goods are dispensed. As it is appropriate to "issue goods" in exchange for something, the role of the receipt was identified, symbolically, by the piece of paper indicating a person's number in line, received while waiting to get the free food products. As discussed below, such a practice was invented outside of the CIS in accordance with a Soviet tradition.

Further, it is very important to add that the concepts—*satovarit'sa* and *otovarivat'sa*—used by participants were constructed from the root of the Russian word for *goods*, and are hence inseparable from the economic terminology. Additional words used in this context were—stocks, procurement, and provider. Also, the question—"what and how much *dayut*?" [is given, Rus.] was used continually. This question functioned in the Soviet context as a synonym for "was sold." However, in the new context, it returned to its literal meaning. In my opinion, applying concepts taken from a previous economic system to the alternative context in which one procures food for oneself and the family makes it possible to conceptualize this activity as an alternative free consumption route. Such a conceptualization corresponds with Herzfeld's (2001) recommendation that such broad, expanded contexts should also be grasped under the concept of "economy."

The extensive use of distribution centers by migrants in Germany versus their limited use by Israelis is especially interesting in the light of findings reported in Cohan's and Kogan's (2005) comparative study of general differences in living standards in Israel and Germany: Considered over a ten-year period, the value of the German social support package awarded immigrants in Germany is seven times higher than the respective value of a similar award made to Israeli immigrants. Accordingly, one would expect Israeli participants would be more likely to search for and use alternative resources to support and to improve their economic standard of living. However, though they knew about their existence and location in the city, none of the participants in the Israeli circle investigated frequented distribution centers to obtain free food rations and clothing as did many in the German fieldwork. Rather, they considered such places to be helpful in meeting the needs of poor migrants during the initial post-immigration period, but inappropriate for themselves after many years of residence.

Two possible explanations for this finding can be found in these contexts: First, the standards of living of the reference group with whom participants compare themselves; and, second, development of different political self-consciousness and social self-positioning.

Regarding the first explanation, similar to findings in this study, Cohen and Kogan found that the unemployment rate of immigrants as well as income gap between immigrants and resident population are significantly higher in Germany than in Israel.[40] In other words, compared to the average standard of living of the resident population, immigrant self-perceptions as being more deprived of economic resources (and a lower living standard) are more accurate in Germany than in Israel. Thus, even if objectively, they are capable of purchasing more than compatriots in Israel, their everyday reference group for the sake of comparison is the group of employed resident Germans. This is compounded by the fact that as a result of dequalification, lack of professional recognition, and dependence on the social welfare, the location of Russian-speaking Jews in the stratified socio-political system in Germany is much lower than in Israel (ibid).

Second, social recognition and sense of social contribution to the imagined new collective were significant in different emotional affiliations

---

40 "In Israel the unemployment rate of recent immigrants is 12.3 percent, about 5 points higher than the rate among native residents (7.5 percent); in Germany, the rate is 50.3 percent, about 40 points higher than the rate among the native population (8.6 percent)" (Cohan and Kogan 2005, 262).

that developed in response to each receiving society and the social positioning of each group. Thus, as discussed in Chapter Six, the national myth about the unity of the Jewish people [lit. Am Israel, Heb.] fostered strong intragroup emotional affiliation, and, consequently, an inner sense of duty to contribute to the imagined Israeli collective. In contrast, in Germany, the participants felt somewhat alienated in national terms, lacked professional recognition, were unemployed in large numbers, and as welfare recipients found themselves located at the bottom of the social and economic pyramid. Consequently, participants in the two contexts coped in different ways with "taking from the state" status as "needy citizens," and not finding appropriate ways of personal and professional fulfillment as a result having their qualifications deemed to be inadequate.

Reviving Soviet consumption patterns and artificial scarcity

During my participant observations, both in Israel and in Germany, I regularly heard people speak of the loss of the "right" taste, as something that cannot be authentically retrieved. This seemed to be related to memories about the struggle to procure foods in the SU and capabilities required to do so. In some cases, immigrants in Israel and Germany even spoke of the frustration and senselessness of consumption in the Western society, which seem to be foreign and boring, as it deprived them of interesting stories about the procurement process that, as we have seen, involves individual struggle and use of social skills and networks.

Tamara (Germany): "Now there is nothing special in the consumption of products. Everything you want is already there [she means available on the shelves], and it is very difficult to surprise somebody with the statement 'Ya dostal!' [I got it, Rus.], as for example, 'Ya dostal kurizu!' [I got a chicken; Rus.]."

Faina (Israel): "When you run from shop to shop trying to buy some eggs on New Year's Eve, and you can't find eggs anywhere, and then suddenly you are lucky, you manage to buy two cartons somewhere a long way from home. Well, then you feel that you *are* a *dobitchik* [provider, Rus.]. You know that eggs are needed. You are being useful to your family. They are all waiting for you. You bring the food home and everyone is pleased! A friend of ours who also comes from Russia and who works in England once came to visit us when we were still in Russia, and said: 'You don't understand how lucky you are here. You have to chase down the sausage and when you find it you are overjoyed. What about me? I finish work [in England], just go into the supermarket, and pick out one sausage from among all the different sorts available, with whatever I see at the moment. I go home, eat it all up, and what's the result? No pleasure, no joy, it's a *'boring sausage'* [we all laugh, pause]. I've only understood what he meant since we left, because somehow nothing tastes the way it used to."

Leonia (Germany): "Yes, we obtained everything through struggle and it made you so happy! Each time you realized your expectation [and felt] the pride of success. Whereas here, you buy it and [feel] nothing! You can buy more, as much as you want, and, again, nothing."

Similar to other studies that report migrants' complaints about tasteless local food (e.g., Lynn 1977), these citations reveal in a particularly rich manner that the original taste missing after migration is connected to a significant degree to the procurement process and overcoming difficulties connected with it. For example, Hubert's (1997) studies of Yao food habits claimed that habits and food preferences cannot be separated from prevailing hegemonic life concepts, norms, and practices. Actually, one could assume that abundance would give people free choice as a principally new existential condition that would relieve migrants from the necessity of everyday struggle for basic foodstuffs and be perceived by them as an extremely positive and pleasing situation. Yet, in fact, many participants reported that the task of "selecting one product out of a seemingly endless, abundant array of goods" was seen to be a burden and alienating, as commodities were deprived of their own interesting story (related to their "procurement"). This is similar Kopytoff's (1986) claim that commodities have their own "biography" that can be shared with others and so have added meaning beyond the basic purchase value. Indeed, according to participants in this study, local commodities were deprived of their biographies and this contributed to the immigrants' feelings of inner alienation.

Even if migrants were not ready to replace the current context with the old reality, many still missed Soviet practices that structured a good part of their life and that offered a particular way to personal self-realization that included norms recognized by others as signs of socially competent agency. Sveta (Germany) presented a critical view of this situation in reflecting on what she referred to as the *snatching reflex* of ex-Soviet citizens in the West:

"A Soviet person can't get by without standing in line. If something is available you have to act fast, whatever it is. We learned to do so as a matter of instinct."

Sometimes the Soviet idea of *consumption as a hard work* was echoed in the new context. In my opinion, the citation of Felix presented above ["Nooo, collecting mushrooms in Israel is hard work. It is not as much fun as it used to be."] can also be seen as a reversal of the customary Soviet idea about consumption difficulties: The pleasing and useful process of collecting mushrooms in leisure time in the SU (juxtaposed to usual hard work of standing in lines to "procure" food) is now conceived, in Israel, by Felix, to be "hard work;" a voluntary form of "procurement" (Felix: "until you collect an amount").

Also, in relation to the Russian food store, I could trace the extended use of the elements of the Soviet economic system as well as Soviet terminology connected with scarcity and the *procurement* process as a convincing argument for advancing sales to consumers. In some stores I even discovered the familiar Soviet *kniga zhalob* [book of complaints, Rus.], hanging by a band on the wall behind the sales clerk (picture 3:9), where it was available to every customer, exactly as it was in Soviet stores. While formerly, in the SU, consumers could seek to defend their rights by complaining in written form about the behavior of a certain clerk employed in the state-run store, all the stores in Israel are private. Indeed, in one particular Russian food store the clerk was the owner. This situation could make the presence of this book and the complaints entered therein a senseless exercise. Consequently, the owner changed the book's purpose: Now every consumer could write down personal requests or make comments to the owner about changes they desired and things that consumers liked in particular.[41] Thus, following the findings of Wang and Lo about the dynamics of the immigrant grocery, clerks as well as consumers act as "co-actors in producing" meanings by sharing common symbols (Wang and Lo 2007, 684).

Another exemplar of adapting previous practices in the new context involves worker-owner relations. For example, pictures of two shop clerks with captions that reproduced the Soviet-style hierarchy in the store were found in a Russian store in Israel. One of the clerks was assigned the title—Clerk, the other was entitled—Chief Clerk. In contrast to Soviet state stores in which there were expansive, hierarchically organized store teams, this particular store employed a total of two clerks, only one of whom was entitled to be referred to as the chief salesperson.

Some advertisements appeared to create an artificial sense of scarcity, as for example an announcement posted on the store window (Israel): "Fresh chicken has arrived, get it while stocks last." Even if one could

---

41 See the next chapter for extended discussion of this topic.

claim that similar pronouncements could also appear in any number of non-Soviet Israeli or German groceries, I would suggest that the effect on this target group would be different. As it relates directly to their own, extensive experience and understanding of what it means in practice when the store runs out of stock. Indeed, advertising strategies in Russian food stores, in both contexts, often use sentences well-known to every ex-Soviet citizen, as demonstrated by the following examples gathered during participant observations in Israel and Germany:

Israel:

"This [article] will be discontinued soon, few remain in stock."
"We've got fresh meat!"
"Take more, you can't be sure it will always be available."
"I'll put a piece [of meat] aside for you."

Germany:

"Better take it now, we don't have it [in stock]."
Salesman: "Buy it for me, too. It is really good."
"You can *get* chicken liver here."
When asking for a particular product: "Yes, several people have asked for this sausage. I will get it for you!"
Even if not necessary in the new context, such sentences seemed to continue to be useful and attractive as they revived the reality in which participants could clearly point to their social positions and the cultural affiliations of which they were proud.

Reviving *zakazy* system

The *zakazy* system [orders, Rus.], discussed previously, was revived in Russian food stores in both contexts, as evident in the following signs posted in windows in Israel:

"Special holiday *zakazy*,"

"Purchase *zakazy* here. Prepare your food for home!"

"Special *zakaz*, milky piggies for New Year."[42]

---

42 The "milky piggies" combination is discussed in the Israeli context in Chapter Five.

And, in Germany: "*Stol zakazov* news [place for orders, Rus; an alternative Russian expression for orders]: Pay only Euro30 and receive a can of caviar when you order [...] our *stol zakazov* [...]

"Undoubtedly the favorite of our *stol zakazov* is the caviar. Everybody thinks it is a lovely addition to every festive table. A product whose taste and healthy effects are legendary.

What I find especially interesting is the evidence of syncretism in adaptation of the *zakazy* practice. Whereas Soviet *zakazy* were composed, usually, of highly desired products, often in insufficient supply, and simple basic food products, Russian store owners in both of the new contexts display foods in a particular order. Even in a setting in which there is no necessity to purchase undesired products as part of the set, as *zakazy*, entrepreneurs in these Russian food stores tempt consumers to purchase several additional products in order to "get" highly desired items, like caviar, for an overall lower price.

The use of terms taken from the *zakazy* system was found in other food practices. For example the term *zakazy* was used when people received different free food products within the framework of German churches. Here the meaning seems to distinguish between the highly desired products they received (e.g., meat products, yoghurt, or tins of salad, sausage, cookies, fruits and vegetables) and those received/procured "*v nagrusku*" [obligation, duty; meaning the undesired part of the Soviet *zakazy*] (e.g., jars of sauces, mustard, or greens used much less frequently). Therefore, receiving them was unnecessary, but included due to to a surplus.

Tania who visited me directly after visiting her church supplier[43] itemized enthusiastically her booty:

"This time I got number four [number in line[44]]. It was a *nastoyashii zakaz* [real, authentic, high order, Rus.]:[45] bread with nuts and sunflower seeds, sausage, two biscuits, one yoghurt, potato salad, cream, curd cheese, celery salad, two boxes of chocolates, bonbons, tomatoes, oranges, two aubergines. [pauses] Well, and also, [meaning the undesired, obligatory part of Zakazy] two instant onion soup mixes, rice, sauce, and mustard. I have never been at the beginning of the line before. Now I understand what they [people in the line] struggle for, though the workers

---

43 My flat was located near a church in the investigated city where free food products were distributed once a week where I conducted participant observations.

44 See discussion below about the meanings associated with a particular number in line.

45 Best rank of *zakazy* (i.e. that of Soviet party leaders), discussed above.

assure us [that we] 'all get the same.' However, if you get number sixty you get bread, cans of salad, a lot of greens, and mustard.''

Although everyone could choose products from among those not needed, participants admitted that they usually took all items suggested in the rations, sharing later the unnecessary products among friends. Indeed, the idea of waiting a long time to "get" products and then to refuse some of them was inconceivable, as demonstrated in the following conversation overheard among those waiting in line:

One person from the line turned and smiled at a man who was leaving with half empty bags: "Petya, is it too heavy to carry?"

Another person in line: "Probably he didn't want to take [the entire line laughs strongly; seems to be the joke of the day]. Yes, he refused, that is why there are so few [...] probably only boxes of mustard

Petya laughs and answers: "Didn't you know, this is the year of the goat? We "get" a lot of greens" [people in line laugh even harder].[46]

It is especially interesting that in both the store as well as the church the idea of *zakazy* implied actions either by the store owner or church volunteers who organize the contents of these organized sets of products. The assumption seems to be that these actions are immutable, yet they assume a certain degree of agreement and cooperation by consumers to act within predetermined given conditions. In fact, in both contexts, it was possible to choose between products or to take only desired products. However, according to the *zakazy* logic and the practice of habitual consumption transported from the SU, it would have not been considered to be worthwhile or appropriate to do so. So, according to the participants' perception, *zakazy* remains a positive, desired practice.

Artificially modifying the presentation of food items—for example, by placing an overripe product next to a ripe one in order to make it more appealing—is a well-known and thoroughly investigated tactic in Western marketing. However, in our case, shop owners appear to have adopted strategies used in the SU that will have a strong appeal to their target group. In other words, there are certain elements in consumption patterns of the participants that may seem to an outsider to be not only strange but

---

46 In the terms of the Soviet *zakazy*, greens, which grow easily everywhere, would be categorized as *nagruzka* (an obligation to receive, a duty, in comparison with desired goods, such as meat or cheese).

also irrational as they follow different socio-cultural rules and presuppose certain symbolic codes. Yet, for the participants these patterns supported their interest in managing their household as well as affirmed their ability to *get* goods needed by their family through the available and legitimate means.

Reviving *spisok*

The use of a *spisok* [lit. listing, Rus.] to reserve desired goods was found in both contexts. The three instances found in Israel (sign-up sheets for chicken, Kiev tart, and caviar) were conducted by owners of two different Russian stores who explained that their weekly orders replicated last week's consumers' *spisok*. One reference to the *spisok* in Israel was found posted in a window of a Russian food store: "*Spisok* for ordering Kievski tart" [Kiev tart; a very well-known fancy cake rarely available in the SU]. Fania shared a second case when she related how three days previously she had tried to put her name on the *spisok* at a Russian store in order to "get" small fresh chickens (popular but scarce in the SU, in contrast to frozen chickens; referred to in the SU as "blue birds"). She learned from the shop owner that the *spisok* for the week was full and that it was impossible to place an additional order. In the third case, Nikolai (Israel) shared his experience of visiting a certain Russian food store three times in one week in search of caviar, only to find out that he could not purchase it because the seller claimed Nikolai had not registered for the weekly order. In response to my question—"And what did you do then?," I received the amazingly simple answer: "I just went to another store and bought it there." Upon comparing the prices of the articles registered, it turned out that neither the chickens nor the caviar cost less via *spisok* than in nearby stores. It appears that not only did the participants seek to revive old patterns but also sought to retain their loyalty to certain Russian shops and brands they visit regularly.[47]

Using of a strategy that employs claims of artificial scarcity, when the owner of a store does not have to take a risk in ordering a product that might eventually not be sold, would hardly be possible if there was not a

---

47 This information is confirmed by studies about consumption patterns among Russian-speaking migrants in Israel conducted by Elias and Greenspan (2007), as well as, by a marketing survey conducted by the Neilson Institute. Online references: http://www.newsru.co.il/finance/21feb2008/rus_pokupki308.html, 21.06.2010.

target group that shared a consumption pattern. Furthermore, this seems to be a very convenient arrangement for shop owners who share the same cultural background with this group and can employ terms taken from their joint past.

In the German context, the artificial introduction of a *spisok* for desired goods was found during participant observation of the distribution of free food rations in one of the numerous churches of the city. The analysis of this practice deserves special attention as it reveals a transgression of limits and socio-cultural codes by Russian speakers when interacting with German church workers.

Although the distribution in the observed church began at 11:00—11:30 hrs. people usually started to arrive as early as 4:00 a.m. in order to "get" one of the first places in the line. Participants in line invented an interesting regulation; namely, at 6:00 am a person of Polish origin—the only one among otherwise Russian speakers—appeared with cutout, numbered cardboard pieces. He handed out numbers to those who had waited since 4:00 listed their names on a piece of white paper entitled *spisok*, and released them from waiting until 12:00 hrs.. He stayed in the line the entire period of time and between 6:00—12:00 hrs. and continued to conduct the *spisok* by distributing numbers to newcomers. Numbered pieces of cardboard which everyone received were proof of their place on the *spisok* and *in line*. For his efforts, the distributor *got* number one in line. Of course, such a practice would have been impossible without the agreement of most or all participants waiting in line.

While the *spisok* elicited positive responses and understanding among Russian speakers (the most frequent visitors of this distribution center), the few non-Russian speakers who entered were often confused and unable to decode the rules with ease. Usually they stood in line with the others, but did not receive a number, as this practice was reserved for *Nashi* [Ours, meaning ex-Soviets]; a category of persons seen to be significant throughout different chapters of this work.

Especially interesting were the few cases when needy German citizens visited and entered the center without waiting in line. Though immigrants had been waiting in line and were visibly upset by this action, none of them complained to the Germans; perhaps this is because few spoke German with ease.

After a while, local volunteer workers observed that people came to the center many hours before it opened and they tried on several occasions to explain to visitors that every person would receive the same food ration. These attempts met with failure since participants counter-claimed that those who obtained the first numbers in line received more products (especially sausage or meat cans), since there were insufficient quantities of these products for the 80 or so persons waiting in the line.

After residents of neighboring apartments complained to church officials about the noisy and disturbing sounds made by those waiting in line at 4:00 a.m., church volunteers were forced to take other actions: They posted the following announcement that explained their purpose and expectations of visitors. Printed in German and Russian, they hung the announcement on the wall in the entrance hall. When this did not have the desired effect, the text was copied and distributed among everyone waiting in line:

"Dear Visitors! We are here to help. In turn, you can help us if you take into account the following information: We are not a state institution, but a charity association organized on our own initiative in order to help poor people. We can help only by providing goods and food products that have been contributed voluntarily for the needy by private persons and some businesses in the city. [At this point the German version has an additional sentence not translated into Russian: 'For this reason special requests cannot be fulfilled.']

We want to distribute the products contributed in a just, fair, and equitable manner and to help the maximum number of persons in need. We want to achieve mutual understanding between our German and foreign visitors. Support us in this goal!

You do not have to compete with one another for these goods and stand in line before the Center opens, because the first visitor will not receive any more than the last one.

Please abide unconditionally by our working hours. This will help us prevent discontent and claims made by residents of XYZ [name of the area in the city] [in German version of the announcement: 'to avoid the anger of the city's citizens']. Also, we ask you to take into account that every needy family can only send one of its members.

You are welcome here as long as you are willing to abide by the rules listed above! [Rus.]."

Here we see that the volunteers sought to state in an explicit manner their values and expectations of the visitors, while making reference to disturbing behavior and apparently unfriendly communication between two groups—namely Russian-speaking migrants referred to as "needy persons" and German "residents," who complained about the inappropriate behavior of the Others. In fact, this pronouncement reveals several cultural disjunctions: The behavior of Russian-speaking participants was based on their Soviet experience of the process for "procuring" goods that had taught them that one could never trust state practices or representatives. The volunteers, in contrast, stressed their work as a private aid initiative conducted within a church framework and, indeed, requested that those who receive products show their gratitude by making a small donation to the church. This expectation was repeated every week by the workers and written at the entrance to the hall.

Church volunteers referred to concepts of "equality" and "justice" as perceived through their democratic Christian heritage. In contrast, ex-Soviet participants perceived the use of concepts such as "justice" and "equality" as utopian, even as lies. Frustrated by the promises of the communist regime, ex-Soviet participants hardly believed in the just and equal distribution of goods. And, on the basis of their ongoing experience with this church distribution center, the participants knew that this pronouncement was false, as those who had stood in the line and obtained the first numbers "got" more than those who were at the end of the line. Moreover, through socialization in the Soviet society, the participants had internalized the idea that they had to struggle for "getting" goods they desired—a practice regularly reconfirmed through current practice within the church. Thus, in this context the sentence in the announcement "You do not have to compete with one another for these goods" not only seemed to be false, but also an illusionary, hypocritical assurance, as it asked them to act contrary to what had developed as a shared logic: Namely, "in order to 'get' the desired limited goods you have to struggle for them." The volunteers' perceptions emanated, presumably, from within the conditions of the abundant reality of European life amidst a strong supportive social system that viewed their aid-related work as help rather than as an essential existential struggle for survival.

Finally, based on the participants' Soviet experience, they understood that lining up for desired goods as early as possible was absolutely necessary, if they were to succeed in the struggle to procure goods for their families. For many, the personal decision to stay in the line was one of the few activities within the constraints of the Soviet system that were always considered to be legitimate and that nobody could prohibit. Thus, the volunteers' request—"Please abide unconditionally by our working hours" was viewed by participants as irrational and secondary in comparison to their goal—to provide their family with the products needed. In contrast,

the volunteers were not motivated by material reward and viewed themselves as being responsible, solely, for the distribution and sharing of
goods. And, from their pronouncement one can understand that they believed that they had a responsibility to respond to the neighbors' complaints, the right to prescribe rules, as well as, to request that order be
maintained.

Ultimately, the pronouncement did not achieve its aims. However, it
did expose the unpleasant atmosphere present at the site and led to some
participants feeling shame that their way of acting was inappropriate in the
view of the German volunteers, who as a part of the absorbing society
were "sharing food with poor migrants" and, thus, had a right to explain
what they considered to be appropriate rules. Thus, consequently, for some
participants, the pronouncement did place the volunteers on a higher
plane, in a hierarchical relationship, as we see from this statement made by
a man standing in line a week after the pronouncement was posted:

"How embarrassing! They [volunteers] shared their views and explanations. And *eti*
[them, Rus., contemptuous reference to other migrants by nodding his head to
those waiting in the line] never obey! Instead of waiting in line properly, those who
have 'long hands' go and just stand in front of the line or take numbers twice. It
does not matter if you explain it to *nashim* [Ours; used here negatively meaning
Soviets] or not [meaning it does not work anyway]

Interestingly, no one referred to the unpleasant, condescending tone of the
pronouncement with its underlying assumption—migrants do not know
their way around and make mistakes.

The pronouncement did not have any effect. People still came at 4:00
am and continued the practice of making lists and assigning numbers. So,
the volunteers decided to introduce a new lottery system in hope of elimi-
nating lining up at 4:00 a.m. From 11:30 a.m., a female volunteer stood at
the church entrance with a box containing numbered pieces of paper.
Every person waiting in line could draw a number assigning them a place
in the line. Dozens of people were very upset and frustrated with this system as it removed the possibility of obtaining one of the first places by
waking up early and waiting in line. This disappointment can be seen in the
following citations from the field notes:

One man, seemingly confused, said: "Are these the old numbers or the new ones?"

One woman answered: "The old ones."

He again: "And, do you have a new number?"

The women: "Yes, I was number 8 and now—74."

Another woman in the line: "You stand here from 4:00 a.m. in the rain and dark and then you get the number 69 in this lottery, and nothing remains when it is your turn."

Another man: "Yes, it is not good. Before [in the old system] you came, waited, and then you "*got.*" Now, you never know, never know [people in the line express agreement]."

The new practice resulted in only a slight change in the previous, self-initiated, self-monitored system: People came to line up at 7:00 a.m., so it was still important to organize the line. Sometimes this was accomplished through a renewal of the *spisok* practice or numbers were distributed on small pieces of cardboard. Occasionally, when volunteers decided not to use the lottery system on a particular day, people immediately re-introduced the old system the following week with many showing up, again, at 4:00 a.m.

Undoubtedly, this alternative food *procurement* system was also a kind of social club. During hours of waiting in the line, many of the people who came every week came to know each other, engaged in extended conversations on different topics, including world news, or offered practical advice about managing their everyday life in Germany. Some played cards. Many speculated regularly and shared their concerns about the prospects of success in *procurement* on the certain day, as we can see from these exchanges cited from the field notes:

"I am not sure if the car [carrying the food to be distributed that usually arrived at 10:30 a.m.] will come today, with such rain."

Somebody in the line: "Ask and you will receive."

Another person answers: "I feel like we shall receive soon [smiles, meaning the food is coming soon]."

An hour later: "As I helped unload the car [carrying products], I saw they did not bring much today."

"I heard that today there may not be a lottery!"

"Anyway, if you are over 30, you will get very few things."

An hour later: "What numbers are inside now?"

"Soon come the 30's."

"And what number do you have?"

"45"

"I have 51, so we will look at you [meaning—at your bag of food when you leave]."

"May be it is even better to be at the end of the line because then you get everything that remains."

"This time we 'get' no pineapples [line laughs]."[48]

"Do you usually 'get' only pineapples here?"

[Persons in line laugh even stronger]

"Well, there is nothing to do about it [in the case that there may not be enough], then we will 'get' them at another mountain [meaning, to go another center for free food rations] tomorrow."

"You know how it is. Someone waits in line, then several others come up to him and say that they were together, and you stay behind [them].".

Although it seemed irrational to retain the *spisok* practice, the waiting list, and lining up at 8:00 a.m. when the new lottery system was introduced, these practices assisted in dealing with the question—Who has the right to be the first persons to draw numbers from the box? The self-initiated system whereby numbers were distributed for those in line after 8:00 a.m. assured participants who had been in line that they could draw the other numbers (for their 'real' place in the line) at 11:30 hrs. from the lottery drawing administered by the German volunteer. The volunteers' arguments that someone could come at the last moment and draw the number one place in line obviously did not sound convincing to participants, who discussed among themselves that it was possible that their entire set of numbers (for example 60) could be less than the number of people waiting (approximately 80). Besides, their practice showed that the lottery was not always used by the volunteers. This gave them hope that they could influence an eventual success that they hoped for in the "procurement" process.

---

48 As explained in the Chapter Two, pineapples embody the dream of the *capitalist life*. In the context of free food rations in the church, the juxtaposing luxury life in the West and the actual economic state of people made them laugh about the absurd idea of the most luxury product being distributed for free.

3.5 Contested procurement

In summary, participants in Israel and Germany kept reviving different Soviet practices that had been essential parts of the Soviet consumption process, but which are not part of neither Israeli nor German consumption patterns. Such persistent use of old practices in the consumption- *procurement* process cannot be separated from self-defining and positioning of people who use them. This cannot be reduced by repeating sentences such as that made by Sveta (Germany):

"*Nashi* [meaning—Ex-Soviets] need a line to feel comfortable."

Interactions between different participants in both contexts demonstrated that participants were driven by their wish to be useful to their families. In doing so, they revived, symbolically, their previous status as competent, skilled *procurement* agents.

As long as this process took place within the Russian-speaking enclave (e.g., in Russian food stores), it did not arouse contradictions or irritations among residents, because revitalizing old practices seemed to be desired by those who shared them. However, in the delicate case of the *procurement* of free food rations in German churches, the juxtaposition of the image of the "provider" with the image of a person "asking for alms" involved inner identity conflicts within Russian-speaking participants. Moreover, it reveals transgressions of socio-cultural boundaries at the intersection of different common sets of knowledge and practice shared by different groups who interact in this complex situation. Throughout, it is important to remember the asymmetrical power relations that exist in these interactions; for example, between the members of the migrant minority who have limited economic resources and the volunteers of the dominant group of the receiving society who provide the provisions. In this hierarchical constellation, it is the common socio-cultural knowledge of the migrants that is constantly being challenged, scrutinized, and questioned as if they, the non-Germans, are the ones expected to change, to adjust, to adapt, to adopt, and to integrate themselves.

4 Russian food stores in Israel and Germany: Images of imaginary home, homeland, and identity consolidation

An observation shared by a salesperson in Haifa (Israel) exemplifies the assumption that food and drink as a symbolic milieu "construct the world and reflect the ideal world" (Douglas 1987 referenced by Miller 1995: 148; see also, Kopytoff 1986 and Lupton 1996).

"People ask frequently for something that is not a basic food product, something I have forgotten about, for example, special candies, like *Solotoi Kluchik* [Golden Key, from the Russian version of the children's tale "Pinocchio"]. Do you remember them? So cheap and tasteless. It is not Golden Key they want, but their memories about their childhood and sweet Golden Key candy in their jacket pocket full of holes as they played in the backyard."

Here, Golden Key candy purchased at a Russian food store symbolizes and refers us to the more general question: What do migrant consumers aspire to discover at the Russian food store and will their key fit the imagined door?

Food and drink are often used by different groups to recall memories, to demonstrate identities, or to construct "their own sense of nostalgia for customary sociability" (Miller 1995, 149). Not only is "cuisine a product of double orality, taste, and talk" (Ray 2008, 2), consumption of food can be linked symbolically to multiple identity affiliations through use of visual images, names, and statements displayed on packages. In doing so, food functions along a spectrum between two poles: Nationalization of food that is presumed *to belong to us* versus post-modern Western consumption societies in which everyday mobility requires open-mindedness, culinary cosmopolitanism, and authenticity (Ching Lin Pang 2003, 67). Clifford described this as "traveling in dwelling, dwelling-in-travelling" (Clifford 1997, 36 cited by Döting, Heide and Mühleisen 2003, 5).

The packaging of commodities is particularly characteristic and a key to understanding the connection between food and identity. Herzfeld referred to "packaging [as the] poetics of authenticity" (Herzfeld 1992, 1999, 2004 by Grasseni 2005, 86) and, Grasseni argued that it also symbolizes the "shift toward a marked commodification of taste" (Grasseni 2005, 86).

The original, the authentic, the real, the right one, as well as, customary sociability receive special meaning and significance for people in the state of migration. This is especially the case when people emigrate from societies characterized by economic scarcity and shortages in comparison with abundant Western societies.

We can trace interesting changes in typical but complex processes connected with food that Grasseni defined as "construction of food as heritage, of taste as a skill, of quality of life as quality of food" (Grasseni 2005, 79). In emigrating to Israel and to Germany, Russian-speaking Jews had a particular desire to discover "the land of milk and honey," not only in the common metaphoric sense of economic security and improvement in the quality of life, but in the literal, material sense—as reflected in the family's refrigerator or displayed on the dining room table in a meal prepared in the new society. These material objects manifest the realization of what Appadurai referred to as dreams of "cultural tales," (Appadurai 1988) which can also be called "spread tablecloths" (ibid) or a taste of life abroad. Moreover, complex commercial developments within the Russian food domain abroad point to creative combinations of multiple images of different collective identities, mobilization of well-known, older, as well as different cultural and national new symbols that led to "re-inventing traditions" (Bell and Valentine 1997; Grasseni 2005; Ohnuki-Tierney 1993; Hobsbawm, 1983; Welz 2000) or "creative traditionalisation" (Beck and Welz, 1997). Similar to clothing, migrants try on the different imaginary *home* images, suggested by products in Russian food stores. Some fit their self-identity and seemed natural and/or have always been part of their lives, while others contradict their self-vision.

It is through the act of migration that "naturalization of the arbitraries in the established given order" (Bourdieu 1977, 164) in the land of origin becomes visible and even questioned as the *home system* is questioned and relativized. Based on the assumption that "food has always operated to define homes as well as cultural otherness" (Döring, Heide and Mühleisen 2003, 4), we know that food products and cuisine traveled from the *home* to be "re-embedded in new lands and cultures" (Mintz 2003, 22) and "indigenized" (ibid., 21) or "naturalized" (Kaufmann 2005, 47). Still, I submit, the domestic images achieved in the migration process through food become particularly obvious, meaningful, and may appear as especially controversial or even painful because people leave their homes in multiple senses and at multiple levels (micro, meso, and macro). For example, when participants left behind their Soviet flats (as micro home), they lost—at the meso level—what they perceived to be their immediate environmental societal *home* (e.g. community, friends, colleagues, habitual and loved places); and at the macro level they forsake the constructed image of the Soviet or CIS *homeland*. Consequently, the sense of *homelessness* can and often does appear in all three levels of their life experiences in the receiving society.

Even if the participants performed a transnational style of life achieved, in part, through purchases in food stores that enabled them to enjoy material culture and media from two societies,[49] both Israeli and German participants still reported feelings of being *"uprooted."* Such feelings seem to match concepts related to emigration in the classical literature, as revealed in classical fiction about emigration and in academic studies.[50] In fact, in both fieldwork settings, it was possible to trace continuous, intensive efforts to acquire, to create, and to design a new *home* as a *micro*cosm within the flat; an appropriate, comfortable *homelike* immediate environment that also served to represent and to remind residents of their longing for the *homeland* they missed in the new country. Accordingly, in relating to these impressions, this chapter presents evidence of "telling stories" (Amon and Menasche 2008), reminiscences of life in their former setting, performed by means of food. Such stories included different and sometimes contested images of *home* and *homelands*, and served as "true fictions."[51]

In this sense, tensions between memories and visions of "roots" and "routes" (Döring, Heide and Mühleisen 2003, 7), chosen and undertaken by migrants become visible in constructing, trying, or borrowing different images of the *new home* or the *homeland*. Created, consumed, and subjectively interpreted images of *home* and *homeland* constructed through food products also symbolize a special form of personal agency, namely "thinking through the body" (Boyarin 1994, 25); or, in other words these *Lebenswelten* are so to say *imbodied* through everyday praxis of food consumption. Accordingly, different, sometimes controversial, or even oxymoronic visual images of Russian food product packages from the Soviet past, contempo-

---

49 About transnational praxis, see the next chapter.
50 Regarding conceptualization of "marginal man" (Stonequist 1935, 1937) and the "stranger" (Schütz 1972).
51 Adaptation from Clifford (1986) who wrote about the process of "writing culture."

rary CIS or Israel are mobilized and commercialized within the framework of food stores in Israel and Germany.

Rather than concentrate on the boundaries, exclusion processes, or misinterpretations that evolve in the "culinary melting pot,"[52] this chapter deals more broadly with the complex, changing concept of *home*. The particular focus on food consumption and culinary practice serve as grounding for this discussion and demonstrate the multiplicities and hybridities involved in both food practice and the conception of *home*. That is, based on assumptions about the importance of the symbolic meaning of the consumed product presented in Chapter 1, the present chapter discusses the "place-making practice" (Ray 2004, 5) of food as symbolic representations of "imaginary space" (Doleve-Gandelman 1990) and "imaginative scenarios" (Wilks by Miller 1995, 149) or "common places"[53] of *home* and *homeland* in real praxis. In doing so, we will observe how participants awaken and impart collective and individual memories,[54] embody in material ways symbolic dreams about powerfulness and richness, propose new narratives and manage several national affiliations, and manifest as well as combine consolidation of personal and collective identities while neglecting or viewing others with irony.

Thus, we see the conjunction of three collective identities:—a revived *Soviet* identity, a recently invented *nationalized Russian* identity, and a modified *Jewish identity* exist in a problematic relationship. For example, the prohibitions of Jewish religion and culture and deep internalization of Russified Soviet culture made it possible for the participants to take for granted certain elements in Russian narratives, particularly those deemed historically problematic for Jews. Above all, it was the Russified Soviet culture that accompanied them abroad. However, in the new context of their lives, this *Lebenswelt* encounters an intensive process of *re-nationalization* that is taking place in the contemporary CIS in the form of the exported commodities, as some contradict historic Jewish processes and the participants' new sense of Jewishness that is developing in Israel or in Germany. In

---

52 About the culinary melting pot as misleading myth, see Appadurai 1988.

53 Or "lieu commun," complex organization of space, language structures, topography and rhetoric according to Boym (2000, 22.)

54 About food as "agent of memory," as constituting communities, and constructing collective identity—see Amon and Menasche 2008; Diner 2002; Mankekar 2005; Sutton 2001.

concrete terms, this complex process can be seen in images displayed on food packages purchased in a Russian food store in Israel and Germany.

In analyzing foods and packaging, we must remember that images do not always reflect people's collective identities or "what people think to be so" (Mintz 2003, 19 quoting Thomas 1927). Thus, in certain cases the very popular sentence, quoted and confirmed in numerous works, "tell me what you eat and I will tell you who you are," can be disproved.

The chapter begins with a presentation of how different positioning in the new, macro *homeland* are expressed in the different ways Russian food stores are constructed in both contexts. This leads to analysis of the metamorphosis of the micro and meso *home* in Russian food stores and meanings of the *hostess*, who is assumed to be responsible for the *home* sphere. This is followed by analysis of different images of *home* proposed and purchased in stores, the commercialization of *nostalgia*, as well as, different images and changes in the macro *imaginary home* transferred from the previous context. Along the way, this analysis will address such topics as proletarian food, food as a Soviet communist paradise, and food as powerful political icon of the Soviet empire. These phenomena will be compared with a parallel process in which food consumption embodies a new political icon of the Jewish Zionist *homeland* in Israel. Then, new and borrowed food images of the contemporary Russian homeland will be presented and analyzed followed by a summative discussion of the multiple meanings of Russian food stores.

4.1 Visibility of Russian food stores in Israel and Germany

Before discussing different *home* images constructed within the framework of the Russian-speaking enclave, in general, and Russian food stores, in particular, I would like to point to the different images extant in Israeli and German contexts that seem to be involved on different levels in constructing the concept *home* and *homeland*.

In Israel, there is a large, strong-voiced, powerful, and largely self-sufficient Russian-speaking community characterized by unabashed "noticeable Otherness" (Mittelberg and Borshevsky 2004), whose presence is evident in nearly every sphere of public life. Advertisements appear in the Russian language in Hebrew language print media, often in large letters, making the presence of the Russian-speaking collective in Israel in the public sphere obvious. There are many Russian food stores (pictures 4:1—3 *Gastronom* [Rus. supermarket] and Delicatessen) and restaurants, book and music stores, video rental shops, alternative medical centers, tourist agencies, removal companies, real estate offices, shoe repair and tailor shops, pawn-brokers, cosmetic centers and hair salons, law firms—all established by and adapted to meet the needs of the Russian-speaking community.[55] Individu-ally and collectively, these service providers have significantly changed the visual image of Haifa's streets, for example, and reflect attempts by this group to self-position itself for legitimacy and to play an active role in the new *home*, on its own cultural terms.

In Germany, by way of contrast, the presence of Russian-speaking ser-vices is inconspicuous and almost invisible to non-Russian-speaking mem-bers of society. The names of shops as well as advertisements are most often written in the German language or even in Russian with German letters (pictures 4:4—5; Jakob supermarket and ZUM[56] supermarket; 4:6 advertisements). Russian food stores and Russian restaurants are hardly recognizable participants in the so-called *globalized ethnic food entrepreneurships*; such as, Indian, Japanese, Italian, Chinese, Mexican food stores and restau-rants in the USA or similar multicultural representatives in Germany, such as Turkish, Italian, or Portuguese food stores and restaurants. Small Rus-sian food stores do not make their *Russianness* known on the street to pass-ers-by. Managers of big Russian supermarkets design shop windows to appeal to non-Russian-speaking consumers. Thus, manifest Russian food stores often meld into the variety of other German shops. In remaining inconspicuous, they do not demonstrate their significance, and their legiti-mate Otherness is hardly manifest.

One plausible, albeit partial explanation for differences between Israel and Germany may be the different scale of immigration: Since Russian speakers comprise almost 20 percent of Israel's general population, the community's self-construction as a powerful group that cultivates its Russian cultural affiliation and uses it as an economic as well as a political resource has to be well respected. More succinctly, the *homecoming* policy

---

55 In addition, nearly all service sectors and state institutions employ Russian-speaking immigrants in order to provide special services in the Russian language.

56 ZUM is an abbreviation for Zentralnyi Universalnyi Magazin [Rus.]. It is a food store that sells all manners of food-related products.

Pic. 4:1 Russian food store "Gastronom" [Soviet name for supermarket, Rus.] (I)

Pic. 4:2 Russian food store "Gastronom" inside (I)

Pic. 4:3 Russian food store "Delicatessen" (I)

Pic. 4:4 Russian food store "Jakob" (G)

Pic. 4:5 Russian food supermarket "ZUM" (G)

Pic. 4:6 Advertisement for Russian food supermarket "Grand" with Russian names written in German letters

Pic. 4:7 Advertisement for Russian food store "Teremok" [traditional Russian hut, Rus.] (I)

Pic. 4:8 "Rodnaya Derevnia Ryazhenka" [native country boiled, fermented milk, Rus.] (I)

Pic. 4:9 Mushrooms "Domik v Derevne" [Little house in couutry village, Rus.], name written in Hebrew "Kafri Ubeiti" [my country village and my house, Heb.] (I)

that is at the core of the Jewish "return" to the State of Israel combined with growing legitimization for the multicultural lives of its citizens that has been evolving for decades provide a unique context that not only tolerates but supports, in many respects, development of the self-conscious cultural otherness of Russian-speaking Jews in their new *homeland* [Heb. *moledet*, according to nationalist Israeli terminology].

In Germany, one can hardly speak of a strong, self-conscious group that is proud of its legitimate cultural Otherness in the new *homeland*. This may be due to the migrant reception by the receiving society that is guided by the concept of *"Duldung"* [lit. tolerated, Ger.], as opposed to those who have equal rights to those of the resident host population. Thus, the absence of Russian letters in shop names or advertising may be connected to an operational assumption in the German public sphere that there is no legitimacy for the other languages of all cultural and ethnic minorities, and that all migrants are expected to act through German. Indeed, with the exception of European food restaurants that use Italian or French names, only the largest minority in the investigated city—migrants from Turkey— dare label their enclave through their own language and justify it through use of German subtitles.[57] Even if they have been granted a migration status other than *Duldung*, as *Kontingentflüchtlinge* [contingent refugees, Ger.],[58] Russian-speaking Jews often have the feeling of being tolerated as "Russians" à la *homo sovieticus*, rather than being welcomed to the new *homeland*.[59] Of course, the return of Jews after the Holocaust to the new *homeland* in Germany may be conceptually especially problematic. Additionally, it could be also possible that Russian food stores in Israel are oriented exclusively to the extensive community of the Russian-speaking clientele, whereas Russian supermarkets in Germany appeal to different groups and not solely to the relatively small number and hence economically instable market of Russian-speakers.

Also worthy of note is that Russian food stores in Germany are oriented to the consumption desires of three quite different migration groups: Russian-speaking Jews, Russian-speaking ethnic Germans, and guest work-

---

57 The fieldwork did not concentrate on such multicultural cities as Berlin or Frankfurt, where I suspect this claim might not be as applicable.

58 Or, for example Russian-speaking *Aussiedler* [resettled ethnic Germans, Germ.], who received German citizenship.

59 See Chapter Seven and Eight for discussion of problematic nature of Germany as "homeland" for Russian-speaking Jews.

ers from the CIS. In some cases, such as those encountered during the fieldwork in the investigated city, there were two different Russian food stores. One was popular among Russian-speaking Jews (owned by Jewish migrants from the CIS); the other was popular among ethnic Germans (owned by an ethnic German from the CIS). Although the products available in these competing Russian food stores were very similar, both were involved in the struggle over different collective identities. However, again, these differentiations and confrontations remained, for the most part, invisible to local Germans who often operated through the deceptive, generic term—*Russians*.

4.2 Image of the hostess in the Russian food stores

As mentioned in the previous chapter, in many cultures the domain of food seems to be highly gendered (Bell and Valentine 1996; Brett 1985; Kneafsey and Cox 2002; Lupton 1996; Ray 2004; Starr-Sered 1992; Vallianatos and Raine 2008). Women are often presented as a key figure or "gatekeepers" (Bell and Valentine 1996; Brunner 2008; Vallianatos and Raine 2008) in the construction of *home* (Baxter and Paterson 1983; Beagan, Chapman, D'Sylva, Raewyn 2008; Beardsworth and Keil 1997; Bell and Valentine 1997; Lupton 1996; Murcott 1982, 1986; Starr-Sered 1988; Williams 1985) and are often designated and consequently perceived to be responsible for the important role of feeding the family. With migration, the *home* (at all of its multiple levels) first has to be recreated and to become habitual before it can come to be taken for granted in the new land.

Lora (Germany): "In the beginning, we all [she, her husband and their two sons] were very tense and shouted at one another. The first Novyi God [Russian New Year feast] was terrible. We quarreled. We were so nervous, couldn't enjoy anything. My son said me, 'You have to get a divorce.' It was so bad [pause] I cooked *kholodets* [aspic (jellied meat), Russian festive meal, Rus.], bought champagne [associated with Russian New Year celebration], arranged the *ryumochki* [crystal glass decanter, Rus]. I tried so that it will be like at home."

As homemakers or keepers of the hearth and home, women's agency is involved in constructing the feeling of *home* as well as reproduction and manifestation of family and personal identities. In particular, the food women prepare assumes a significant meaning in the migration process when all identities are questioned and often modified in considerable manner. As found in previous studies about different migrants' groups,[60] Russian-speaking female Jewish participants in Israel and Germany continued to play a crucial role in the process of cultural preservation and continuation through the food they prepared and displayed on the dining room table. In particular, Russian-speaking Jewish women in Israel and Germany were given a new role as cultural brokers, as the food they prepared involved reinventing the habitual cuisine as well as innovating and combining different images and identity symbols on the plate. Moreover, the image and role of the woman as hostess and homemaker was often instrumentalized in Russian food stores in Israel and Germany. In the following examples, one can trace how some advertisements in Russian for products play with the images of the well-fed family, the role of mothers or grandmothers as hostess or homemaker, and presumed retention of the family's cuisine traditions:

– Hostess Crêpes with Potatoes and Mushrooms (G); Dream of the Hostess—Russian Mustard (G); Dream of the Hostess, Mayonnaise—Dreams come true! (picture 4:7); Hostess Squash Paté (I); Hostess Aubergine Paté (I); "Godmother, help yourself. People, be kind, help yourself, eat fully....Vermicelli" (I); "Mother—Butter" (I); Family Ice Cream (G); Family Cookies (G); "Full Father—*Pel'meni*" (G); Grandma's—"Company manufacturing oatmeal cookies, gherkins, cheese" (I).

Moreover, an actual change in the post-migration role of women as hostess or homemaker seems to have evolved. In comparison with what was available in the SU, the material abundance available in Israel or Germany enabled women to develop a wide variety of different ways to improvise and innovate. First, abundance was the basis for one of the most significant changes as it reduced the need for overstocking and the intensive preparation of food as well as seasonal preparation of jams, pickled vegetables,

---

60 This corresponds with findings of studies about the important role of female migrants in the process of preserving original culture through food practices; for example, Starr-Sered's (1992) study of older religious female migrants from Iraq in Jerusalem; Gandelman's (1990) study of Ethiopian Jewish female migrants in Israel 1990; Amon and Menasche's (2008) research about Jewish Sephardic Jewish families in Brazil; Vallianatos and Raine's (2008) study of Arab and South Asia immigrant women in Canada; Kneafsey and Cox's (2002) study of Irish women in Coventry England; Williams (1985) study of Mexican Women in the USA.

and marinades for winter. As a result, self-prepared, pickled tomatoes became an exception and not a common dish on the festive table laden with
homemade food. Furthermore, for the first time, formerly exclusively
homemade dishes could now be purchased in the Russian food store.
Thus, in addition to numerous and different types of ready-made jams,
pickled vegetables and marinades—all labeled *homemade*, semi-prepared
dishes were available for purchase in Russian food stores—though most of
these dishes had been prepared at home prior to emigration. Other products available for purchase, previously made at home, included: pies, *pirozhki* [patties Rus.] filled with meat, cabbage and eggs, potatoes or mushrooms; *vareniki* [dumplings Rus.] filled with potatoes, cheese, mushrooms
meat, curd or fruit; *pel'meni* [small ravioli-like dough pockets, Rus.] filled
with meat; bell peppers stuffed with mushrooms; cabbages stuffed with
meat; *blini* [crêpes, Rus.] filled with sweet cheese, mushrooms, potatoes or
meat; a big variety of popular, homemade cakes; and jars of soups such as
borsch and shi, generally still made in the home.

The option to purchase such products had a number of consequences.
First, in the pre-migration home, the quality and aesthetics of dishes prepared or purchased as *homemade* implied and signified the social competence of women. In contrast, in both post-migration contexts it was for the
first time legitimate to serve semi-prepared dishes at a family celebration,
since time involved in preparation became a valued factor and new understandings and assessments of what was important in constructing the appropriate and legitimate dining table at home emerged. The availability of
so called *homemade dishes* or cakes from the Russian food store also made it
possible to purchase the desired image of the k*hozyaika* [hostess, Rus.],
brought from the SU and now embellished by a variety of products and
material abundance.

Finally, an ironic note; the idea of public kitchens presented in the Soviet iconic classic—*On the Tasty and Healthy Food Book,* with its projected
images of the lives of future communist women who will not have to
spend leisure time cooking in the kitchen, was partially realized post-migration in Israel and Germany through purchase of *homemade*-like dishes in
Russia food stores, prepared by profit-making *public* kitchens.

4.3 Longing for the REAL home via food

> "We are forever mired in polarities
> of dread and desire for home and
> homelessness."
> *Krishnendu Ray (2004, 3)*

> "The only place in this universe
> where we might feel at home is with
> the realization that if we are not at
> home you can realize your home."
> *Jonathan Boyarin (1994, 4)*

The displays of *homemade* products in Russian food stores may well arouse the most desired, craved image among many migrants—the image of *home*. Although it is not clear whether one can point to this or another material object as triggering nostalgic feelings for *home*, numerous products available in Russian food stores in both contexts employed the phrase that signals the importance of the concept of *homemade*, this includes the following products:

- Israel: Homemade Marinated Pickles and Tomatoes, Homemade Butter, Homemade Cheese, Homemade Marinated Vegetables, Homemade Sour Cream, Homemade Bread, Pickled Fairy Ring Mushrooms according to the Home recipe, *Sauerkraut* [usually homemade product], Pasta house in the Country.
- Germany: Homemade Sour Cream, Homemade Liver Sausage, Homemade sausage, Homemade Marinated Vegetables, Homemade Pickled Cherries, Domestic Doctor Raspberry Jam, [61] My Family Chocolates, manufactured by Russian chocolate makers, stamped *Domashnii ochag* [lit. hearth and home, Rus.], Cellar of Lyonya [Rus.],[62] Pickled Vegetable Salad—In the cold winter evening come down to the cellar."

The use of the *homemade* in the names of products in both contexts symbolizes domestic traditions associated with the time invested in preparing, stocking, and storing foods. Even though *homemade* is a concept employed with products sold in non-Russian Israeli or German supermarkets oriented to the general audience of consumers, these symbols have a special

---

61 Raspberry jam added to the tea is widely known for healing colds and flu-like symptoms.
58 The cellar is the traditional place for preserving and storing products in Russia.

meaning for those in various stages of migration, including association with classic components of being homesick and feeling homeless.

The longing for home was a dominant motif in the microcosm and meso-home outside the closed environment in the new country, in both the German and the Israeli contexts. The latter case proves the partial power and validation of the official Israeli narrative about encouraging Jews from all over the world to return *home*. The feeling of "being up-rooted" exacted by the emigration experience was articulated frequently by migrants who referred to such loss through the image of the original home as a bulwark that cannot be reproduced. In this regard, it is also important to stress that the Russian term equivalent to the Hebrew *aliya* [lit. ascend, or go to Israel, Heb.] lacks the *homecoming* connotation, hence Russian-speaking migrants use it in sense of "arrival in Israel" or "immigration to Israel" rather than in the sense intended in the hegemonic narrative as *returning to Israel* or *THE Country*.

Felix (Israel) reflecting on the immigrants' experiences: "Now, if I move to another country, I won't have the feeling of being disconnected from my home [probably meaning both micro-home and homeland], because I've already been disconnected and that feeling remains with me."

Vera (Israel): "Here there is no feeling that your flat, even if you buy it, will remain your home and will become a part of you for your entire life [referring to her feeling regarding her state flat in the SU]."

Lena (Israel): "Everything around, outside, isn't the home—nature, people, and climate. Even the home you've built [here]…can't keep out all the things, it can't oppose them. These things infiltrate your life. That's why no matter how hard you try to create something of your own here; it doesn't feel at all like home [in all three levels]."

The last quote is remarkably similar to a statement made by Galina in Germany:

"Everything is different here. There is different light in the flat, and the water tastes different. Furniture you always liked suddenly does not seem to be so nice. I am always trying to create my world in my flat, to make it my home, but it cannot thwart the environment…The harder you try to create your home, the more your attempt to do so is doomed to failure […] When somebody [Russian-speaker] comes to your flat and is curious, he asks immediately: "Nu, show me your home!" What should I show? There [in St. Petersburg] I could tell a story about every object, but here there is nothing to say. It has no meaning and significance. It is just stuff from the *Flohmarkt* [fleamarket, uses German word] that you purchase quickly and just as easily dispense of, because there is nothing that connects you to it."

Participants in both contexts spoke about "roots" that "remained there" [in the SU] and about themselves as "uprooted, removed, or rooted out" through emigration. Such roots are also associated with material objects that surround the migrant in his/her new, immediate environment, which as Galina put it, have become "just stuff from the *Flohmarkt*." The image of home, in contrast, was epitomized in both contexts through repeated use of the word *nail* as a metaphor, as Kolia (Israel) stated: "I want to have a home where I can bang a nail into the wall wherever I want."

At the same time, there were differences in the two contexts. First, there were significantly different situations at the practical level of property ownership. Whereas almost all participants in Israel possessed their own flats, when the fieldwork was conducted, only one family in the German context owned their own home. The remainder lived in rented flats, most subsidized by the state, that were only nominally perceived to be "their home."

Also, in the terms of the new *homeland*, participants in the Israeli case seemed to use the term home (as applied to Israel as the Jewish home) more easily than did their compatriots in Germany. None of the participants interviewed from the latter group referred to Germany in the sense of *being at home*; rather they claimed that there was an incompatibility between "living in Germany" and "feeling at home." Moreover, in the Israeli case, feeling at *home* (as in *homeland*) was achieved through comparison with, and often critique of, non-Jewish Israeli citizens (referring to non-Jewish Russian speakers, Muslims or Christian Arabs) or Jewish ex-Soviet compatriots living in Germany. That is, speaking about such persons was a unique, symbolic opportunity to define their own home through juxtaposing it to or by excluding Other groups.[63]

At the meso- and micro levels in Israel, and even more so in Germany, Russian food stores seem to aspire to present an alternative version of "imaging the lost home."

Lora (Germany): "I did not know a word in German when we arrived, except *Hände hoch*! [hands up, Ger.]. And then we entered the Russian store and finally I saw an announcement about a translation service. There one can breathe again; everyone gets charged by the warmth. You feel at home."

---

63 This phenomenon is addressed in the Chapters Six, Seven, and Eight.

Especially interesting and strong is the link Lora made between the feeling of *being home* and feeling alive, as when Lora [who suffers from asthma] described her perception of the Russian food store as home and as place where "one can breathe again"—one of the absolute basic conditions for life. In this context, the store is associated with trust, comfort, habitual behavior, and familiarity—all contributing to the sense of a lost environmental *home*. Support of this interpretation was found in a statement by Larisa (Israel) when she referred to the Russian store as "an oasis where your language is comprehended, there is a correspondence of times and tastes, and of course it is an information center."

Similar to the metaphor employed by Lora, the "oasis" metaphor stresses particularly well Larisa's feeling of alienation in Israel, predetermined by the language deficits and reinforced in the new environment by regular supermarkets; places that were alienating and stressful places for many participants during the first stage, and for many years after immigration.

In a related manner, Luba (Germany) spoke at first about her frequent visits to the Russian food store (not cited here) and then elaborated upon her feeling of alienation in regular German supermarkets:

"I felt inferior on the streets and in the stores. I was ashamed to enter stores. They [German speakers] ask there: *'Was kann ich für Sie tun?'* ['Can I help you?,' uses Ger]. I was intimidated immediately. I was ashamed to enter [regular] stores. I was ashamed of myself. When I buy something [uses present] in Lidl or Aldi [relatively inexpensive German supermarkets], I always count the change exactly and *never let anybody* ask. I especially afraid of the question: *'Kommen Sie zurecht?'* [Are you managing OK? uses Ger.]."

For Luba, routine questions from native speakers in Israel or Germany, such as "Can I help you?" or "Are you managing OK?"—caused apprehension because she felt unable to manage in the new environment and would not reveal it to anybody. In contrast, in the Russian food stores, language is not a problem and she understands the unwritten rules of behavior. Consequently, she is self-assured and performs mature acts of social agency. Thus, in both the German and the Israeli contexts, the participants trusted and felt comfortable in the intimate atmosphere of the Russian food stores, but totally alienated in the non-Russian stores, as we see from the following quotes:

Katia (Germany). "The usual supermarket is cold, faceless, and official, while the Russian food store is *rodnoi* [native, home, relative (like part of your family), Rus.]

and close by. Every word that is written or that I hear has its comprehensive meaning. You come there like it was your own home, where everything is intimate, close, and trusted."

Felix (Israel): "You have to choose. We never had such a problem before. You don't know what you should choose. That is really a pity. You are afraid to make a mistake because you don't have a lot of money, and you have to try to save every shekel. You're afraid to ask, so you just take something and go home. Once I bought canned fish in tomato sauce. We opened it at home and it was something that we had to throw away. At the beginning it was more extreme. You feel like you are inside a mussel, even until today it is not quite as comfortable in comparison to a Russian food store."

Lena (Israel): "In the [regular] supermarket you feel like a nameless person, from nowhere. Everything seems so chaotic and you feel like you are in an aquarium. The products have no face. They are foreign and you are apathetic to them."

The idea of the space of the Russian food store as a kind of a comfortable, inclusive, safe home is epitomized, as well, in some store names. For example, an advertisement for a new Russian food store in Israel adopted the traditional Russian name *Teremok* [wooden hut, Rus.; see picture 4:7]. This name is strongly associated with one of the most well-known, traditional Russian fairy tales for small children by the same name about the search by different animals for a home. Once an empty house, the *teremok* is discovered by a fly. Other animals—consecutively larger, from a fly until a bear—seek it out. Every animal knocks on the door and states: "Who lives in the *teremok*?" One by one all those who have been allowed in and live inside identify themselves and then the new animal asks: "Can I live with you?" In the beginning, the other animals hesitate because space in the new home is filling up, but each time they finally permit other animals to stay with them, that is until the bear squeezes in and the entire teremok collapses. This notwithstanding, naming a Russian food store Teremok evokes an association with hospitality and a place where Russian-speaking consumers can find a *home*.

The strong image of home with its warmth, comfort, and hospitality within the Russian food store seems to be much more important for Rus-sian-speaking consumers in both Israel and Germany than where certain products have been produced. Consequently, the Russian food store provided products that satisfied participants' tastes ["home food is tasty"] in a homelike and hospitable atmosphere that—valued added—reinforced the delicious nature of the home-associated food products over regular, seemingly tasteless, local products.[64] Accordingly, making reference to where a certain product was purchased was often perceived as a convincing argument reinforcing the desired taste and quality:

Karina to the guests (Israel): "Taste the pickles. They are from the Russian food store. Really tasty!"

Lena to her guests (Israel): "Spread the butter on the bread. It's real butter from the Russian store. Look how yellow it is!"

Katia to her guests (Germany): "I looked a long time for the right *vitchina* [ham, Rus.]."

An image of a meso as well as micro *home* are stressed explicitly in products available in the Russian food store through depiction of a house on the product or combination of the words *home, house, country* or *village.* For example, a pastoral village house appears on Village Sour Cream (I), Village Liver Sausage (G), Village ham with garlic (G), *Khutorskoye* [small farm, Rus.] sunflower (G). Many other products include the theme of searching for embodiment of their own home in the new homeland; for example, when a childlike picture of a village appears on *Rodnaya Derevnya* [native country, Rus.] *Ryazhenka* [boiled fermented milk, Rus.] (G) (picture 4:8).

Use of product titles to embody the search for home involves an interesting turn in the case of Israel given the goal of the hegemonic nationalist enterprise of Jewish "homecoming" as the context into which migrants immigrated. This can be seen in a comparison between labels in Russian versus Hebrew on some products available in Russian food stores. For example, the Russian name for a package of mushrooms—*Domik v Derevne* [little house in the country, Rus.]—is accompanied by depiction of country house, which may arouse the consumers' associations with a Russian dacha. However, the Hebrew label states "kafri ve beiti" [my country village and my house, Heb.], associated with the Zionist idea of a home in the native [Israeli] *homeland* (picture 4:9). Similarly, the nylon packaging of Engel bread, baked in the mountain city of Jerusalem, states "rodnoe selo" [native country village, Rus.] accompanied by a picture of a field with harvested yellow sheaves associated with vast Soviet expanses, along with the Hebrew "hakfar sheli" [my country village, Heb.] appeal to Jewish Israeli

---

64 The migrants' complaints about tasteless local products purchased in the regular supermarket were pointed out in other studies; see Harbottle (1997) about Iranian migrants in England; Bell and Valentine (1996) about different migrants in Australia; Mankakar (2005) about Indian migrants in the USA.

village (picture 4:10). Thus, a Russian-speaking consumer whose eye is likely to perceive the Russian text first and then the Hebrew receives two conflicting messages from the product's packaging, each having different ideological meanings regarding the Soviet versus the Zionist *national home*. Such commercial messages are hardly compatible as the nationalist terminology is absolute and each demands loyalty to the "right" national home.

Similarly, the packaging of the Israeli *Pa'am* Rye Bread [once, then, at that time, Heb.] displays a rye field with a huge combine harvester gathering the yield from the Jewish Israeli earth. The bread's bakery is called *Ahdut* [unity, Heb.], a word associated with the concept of *ahdut ha'am* [unity of the Jewish people, Heb.]. However, the Russian statement on the package is "rye bread of the past" (picture 4:11). Thus, even if Russian consumers understood the reference to the Zionist value stated in Hebrew, they are more likely to relate it to the promises of communism in the SU and one of its central symbols—the harvester collecting an abundance of wheat, as depicted on one of the first pages of *On the Tasty and Healthy Food Book* (picture 4:12), discussed in the previous chapter.

Another interesting example is *Vladimirskoe* oat cookies, [city Vladimir, Rus.] produced by the manufacturer—Russian Style, as one of his products in of its Golden Ring of Russia[65] series for export to Russian food stores in Israel. The insignia of Russian Style combines the Israeli and Russian flags and the two states' emblems so that half of the Israel's Magen David is added above the Russian two-headed eagle. The package includes a text with a long description of the town of Vladimir, presenting it as a representative of the traditional Russian cultural heritage. One could imagine that the last two sentences would be especially confusing for non-Russian speakers living in Israel:

"[…] all together, they [reference to towns known as the Golden Ring of Russia] represent the treasure of Russian culture. These are the centers of spiritual culture, our past, present and future. Here, your soul touches the past and looks for spiritual revival… Let your return to Russian Style start with the Golden Ring of Russia

---

65 The Golden Ring of Russia refers to several Russian cities that are proclaimed to embody the cultural Russian Christian prerevolutionary heritage and are well-known as tourist travel routes.

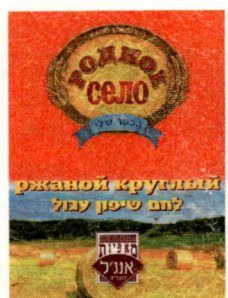

Pic. 4:10 Bread "Rodnoe Selo" [Native country village, Rus.], name written in Hebrew as "Hakfar Sheli" [my country village, Heb.] (I)

Pic. 4:11 "Rye Bread of the Past," [Rus] in Hebrew "Pa'am Rye Bread"

Pic. 4:12 First page of the On the Tasty and Healthy Food Book from Stalin's times

Pic. 4:13 "Khleb Ieruslalimskii" [Jerusalem bread, Rus.] (I)

Pic. 4:14 "Russkii Rzhanoi Khleb" [Russian rye bread, Rus.] (I)

Pic. 4:15 "Kvas" [Russian traditional drink] produced by an ultra-orthodox Jewish firm "Shai Kfar Habad" [Gift of Habad Village, Heb.] (I)

Pic. 4:16 "Kashtan Rye Bread" (I)

Pic. 4:17 "Rzhanoi Khleb Derevenskii" [Village country rye bread, Rus.] manufactured by "Yehudit" [Jewish, Heb.] (I)

Pic. 4:18 "Ierusalimskii Lev" wheat vodka [Jerusalem Lion, Rus.] (I)

products because that is what nourished our courage and gives us the impulse to live, create and love. [Rus.]."

The fact of their contemporary residency in Germany and Israel suggests that the Russian cities included in the Russian Golden Ring route were not what consumers' sought in immigration, as proclaimed on this package, nor where they desired to make their future home. However, even if functioning within this contradiction, Russian cultural food symbols, whose literal reference is a revival of the Russian empire could also *nourish*, symbolically, Jewish migrants in Israel and contribute to their sense of collective difference and sometimes contradictory affiliations.

Whereas some marketing agents instrumentalize cultural Russianness, others commercialize the Jewish religious tradition and Zionism through symbols of the new *homeland*. As discovered during the fieldwork in Israel, different areas connected with food produced evidence of what Raviv referred to as the consumption of food products as an "act of patriotism" (Raviv 2001, 2). For example, Russian Israeli food magazines include articles about the history of "the taste of the motherland"[66] that discuss the development of Israeli food habits and Israeli food stores, from the pre-state period and on. Additionally, both products produced in the CIS for Israeli Russian speakers as well as products produced in Israel for this population frequently combine Russian and Israeli religious or Zionist symbols on the food packages. Similar examples include the following:

Khleb Ierusalimskii [Jerusalem bread, Rus.] baked by Libo Bakery; packaging includes a kosher stamp and picture of a street in Old City of Jerusalem (picture 4:13).

Russkii Rzhanoi Khleb [Russian rye bread, Rus.], baked by Village Product; packaging includes kosher stamp and depiction of religious Jewish male with beard and skullcap, blowing a shofar, with crown and Star of David above his head (picture 4:14).

Kvas[67] [Russian traditional drink similar to malt] produced by an ultra-orthodox Jewish firm Shai Kfar Habad [Gift of Habad Village, Heb.]; the packaging portrays Russian wheat stalks and a statement announcing the coming of Messiah (picture 4:15). Interestingly, the package displays an exact replica of the home of the Lubavich Rebbe in Brooklyn

---

66 "Taste of the motherland" in the serial *How was it? Delo vkusa*, 21—23.
67 A mildly acidic, sweet, dark-colored drink produced by fermenting wheat with water and sugar (Tempest 1997, 3).

constructed in Kfar Habad village, near Tel Aviv, after his death. It
symbolizes Habad believers' hope of the Messiah's coming.

Kashtan Rye Bread [marrone, Rus.] produced by Ta'anug [pleasure, Heb.,];
packaged in the national colors of Israel—white and blue—with two
Israeli flags and the number 50 [for 50th jubilee anniversary of the State
of Israel] (picture 4:16).

Rzhanoi Khleb Derevenskii [Village Country rye bread, Rus.] manufactured by
Yehudit [Jewish, Heb.], packaged with the emblem of the Magen David
with two wheat stalks (picture 4:17).

Ierusalimskii Lev Wheat Vodka [Jerusalem lion, Rus.] portrays a lion, the
Jewish symbol of the city of Jerusalem (picture 4:18).

Jerusalem Chocolates, manufactured by Laima, a Lithuanian firm, portrays
a large picture of the Western Wall with orthodox men praying and the
flag of Israel (picture 4:19).

A related, an interesting phenomenon can be found in a recent book—*On
a Tasty and Healthy Life*—by Okun' and Guberman (2003) published in the
Russian language in Israel. The title of this book is related to the famous
Soviet cookbook *On the Tasty and Healthy Food Book* (discussed in the previous chapter). In giving names to recipes for festive meals, developed especially for Russian-speaking Jews living in Israel, the authors selected such
ironic titles as Oslo, Intifada, or Primaries. Also included in the "semiotic"
kitchen (Okun' and Guberman, 2003) are recipes for—The First Zionist
Congress in Basel hot chocolate, Trotzki Red Borscht, *Halutzim* Salad
[Jewish pioneers in pre-state Israeli, Heb.]; *Kibbutz Galuyot* Paella [Diaspora
unification, Heb.]; *Hok Hashvut* Pancakes [lit, Law of Return, refers to law
granting Jews special status in repatriation to Israel, Heb.], *Giur* Bouillon
[conversion process to Judaism boullion, Heb.]. Especially interesting is
the authors' explanation for "Repatriate Pullet," in Russian:

"Wine symbolizes the land of origin. The mixture of mango, oranges and lemons,
olive oil, and bananas—the historic motherland [typical expression of Israel by
Russian speakers, referred in Heb. as moledet]. Detachment from the pullet symbolizes separation from the prehistoric motherland [here the SU], arrival in the
new Motherland, and the challenges of absorption. After experiencing difficulties,
the chick swims and enjoys a new life—in the sauce. The grill is the energy of the
sun in *Eretz Israel* [promised land, Heb.] [Rus.] (ibid, 209)."

No references were found in the German context to the use of the national
German narrative or evidence of food consumption as an act of patriotism.
The images of home were composed of different components of the

Pic. 4:19 Chocolate box "Jerusalem" manufactured by "Laima", a Lithuanian firm (I)

Pic. 4:20 "Nostalgia Chocolate" tart (I)

Pic. 4:22 "Birch Sausage" (G)

Pic. 4:23 "Baikal Drink" [name the river in Siberian] (I)

Pic. 4:21 Advertisement of "Cold Valley Vodka, Real Ukrainian" (I)

Pic. 4:25 "Borzhomi Water" (I)

Pic. 4:26 "Yessentuki Water" (I)

Pic. 4:24 "Wonder Berry Juice" (I)

Pic. 4:27 Pickled vegetables "King's meal, the very same taste" (G)

Soviet past and post-Perestroika present Russianness.[68] However, ideas about the components of *home* in both contexts were performed especially within the walls and microcosm of the Russian food store. Here the images performed seem to have been intensively sought, produced, and in both cases only partially founded. The subjective memories, tastes, and expectations concerning the feeling of home contributed to the broad variety in production of certain products and imitations of what is remembered or assumed to be their authentic origins. However, while such past experiences are often idealized, "sanitized" (Stern 1992, 11) and "fictionalized" (Lupton 1996, 50) they turn out to be crucial in the consumers' determination of considering a particular product to be one they liked, considered to be "authentic" or a "fake."

In conclusion, well-known food Soviet products that were used traditionally, or dreamed of, were given significance in the present. These products encapsulate the illusionary harmonious nostalgic image of the "original home" invoked through the Russian food store.

4.4 Commercial promotion of nostalgia

Loss of feeling at *home*, on different levels, combined with subjective memories motivated the participants to long for the *real, original, authentic, same*, but also *the right* and *that* taste. Such yearnings were based on idealized, positively connotated images of *home* and "rosy recollections" (Lupton 1996, 50) of past experiences. In analyzing the concept "nostalgia" Boym (2001, 41) found, that it places different stresses on restorative and reflective components, namely on *nostos* and *algia*: "Restorative nostalgia puts emphasis on *nostos* and proposes to rebuild the lost home and patch up the memory gaps. Reflective nostalgia dwells in *algia*, in longing and loss, the imperfect process of remembering" (ibid). Both of these components are present within Russian food stores and in the participants' consumption in Israel and Germany. The restorative process—*nostos*—was present when migrants actively invested time and effort in the search for certain products, as well as to revive, re-produce, re-create and re-build *desired tastes* and identity images. The reflective process—*algia*—was present

---

68 As proletarian Russianness, Russian empire, Russian paradise, current Russia, all presented in this chapter below.

when migrants came to realize that this task was doomed to fail, but continued to long for and remember the *original, real, authentic, natural images*, and *tastes*. The following excerpt of a discussion reveals the manifestations of these two components:

Luba to Katia (Germany): "What do you miss most?"

Katia: "Different tasty cakes and cookies, éclairs, *korzinochki* [small cakes with cream, Rus.] that cost 22 kopecks. Here everything is *Kuchen* [cakes, Ger.]. I miss bread, especially biscuits. There is a lot of bread here, even in the Russian store, but all these are only names."

Luba: "I have no problem with bread, but ice cream, it is just really not the same!"

Ella (Israel): "You know I miss *tulskie pryaniki* [Russian honey gingerbread produced in the city of Tula, Rus.]. Once in half year I want to believe in the miracle, and I buy some at the Russian food store—but no, it is never the same!"

Yuri (Israel) turns to the hostess: "Do you remember *belyashi* [fried pirozhki, pockets filled with meat, Rus.] that they used to sell at the entrance to the Metro? I can still taste their flavor."

Katia responds (his sister who lives in Germany, but is visiting in Israel): "What's the big deal, they are easy to make!"

Yuri: "No, that wouldn't be the same...."

Katia (pondering) comments: "It's you who are no longer the same..."

Luba, Katia, Ella, and Yuri are convinced that there is an irretrievable, original taste of bread, cakes, ice cream, honey gingerbreads, and belyashi. The main reason for their unconditional claim, I submit, is that the taste of certain products has been perceived and recalled through cultural interpretation ground in certain situations in a social context. Now, all these products are relocated within a completely different social environment, displaced in significantly different everyday situations, and deprived of their original, familiar physical context. Thus, the physical context, and its loss, has a dynamic influence on the participants' judgment. For example, whereas in the SU many persons claimed that it was nearly impossible to find out what meat was stuffed in belyashi, many speculated that it was a suspect mixture of cheap and fatty meat, and hence this product's ironic nickname was "ear, nose and throat." However, in the new context, Yuri's description employed a nostalgic (stress on *algia*) image of belyashi sold for ten kopecks in the St. Petersburg underground where Yuri was born, lived for most of his life, worked as a highly successful mechanical engineer of respectable social status. Consequently, de-contextualized *belyashi* cannot be reproduced in their original form because they are detached from their socio-cultural location. Therefore, they cannot have the same taste and meaning.

Presuming nostalgia to be an inevitable part of the emigration process, newspaper advertisements in Russian used statements, such as: "food we have lost;" (I) "the main salad of the SU;"[69] (I) "Soviet taste of the most famous Moscow Ice Cream;" (G); "mackerel roasted in oil—quality traditions since 1949" (I). Not only do these product names and references articulate nostalgia, they promote it directly through over use of the stereotyped word "nostalgia." Thus, Russian-speaking commercials in both contexts strove to revive the concept of *nostalgia*, knowing that it was well-known to consumers from books about Russian emigration to France or to the USA during the 1917 Revolution. Above all else, the word *nostalgia* and the birch tree were used to symbolize the myth of sentimental longing for the lost *homeland* and irretrievable past while living in the new country.

Products using the theme of a lost imagined world offer migrants the possibility to realize it once again, to sympathize with it, and even literally to *imbibe* nostalgia (i.e. to internalize its taste). Among the examples of this phenomenon are: Nostalgia Ice Cream (G); Nostalgia Chocolate Tart (I) (picture 4:20); Russian restaurants and food stores called "Nostalgia" (both in Israel and Germany).

An additional example of a primary albeit clichéd Russian symbol for emigration nostalgia, the birch tree, appeared on packages and commercialized nostalgia. For example, Cold Valley Vodka (I) employed actual Ukrainian advertisements in which the bottle was displayed against a backdrop of birch trees in the winter with a silver sword lying next to a large stone on the snow (picture 4:21). Such a portrayal is especially exotic in the warm Israeli climate. Other examples include Birch Juice (Israel and Germany), restaurants or Russian food stores with the name Birch Tree (both in Israel and Germany), vodka made from buds of the birch tree (G), Birch Russian-style Mustard (G), and even Birch Sausage (G) (picture 4:22).

The name *Berezka* [birch, Rus.] on Russian products and as a name for Russian food stores has an additional nostalgic connotation. Soviet stores for foreigners from the capitalist West, where commodities were sold for Dollars instead of Soviet rubels were called *"Berezka."* These shops, which

---

69 Refers to a potato salad (with pieces of meat) and mayonnaise called Olivier, which was and remains for many families an essential part of every festivity around the dining table.

have almost never been visited by the participants had a strong image of the Western material paradise. Thus, *Berezka* embodies an interesting symbolic combination: it is desirable both as being something nostalgic and traditionally Russian and missed and simultaneously as being foreign, capitalist, Western and also missed.

Nostalgia functions very selectively as a mechanism in reconstructing images and histories in terms of longing. "The good old times" are often "sterilized" negative events and memories that have been idealized. For example, portrayals of landscapes can include motifs such as fields, seas, and mountains on labels of drinks such as Baikal (I) (picture 4:23) or berry juice (I) (picture 4:24) and pictures of well-known health resorts on bottles of the spa's mineral water Borjomi or Essentuki (I) (picture 4:25—6). All these names seek to arouse nostalgic feelings for missed landscapes and "good Soviet times." This recalls Barthes analyses of references to "good times" in French images (Barthes 1984, 1997) as well as Grasseni identification of this theme in the use of idyllic Alpine landscapes as visual strategy in promoting Italian food products (Grasseni 2005, 84). Food and the dining table were employed in the 19th century Russian literature to present the "idyllic life," the "happy ethic of consuming" (Leblanc 1999, 263) and the spirit of community in the age of industrial revolution.

Thus, as we can see from these comparisons, *nostalgia* was not limited to emigration; rather it has been addressed and commercialized frequently in the post-modern world (Boym 2001). Furthermore, nostalgia has been used to refer to something that people never experienced in their lives as in the case of the use of pre-Russian revolution symbols; for example, pickled vegetables called Kings' Meal, the Very Same Taste (G) (picture 4:27) or dry red wine Nostalgie, Isabella that displays a post-Renaissance portrayal of noble women under the product name—Nostalgie—printed in Russian letters but pronounced in French (I) (picture 4:28). In this sense Nostalgie relates not only to creating past but also to creating the present with producing products which claim/pretend to be "*mnemonische Erinnerungsträger*" ["mnemonic commemorative carriers", Ger.] (Berdahl 2002).

Although the motif of *commodified nostalgia* plays a significant role in Russian food products and stores, its direct articulation as well as commercialization also aroused negative feelings among some participants.

Pic. 4:28 Dry red wine "Nostalgie Isabella" (I)

Pic. 4:29 Tart "Horne of Plenty" from the cookbook, Culinary, dating to Stalin's times

Pic. 4:30 Tart advertised by Russian food store "Jakob" (G)

Pic. 4:31 Tart "Pineapple" from the recipe book, Culinary

Pic. 4:32 Tart "Pineapple" by the Russian manufacturer "Bron" (I)

Pic. 4:33 "Glory Chocolate" from On the Tasty and Healthy Food Book

Pic. 4:34 "Glory Chocolate" sold in Russian food stores (I)

This may be due to their unwillingness to purchase the melancholy associated with nostalgia for these products or because they felt that their feelings were being manipulated for commercial purposes, as perceived by Ella:

"I visit a Russian food store regularly, but I don't like its atmosphere of false nostalgia and the proprietors exaggerated display of success. Russian stores were created not by altruists, in order to make us rich and happy, but by business people, who understood well the distribution of relationships and power and utilized our habits and fears and inexperience in the new circumstances in order to become happy and rich themselves"

Ella's critical statement corresponds well with the statements presented in chapter Two, i.e. maintained Soviet thinking structures such as critique of an economic interest as prime interest managing the agency and assumption about some given spiritual structures which are supposed to care for happiness and prosperity of the individual.

Along with different aspects of nostalgia and its instrumentalization, entrepreneurs developed a variety of other products that appeal to the consumers' longing and expectations of *nastoyashee* [something real, original, authentic, the same, Rus.] by use of motifs that create an association of a food product as *real*. This involves a juxtaposition between an illusive construction referring to as *nastoyashee* in the past and the alienating present. A related incident occurred with Lida (Israel) noted, excitedly, after smelling an Israeli apple—"Wow, this is a *nastoyashee* apple!" She then passed it along to other participants seated around the table who smelt the apple one after the other, each acknowledging what she meant. Reuven,[70] the only Israeli-born participant present in the group, observed: "Wow, what nostalgia there is here!" Then he turned to me, smiled, and added (in Russian, imitating their pronunciation of the word *nastoyashee*): *"Nastoyashee* [for them] means *Russian!"*

The longing for *nastoyashee* epitomizes both *nostos and algia,* as used extensively in the Russian food store. Advertisements and packages frequently include this word to arouse both nostos and algia, for example: *Nastoyashii* Bread of Volodya Brodyanski (I); *Nastoyashee* Moscow Ice Cream (I); *Nastoyashee* Russian Cooked Beef Stew (I, G); *Nastoyashee* Russian Stew [meat] (I); *Nastoyashii* Peasant White Cheese (I); Red Blueber-

---

70 Reuven, the husband of a daughter of one participants' family studied Russian and is able to take part in a Russian conversation.

ries—*Nastoyashee* Russian Jam (I); Natural [also used in Russian language as synonym for real] Vitaminy—*klukva v sakhare* [cranberries in sugar, Rus.] (I); Natural Russian White Cheese (G); Natural Humpback [pink] Far-eastern Salmon (G); Natural Liver or Codfish [both—well known Soviet products] (G); Russian Kvas [Russian traditional drink, similar to malt, Rus.], "a sip from childhood" (I, G); Pearl of Russia—The *Nastoyashee* Moscow Ice Cream (G); Russian Frost Ice-Cream displayed with a king's crown (I); Bochkarev—the *Right* Light Beer [unusual usage if "right" applied to beer] (G); "Ice cream—the very same taste" (G); "the very same Indian tea, a sip from childhood" [symbol of well-known Indian tea in SU(I, G)]; "Pickled Gherkins"—the very same taste!" (G); "Indian Summer—Pickled Spicy Tomatoes," the very same taste!" (G).

Similarly, "Russian Chocolate Milk with Hazelnuts" (G) displays hazelnuts on the package against the background of the Kremlin along with the statement:

"You hold in your hand nastoyashii chocolate. Russian chocolate is the [right] choice of real gourmet and fine gastronomic sweets. We hope you appreciate [...] the delicate taste of our highly qualified product."

Use of *nastoyashii* in product advertisements is not arbitrary, rather it is deliberately chosen to represent selected traditional, mostly Russian Soviet products; usually those, not available in a non-Russian grocery in Israel or Germany. For example, the breads or ice cream, which Russian speakers claimed tastes different in Israel, are categorized as *simple* Soviet products and are expected to be quality goods, affordable to anyone, whatever their economic means:

Faina (Israel): "We can afford nastoyashii bread."

Lena (Israel), hinted at her limited consumption capabilities due to low income: "Do I have to accept it that I cannot afford to buy normal [good] nastoyashii bread? I will not limit bread! [as a basic food]."

Other product names and advertisements related to their origins in the SU in a manner similar to *nastoyashee*. Whereas in the SU these were considered to be taken for granted, habitually used products, in the new country they assumed a special, even exotic meaning. For example, in the SU, canned beef or pork stew might have to be used instead of fresh meat in order to assure a full meal when fresh meat was unavailable or too expensive. Post-migration, these canned products remained popular among migrants, with greater stress placed on its *sameness* or *originality*, by comparing them to the well-known canned products in the SU. Hence it was viewed as something unique or out-of-the-ordinary in Israel.

Similarly, since many berries available in Europe are not grown or popular in Israel, they can be seen as an exotic product imported into Israel from a country with a colder climate. Thus, as a very popular product in Russian food stores in Israel, berries symbolize Russian nature, missed after migration. For example, there is Nastoyashee Russian Jam [red blueberries] and Natural Vitamins [cranberries in sugar]. And, while ice cream in general is not an unusual product in Israel, the exotic packaging of Russian Ice Cream was designed to appeal to Russian-speakers pictures of cold winter with flakes of snow, snow covered Russian traditional country houses and fir trees and streets, all foreign elements in the Mediterranean reality of an Israeli.

Symbols of realness and originality seem to correspond to tendencies described by Barthes in his analysis of symbols and consumption practices in France. There he found that loyalty to a certain brand is justified through "a set of 'natural' reasons" (Barthes 1997, 21). Yet, during the migration process, the "naturalness" of things and artifacts was specifically questioned, challenged, and modified through ongoing comparisons with products familiar from the past. Consequently, the taste recalled through use of concepts such as "natural," "authentic," "original," and even "right" and "real," was at best categorized by participants to be "just like the original," the "authentic," or the "natural" formulation, which in addition to similarity also implied some difference and consequently not absolute similarity.

Also, advertisements that employed the phrase "a taste of childhood" (both in Israel and Germany) pointed to an invented continuity as well as irreversibility of a past experience. For example, bread brought as a gift by visiting tourist from the CIS to relatives or hosts in Israel or chocolates in Germany remained on the table, while the local bread or chocolates were gratefully consumed, accompanied by statements such, "it is just like them [the real];" or the taste of an original product, exported directly by the original CIS manufacturer was viewed as fake, while a product with the same name produced in Israel or Germany was categorized as "exactly alike." In fact, the main criterion for determining the successfulness of a certain food commodity was the use of a personal subjective statement, such as "it is exactly like" or "it is not like…". It is interesting that different people in both contexts pointed to the same products from the Russian food store and stated [it is] "exactly like…!" or "a miserable fake!" or "has nothing to do with original!"

Boris (Israel) tasting salami as it was sliced at the table: "Tasty, but no, it's not it."

Faina (other guest): "No? I find it is exactly like them [meaning those she remembered]."

Ella (hostess): "No, there [in the SU] it was nastoyashaya Hungarian salami, not like here [in Israel], even in the Russian food store […] I remember I was in Moscow once [for a business trip]. Suddenly I saw the line for these sausages, but I was hurrying, don't know why. Even today I am sorry that I did not line up for them [laughs] [All the guests laugh with her]."

In another situation, in Germany, participants compared *zephyr* (chocolate covered marshmallows):

Sveta (Germany): "Just try it! It's exactly them!!! [meaning, based on her memories of its taste]"

Rita, takes a bite and is obviously disappointed: "It has nothing to do with it, it is just a miserable fake! You can't find anything exactly [imitates the pronunciation of the word by Sveta] like it here, anywhere."

In fact, the assumption about irretrievable taste is quite a convenient commercial condition that can lead to experimentation with products by using well-known images that can be recalled from the past in order to promote different commodities. Thus, in Russian food stores the criterion of something being "like," could be applied to a variety of different imitations of certain food products, creating what Barthes called the "spirit of the product" (Barthes 1997).

4.5 Images of the Soviet paradise

Highly politicized in the SU, food retained many of its characteristics after emigration. This seems particularly evident in the following discussion.

Different symbols of realization of the dream of the Soviet paradise, promised in the *On the Tasty and Healthy Food Book*, discussed in the previous chapter, were found in Russian food stores, consumption patterns, and festive dining room settings of participants in Israel and Germany.

In comparison to their lives in the SU, the participants in both contexts acknowledged the improvement in their material conditions, as evident in their everyday diet and occasional luxurious festive settings. It seemed that a visit to the Russian food store was more than a means to acquire commodities. In fact, as described by participants it was more like an adventure involving a "hunt" for a variety of symbols of a wealthy, powerful, and rich life often dreamt of but seldom realized in the SU. The pictures used in advertisements and displays of Russian food stores were identical to or very similar to illustrations in the original, politically-laden version of the Soviet book. In some cases pictures on tins of food products were almost identical to pictures in the book. Products mentioned in the book as well as commonly known hard to find products in the SU—such as sturgeon, beluga, carp, mackerel, calamary, crayfish, shrimps, catfish, squid, trout, and especially cod-liver, pink salmon and sprat—were available in numerous variations in Russian food stores in both Germany and in Israel. As there is no universal consensus about expensive and prestigious food, some of the food products mentioned above did not necessarily have a high status in the local dominant market in Israel or Germany and were in good part affordable and even cheap. However, within the framework of the Russian food stores, they remain prestigious and special.

Chocolates and cakes embellished in a special Soviet style in Russian food stores as well as the participants' desserts trays also resemble pictures in the books from the period of Stalin; for example, the very prestigious tart, Horn of Plenty, displayed with roses, leaves, and mushrooms made from cream displayed in a well-known book of Stalin's times *Culinary*[71] (picture 4:29) is similar to a tart advertised by the Russian food store, Jakob, in Germany (picture 4:30); and Pineapple Tart, made with pineapple and cream in *Culinary* (picture 4:31) is exactly like the Pineapple Tart sold by the Russian firm, Bron, in Israel (picture 4:32). In some cases one can find exactly the same pictures, as for example Glory Chocolate"[72] from *On the Tasty and Healthy Food Book* (picture 4:33) in comparison the same chocolate, sold in Russian food stores in Israel (picture 4:34); or very similar images, as in the case of sweetened condensed milk, condensed milk

---

71 Brunnek, N., Gavrilova, N. et al. 1955; 2002. Numbering 960 pages, this book was reprinted numerous times, remains popular to this very day and similar to *On the Tasty and Healthy Food Book* was brought by some participants to Israel and Germany.

72 The Russian word *slava* can also be translated in English as "honor" which is easily associated with military honor.

with cocoa, or coffee from *On the Tasty and Healthy Food Book* (picture 4:35) with imitation products available in Russian food stores in Israel and Germany[73] (see three among numerous examples on pictures 4:36—8).

Additionally, one can find other previously scarce, highly desired sweet products in Russia food stores in Israel and Germany not mentioned in the book but well-known by every ex-Soviet citizen.[74] Not only were the original products available but there were numerous imitations. In fact, it seemed that the number of imitations was an indication of the degree of prestige attained by a certain product; for example numerous imitations of sweetened condensed milk, mentioned above. In addition, there were 15 imitations in Israel and 13 in Germany of *Mishka Kosolapyi* [clumsy bear, Rus.] a very prestigious Soviet chocolate (pictures 4:39—53, from Israel; and 4:54—66 from Germany).

Also, dining settings depicted in the *On the Tasty and Healthy Food Book* were similar to the luxurious festive settings set for opulent celebrations to which I had been invited during the fieldwork, including birthdays that had to accommodate all guests, many of whom considered themselves to be "spiritual" intellectuals and had an ambiguous view of exaggerated, opulent festivities. For example, Larisa (Israel), upon looking at the table overflowing with an abundance of food and delicacies, smiled and offered a "complimentary" remark to the hostess:

"Wow, to lay out such table seems so decadent [meaning too opulent, too much of a hedonistic banquet]. You are really bourgeois!"

Here, too, the realization of the old dream is achieved through well-known guidelines offered in the book, including—crystal glasses, heavy silver-plated cutlery, crystal bowls for salads, and in one case even the same two stacks of plates. The table also displayed many images from the past, such as: numerous bottles with alcohol beverages, (especially Armenian cognac and Georgian wine Kinzmarauili and Khvantzchkara—both drinks dating back to the Stalinist period served now in plastic bottles with soft drinks), red caviar, green and black olives, big bowls of fruits, well-appointed

---

73 33 imitations of sweetened condensed milk were found altogether in Russian food stores in Israel and15 in Germany.

74 Such as Kiev Tarts, Bird's Milk, Evening Prague; or chocolates truffles such as Clumsy Bear, Bear in the Forest, and Bear in the North, Inspiration; chocolates Karakum, Bunny.

Pic. 4:35 Sweetened condensed milk, condensed milk with cocoa or coffee from On the Tasty and Healthy Food Book

Pic. 4:36 Sweetened condensed milk sold in Russian food stores (I, G)

Pic. 4:37 Sweetened condensed milk with cocoa sold in Russian food stores (I, G)

Pic. 4:38 Sweetened condensed milk with coffee sold in Russian food stores (I, G)

Pic. 4:39—53 Imitations 1—15 of highly prestigious chocolate "Clumsy bear" (I)

Pic. 4:54—66 Imitations 1—13 of highly prestigious chocolate "Clumsy bear" (G)

dishes with fish or meat. Additionally, traditionally Soviet festive salads with cooked vegetables mixed with mayonnaise and embellished with peas and parsley are displayed.

Thus, Russian food stores made it possible to realize, for the first time, the "tablecloth spread" of the illustrious Russian fairly-tale with its powerful and magical ability to produce the desired abundance of dishes, wines, fruits, and gourmet delicacies. Through symbolic realization of the ideal image of the appropriated home and the communist food paradise, promised in the Soviet homeland, migrants could participate in its imaginary political power and richness, albeit in the Western "now and here."

4.6 Image of Soviet proletarian food or the *imaginary proletarian home*

A longing for ordinary, simple Soviet food, too, was observable, though in the new context its meaning was transformed. Suddenly everyday food and dishes associated in the SU with lower class persons, even those in poverty, which some participants had never consumed in the previous context, became desired, exotic, and consequently rose in status. In this process, products, which had always available and affordable in the SU, became *exótikos* [foreign, exotic, Greek], simultaneously representing, on the one hand, the symbolical continuation of the Soviet past and well-known folk products while, on the other hand, distancing the past through exoticization of these products.

– Among the wide variety of *proletarian products* found in both contexts were the following products well-known from their lives in the SU: *Taranka* [salted dried fish, Rus. usually eaten with beer] (picture 4:67);[75] Kvas [Russian traditional drink similar to malt]; and cans of fish such as anchovy, capelin or pig-fish in tomato sauce, dog-fish, herring,[76] different kinds of vegetable, zucchini and aubergine paste (picture 4:68). Well-known Soviet names were given to processed cheeses; such as— *Yantar* [amber, Rus.] or *Druzhba* [friendship, Rus.]; the latter includes a

75 This product was often referred to by non-Russian speakers in Israel as inedible.
76 Herring, potatoes, bread, and oil were also mentioned as simple proletarian food by Glants and Toomre (1997, 18—19).

depiction of the globe (picture 4:69), suggesting friendship among different [socialist] peoples. Other foods included: honey; gingerbread, *pel'meni*, [small pasta pockets filled with meat, Rus.]; semi-baked pea soup or berries in briquette form; *baranki* [Russian bagels, Rus.]; sunflower seeds; *Barbarise, Zabava* [entertainment, Rus.] (picture 4:70) or *Zolotoi Kluchik* Bonbons [Golden Key from the story about Pinocchio, Rus.] mentioned in the first quote of this chapter (picture 4:71).

Overall, Russian food stores in Germany stocked an especially extensive assortment of proletarian food. One explanation for this phenomenon might be the fact that migrants had unlimited choices of different gourmet products in regular German supermarkets, making it more difficult for the Russian food store to compete with the local supermarket. The opposite was the case in Israel, as the presence of a non-kosher delicatessen is a specialty of Russian food stores, along with other alternative foods available there. This can be seen clearly in Tiv Ta'am, an extensive and rapidly expanding chain of general grocery stores.[77] However, ex-Soviet citizens living in Israel also consume folk products or proletarian food.

Sometimes products dear to the Soviet working class are advertised through a combination of symbols that in the original context, in the SU, was absolutely unthinkable; for example: packaging of *Doktorskaya* Sausage [doctoral, Rus.],[78] a cheap readily available sausage, was decorated with three king's crowns and the words "delicacies of the kings' crown" (G) (picture 4:72); and *Varenaya* Sausage [lit., cooked, Rus.], one of the cheapest sausages available in the SU, was referred to on the package as an "Elite cooked sausage. High cuisine." (I).

The participants expressed a longing for basic products that reminded them of memories of different stages in their lives and social events in the SU. Felix (Israel), for example, read me a passage from the newly edited

---

77 See Chapter Five.
78 Introduced by Anastas Mikoyan as ideal diet for factory workers, as it was thought to be nourishing, healthy food during the food scarcities and shortages after WWII in the 1950's. He derived it from the German model of *Frankfurters* (Fitzpatrick 1999 by Klumbytė 2010, 26). Klumbytė mentions that "during the Soviet era, sausages produced and consumed in Lithuania and other Soviet republics were integral to Soviet modernity" (Klumbytė 2010,25) with "its massive drive for industrialisation and the creation of an industrial proletariat" (ibid., 25—26, citing Kotkin 1995).

Pic. 4:68 Proletarian food: aubergine paste (I)

Pic. 4:67 Proletarian food: "Taranka"
[salted dried fish, Rus.] (I)

Pic. 4:70 Proletarian food: "Zabava
bonbons" [entertainment, Rus.] (G)

Pic. 4:69 Proletarian food: Processed cheese "Druzhba"
[friendship, Rus.] (I)

Pic. 4:72 Proletarian food:
"Doktoskaya" sausage [doctoral,
Rus.], with words "delicatessen of
kings' crown" (G)

Pic. 4:71 Proletarian food: "Zolotoi kluchik"
[Golden Key from the story about Pinoccio, Rus.] (G)

Pic. 4:73 Proletarian food: Laminaria (kelp) (I)

edition of Okun' and Guberman's *On the Tasty and Healthy Life*, mentioned above. A passage with which Felix expressed his strong identification with the passage in which the authors revealed their mixed feelings about the proletarian foods that while eaten frequently and desired were often reviled. He noted that it reminds him of experiences from previous periods of his life and his earlier social position:

"Do you remember *kisel'* [jelly dessert or drink made from berries, also fool, Rus.]. Nothing was more disgusting [...] Early in the 1990's, someone brought me two compressed briquettes of kisel [referring to pre-cooked berry briquettes] from Peter [St. Petersburg; an informal, beloved name for the city, used by its inhabitants]. I prepared and tried it. It had not changed at all. It was still the same vile, abhorrent slumgullion. It smelled like the polish on school floors and the factory cafeteria. Nobody was willing to eat it except Willi [his friend] and I: We were disgusted, but we devoured the entire pot while tears of happiness flowed down our cheeks [Rus.] (Okun' and Guberman 2003, 89)."

Yelenevskaya (2005), in her research of Russian-speaking migrants in Israel and Germany, related an additional example of an interviewee who went specifically to a Russian food store in order to purchase herring that had many bones, so that eating them would be uncomfortable enabling him to "experience again the various discomforts associated with the old country" (Yelenevskaya 2005, 278).

The artificial revival of difficulties, detailed here and in the previous chapter, relates a nostalgic element of longing for certain products and difficulties that caused people to complain in the past—a phenomenon found not only among Russian speakers.[79] Indeed, it may well be the case that longing for cheap proletarian food and for the discomforts of the old system may be only meaningful and possible amidst positive associations and emotions that are aroused with revived memories about difficulties and discomforts. For example, a number of well-known products can arouse memories of skills such as knowledgeable agency, socially respected positions, and cultural competence. All three skills are especially needed in post-migration adaptation to the new context. The following example reveals this difficulty. Nikolai (Israel) sought to amuse a friend visiting from the CIS by pointing to the unlimited assortment of foods available of the Russian food store, where one can "get" everything:

---

79 Raviv described a similar longing for food that exists in Israel concerning *luft-* (canned minced beef, Heb.), the IDF's version of "Spam," recently removed from the list of army rations." (Raviv 2001, 4).

Nikolai: "Here [in Israel] I can "get" anything."

Disbelievingly, a guest asks: "Anything?"

Nikolai: "Yes. I tell you! If I feel like having *kobachkovaya ikra* [a cheap Soviet zucchini paste, Rus.] from a can, you know, like they [Soviets] serve at cafeterias in a factory, I can "get" it or if I want sprat in tomato sauce [also canned], no problem! I go to the Russian store and buy it!"

This example is especially interesting because Nikolai relates to proletarian food as a symbol of "real" abundance after ascertaining that all the products migrants dreamed of attaining pre-migration are available and affordable. It is also a demonstration of his economic status that he uses to display before his guest, similar to a statement he quoted from the Soviet past: "economic status and possibilities are seen well through your refrigerator." However, in doing so he does not use accepted Soviet symbols of prosperity and wealth, such as caviar or salami. Rather, as we see in this example, Nikolai flaunts his economic status by drawing attention to the surprising array of possibilities unexpected by a visitor from the CIS: how easy it is to obtain simple Soviet food products—the epitome of ordinary Russian life—in Israel.

In addition, there are some food products that had such low status or that were directly indicative of proletarian affiliation that they were not consumed by participants in the past, yet were purchased by migrants in the new context. A similar tendency was found by Mankekar (2005) in her research of Indian groceries in the USA. Among such products, consumed by Russian speakers in Israel and Germany, one can mention semi-prepared bricks of berries (jelly), peas soup, *suchari* [dried bread, crackers, Rus.], semi-baked *pel'meni* [small pasta pockets filled with meat, Rus.] and the most symbolic of all *laminaria* [kelp] (picture 4:73) a product nearly always available, even when Soviet stores were empty during difficult times, associated with food eaten by alcoholics.

Boris (Israel): "*Laminaria* was bought only by alcoholics as an appetizer, you know, because it was the cheapest food they could afford to eat after drinking."

Felix (Israel): To eat *laminaria* meant to descend to the depths of society, so deep that there was no way back. Nothing was lower than that".

Different variations of laminaria found in both contexts are evidence that it had become among the most exotic of food products, signifying Soviet reality in a most original way. Other new products of revived Soviet proletarian food include; "Miner Beer—beer for *nastoyashii* men" (Germany). Here, the product's name is portrayed alongside an image of a miner gazing off into the distance. This is a typical way of depicting workers and peasants in the realistic genre of socialist pictures. The miner's gaze is referred to in Soviet propaganda language as "looking to the radiant [promised, communist] future" [they will realize through their work]. Although none of the participants in either research context reported having dreamed of participation in this endeavor, such products create a new affiliation, albeit from abroad, with the image of the Soviet proletarian *home*.

It seems that the status of these products increased significantly as they became more popular and expensive in both contexts. Such a mixture of class manifestations contradicts Bourdieu (1984), as well as, Beardsworth and Keil's (1997) claims that food maintains class distinctions. Bourdieu claimed that "members of the established petite bourgeoisie were likely to say that on special occasions they serve their friends 'simple but well presented meals,' while the new bourgeoisie preferred to serve original, or exotic meals or pot luck" (Bourdieu 1984, 179). Particularly interesting were similarities between the use of proletarian food by Russian speakers, who belonged to the intelligentsia stratum and socialist food habits of workers in England, presented in the research of Beardsworth and Keil (1995). However, we are dealing in the contexts investigated not only with the intelligentsia's continuing consumption of proletarian food, but with a further voluntary adoption of food products associated with the Soviet working class and their consumption, along with products and dishes symbolizing the Soviet elite or bourgeois upper class.

Indeed, participants served food dishes from different classes on different occasions. In doing so, the table setting appeared as it did on other festive occasions (n.b., including use of crystal glasses, silverplated cutlery, and porcelain cups) as proletarian dishes—potatoes with herring, *pel'meni* or beer with salted dry fish *Taranka* – were served at family meals. On the one hand, such meals were often a manifestation of the proletarian spirit juxtaposed to materially rich, hedonistic "capitalist" festivities.[80] On the other hand, I noted how migrants were continually tasting, interested in, and improvising creatively with the abundance of food products available in the new contexts and tried to present themselves as belonging to the

---

80 See discussion in Chapter Two.

elite intelligentsia through bourgeois upper class cuisine. Such polarized food habits were observable during the fieldwork in both contexts, pointing to a combination of significantly different kinds of cultural habitus and simultaneous affiliation to different classes with its different values by the group of ex-Soviet Jewish intelligentsia.

4.7 Images of the Soviet empire and the Soviet political iconography of food post-emigration

Different images of *home* and *homeland* and collective affiliations displayed on food products at Russian-speaking stores often represent older narratives that are given new post-migration meaning. In fact, the esprit of the unconquerable Soviet empire narrative with its 15 republics led by Russia continues to be salient in the Russian-speaking enclave. Even if the powerful empire no longer exists physically, symbolic and often stereotypic revival serves as active signifiers for ex-Soviet citizens abroad. This is apparent in the food products consumers purchase adorned with images of the powerful Soviet empire and "patriotic gigantomania" (Genis and Vail 1992; Solodkina 1996). Here, the symbolic stress on the richness and power of the Soviet empire serve a compensatory role for migrants who are usually perceived to be a marginal minority by the receiving society and lack political, social, and economic resources. Thus, "one sixth of the dry land," a common symbol referring to the richness, expansion, and power of the Soviet empire, is a phrase referred to frequently by Russian and non-Russian-speaking entrepreneurs, as it is assumed to have a positive connotation for ex-Soviet emigrants. Renaissance of nostalgia for idealised images from the socialistic past are not exclusive for Russian-speaking consumption patterns for ex-Soviet migrants abroad as they can also be found in other researches as for example in Daphne Berdahl's analysis of "Ostalgie" [a combination of the German word "Ost" which means East and "algia" from "nostalgia", Germ.] in the former GDR (2002) or Neringa Klumbyté's analysis of renaissance of the Soviet sausage as a form of political engagement and critique of the postsocialist neoliberal state in Lithuania (2010). In both researches as well as in my fieldwork one can observe the revival of positive associations with ex-socialist commodities as detached of their original ideology and connection with their political context and the memories about opressions and a totalitarian regime. In all cases we deal with the revival of active reminiscening, whereby certain memories fall into oblivion ("forgetting") (Berdahl, 2002; Klumbyté, 2010).

In Israel, for example, an advertisement for Tnuva, a very well-known Israeli food concern specializing in dairy products, appeared in the Russian language magazine *Delo vkusa* [Taste matters, Rus.] just prior to the Jewish holiday of Shavuot, when traditionally dairy products are a main ingredient in dishes prepared at home for the festive meals. The design of the advertisement contains multiple images of the Soviet empire. The text starts with a rephrasing of the Soviet national anthem from—"The indestructible union of free republics"—to a text written in large red letters: "The indestructible union of the people's recipes, a nostalgic culinary collage" (*Delo vkusa*, 2007). The nation's red flag displayed on the right of the text is accompanied by an egg beater and ladle instead of the original sickle and hammer. 15 recipes, one from each of the 15 ex-Soviet republics, appear against a backdrop of a map of the SU. Renewing a clichéd canon of the Soviet empire, Tnuva marketing staff revealed their actual intention: "Discover new possibilities for using Tnuva milk products" (ibid). The introduction begins with two sentences typical of the dominant Israeli discourse including expectations of the changes imposed on migrants: "When we came to Israel from the former SU, we discovered new products, new dishes, and a new Israeli kitchen. However, memories of the Republics, where we were born and grew up, have been preserved—until today—in our family's recipes from there" (ibid).

The idea of the intra-international Soviet Union driven by the political claim of the "solidarity of 15 republics" with "Russia leading" was a motif of advertisements reproduced for migrants through stereotypic national culinary representation in food products in stores and dishes prepared and displayed on the festive settings; for example, plov or manty (Uzbekistan), leche (Georgian), borscht (Ukraine), shi or rassolnik (Russia). This process was characteristic of marketing strategies employed to attract Russian speakers abroad, as well as, in contemporary advertisements in the CIS.

In discussing transformations in contemporary Russia and state paternalism in commercial developments of Russian market, Sandomirskaya argued that "discourse of the motherland has not expired, but, on the contrary, has become more vital" (Sandomirskaya 2004, 124—5). This involved a "large-scale sale of the motherland" (ibid) advanced through "commercially developed patriotism," "commercially beneficial visibility of empire" (ibid) [...] "transformed into a commercial logotype, into a trademark" (ibid) that sought to arouse consumers "patriotic lyricism as compensation of the moral and social loss [...] declassé and marginalized in the new capitalist conditions"(ibid). While this strategy seems to be typical for consumers in contemporary Russia, it was employed with Russian speakers abroad as well. In fact, symbols of Soviet achievements and its military power that emphasized valor, honor, and pride were displayed frequently on the wrapping paper of products found in Israel and Germany. Participants expressed the belief that these images and the strong personal emotions they arouse are inseparable, become part of a commodity's identity, or what they refer to as a "commodity's biography" (Kopytoff 1986) that is inevitably purchased along with the product.

For most of the participants, in both contexts, political icons on food products had more of a nostalgic than grotesque effect, as they might have for an outsider. That is, while an outsider might interpret use of such symbols as *gross political propaganda*, people who lived in the SU connect the product and its political image with their own personal meaningful memories and experiences that add a multi-biographical dimension to the products. Consequently, for participants, a commodity's multi- biographic character and their personal memory of its taste and experiences consuming it in the SU have more impact than the product's obvious *political biography*.

Moreover, whereas in the past, Soviet political ideas were sacred and unassailable properties of the state, the revival of these ideas in association with consumption sought to serve people in a new way, through illusions of power and security borrowed in stereotypic manner from the good old days. The following examples demonstrate this phenomenon. A participant in Israel received a present from a visiting Russian friend: A souvenir bottle of Red Army Vodka shaped like a bombshell encased in a wooden box [like an ammunition casing] stamped with the red star (picture 4:74). The background on the label displayed the Soviet newspaper *Komsomolskaya Pravda* [Komsomol Truth published by the Communist Youth Movement,[81] Rus.] attached to two military decorations—"Order of

---

81 Komsomol, Youth Communist Movement, charged by the state with socialization and rites of passage of Soviet youth (van Gennep 1909), considered to be an honorable act forced on scholars in the SU in an official ceremony. Participation was necessary in order to enter all high schools as well as to become a member of the Communist Party.

Pic. 4:74 A souvenir bottle "Red Army Vodka" (I)

Pic. 4:75 Advertisement tag, attached to the bottle "Red Army Vodka" (I)

Pic. 4:76 Advertisement of the Russian restaurant "USSR" (G)

Pic. 4:77 "Soviet Sunflower Oil" (G)

Pic. 4:78 "Rodina Vodka" [Motherland, Rus.] (G)

Pic. 4:79 "USSR Ice Cream" (I)

Pic. 4:80 "Chaika Chocolate" [Seagull, Rus.] (G)

motherland War" [WWII] and "Order of Lenin"—along with Lenin's portrait, and a picture of the first Soviet astronaut Yuri Gagarin—celebrating the second grand Soviet achievement after the victory in WWII (picture 4:75).[82] Here, some of the most meaningful symbols of national pride have been mobilized in the packaging of one product. The participants showed it to me with a smile at one of the meetings. Then, I received the following reply from Faina (Israel) to my query if there is certain irony intended in the product?

"Not at all. Alex [a Jewish friend since elementary school in the Ukraine living in Moscow] brought it as a cool, expensive present of the new Russia. It arouses a smile because of the package and vodka, but it exudes power."

The participants' smiles when viewing this product were significantly different from the laugher it aroused among non-Russian-speaking persons with whom I shared this example at an academic conference. Yet, though amused by a product produced by the country to which they once belonged, which as Faina said "exudes power," participants in the study continually stressed its delicious taste and that all the associations with the military power of the big Soviet empire lacked importance. In contrast, for many outsiders, it is impossible to ignore, or neglect the political icons displayed on the products. Therefore, in their eyes it seems that Russian-speaking consumers are being manipulated and spoofed.

Other examples include an advertisement of the Russian restaurant USSR in the investigated city in North Rhine/Westphalia (G) (picture 4:76) and the packaging design on Soviet Sunflower Oil displayed in a Russian food store (G) (picture 4:77). In both cases the original Soviet state emblem is associated with the direct reference to the past, powerful empire in the advertising picture. Also *Rodina* Vodka [motherland, meaning here Soviet motherland; Rus.] (picture 4:78), USSR Ice Cream (I) (picture 4:79) or Soviet Salami (I) are wrapped in red wrapping paper that includes the Red Star, hammer, and sickle. While this may appear to the non-Russian speaker to be ironic, it arouses mostly positive associations among participant/consumers who connect them to past official Soviet symbols.

Faina (Israel): "Even today it is pleasant and enjoyable to look at this emblem. It is powerful. It has no negative connotations, like the repression associated with portraits of Stalin, for example. It has great power! "

---

82 See Chapter Seven.

Manifestation of pride in the Soviet empire and its achievements is not always expressed through a pompous, grandiose display of key Soviet symbols such as the Red Army, Yuri Gagarin, and *Pravda*, as it could also be hinted or stated indirectly. For example, the popular Soviet design that appears on the package of *Chaika* Chocolate [Seagull, Rus.] (G) (picture 4:80) seems at first glance to be naïve and unrelated to politics: A seagull is portrayed flying in blue skies with the sun in the background. However, people older than 50, socialized in the SU, know the story of how this brand of chocolate became to be available. Dedicated to the first female astronaut in the world—a Soviet woman named Valentina Tereshkova, the name of the chocolate immortalized her "seagull" call sign. Also, the name of the *Legenda o Burevestnike* Bonbon [Song of the Petrel, Rus.] (I) (picture 4:81) seems innocent, but it too is connected to a strong political message. This product's name refers to a well-known revolutionary poem by Maxim Gorki of the same name, written as a call for revolution, and was for a long time a part of SU school curricula. The flight of birds soaring in the sky against the background of the sun initially associated with the future of the Soviet state evolved into pride in the awakening Soviet socialist culture. Pride in the Soviet motherland also appears in Icebreaker—a bonbon (I) (picture 4:82); *Krasnyi Oktyabr* candy [Red October, Rus.] made by the manufacturer Krasnyi Oktyabr' (I) (picture 4:83); the bonbon *Severnaya Avrora* [The Northern Aurora, Rus.] manufactured by confectionary firm Krupskaya [named in honor of the Lenin's spouse] (I); and, Artek Waffle (I, G)—the name of the most known and prestigious international socialist pioneer camp for children in the SU, which none of the participants in this study had ever visited. Indeed, as Larisa (Israel) stated smiling: "At least [we can] eat a dream". The wrapping paper (picture 4:84) displays the original words in Russian of a pioneer children's song that has been transposed from "let the sun always be there" to "let it always be tasty."

Conversations with the participants about these products did not elicit comments or questions about the use of political symbols or slogans in advertising, such as: *Rot Front, Bolshevik, Kommunarka* Chocolate [female communist, Rus.], *Kievskaya fabrika imeni Karla Marksa* [Karl Marx Kiev Factory, Rus.]. Rather, their presence seemed to be taken for granted, omnipresent, and set on labels. This is similar to the perceptions extant among the host resident populations of well-known companies—such as Nestle in Germany or Elite in Israel. Consequently, we can conclude that the contents on these labels do not appear to have been the focus of

Pic. 4:81 Bonbon "Legenda o Burevestnike" [Song of the Storm Petrel, Rus.] (I)

Pic. 4:82 Bonbon "Icebreaker" (I)

Pic. 4:83 The candy "Krasnyi Oktyabr'" [Red October, Rus.] manufactured by "Krasnyi Oktyabr'" (I)

Pic. 4:84 "Artek Waffle"]socialist pioneer camp, Rus.] with statement "let it always be tasty" (I,G)

Pic. 4:85 "Jubileinoe Tradizionnoe" biscuits [Traditional Jubilee, Rus.] manufactured by the "Bolshevik Company" (I,G)

Pic. 4:87 "Skhidny Soloshi Bonbons" [Sunrise sweets, Ukr.] manufactured by "Rodina" [Motherland, Ukr.] with the slogan—"Ridnishe ne buvaye" [it cannot be closer, more native, trusted, Ukr.] (I)

Pic. 4:86 Canned beef stew (I)

questioning or reflection. Thus, even after migration, migrants' frustrations with the Soviet regime and their consciousness of the failures of the SU were not associated with symbols of the regime used in names and packaging of products; for example, *Jubileinoe Tradizionnoe* Biscuits [Jubilee, traditional biscuits; named after the 50th anniversary of the SU; Rus.] manufactured by the Bolshevik Company (picture 4:85). Indeed, Krasnyi Oktyabr and Fabrika Krupskoi were perceived by participants in the two contexts as trusted and prestigious Soviet manufacturers of quality food products. *Lubimyi* Chocolates [Lovely, Rus.], *Mechta* Bonbons [Dream, Rus.], *Krasnyi Oktyabr* Chocolate—all produced by the Red October company—did not elicit any questions, signs of an identity conflict, or even an ironic smile by the participants who consumed them. Rather, they remained among the category of "desired and tasty" products. Indeed, these sweets escaped any sign of irritation or questioning of the political terms embedded in these products even among cynical participants who were critical of political associations connected with their life in the SU. For example, the following is Larisa's (Israel) reply to the author's question about feelings aroused by political images on the products:

"First of all we [Russian speaking consumers] don't think at all about the Revolution when we buy a chocolate of *Krasnyi Oktyabr* [Red October], [pause] nor about the dream of the Soviet regime. It is dead, many people are dead, but Dream bonbons are still there and popular. And, these chocolates—*Krasnyi Oktyabr*—are for me, first and foremost, about very good quality. That is what counts."

Unencumbered by any previous personal associations with these products, nor the perception that the product has a *cultural, social,* or *subjective biography*, outsiders perceive there to be an exclusively political message in the marketing and packaging, and hence claim that this is an example of pure indoctrination. In contrast, these products were not perceived by the participants to be frozen political categories with stagnant, one dimensional meaning—as *Red October, Rot front* or *Bolshevik*. Rather, they represent quality brands that are strongly connected to their recollections, memories, and experiences during their life in the SU. As such, these products are embedded in and signify certain stages in their personal lives, contextualized through memories, which remind them of certain events in the past that are still alive and real for them.

Sveta (Germany): "This is one of the few positive things that remain with me from the Soviet past, the taste of delicious products […] I don't think about the Revolution, Red October, Bolsheviks, or Krupskaya when I eat cookies. For me, they are just delicious. It reminds me of the work required by *zakazy* [orders], celebrations with friends, and experiences as a young person—and getting them when you have the luck to find a desired product."

Larisa (Israel): "For them [non-Russian speakers, foreigners] these are just words that have only a political meaning and the idea of brainwashing. They don't make any personal sense [...] For us [ex-Soviet migrants], this is all of our life and memories, and besides they are really good cookies [pointing to Jubilee Biscuits]."

The claim—"for me it's just delicious"—was constantly repeated by many participants in both contexts as the simplest, most convincing explanation for their selection. Yet, broader social, cultural, as well as political factors connected with products should not be neglected. Although the participants claimed to have been "immune" against the Soviet political indoctrination imposed on them, in certain sense such propaganda work was revealed to have been quite successful, as they were hardly critical of it and many slogans were taken for granted (i.e. internalized) and even post-migration were not perceived to be propaganda.

Moreover, commercials today instrumentalize these positive emotions and personal memories by use of familiar propaganda slogans. The strategy in reviving key political Soviet trade slogans—such as "Soviet means the best"—as a mark of quality products was well-known to all participants and seemed to work. Indeed, the use of political symbols in the design of Russian food products appears to be a strategy to convince consumers of the quality produced by familiar firms that are recognized and legitimate in the SU. Moreover, the use of Soviet symbols and narratives in products sold in stores in the CIS as well as within Russian-speaking enclaves in Israel or Germany contributed to the symbolic continuity between the Soviet past and present. Here, as Barthes demonstrated, the fragmented and often de-contextualized revival of the *good old days* was generally typical in advertising commodities (Barthes 1997). Klumbyté in her analysis of Soviet sausage in Lithuania considers sausage with Soviet images as a

"semiotic phenomenon that is embedded in and expressive of social, political, and economic contexts... as a quintessential historical commodity (which) both shapes and is shaped by history... Its [sausage] biography is that of an imaged 'Soviet' sausage that exists in replicas or tokens" (Klumbyté 2010, 25).

Overall, I found few cases of participants distancing themselves from the tendency of the stereotypic reproductive use of old well-known political slogans and symbols. Whereas all participants were harshly critical of the Soviet system, only few were so in relation to food commodities. Indeed, many participants seemed to perceive the irony related to the Soviet system and Soviet motherland only when it was explicitly pointed out to them; that is, only when one could not find any other way to interpret the packaging.

Self-distancing occurred only in cases when exemplars of package design included elements of the Soviet past that participants perceived to be new and significant innovations. For example, participants noted the claim made on a package of Wild Russia that there was a "bad new taste" being advanced by entrepreneurs post-Perestroika in Russia and abroad. In this process, combining new elements with old Soviet symbols involved the clear and explicit use of irony in relation to symbols of the Soviet empire; such as, *Sovdepovskoe* Champagne [an ironic slang name for the Soviet Union, Rus.] (G); canned beef stew (I), whose packaging included placing a cow in the middle of the insignia of the USSR instead of the original globe, sun, hammer and sickle, and red star (picture 4:86); USSR Ice Cream (I) employed an oxymoronic design in which the hammer and sickle appear alongside a crown and the product's name—Kings Ice Cream (picture 4:79); and, in designing the label of *Skhidny Soloshi* Bonbons [Sunrise sweets, Ukr.] (I) (picture 4:87), marketing designers may have glossed the ironic meaning, especially in the emigration context, for it includes the manufacturer's name—*Rodina* [motherland]—along with the marketing slogan *"Ridnishe ne buvae"* [it cannot be closer, more native, trusted, Ukr.], accompanied by the *Shrek* cartoon character of a laughing donkey.

Among the most striking examples of commercialization of Soviet political history and Soviet motherland are wrapping papers of products that display portraits of communist leaders. Some producers seem to have intended their use to be ironic, while others had a more serious goal—to arouse pride association with the country's history. Yet, in the case of both aims, these portraits aroused ironic or cynical comments among most participants. For example, a pennant with a portrait of Lenin wearing a *kipa* [*yarmulke*, skullcap, Heb.], painted on the portrait by the shop owner, was hung on a wall in a central location inside a Russian food store in Israel. The shop owner added the following familiar, highly politicized statement beneath the pennant: "To the winner of the socialist competition" (picture 4:88). De-contextualized, the transformation of this pennant was taken *from* its original, generalized use as an award granted shop managers for "especially successful socialistic practice" *to* a "self

Pic. 4:88 Soviet pennant with portrait of Lenin in a Russian food store (I)

Pic. 4:89 Devaluation of Lenin's image giving the finger in a Russian food store (I)

Pic. 4:91 "Triple Aftershave" displaying of portraits of Lenin, Marx and Engels (G)

Pic. 4:90 "Lenin Sausage" accompanied by "Bon Appétit, comrades!" "History of the Motherland in sausages" (G)

Pic. 4:92 "Nostalgia po Doktorskoi" [Nostalgia for Doctoral sausage, Rus.] displaying the portrait of Brezhnev (G)

Pic. 4:93 "Russian Vodka" displaying photo of Michail Gorbachev and words: "the first and the last president of the USSR" (I)

granted" award that the shop owner in Israel displayed to "honor" himself. The principle applied here was to give old signifiers a meaning in a local context. Hence, by including familiar Soviet signs of quality in the new context of a Russian food store, the pennant's intended message sought not only to announce that the store offered quality products, but through the use of humor to play an ironic spoof not only on Lenin, but also on ultra-orthodox Jews.

Postcards displayed or offered for purchase in Russian food stores in Israel are another example of the use of political symbols in an ironic and cynical manner. One postcard, designed in the early socialist style, stated: "Even Lenin says to you: 'Learn, Hebrew!'" Another postcard tacked up on the wall near the entrance to a Jerusalem Russian food store portrays an image of Lenin *giving the finger* (in a gesture of contempt). The shop owner reinforced this message by posting two other postcards on either side: One shows a child naked from the waist down looking for presents under a Christmas tree; the other is of a humorous reproduction of a Russian bank currency with the portrait of a monkey in the middle (picture 4:89).

Other examples of the use of political portraits in advertising products include Lenin Perfume (G) and Lenin Sausage. (G) (picture 4:90). The latter contains the richest display of symbols collected in this study, including a Soviet state emblem with the slogan: "Bon Appétit, comrades!" followed by this interesting statement:

"The history of the motherland in sausages, made according to the original recipe since 1923. The very same taste! This is something to depend upon, from someone we can depend on, and something to snack on [as appetizer while drinking alcohol, Rus.]."

Such products aspire to create historical continuation and participation by consumers in a presumed collective history through all its contortions. Yet, in doing so, unique, even oxymoronic concepts are combined: "The history of the motherland" [a sacred, reverent term in the national glossary] and "sausage," an embodiment of a basic need—raises questions about the value attached to this motherland's history. Continuing in the Soviet tradition of the politicization of food consumption, the marketing copywriters chose the most exaggerated, discredited, and unexpected form: The history of the Soviet motherland is to be rewritten through the sausage and remembered through the portrait of the founder and leader of the Soviet Union.

All these examples utilize one of the most central and important symbols of socialism and the Soviet system—the image of Lenin. In doing so, this image had been transformed from being sacrosanct and unquestioned to commercialization with mixed messages. In its contemporary transformation, it symbolizes simultaneously: a common history and collective experience, the collapse of the USSR, the failure of the vision that all the USSR promised would be realized by the communist state, and through its modification a signifier of how the sacrosanct can be transformed into the profane and ridiculous. Such a presentation could also be viewed as realization of the newly attained right of ex-Soviet producers, entrepreneurs, and consumers to transform the sacred into the subject of irony. This also demonstrates the immigrants' sense of the triumph of life that survived the repressive state in which they lived and that they feared during their former life in the SU. Still one wonders if this process might also be a form of self-distancing from the old values of the motherland/homeland, since the creators, entrepreneurs, and consumers revitalized these terms in the new contexts of Israel and Germany?

Not only images of Lenin were revived on packaging of food products. Two interesting examples from the German case study exemplify the use of other historical figures: Triple Aftershave is advertised by displaying the portraits of Lenin, Marx, and Engels (all with beards! picture 4:91). And, the imported *Nostalgia po Doktorskoi* Sausage [Nostalgia for Doctoral sausage,[83] Rus.] (picture 4:92) packaging was transformed by marketing designers who used the portrait of Brezhnev,[84] adorned with military decorations, and the depiction of another sacred, key symbol of the Soviet regime—the Vera Muchina sculpture *Worker and Peasant*—with a hammer and sickle.[85] The skin of the sausage displayed a sentence that has a double meaning: "Sausages have taste and quality. Who could forget?" Like Lenin Sausage, where Lenin's portrait sought to arouse consumer irony through the statement—"the history of the motherland in sausages," this marketing approach seeks to evoke nostalgic feelings for the Soviet era with its illusory sense of a safe society, reliability, and a quality Soviet life. Yet, *Doktorskaya* Sausage traditionally belonged to the category of proletarian

---

83 Doctoral Sausage is a popular Soviet sausage belonging to the category "proletarian" food. This sausage is discussed further in Chapter Seven.

84 Secretary-General (Premier) of the Soviet Union between the years 1966—1982.

85 The sculpture (and its symbol) was displayed in representing the USSR at the 1937 Paris World Fair, in which the USSR participated for the first time.

food (i.e. it had a reputation as a simple product) and since the 1980's the quality and amount of meat in this sausage was often doubted by the intelligentsia stratum investigated in this study.

As Tamara (Germany) stated: "Sometimes it had a suspicious rose-gray color that you thought could not be meat."

Katia (Germany): "My ex-husband was a vegetarian, but he still ate *Doktorskaya*, because he was absolutely convinced there was no meat in it anyway."

In spite of the potential irony about the taste that some ex-Soviet citizens would like to forget and doubts about the quality of the meat in this product, *Doktorskaya* Sausage remained very popular after emigration and was still consumed frequently by participants in both contexts.

Finally, the label of Russian Vodka (I) displays a map of the SU, the Soviet state emblem, and a picture of Mikhail Gorbachev accompanied by the statement: "The first and last president of the USSR" (picture 4:93). The portrait of Gorbachev on the bottle of vodka hints at an additional ironic meaning: Gorbachev's reputation and legacy was earned, in part, due to his active struggle against alcoholism in the SU. Thus, his depiction not only reminds consumers of the end of the Soviet epoch, stressed its collapse, the failure to achieve its goals, and symbolizes the triumph of life after the regime.

Placing this secondary use of political symbols in context requires understanding how different historic processes are reflected in food design and advertizing strategies in the former SU, Israel, and Germany. The Israeli and German economic markets, in which Russian-speaking enclaves were built and developed, are hardly comparable in terms of the main symbols employed in advertising and marketing food products to the commercialized use of political symbols of products usually found in Russian food stores. Furthermore, here, too, it is useful to differentiate between Israeli and German contexts. In Israel, national and Jewish religious symbols do appear on the packaging of food products found in local food markets; for example, the six-pointed Star of David, the colors white and blue (similar to the Israeli flag), or Jewish religious symbols such as the menorah, candles, or certain food products connected with particular holidays. Collectively, these symbols are integral to and representative of the hegemonic Jewish—national political narrative, reinforced by appearing in everyday life consumption products.

During the 1920's consumption of local food products by Jews distributed under the label *Totzeret Ha'aretz* [lit. products of the land, but this ideologically driven labeling refers to THE land (of Israel), Heb.] was considered to be an "act of patriotism" (Raviv 2001, 2) and this value played an important role in the promotion of products. Though not in the scale of the 1920s, today there are still many products that incorporate symbols of politically loaded images related to the central concept of the Jewish homeland. For example, in honor of the 60th jubilee anniversary of the establishment of the State of Israel in 2008 special marketing of products via use of national symbols appeared in regular Israeli supermarkets, such as a package of regular Elite Turkish coffee that displayed an Israeli flag prominently along with the statement: "Roasted and ground Turkish coffee—60 years of coffee roasting in Israel" (picture 4:94).

Also, a box of the Elite company's chocolate named *Mahadura Nostalgit* [double entendre: nostalgic campfire or another nostalgic version of a product, Heb.] depicted gun-toting, uniformed soldiers from different military units eating chocolate (picture 4:95). The statements on the package read: "Nourishing and delicious;" and "Give them the best, give them Elite [name of a leading Israeli chocolate and food manufacturer, Heb.]. Placed in the context of the depiction of the soldiers, the product's name and the military images can have a number of interpretations: Nostalgia for the period of the pre-state military divisions known as the Palmach that was well-known for meetings, parties, and romantic encounters around a campfire; and production of an earlier version of chocolate produced by Elite at the time of the War of Independence. Another packaging version of chocolate in the same series depicts male and female soldiers sharing, presumably, Elite's Mahadura Nostalgit (picture 4:96). Interestingly, as an aside, only the content information about the contents, calories, and allergenic ingredients have been translated to Arabic, not the name of the chocolate bar, as the nostalgic associations are connected to the military connotations by non-Jewish Israeli citizens, for whom such an image would hardly be nostalgic.

In Germany, by way of contrast, direct use of national symbols such as the German flag, the state emblem, or military symbols seems to be taboo, probably as a consequence of German actions during World War II. Associations with this horrific history do not seem to permit any public,

Pic. 4:94 Turkish coffee with Israeli flag accompanied by "Roasted and ground Turkish coffee—60 years of coffee roasting in Israel" (I)

Pic. 4:95 A box of the "Elite" chocolate named "Mahadura Nostalgit" [nostalgic campfire or version, Heb.] with the words "Give them the best, give them 'Elite'" (I)

Pic. 4:96 Another packaging version of chocolate in the same series "Mahadura Nostalgit" from "Elite" (I)

Pic. 4:97 "President" chocolate (G)

Pic. 4:98 "Putinka" vodka [adaptation of the name of the Russian President Putin] (G)

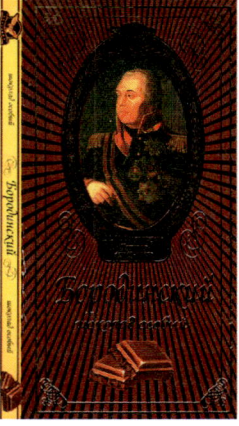

Pic. 4:101 One box of chocolates from the "Borodino" series; displays portrait of General Kutusov, who led the Russian battalions into the Battle of Borodino (1982) (I)

Pic. 4:100 "Lights of Moscow" chocolate deluxe with the marketing logotype "Buy Russian" (I, G)

Pic. 4:99 "Russia" coffee mug (G)

Pic. 4:102 One side of insert paper enclosed in box of "Borodino" chocolates; statement reads: "Not in vain, all Russia knows" (I)

commercial use of the state's national symbols. Thus, the local non-Russian food market is strongly separated from the political sphere.

In conclusion, even the commoditization of political symbols in Israel cannot compare to practices in the former SU where, as we have seen, pictures of former premiers or political leaders can appear on the wrapping paper of food commodities. Presumably, advertising designers and manufacturers assume that such displays will attract consumers or arouse associations with the taste, or purchasers' previous experiences with the product. Moreover, the degree of politicization of the commercial market, the ideological control displayed in the case of the SU, and the degree of commercialization of political symbols found in Russian food stores in Israel or Germany may be seen as a unique phenomenon, one that may well echo the totalitarian system.[86]

4.8 Nationalized Russia in food products and *gastronomic Slavophilism* of ex-citizens abroad

An intensive, new process of reconstructing Russian national identity or Russian nation-building started following the collapse of the SU (Lerner 2006, 22) and continues today in parallel with the reconceptualization of Russian ethnicity as "the affirmation of the 'great Slavic-orthodox nation'" (Calloni 1999, 121). Lerner claimed that we are witnessing the "need to build Russia for Russians while simultaneously maintaining the claim to be a homeland for an extensive Russian-Soviet cultural linguistic multi-ethnic Diaspora" (Lerner 2006, 22). The traces of both the aspirations to construct a great Slavic-Orthodox Russian nation, as well as, to preserve the Russian-Soviet cultural political narrative (including numerous different internations of the former SU) can be seen in many different spheres of public space. This was particularly the case during the fieldwork in Israel and Germany where it became evident, in unexpected areas, such as material food culture exported from the CIS to Russian food stores abroad.

The phenomena of *nationalization of food products* and *food nationalism* has been investigated in different contexts and recognized by scholars to be very significant (Bell and Valentine 1997; Caldwell 2002; Golden 2005;

---

86 For further discussion of this topic see also Chapter Seven.

Mintz 2003; Raviv 2001; Wilk 1999).[87] Studies have found that the process of nationalization of food and naturalization of its outcomes can take place within a very short period of time and involve mobilization of different symbolic cultural resources in introducing and establishing new ones, creating the fiction as if they were always there.[88] However, processes of establishing certain food products and meals as essential components of a homogenized *we* culture to mark and signify collectives are in no way new phenomena in the current Russian context. Analyzing Russian fiction of mid-nineteenth century, LeBanc pointed to what he named "gastronomic Slavophilism" (LeBlank 1999, 244). The visual design of food products presented thus far serve as evidence of the presence of these processes in the Russian context and their transportation by former SU residents to new contexts.

Two parallel processes are involved in these phenomena. First, the newly nationalized Russian mobilization of shared symbols of national pride taken from the Soviet period. And, second, introduction of new images from the old Russian traditions, such as: Slavic folkloristic and orthodox Christian symbols, symbols of nobility and feudality, symbols of Russian Tsars and empresses, motifs of old Russian fairytales and legends about Russian heroes, conquering foreign enemies (such as Tatars and Mongols) and saving the Russian land.

Many of these national and sometimes nationalistic trends that have been emerging in Russia since the demise of the USSR were carried on by Russian-speaking consumers in Israel and Germany. Here I would like to concentrate on two main aspects: First, verbal articulations of *being Russian* through use of nationally loaded symbols on food packages; and, second, exemplars of recently invented national symbols retrieved from history. In particular, we shall focus on especially controversial aspects that demonstrate how the process of rewriting Russian and Ukrainian history on food packages contradicts the history of Jewish history in this region. Consequently, as developed below, numerous food products imported by Russian-speaking migrant entrepreneurs to Israel and Germany export the national/nationalistic signs that receive another and a different meaning from the initial one in the new context.

---

87 See Bell and Valentine 1997; Caldwell 2002; Golden 2005; Mintz 2003; Raviv 2001; Wilk 1999.

88 As for example nationalization of Balizean through food practices in the research of Wilk 1999.

"Russia—The generous soul" or "Buy Russian!"—Direct references to
new national Russianness

National and nationalistic signs that directly articulate *Russianness* and positive features ascribed to *being Russian* were found frequently on food
products exported from the CIS in Russian food stores in Israel and Germany. The symbols that appeared most frequently on these products are
the flag and emblem of the Russian Federation and references to Putin, its
president; for example: on the package of President Chocolate (G) (picture
4:97); on the label of *Putinka* Vodka [improvisation of the name Putin] (G)
(picture 4:98); and on the Russian Coffee Mug (G) (picture 4:99).

A second observation is of the prevalent, indeed especially conspicuous, use of symbols of richness and gold motifs found in products exported from Russia. It seems that during the transformation processes
after *Perestroika*, and in particular in local interpretations and re-definitions
of living according to the new capitalism, the use of gold and other symbols of material richness became a legitimate means of constructing the
new image of the Russian nation. These new motifs are accompanied by
continuation of the Soviet tradition of the highly politicized nature of
commodity design. The packaging of the Lights of Moscow and Chocolate
Deluxe, for example, portray the Red Square, the Kremlin, the Duma
building with the state flag, gold domed roofs of the church (Vasilii
Blazhennyi) and the trademark "Buy Russian" (I. and G; picture 4:100).
This use of motifs of gold and richness confirms Sandomirskaya's finding
of the use of golden depictions of the Russian capital in relation to construction of the *Russian motherland*, which she stated as follows:

"My dear capital, my golden Moscow' [citing popular Soviet song], the epithets *dear*
[expensive, same word in Russian] and *golden* should be understood literally nowa-
days" (Sandomirskaya 2004, 132).

Transformation processes of Russian nationalization were found in many
different food products imported from the CIS and in particular from
Russia, reflecting the *Buy Russian!* campaign conducted in Russia since 1998
(Caldwell 2002, 295; Caldwell 2005). In fact, the effectiveness of this campaign in the current Russian context is evidenced in data from a representative 1998 survey finding that 92 percent of Moscow's citizens consume
exclusively local Russian food products (Althanns 2006, 169). Both the *Buy
Russian!* campaign and logos such as *Russia-Generous Soul* (ibid) mobilized
the nationalistic rhetoric of inclusion and exclusion. Interestingly, some but

not all of the motifs and campaigns promoting Russian nationalization are not local; for example, the logo "*Rossiya shedraya dusha*" [Russia—generous soul, Rus.] is found on chocolates produced by a Swiss firm in Russia—Nestle-Russia (ibid). McDonald's makes extensive use and supports the *Buy Russian!* campaign when it makes reference to the concept of *nashi*[89] [lit. kind of Ours, our people, Rus. refers to the new Russian nation. This concept does not exist in English but is a key symbol in Russian] (Caldwell 2005). Kehrer identified a similar strategy of nationalization or localizing an international product in Egypt. For example, marketers there advertised Procter and Gamble's Ariel detergent with the slogan: "100 percent Egyptian" and "produced by Egyptians" (Kehrer 2005, 89).

In order to provide the reader with an opportunity to assess the scale of these phenomena, the following list includes selected exemplars of food products exported from Russia to Israel and Germany that address make direct reference to, stress, and seek to reinforce *Russianness*:

– Red October—Traditional Russian Quality Chocolate (I); Sweet concentrated milk with the sentence "The best quality 100 percent *Rossiiski* [of Russian state, Rus.] product" displayed with a map of the Russian Federation (I) on the label; Monarch Ketchup (I and G) with "*Otechestvennyi* product" [Product of the Fatherland, Rus.] stamped on the label; *Lyubite Rus* Vodka! [Love Russia; "Russia" appears in pre-revolutionary version] (I) an annotation attached to the bottle states: "Our production is *istinno* [authentic, original; Rus.] Russian" liqueurs and vodkas; Russia Truffle Chocolates (I); Russian Frost Ice Cream displayed with a king's crown (I); Pearl of Russia Ice Cream (G); *Rossiskie* Cigarettes [of the Russian state, Rus.](I); *Russkoe Chayepitie* Tea [Russian tea-drinking, Rus.] (I); Russian Standard Vodka (G) with annotation on the label ending with the sentence: "We invite you to raise your standards to Russian Standards;" Russian Kvas [malt, Rus.] with the emblem "1000 years of Russian kvas" (G); Russian Croutons (G); "Vivat Russia!" Chocolates (G.) depicting Catherine I, the first Russian empress; Russian-style Cigarettes (G); Russian ornaments on packaging of chocolates of prestigious manufacturer Babayevskoe (G); Russian Ornaments Biscuits made by Bolshevik (G); Russian Chocolate with pictures of Moscow and Kremlin from 1860 (G); Traditional Russian Horseradish

---

89 About actualization of this concept by the participants constructing different collective affiliations, see Chapters Six and Seven.

(G); *Russkaya Kasha* [Russian buckwheat, Rus.] with an award medal for quality displayed, accompanied by the Russian flag (G); Veda Vodka—with ambiguous sentence "pure Russian vodka" (G); Russian Diamond Vodka, Premium Genuine Russian (G).

Interestingly, most of the information on the packaging and labels examined in this study did not stress Russia as the *geographic* place of production, but rather ethnic Russianness in the sense of the Soviet meaning of nationality as inborn and essential [as discussed in Chapter 6]. Indeed, through the use of the *Russkost* concept [Russian ethnic affiliation, Rus.] on food product labels, we can follow the aspiration of naturalization of the national habitus of *being Russian*, referring to hundreds or thousand years of Russian tradition through an emphasis on superb quality and unique traditional recipes—as if it they have always been there. Such naturalization of nationalization has been affirmed in many other studies of *culinary nationalism* (Bell and Valentine 1997; Caldwell 2002; Golden 2005; Mintz 2003; Raviv 2001; Wilk 1999).

In addition to the exportation/importation of *Russianness* into stores in Israel and Germany, numerous food products with the aspiration of *being Russian* or stereotypical representation of *Russianness* are produced in Israel and Germany for Russian-speaking immigrants. However, none of the participants in either context identified differences between images of *Russianness* initially produced for Russian citizens in Russia and those produced in the receiving society for Russian-speaking population.

Yet, independent of where *Russianness* was produced, "Russia shopping"[90] undertaken abroad was perceived by consumers in ways different from consumers of similar products in the Russian Federation. In particular, the findings suggest that the act of "tasting nationalism" (Caldwell 2002) abroad was significantly limited, smoothed over, and relativizied due to the physical distance of participants from their former national borders as well as through the very act of voluntary emigration, which in national terms could be questioned vis-à-vie their patriotism and loyalty to their land of origin. Consuming the manifestations of *Russianness* from abroad and being independent of the Russian system allowed participants the opportunity to distance themselves from it and to criticize it. Thus, construction of *Russian motherland* as total signifier appears to have lost its totalizing nature, post-emigration. Furthermore, in looking for the *authentic*

90 An adaptation of "India shopping" coined by Mankekar (2005).

and the *Russian*, the participants often overlooked or neglected national (istic) Russian signs and rather perceived only the fragmentary image of *Russianness* proposed in the stores and, in particular, stereotypic, all-encompassing signifiers of their collective cultural affiliation exported to and aimed for preservation in Israel or Germany.

Thus, direct manifestation of *Russianness*, even if nourished by contemporary Russian nationalized symbols, was employed by ex-Soviet Jewish participants abroad as an empirical category even if it became a stereotypic homogenized cultural marker of immigrants. Additionally, in the German case, symbols of nationalized Russianness may signify an imaginary homeland with which they can affiliate partially and which citizenship the participants mostly possessed in contrast to the participants in Israel who had the Israeli citizenship and could "try" the national Israeli narrative about the new homeland, proposed strongly to immigrants.

"Tell me what you eat and I will tell you who you are NOT"

As we have seen, images placed on packaging of food products have been among the many strategies applied to strengthen national *Russianness* (or *Ukrainianness*) in contemporary Russia and Ukraine. Here, historic images have been adapted and used in a manner that glorifies the power, richness, and heroic valor of the pre-revolutionary Russian empire. The images portrayed and narratives they represent create a symbolic-historic continuity with the past that is intended to strengthen the contemporary Russian nation, if only symbolically. In doing so, the intention seems to be pedagogical—such packaging seeks a development of a collective identity after the collapse of the SU and strengthening the citizens-will amidst the general morass of uncertainty and disorientation (Sperling 2001 cited by Althhanns 2006, 169).

However, rewriting history and exchanging one dominant Russian or Ukrainian group for another does not mean that the new version of history will reflect, automatically, the history of minorities, living (or previously living) in these territories. Indeed, the very elements cultivated in the emerging new Russian public discourse and selected for display on packaging have been problematic or controversial in relation to historic representation of Jewish life in Russia. Indeed, some of the images and narratives revived by dominant Russian groups correspond coincidentally to or in some cases are in direct contradiction to the historical facts of Jewish participation in the narrative. Furthermore, in general, reviving any historic events as part of nationalizing process would be problematic from the Jewish point of view, as this is a history whose main characteristic was the strong discrimination of Jews.

The following three examples of commercialization of historic Russian heroism correspond, coincidentally, with or are an obvious contradiction to Jewish history.

First, Borodino Chocolates (I) are named after the famous Battle of Borodino waged by the Russians against the French in 1812.[91] The packaging displays Russian commanders—Generals Kutuzov, Uvarov and Tuchkov who led the Russian battalions into the battle at Borodino (one of a series of portrayals; pictures 4:101). These portraits appear on the external packaging as well as on an additional explanatory insert placed inside the package: On one side of the insert is an art painting that memorialized the famous battle including the statement that appeals to Russian valor: "Not in vain, all of Russia knows." (picture 4:102) On the other side of the insert is a portrait of a general accompanied by his biography with emphasis on his valor, heroism, and courage in thwarting the French military advance, causing them to panic, and finally to flee. Presumably, this historic narrative is to be internalized, literally, through the taste of the sweet chocolate. However, not one word is mentioned about the fact that the Russians actually lost the battle.

Historically, the public discourse in advance of the 1812 war included expressions of suspicion about potential disloyalty of "all yids" (Kandel 2002, 281). Thus, the Russian emperor ordered that Jews be placed under special observation. Although generally Jews did not serve in the Russian army, they were faithful to the Russian Empire. In fact, they provided important intelligence information about the locations and movements of the French troops during the 1812 war (ibid., 282—283). Such "amazing loyalty" (ibid, 283) was noted by many Russian generals and even by the future Czar Nikolas I [whose reputation was that of an anti-Semite] who upon traveling in the Russian Western provinces made very disapproving notes about Jews, but also remarked that they "were perfectly loyal to *us*

---

91 This was the last battle before the fall of the Russian capital to Napoleon. This battle was eternalized for Russian speakers through the famous poem by Yuri Lermontov "Borodino," (1837). He dedicated his poem to the valor, heroism, and dignity of Russian soldiers, when despite defeat of the Russians, Moscow was set afire by the Russians rather than surrender to Napoleon.

and *even* helped where they could, even at the risk of their lives" (ibid). Indeed, in spite of Jewish valor and heroism during these events, the dominant narrative related to this period is solely about Russian heroism. Even today information about Jewish participation in these events remains known to few Russians as well as Russian-speaking Jews. Accordingly, it was not unexpected that participants made no connection between their Jewish identity and the narratives depicted on what was known to them simply as Russian Chocolate.

On the label of Monarch Ketchup, the second exemplar, the word for *ketchup* is printed in pre-revolutionary Russian orthography—*кетчупъ* (picture 4:103). The label displays portraits of Peter I and Catherine II within a gold frame set against the background of a sketch of St. Petersburg and a pre-revolutionary emblem of Russian empire. Though the following discussion will focus on the meaning of Peter I and Catherine II for Jewish history, we would be remiss in not noting the oxymoron nature of this combination of symbols—ketchup as a cheap American fast food and the rich traditions of a Czarist Russian food.

During the regime of Peter I, the city of St. Petersburg depicted on the Ketchup bottle remained closed to Jews. The sole exception were Jews, who converted to Christianity, some of whom occupied prestigious positions at the court and therefore were allowed to live free in the capital (ibid., 191—193). Thus, in his famous 1702 manifest, in which he invited qualified masters to Russia, Peter I made one exception to his invitation— everyone except Jews (ibid., 192). By way of background, we note that while living in Holland, Peter I had invited different masters to come to Russia. Some Amsterdam Jews also wanted to settle in Russia offered to guarantee numerous benefits to the Russian treasury and even proposed a first payment of one hundred thousand guldens (ibid., 191). Peter denied their offer and provided the following explanation:

"You know Jews, their character and features. You also know Russians. I know both and believe me, the time to unite these two folks has yet not arrived. Tell them that I am very grateful for their proposal and understand how worthy it would be to accept it. However, out of concern for them I take pity upon them should they settle among the Russians" (ibid) [Rus.].

After the death of Peter I, Catherine I (depicted on the Vivat Russia! Chocolates (picture 4:104) ordered the deportation of the Jews from the pale. Only Jews who converted were allowed to live in the Russian territory (Kandel 2002, 194). Later, when Catherine II (represented on the right side of the bottle of Monarch Ketchup, picture 4:103) confronted the "Jewish question," she continued this tradition in the face of all the members of the Senate who voted to grant the Jews permission to live in Russia. Catherine II aspired to protect Christianity and on December 4, 1762 she signed the manifest that enabled any foreigners, "except yids," to settle without objection in Russian territory (ibid., 198—199).

Although some participants knew about the anti-Semitism of certain Russian emperors and anti-Jewish discrimination prior to the revolution, none ever used this knowledge in discussing what was problematic for their self-identification as cultural Russians. In doing so they were either ignorant of or repressed the historical record of discrimination against Jews and their forced conversions throughout the history of the Russian empire. On the contrary, like many others they associated Peter I with being the great benefactor of Russian culture who built St. Petersburg—a key symbol of their pride in the Russian culture. Some participants even cited that one of the most trusted generals of Peter I, was a converted Jew (the stress placed usually on the last word—Jew, not on converted).

Representations of historic emperors as glorious heroes as well as numerous nobles and Czars as symbols of contemporary nationalized Russia on food packages may not have led to less consumption of these products. However, the question of economic profits is not our sole concern. Rather, it seems that the use of numerous symbols of nobility and mentioning different Czars on food packages in Russian food stores in Israel and Germany had different roles. Lacking wealth, power, and prosperity, these symbols stand in juxtaposition to the ongoing struggles of these migrants. Thus, these mythic biographies epitomized the high social and economic status that participants lacked.

The packaging of *Vechirnii Kyiv* Chocolates [Kiev in the Evening, Ukr.] (picture 4:105), sold in Russian stores in Israel and Germany and considered to be a quality popular product, also exemplifies the revitalization of a nationalized folk narrative in the contemporary Ukraine. The product is adorned with images of Cossacks and their leader—Bohdan Khmelnitski, revered symbols of the historical roots of the Ukrainian nation. Indeed, it is a picture of the large pedestal of Khmelnitski located in the Ukrainian capital—Kiev—that is depicted on the package. Historically, Cossack movements and Bohdan Khmelnitsky himself were responsible for the

Pic. 4:103 "Monarch" Ketchup displaying portraits of Peter and Catherine II (I, G)

Pic. 4:104 "Vivat Russia!" Chocolates displaying portrait of Catherine I (G)

Pic. 4:105 Box of "Vechernii Kyiv" chocolates [Kiev in the Evening, Ukr.] displaying the sculpture of the national Ukraine hero and Cossack leader—Bogdan Khmelnitski (I)

Pic. 4:106 Pelmeni [dumplings filled with meat] with an image of Cossacks (I)

Pic. 4:107 Vareniki [dumplings filled with potatoes, cheese or mushrooms]with the image of Cossack (G)

massacre of many thousands of Jews during the 17th century.[92] Yet, images of Cossacks appear very frequently on the packaging of food products, even on those manufactured in Israel and Germany for Russian speakers; for example, *pel'meni* or *vareniki* [dumplings filled with meat, potatoes, cheese or mushrooms] are a revered Ukrainian national dish (I and G) (pictures 4:106—7).

Only two participants, both members of the same family in Israel, pointed out the strangeness of selling images of Bohdan Khmelnitski to Jews in Israel. In spite of this critique, they consumed these products, stressing their taste. In response to my explicit question regarding this phenomenon that I posed to participants, the typical answer was that the connection I am trying to draw is artificial as it is taste that plays the decisive role. Indeed, based on these interviews, connections between these products and the historic meanings of packaging were not perceived. For example Katia (Germany), a history teacher who probably knew more than any of the other participants about contradictions between such images and Jewish history, stated:

"We buy for the taste, you know. And when such associations [meaning with Jewish[discrimination] appear, you try not to connect to them, to erase them, to tuck them away as deep as possible."

From this citation one can see how different Jewish, Russian, or Ukrainian narratives are separated and dissociated from one another. The painful history of the Jewish Diaspora is not concealed. Faced with contradictory narratives, there appears to be, on the one hand, repression of the most unpleasant ones and any associations with them; and, on the other hand, stress is placed on consumption of taste alone or references to positive connections with cultural *Russianness*.

Consumption of nationalized Russian or Ukrainian food symbols by Russian-speaking Jews abroad does not mean that they identify with these symbols or the nationalization process. Quite often the opposite is true. All the participants, in both contexts, were highly aware of anti-Semitic trends involved in contemporary nationalization processes in Russia and in the Ukraine. In fact, many participants in both contexts mentioned that awareness of these processes was central in their decision to emigrate.

On the basis of these three examples and others, it appears that we have a situation that contradicts the frequently quoted statement that ap-

---

92 Kandel 2002. Some sources claim that he was responsible for the death of 300,000 Jews.

peared in Brillat-Savarin's *La Physiologie du Gout* (1826)—"tell me what you eat and I will tell you who you are."[93] Here it appears that it does not reflect the self-identification of Russian-speaking participants as Jews in Israel and Germany. In fact, at certain points it seems to be in direct contradiction to their Jewishness. If so, then participants neglect or de-contextualization of nationalistic messages require an explanation. At its core their behavior involves developing a strategy to cope with a combination of controversial and contradictory narratives and identities: Their cultural Russianness, long periods of Soviet repression of Jews, Jewish culture, study of Jewish history, and accordingly the development of understanding their own ethnic Jewishness.[94] Moreover, through particular individual subjective association and interpretation of the food product (and stressing certain selected food biographies), we can trace another parallel process; that is, modification of original images according to the ideas and needs of ex-Soviet Jewish consumers abroad. In turn, these new images become a part of their present collective and individual identity as Russian-speaking Jewish migrants in Israel or Germany.

4.9 Meaning of Russian food stores in Israel and Germany

In concluding the various aspects addressed in this chapter, I would like to suggest several general interpretations of the meaning of Russian food stores for the groups investigated.

Realization of dreams

Russian food stores enabled immigrants to *taste capitalism* through familiar ways based upon past experiences in the SU, especially through the essential process of "procuring and getting" desired food items. Furthermore, certain aspects of the abundance they once dreamed of attaining were realized in Russian food stores in the two contexts. This includes food products that were highly desired and prestigious in the SU that most participants might never or very rarely been able to afford when living in the

---

93 See quote of Kershen 2002.
94 See Chapter Six for discussion of the sense of their ethnic Jewishness.

SU. Thus, paradoxically, it was only after emigration to the capitalist society that certain food products that embodied communism's dream—as expounded in the *On the Tasty and Healthy Food Book*—were available, affordable, and purchased regularly at Russian food stores by migrants.

Indeed, shopping, itself, became a very pleasurable activity, in particular because they were able to realize desires and dreams that were impossible to achieve when living in the SU. Applying the analysis of Jackson and Holbrook (Jackson and Holbrook 1995, 1919—21), the participants allowed themselves to be self-indulgent and to splurge for delicacies and fancy foods, especially when this allowed them to treat family members. Furthermore, attaining exemplars of abundance enabled participants to consume "cultural tales" (Appadurai 1988) including the dreams of the *spread tablecloth* and *taste of life abroad*, referred to previously. Such food consumption epitomizes the materialization of the desires of those who opted for economic emigration to Israel and Germany (i.e. to desire the land of "milk of honey" in the literal sense). Overall, then, one major outcome of these processes was that all participants in both contexts claimed that their post-immigration diet had improved significantly, even though most participants believed that their social status had declined since their arrival in Israel or Germany.

Russian food stores as a social club and new participation

Different images of products purchased in Russian food stores are inextricably linked to a projection of the social status. Restated through the terms of Douglas (Douglas 1966; 1975; 1985), the act of consumption can be conceived to be an act of social attachment in two key ways: First, in the sense of marking group borders in the new society; second, no less important, in the sense of performing a respectable, past action associated with the social status that is recognizable through common cultural terms shared by participants, who in this case belong to the educated intelligentsia stratum. This atmosphere of support and sodality helps preserve dignity and recreates the lost social status disrupted through the change of environment by those who recognized this status in the past.

Therefore, as a social act, shopping in the Russian food stores is a special type of cultural performance. People visited the shops in both contexts in order to procure desired products and to demonstrate competence as mature social agents and knowledgeable consumers. No less important, they did so because of the personal contacts and interactions they performed there with other clients and the clerks. As a result, Russian food shops have an informal atmosphere where there is much talking and laughter. Furthermore, whereas in certain other situations "personal service could be a source of anxiety" (Jackson and Holbrook 1995, 1922), consumption in Russian food stores is characterized by a personal, friendly service and humane treatment conducted through well-known behavior patterns that are greatly appreciated and desired by clients. Indeed, the framework of Russian food stores can be seen as a kind of social club that people visit regularly and which play an important role in their lives. However, in contrast to other clubs, this club does not require registration nor does it have formal membership rules.

One particularly interesting characteristic of the Russian food stores observed during the fieldwork was that people who came to the shops often talk about their past and present experiences. Some customers explained that they had a routine of coming to the shop on a set day in the week so that their conversations were ongoing, and in some cases they did not even purchase anything. Here, Slava (Israel) explained his reasons for going to a Russian shop he visits regularly:

"Simply to meet acquaintances and to enjoy an informal atmosphere with nice educated people."

Visitors of the Russian shops also exchanged information and recommendations on a wide range of topics, for example: Russian-speaking doctors, new books, films in the Russian language, interesting TV programs, worthwhile activities or clubs for children, Russian-speaking guided tours, and stores offering good discounts. People shared anecdotes and news about themselves and children attending the university, gave one another advice regarding the contemporary difficulties or problems, and discussed cultural or political events, posted or came to view personal announcements or discuss newspapers articles in Russian.

Moreover, it would be mistake to claim that these *imaginary home*s and *homelands* in the shops were a kind of vacuum in which the participants reproduced and lived in a hazy past, unconnected to contemporary events. On the contrary, local events in Israel and Germany as well as those taking place in the contemporary CIS were discussed intensively in the Russian food store social club and, accordingly, new forms of reference were created. This was especially the case in the Israeli context as significantly different national images and contemporary Slavophil Russia and Zionist,

Jewish Israeli nationalized narratives were simultaneously consumed and re-activated in Russian food stores in Israel.

Emotional feelings such as closeness and the sense of community developed and characterized the service provided by Russian-speaking clerks, according to new local standards. Such an atmosphere was preferred by participants to a visit of the regular supermarket. This preference substantiates Gold's findings in his study of Russian-speaking migrants in the USA (Gold 1997, 264). This finding is reflected by the statement of a clerk in an Israeli Russian food stores as he described what his work entails, given the social atmosphere created in the store by consumers and staff alike:

"People come here to talk, to remember. They share with us what is happening to them, tell us about themselves: Whose child is in the army. Who has left on vacation? Who is working where. They talk about their problems. It really is not like it was in the Soviet stores, you do remember? [Referring to the unpleasant nature of service in the Soviet store and the stressful struggle involved in "attaining" everything].

People come here even if they don't want to buy anything. They come in and say "Shalom" [Hello, Heb.]. They know that we will greet them warmly, that we will talk to them. People are not, after all, having a good time [many are unemployed]. We [my wife and I] are, for example, also medical doctors, but we have not yet been granted our license [to practice in Israel]. We know almost all of the consumers by name and we know what is happening in their families. Who had their teeth fixed; who rebuilt their flat; who bought a car; who retired."

Similar to other studies, the clerks in Russian food store functioned as "cultural ethnic brokers" (Darieva 2004, 38) and as communication sources in regard to intercultural questions (Mankekar 2005). Moreover, it seems that these clerks served an additional role as surrogate social workers or demi-psychologists for migrants. I observed that they were ready to listen to various and often endless accounts of problems and difficulties encountered by new and regular customers, and to offer their advice. For example, when I stated my amazement that a clerk (Israel) knew my name after my first visit, he explained:

"My function is to know all these things, not only the products' prices, such as— names of customers' relatives, phone numbers of different institutions—for example *Misrad Haklita* or *Bituach Leumi* [The Ministry of Absorption or The National Insurance Institute, uses Hebrew amidst Russian statement.] because people ask me. I am trying to create a home atmosphere here. So, I have to know all these things."

Some clerks were shop owners. Of course, their behavior "as if social workers" disguised to a certain degree their direct financial interest to sell their consumers as many food products as possible. However, I observed that quite often economics assumed a secondary role to social interactions and exchanges. On the other hand, I also noted how on occasion this trust was occasionally"exploited" for economic purposes in both contexts; for example, when during an enthusiastic discussion in Germany about local politics in Israel or global news the clerk/shop owner recommended, in a subtle but nonetheless insistent manner, this or another product, offered installment payments, if more products were purchased, or advised a customer to *trust* him about the quality and popularity of a certain food product. Shop owners played an especially important role as they *selected* and made available different *home* and *homeland* images to their consumers via the products they agreed to sell in their shops. Nevertheless, this role is not omnipresent. Through their preferences and items they purchase consumers are co-actors in producing and performing collective identities and certain imaginary *home* and *homelands* images available at a certain store.

Imaginary 'homes' and homelands

Russian food stores should not be considered to be a unique or self-sufficient phenomenon, they are rather part of an evolving and growing Russian-speaking enclave comprised of different institutions where participants meet and create their communal life. As found in studies conducted in other such communities,[95] the decision to frequent a Russian store does not mean that consumers intend to go back to the original society. Rather, by participating in the institutional life of the enclave they are involved in creating and sharing a new symbiosis with different *home* and *homelands* narratives that evolve continuously and gain legitimacy in the multicultural society.

In his research about food consumption among Russian-speaking Jews, Ben-Sirah identified *habit, taste, pleasure*, and *price* as more central factors than others for explaining consumption patterns among this group (Ben-Sirah 1993, 34). Markowitz (1991), in her study of this population in Israel and USA, pointed to the especially important role of money in the consumption process of migrants in a society of abundance. Other researchers

---

95 As for example, "India Shopping" (Mankehar 2005).

who investigated immigrant grocery stores found that ethnic affiliation more than economic rationality plays a central role in the consumption of food by immigrants (Kunow 2003; Lynn 1997; Mankekar 2005; Wang and Lo 2007).

In contrast, this investigation found that the key criteria applied in choosing among products in Russian stores are visual images (especially those of different *homes* and *homelands*) attached to/associated with the product, together with the consumer's subjective perceptions that are grounded in memories and tastes associated with an exact or a similar product. This was the case, in both contexts, for employed consumers as well as those supported by welfare. This claim was confirmed several times during conversations with clerks in Israel and Germany.

It was interesting to find that the criterion of "healthy food," often claimed to be one of the most important criteria in Western food consumption (Jenkins 1991), did not play even a secondary role in the purchase of products by the participants in Russian food stores. Intensive consumption of festive salads traditionally prepared with much mayonnaise as well as preferences for the "right" sour cream (i.e., containing at least 30 percent fat) or canned meat and fish products remained prevalent in both contexts. Of particular note was the finding that participants from Russia, but especially from the Ukraine, consistently purchased certain products (e.g., unrefined sunflower oil or chocolates made by certain companies) that were produced in specific areas, in particular Pripyat' and Gomel, located very near Chernobyl. Customers overlooked the production location in all the cases observed. Furthermore, I became the subject of their humor when I inquired if they knew where the product was produced. For example, several participants argued I emigrated too long ago and consequently had distanced myself from what is "natural" for them and, as a result, pay attention to other "strange" things. It was obvious that the desired images of home of these products were much more important than their intake of extra calories, cholesterol, or even possible radiation.

Russian food stores present what Kunow called "proxy for home" (Kunow 2003, 158) by offering multiple narratives and *home scenarios* on the packages of products for sale in these shops. However, I claim that this remains a kind of *imaginary home*. In this sense, Russian food stores' *real praxis* is above all a "place-making practice" (Ray 2004, 5) performed by displaying different food images of imaginary *homes* and *homelands*. The physical walls of Russian food stores create special microcosms where customers can feel comfortable, embraced, and safe in a home that symbolically replaces the migrants' feeling of *homelessness*, which prevails on different levels. All participants stated that the Russian labels on foods and announcement boards had a pleasant effect; clerks who speak Russian were often perceived, sometimes deceptively so, as people "who speak your language" in the broad cultural sense. Thus, in answer to a question posed to a consumer in Israel: "Do you speak Russian?" a clerk answered, proudly: "Yes, and without an accent!"

Thus, Russian food stores in both contexts were perceived to be a setting that created an atmosphere of affiliation with one (presumably) homogeneous group where all share common symbolic cultural codes. The use of the sentences reproduced from the previous Soviet deficit system, which in the new context might seem to be redundant, elicited feelings of trust and closeness in participants. For example, a clerk in Israel stated:

"No, we don't have this chocolate now, but I will *get* it for you!"

One participant [Larisa, quoted above] described Russian food stores as: "An oasis of comprehensive language, correspondence of the times and tastes and of course an information center [...] where [as Lora, quoted above] one can breathe again."

Incorporating multiple elements from the contemporary local environment, Russian food stores still seem to embody the illusion of a *hermetic bastion*, a vacuum-enclosed microcosm understood completely by its participants. Cultural consumption practices retained within Russian food stores as "common places" (Boym 2002, 22) with its "place-making practice" (Ray 2005, 4) seem to function as cohesive, stabilizing, empowering, and affirmative not only in the first years, but for many years after immigration. The physical walls of the Russian food stores that serve as a kind of *home* symbolically demarcate the borders between *inside*, with its comfortable trusted atmosphere, and the significantly foreign *outside* world of the receiving host society. In contrast to the comfortable trusting atmosphere that many participants perceive exists in Russian food stores, regular shops and supermarkets seem to be a "stressful environment"[96] not only during the first stages of immigration.

The atmosphere and food products of the Russian food store with their meaningful and comprehensive meanings and labels not only aim to bring Russian-speakers to their past *homes* and *homelands*, symbolically, but also

---

96 Jackson and Holbrook (1995: 1923) described elderly English ladies' perceptions of big supermarkets.

created new kinds of *home* and compensational images of *homelands*. Both imaginary images of *home* and *homelands* serve as effective *placebo pills* against longing for an irreplaceable home of an irreversible past, and propose a comfortable new alternative. In doing so, Russian food stores facilitated transition difficulties involved in emigration with the accompanying feelings of flux and continuity in these different "social worlds" (Schütze 2002).

Revived images of the *Soviet empirical homeland*, contemporary *nationalized Russian homeland*, *Israeli Jewish Zionist homeland*, *proletarian home*, *elitist cultural Russian home* or *nostalgic home* can be purchased in Russian food stores in different combinations. Similar to clothing, some *home* images and *cultural tales* "fit" exactly the self-vision of consumers with their subjective sense of one of the most meaningful self-identities; while others are satisfying, combinable, and compatible with prevailing self-definitions. And, while certain others are contradictory to some aspects of their self-identity and so provoke a feeling of "what you eat is not what you feel you are," the participants always tried to find a strategy to cope with contradictions, to bridge discrepancies, or neglect certain (especially controversial) messages and fragments, while stressing others.

5 Russian food stores in Israel and Germany: Different national symbolic participations and *virtual transnational enclave*

Building on discussion of multiple imageries found in Russian food stores in Israel and Germany discussed in the previous chapter, the discussion here demonstrates that Russian food stores are a controversial transnational framework. As we have seen, the different national narratives that coexist in this entrepreneurial framework often appear to be in competition in migrants evolving collective identities, in both Israel and Germany. Thus, rather than a cosmopolitan and globalized[97] homogeneous praxis, this study found a transnational view that includes combinations of multifocal, contradictory, and even mutually exclusive national and cultural narratives, myths, and images.

This finding stands in contrast to the "national foods" that are usually taken for granted by members of dominant groups and contribute to the socialization into a one-dimensional concept of a *nation*, or what Mintz (2003) referred to as "artificial sticking together." According to the "cultural logic of invented traditions" (Welz 2000, 178 [Ger.]), a "national cuisine" (Mintz 2003) or "national larder" (Hughes 1995 by Bell and Valentine 1997, 178) seems to be very important politically and highly emotional on the *iconic* level (Mintz 2003). Consequently, certain food products or meals symbolize the uniqueness of the nation and mark the frontiers of the *imagined national collective*. Purchasing food products as well as preparing and imbibing dishes define those who belong to it and those who do not or are "not quite" part of it. Therefore, *food nationalism* is the attempt to attach deep, nationalist sentiments to certain products that signify "our" nation, as opposed to "filthy foreign food" (Attar 1985 by Bell and Valentine 1997).

---

97 Pécoud (2001), for example, argued that cosmopolitanism seems to be an important, necessary resource for migrants' entrepreneurship in their everyday praxis.

After reviewing the research on food and nation (e.g., Allison 1997; Appadurai 1988; Golden 2005; Kunow 2003; Mintz 2003; Möhring 2007; Raviv 2001, 2002; Wilk 2008), the approach of Bell and Valentine to the interpretation of culinary cultural capital was adopted. These authors argue as follows:

"Like a language, food articulates notions of inclusion and exclusion, of national pride and xenophobia. On our tables and in our lunchboxes, the history of any nation's diet is a history of nation itself, with food fashions, fads and fancies, mapping episodes of colonialism and migration, trade and exploration, cultural exchange and boundary-marking" (Bell and Valentine 1997, 168—9).

While the link between food and nation (e.g., nationalizing food) has been broadly investigated over the last ten years, no studies were found that investigated how immigrants simultaneously construct and modify several national narratives through food practices. An investigation of this phenomenon involves, among other things, reflecting on the dichotomized terms of *local* and *global*.[98] Such an analysis can be advanced by focusing on ongoing processes involved in redefining collective national identities that occur through the flux and influence of migration as multiple national and ethnic food symbols transported by immigrants from their society of origin are interwoven into an evolving puzzle that relates to the dominant notions of collective identities in the receiving society.

In reviewing this literature, no studies were found that explicitly examined the coexistence and coalescence of multiple contradictory national narratives involving transnational food practices of migrants. In focusing on this phenomenon, this chapter presents findings that relate to the following questions: What meanings and roles do different national food symbols and images receive in migrants' practice? How are these used and how do they change? How do images of ethnic, religious, or nationalist Jewish, cultural Russian-Soviet, contemporary national Russian, and religious Slavic Orthodox Christians coexist within the cultural transnational framework of the Russian food store? How do these multiple images reflect and also contribute to the construction of migrants' complex collective identifications? How do these processes influence the dominant collective images in the receiving society?

---

98 As for example in the prominent work of Herzfeld who discussed how the local "overcome[s] the global at the level of the social organization of taste." (Herzfeld 2001, 94).

Two principal aims are achieved in answering these questions in this chapter: Grounded in the investigation of Russian food stores in Israel and Germany, the first part of the chapter presents an analysis of the meaning and roles of two key symbols of Russian (as well as Ukrainian) *national* foods—pork and caviar, as transported and practiced by Jewish migrants in the Israeli and German contexts. The analysis will discuss how these two foods crossed national borders and were manifest in controversies that contributed to the transformation of collective identities. The Russian-speaking enclave established in both contexts over the last 18 years is the focus in the second part of the chapter. Analyzed via the transnational theoretical perspective presented in the previous chapter, the research found that it is reductionist to apply the one-dimensional label of *Russian* to these food stores, as in reality this framework combines multiple and sometimes what can appear to be contradictory cultural images and national narratives. Accordingly, when considering what is referred to, strictly, as *Russian food stores*, we should respect the customers' perspective, most of whom do not see themselves as *ethnic Russians*, but rather as *ethnic Jews*.[99]

In addition, this chapter demonstrates that the enclave frameworks, in general, and Russian food stores, in particular, differ from concepts discussed in the literature, such as "transnational entrepreneurship" and "ethnic entrepreneurial niches."[100] The concept of *transnational entrepreneurship* usually refers to transnational economic action by migrants. This can involve transferring funds to family members or friends who did not emigrate, importing goods for sale in the receiving society (e. g., in Russian food stores), or investing in enterprises in their country of origin. In this regard, immigrant enterprise in the reception country is usually referred to as "ethnic business" or "ethnic entrepreneurship" (Guarnizo 2003). However, this study found that it is problematic to apply concepts such as *Russian ethnic food*, *Russian ethnic business* or *Russian ethnic entrepreneurship* to those who see themselves as ethnic Jews and not Russians. Indeed, the findings suggest that the phenomena analyzed are a special type of transnational activity within the enclave. Therefore, we can conclude that two concepts "transnational" and "enclave," which at first sight seem to contradict each other, should be combined. Moreover, in both contexts, but especially the

---

99 Further delineation and discussion of this concept is presented in chapter Six.
100 See, for example, Kloosterman and Rath (2003).

Israeli one, the transnational enclave functions as a *virtual transnational enclave*.

The analysis will demonstrate that the two contexts—Israel and Germany—are very different from one another: Each context has a strong influence on every event and phenomenon, including formations like enclaves.[101] Furthermore, transnational activity and the enclaves developed in parallel, apparently without inter-connection with one another.

The basic assumption of this investigation is that consumption and the migration process are acts of personal and collective agency. The view adopted here is shared by other scholars who assume that people are *knowledgeable, responsible, mature agents* (Kivisto 1990; see also Bodnar 1985; Stonequist 1935, 1937) and *knowledgeable consumers* (Jackson and Holbrook 1995). Consequently, food practices and food images are assumed to be manifestations of collective identities that are reshaped and transformed by immigrants through everyday practices and interactions within the transnational framework. The effect of personal and collective agency is especially apparent in the case of Israel. There we find that the ethnic Jewish transnational enclave has transgressed a number of key national-cultural rules over the last 18 years, since the immigration of ex-Soviet Jews. For example, the growth of a broad range of non-kosher food stores; a long, continuous struggle to gain recognition of pork as a legitimate practice of the Jewish national collective; and how changes in political participation influence local hierarchies of power in relation to food habits of resident populations.

5.1 Special national key symbols crossing borders and manifestations of identity: The symbolic meaning of *pork* and *caviar* in different national contexts

Various types of food consumption can be understood as codes for individuals views and behavior. These codes can be deciphered in terms of defining group boundaries, social status, political position, and economic class. In a migration process, people are also exposed to different cultural meanings associated with particular products. Hence, one key question

---

101 On Israel, Kimmerling (2004).

is—how do they cope with these differences? Let me start with citations from my field notes about two situations observed in Israel:

Esti (veteran resident in Israel): "What are these *blini* [crepes, Rus.] filled with?"

Ella (a participant who immigrated to Israel in 1992 answered with a big, proud smile and challenging tone): "I don't know what filling you [veteran residents] put in them, but we [migrants] fill them with caviar."

Valentina: "Russian food stores are not only for the usual kinds of foods [regularly consumed items]. Formerly it was a cheap store, now it is more expensive than the normal supermarket—with caviar, bacon, and [smiles] "*ryl'ze v pushku*" [lit: pork's face in a trough; she uses this Russian proverb to refer, playfully, with the idea that Jews are lured to eat pork because of its taste, and hints that such consumption is not viewed as appropriate by veteran residents]."

These two citations reveal a strong emotional attachment to certain food products that connect shared symbols and one's own personal biography and associations. And, in referring to certain products—caviar and pork, they erect a border between "we" and "them," and question what is appropriate and legitimate for "us" and "them." Moreover, the two quotes can be perceived as challenging collective positioning: Ella attempted to present migrants as opulent eaters, as a rich group who usually add caviar to the *blini*. Valentina dealt with the oxymoron—Jewish pork—humorously, countering that ex-Soviet Jews in Israel are made to feel guilty for their consumption of pork.

Pork sausages and caviar became central signifiers of Russian food stores in both contexts. However, both are used in Israel in a particular way—as key symbols in advertisements for grocery stores where they can be purchased (e.g., the Russian store Teremok or the non-kosher meat factory Valdman; see picture 5:1—2). I found the following two signifiers on the wall by the entrance to one food store in Israel, where they seemed to serve as a manifestation of the store's identity. Displaying on the wall was a framed picture with two pigs, a hanging mobile with silver pigs, and a framed picture with the sentence—"Life has been a success!"—written in black caviar over a background composed of red caviar (picture 5:3).

By examining pork and caviar purchased in Russian food stores in Israel and Germany, the analysis presented in this chapter demonstrates how different key symbols of these products are encountered in the culture of origin and in the country of immigration. And, accordingly, the analysis demonstrates how different "cultural tales" (Appadurai 1988) expressed

Pic. 5:1 The Russian store "Teremok" (I)

Pic. 5:2 The non-kosher meat factory Valdman (I)

Pic. 5:3 "Life has been a success!" written with black caviar on the background made of red caviar, photo taken in a Russian food store (I)

through food products symbolize different national markers and national myths encountered in the consumption process of Russian-speaking Jews in Israel and Germany.

Purchase and use of culturally and politically-loaded food products that present different *national tales* involve an encounter between collective identities and symbolic social self-position in relation to them. Thus, consumption of special food products such as pork or caviar can serve as a marker of the *imagined community* (Anderson 1991) of a group of migrants or imagined status markers of this community to which collective affiliation is permanently negotiated, rebuilt, and redefined. During my fieldwork in Israel and Germany, both pork and caviar appeared as very powerful *key symbols* with rich and often controversial meanings.[102]

Moreover, these two products have a strong cultural meanings in all three societal contexts considered in my research (in CIS, Israel and Germany), even if particular meanings differed. These two products epitomize different stories about collective identities, but share one significant common characteristic, socially: While migrants wish to continue to consume these products as normally is the case in the former SU, both caviar and pork are considered to be contradictory in the context of the receiving societies (in Israel and in Germany) As I describe it below, pork played a central role in the concept of national identity in Russia and Ukraine, but it attains a different meaning when ex-Soviet Jews consume it in Germany and especially in Israel, where its image does not fit dominant local dictates of what Jews should or should not eat.[103] Caviar, as an elitist national Russian symbol brought to Israel and Germany, also becomes contradictory when used by immigrants whose political and economic status in the new society is low. Thus, the former exclusive power of caviar serves a new function and/or provides symbolic support for those who are deprived of economic and political powerful resources.

---

102 Applying key symbols, per Ortner (1973).

103 Whether animal derivatives are considered to be kosher depends on their nature as an animal, slaughter procedures, and manner of preparation. The pig is considered to be a non-kosher animal because it does not fulfill two Biblical criteria for kosher food: the animal must have cloven hooves and chew its cud. Since fish require scales and fins to be considered kosher, black caviar is not kosher because it is issued by the sturgeon, a fish that lacks scales. In contrast, roe/caviar from salmon is considered to be kosher.

5.2 Pork

Israel: Consumption and special cultural meanings of pork

Field notes:

Waitress in a non-kosher restaurant: "Would you like white meat? [Heb., synonym for pork]"

Alex: "Yesterday I was sad, so I went to the Russian food store and bought sour cream and bacon."

Until recently, one of the abrasively unique characteristics of Russian food stores, as distinct from most other Israeli food stores, was the absence of any *kashrut* restrictions (i.e., religious laws that define the use of kosher/non-kosher foods). Since they do not observe Judaism's restrictions regarding food, Russian food stores drew, principally, on a distinctive collective identity. Yet, at the same time, they were strongly influenced by food preferences of the secular, non-Russian speaking Jewish population in Israel, the majority of which is culturally of European origin (Ashkenazi). Thus, today, 15—17 years since the first Russian food stores appeared, there is a sizeable economic market oriented to Russian food culture (Kimmerling 2004) and tendencies toward secularization of Israeli food consumption. Both of these phenomena can be seen in transformations of Tiv Ta'am [Quality Taste, Heb.], a non-kosher grocery store chain with 24 branches, at last count.[104] Tiv Ta'am was founded to serve, primarily, the Russian-speaking population, however its significant growth, expansion, and transformation occurred when its reputation as a quality, non-kosher supermarket attracted growing numbers of secular Jewish Israeli customers.

Similarly, the last wave of Russian-speaking immigration contributed significantly to the legitimacy of new Israeli non-kosher eating preferences in the public sphere, which previously were the preserve of a small number of restaurants known to serve *white meat* (i.e., pork) and the private sphere. Ben Porat (forthcoming) claimed that the significance of success in the long struggle of the Zionist secular Israeli population against religious coercion, for example in the law prohibiting the sale of pork, epitomizes the struggle for freedom and citizens' rights in Israel.

---

104 Tiv Ta'am is the only supermarket in Israel, in the Jewish sector, open on Saturday, the traditional Jewish Sabbath.

In the Israeli context, pork is perceived by at least half of the population, which consumes exclusively kosher foods, as neither Jewish nor eatable (Gutman, 2002 by Ben Porat, forthcoming; Shimron 2002; Wolffsohn and Bokovoy 2003). Additionally, there are many other people in Israel who neither observe the laws of the kosher kitchen nor eat pork. Contextually, pork has a rich historical involvement in Jewish life in the Diaspora as it is associated with the persecution of Jews over thousands of years when, despite the threat to their lives, many refused to surrender to pressure by dominant non-Jewish ruling groups and refused to eat it (Ben Porat, forthcoming, citing research of Barak Eres, 2003).

Although approximately half of the total Jewish-Israeli population today *keeps* kosher exclusively [105] (i.e., observes the kashrut laws), very few non-kosher food stores existed to serve the other half, the secular population, prior to the arrival of the last migration wave from the former Soviet Union. Thus, until recently, the kosher supermarket was supposed to (and symbolically did) represent the central element of Jewish Israeli culture. However, the last immigration wave from the CIS was involved in the broad and rapid development of non-kosher markets in Israel. Amidst various confrontations between inner Israeli groups, this innovation continues to have an impact on Israel's cultural character in significant ways. For example, just as *Döner* has come to be perceived in Germany as a synonym for *Ausländer* [foreigners, negatively loaded word, Germ.], in general, and for *Turks* in particular (Ayse 1999), so the sale and significantly increased consumption of *basar hazir* [pork, Heb.] in Israel has become metonymic for *Russians/ Russianness* in Israel.

The significant changes caused by Russian speakers in Israel are welcomed by some, but reviled, argued against, and denied by others. The religious and *masorati* [traditionalist, Heb.] segments of the Jewish-Israeli population perceive non-kosher food stores as *anti-kosher* and as a Russian

---

105 Ben Porat (2007); Gutman (2002); Shimron (2002). Different studies claim that between 50 and 56 percent of the Jewish Israeli population eat kosher and between 50 and 54 percent do not eat *teref* products (i.e. products defined by rabbinic law to be impure). The last numbers—56 percent and 54 percent—were cited from Gutman (2002 in Ben Porat, forthcoming). According to Dahaf-Survey (2001), 50 percent of the Jewish-Israeli population describes themselves as orthodox, religious, or traditional (Wolffsohn and Bokovoy 2003). Consequently, one can assume that at least 50 percent would not eat pork, as doing so is a violation of religious laws as well as the Jewish traditional orientation. Yet, on the other hand, 50 percent reportedly do not keep kosher and eat all manner of food, usually when travelling abroad.

intervention in the *proper* Jewish-Israeli collective. This view is shared by some Israeli researchers. For example, the social scientist, Mordecai Friedman, warned the Jewish-Israeli reader in his 1995 article "Cultural integration of the immigrants from the CIS" about the potential influence of Russian migration on Israeli society, in general, and its impact on the constellation of collective Jewish cultural identity, in particular. Friedman includes the following observation about Russian food stores among his claims about the negative expression of undesirable influence:

"Immigrants from the CIS have opened hundreds of shops that sell pork. State laws forbidding the sale of pork are insufficient to prevent the increasing number of factories and enterprises of this kind" (Friedman 1995, 65) [Heb.].

Thus, both historically and in contemporary Jewish Israel, pork is a key anti-cultural symbol[106] of collective Jewish identity employed to establish the desired boundaries between the excluded—those (foreigners) who consume pork—from *proper* Jews who refrain from consuming it. Again, as stated by Friedman:

"Until now it was appropriate in Israel that 90 percent of the population did not consume pork and one could hardly find shops selling pork. Today, in contrast, every citizen can identify shops that declare in Russian and Hebrew that 'the pork era has arrived in our land'" [Heb.][107]

Representing a taboo symbol, pork was traditionally perceived by Jews as one of the most central images of impurity. As such, it functioned to draw clear boundaries around the Jewish collective. And, further, following Mary Douglas, pork can be seen to reflect a given social order and status claims (Douglas 1966). The negative connotation and impurity connected with this meat is mediated by means of the non-naming of the product; that is, it is usually identified in Hebrew on the packaging, wrapping papers, ads, and in some menus in non-kosher restaurants discreetly and non-descrip-

---

106 I refer to the concept key-symbol of Ortner (1973).
107 Friedman (1995, 65). Note: By "Israeli" Friedman means Jewish Israelis. This is a gloss commonly made by Jewish Israelis who in doing so neglect to recognize that nearly 20 percent of the state's citizens are Arabs of Christian or Moslems faith. Christians eat pork and, consequently, grocery stores in their communities sell pork-related products. Until Tiv Ta'am and other Russian food stores made pork products available, these Christian stores were one of the main sources for procurement by secular Jewish Israelis of these products.

tively as "white meat," "white steak," "other meat;"[108] or with the Russian word *salo* [bacon] written in Hebrew letters on the labels of products in non-kosher stores (picture 5:4).

The oxymoronic "Jewish pork" problem was treated in a number of creative ways. Some restaurants employed shared knowledge and language about deviance from a norm. For example, Nest, a Russian-speaking restaurant in Tel Aviv, named a menu *Tainaya Vecherya* [lit. Secret Supper, Rus. reference to the Last Supper]. Here spareribs, basted using a "secret" recipe, are assigned an interesting role as the item diverts attention from a transformative process that the dominant Jewish-Israeli culture expected of recent arrivals—the Russian-speaking Jews. This process involved avoidance of the ongoing confrontation between two contradictory concepts: the abitual consumption of pork, as accepted in non-Jewish European Diaspora culture, was to be abandoned in favor of *proper Jewish-Israeli behavior.*

Other strategies were employed to cope with contradictions between Jewish religious tradition and secular Jewish identity. For example, on Kibbutz Mizra,[109] the main producer of pork meat, pigs for slaughter live on raised wooden planks so that this *ta'meh* [impure, Heb.] animal does not touch the holy earth of Israel.

As the consumption of pork became more visible and grew in scale throughout the 1990s, so the ferocity and passion of statements made by Knesset members from orthodox religious parties and religious citizens intensified. In their view, the pork industry and pork consumption threatened their attempts to impose and preserve an illusionary image of a homogeneous country embracing Judaic tradition and culture. In ways similar to the language used by Professor Friedman, this rhetoric employed abusive images to refer to those who consume or produce pork meat. Members of Kibbutz Mizra were blamed by one Knesset member from a

---

108 It is interesting to note that despite the fact that a half of the Israeli population eat kosher, 75—80 percent of Jewish-Israeli restaurants are not kosher (Ben-Porat 2007). This may be explained through the Israeli stratification system in which the secular Ashkenazi population is in a position to afford most restaurants (concentrated at the center and the north of the country rather than in Jerusalem).

109 A kibbutz located in the northern part of Israel in the Yezreel Valley that has been producing pork since before the establishment of the state. It could neither sell its products in most Jewish Israeli shops nor advertise them publicly until the massive Russian-speaking Jewish immigration to Israel.

Pic. 5:4 Russian word "salo" [bacon] written in Hebrew letters on the labels of products in non-kosher stores (I)

Pic. 5:6 The advertisement at the opening of a branch of the non-kosher super-market chain Tiv Ta'am (I)

Pic. 5:5 Advertisement in Russian language of Ma'adanei Mania [Mania's Delicatessen, Heb.] (I)

Pic. 5:7 Basket with pork sausages (including one entitled "Soviet"), wheat spikes (Soviet symbol for harvest and abundance), apples and wine (traditional Jewish symbols at Rosh HaShana/New Year meals) (I)

Pic. 5:8 Pork in spicy marinade (G)

Pic. 5:9 "Dovgan" beef or pork pickled in spicy marinade (G)

Pic. 5:10 "Jakob Supermarket" with advertisements of minced pork meat and pork liver (G)

Pic. 5:11 "Schulga" pigs' hoofs (G)

Pic. 5:12 "Schulga" smoked piglets—very tasty! (G)

Pic. 5:13 "Gallina Blanca" Lard—very tasty! (G)

religious party for producing and acting like pigs.[110] Religious citizens in Carmiel held up placards—such as "*Pigs, go back to Russia!*"—during a demonstration against non-kosher stores. And, some Russian food stores have been set afire in Jerusalem, causing owners to block off the façade of their store with iron grating.

In this discourse, people who consume pork are reproached for transgressing laws that underpin the *imagined community of Jewish Israelis.* Furthermore, they are represented as having internalized into their personality, through eating, a number of harmful characteristics associated with pigs in popular Jewish culture. Such arguments seem to assume that consuming a polluted, forbidden substance, as defined by religious law, causes a symbolic transformation of a person's spirit and personality, and for this they should be socially and culturally ostracized. Thus, in common parlance, "Russians" often means persons with negative attributions of pigs. This rhetorical device of metonymy is employed and largely adopted in popular culture by non-Russian, Jewish Israelis.

Thus, clearly, food matters in Israel. Indeed, the evidence suggests that far from being a private matter of individual choice, as in the maxim "you can't argue with taste" (i. e., taste is a private matter), the aspiration to define, preserve, and reinforce collective identities includes imposing a national cuisine. This affirms Mintz's (2003) claim that persons or a group who eat similar foods are also perceived to possess similar features. Hence, such persons assume that they are more alike us in other respects and we will have more in common with them, in general, in contrast to those who eat in a manner different from us and who seem to be different (Mintz 2003, 28).

While one segment of the non-Russian speaking population enjoyed the secularization process of Israeli food practices and the possibilities afforded "to taste [foods] from all over the world" (as stated in the logo of the Tiv Ta'am supermarket chain), many individuals from different groups and Jewish religious parties criticized and issued new threats in their efforts to preserve what they perceived to be the traditional and moral image of what is "properly Jewish." For example, residents solicited signatures against an attempt to open a new branch of Tiv Ta'am in a Haifa neighborhood in 2006. They claimed this chain was a non-Jewish practice

---

110 Macintyre (2007): "Kosher wars: how a right-wing billionaire is challenging a secular Israel," *The Independent*, published: 12 June 2007. http://news.independent.co.uk/world/middle_east/article2646291.ece

imposed on their lives. Similarly, in 2007, the media carried debates over plans of a Russian immigrant and billionaire, Arkady Gaidamak, who disclosed in an interview that following his recent purchase of 51 percent of the stock shares of the non-kosher Tiv Ta'am super-market chain and that he was going to purchase the remaining shares and then make the entire chain abide by such Jewish laws as kosher laws and Shabbat closure,[111] as well as to open new branches in Jerusalem.[112] After hot and often strident exchanges in the media, in which Gaidamak openly referred to Jews who ate pork as "pig-faced," he retreated from his plans and the transaction did not take place. Different kinds of pork products as well as other non-kosher food products such as non-kosher cheeses, shrimp, mussels, Strauss eggs or lobster appear on the Israeli market, but still did not become a part of the *normative Israeli-Jewish local cultural-symbolic landscape.* For example, the Israeli journalist Orna Efet, calls her newspaper article *Lavan baeinaiim* [lit. "white in the eyes," Heb.,]. The title plays on words with the expression "everything went black," which in Hebrew can also be used here to express every kind of shock. The author replaces it by "everything went white," because in Israel pork is usually called "white meat." In her article she presents consumers of non-kosher products as "gluttons of shrimp and pork sausages" and describes the development on the Israeli non-kosher market 17 years after the beginning of the change as follows:

"The non-kosher Israeli market has experienced a real boom during the last years. In Israel pigs, rabbits and ostriches are grown, non-kosher fish is cultivated. In *our state* [lit. 'baarez'-Hebrew] terefah [non-kosher] sausages, salamis and meat products are produced, red and black caviar, expensive cheese, shrimp, mussels and lobsters are imported here…'Today only 7 percent of Israeli people [means resident population] consume non-kosher food products'—says the general director of the network 'Tiv Taam'—Dubi Shneidman. 'According to the statistic 50 percent of our population lead a secular style of life. All of them are our potential clients'…" [Heb.][113]

This citation illustrates a highly emotional and political topic: namely, who has the right to define what is "*our state*" and the right to change it. It seems

111 Ibid.

112 *Ynetnews*, Ofer Petersburg "Gaydamak acquires non-kosher supermarket chain," published: June 10, 2007. http://www.ynetnews.com/articles/0,7340,L-3410650,00.html. Note: Gaydamak's actions coincided with the run-up of his campaign for mayor of Jerusalem; a city in which religious Jews are the majority.

113 Orna Efet, "Parmesan dwellers/convent/tenement. Consumption boom on non-kosher market", *Idiot Aharonot,* 15.02.2007.

that there are culturally-sanctioned proclivities and, accordingly, attempts
to attain strong political mandates in Israel to impose and regulate the food
preferences of the Jewish collective. In doing so, attempts are being made
to assert that the political aspect is not only connected to the Jewish religious tradition, but also interpreted to be national signifiers. In this sense
the non-kosher character of Russian food stores continues to be seen by
the dominant Jewish community in Israel not only as a challenge to the
presumed religious consensus about the *proper* and desired homogeneous
image of *being Jewish*, but also as a provocation by the Jewish Russian community, and their representatives, to express a non-Jewish identity and
acceptance of not belonging to the Jewish collective.

Yet, for Jews from the SU, Jewish affiliation has a completely different
meaning. This meaning grew, primarily, through historical circumstances as
well as the values and ideologies of their politically driven socialization. In
their view, consuming pork does not contradict their Jewishness. For most,
food consumption and habits, in general, and *kosher* food regulations, in
particular, are associated with a concept of Judaism symbolized by their
grandparents' religiously-centered, pre-Revolution life in small shtetls.
Given their negative, socialized view of religious-driven practices, they
aspire to distance themselves from this world as far as possible. Hence, the
taboo on the consumption of pork was viewed as obsolete or religious
atavism that could not be a part of a new socialist life. Contrary to the
absolute taboo of pork in traditional Jewish culture and the collective historical experience in which Jews were humiliated by being forced to consume or to come in contact with this taboo product throughout the centuries in Europe,[114] culturally assimilated and atheist Soviet Jews did not
consider it to be taboo in any sense. Thus, the question "Don't you eat
pork?" was transformed and viewed humorously by Russian-speaking
Jews. This, even though it remained a rhetorical anti-Semitic question used
by non-Jewish outsiders, as an exclusion mechanism that had little to do
with actual everyday practice, but rather was a way to confirm generalized
Otherness.

---

114 Diemling, for example, in her analysis of anti-Semitic descriptions of Frankfurt Jews in
    the 18th century portrayed different kinds of pranks by Christians who forced Jews to
    drink from cans greased with lard or put bacon and pork sausages on the prayer bags of
    Jews in the synagogue (Diemling 2005, 86).

Thus, a kosher kitchen in general and the symbol of pork in particular were not a concern in SU Jews' everyday lives.[115] To be a Yevrei, a Jews in the Soviet sense of nationality—was considered to be and remains a matter of birth. It does not have to be established through the daily performance of rituals or traditions. Shternshis (2006) concluded that, for Russian-speaking Jews, there is a significant dissociation between kosher food practices and their *being Jewish*. Accordingly, it is very interesting to note how pork developed a new meaning among Soviet Jews, quite distant from being a central key symbol of impurity used to draw the boundaries of the Jewish collective and to define the limits of those who belong and those who are different. In the interviews conducted in Israel and Germany with people who grew up in Russia or the Ukraine, pork symbolized a "successful household," "the warmth of home," "the wealth and prosperity of family life." For example, the participants from the Ukraine frequently associated food with the family that eats borscht, the main soup in the Ukraine, made with pork, vegetables, and beet root. Also, lard [juicy fat pork] is considered to be a particularly tasty food that gives strength and is needed for the children's growth. The participants spoke repeatedly about pork as the "right," "real," "authentic" meat. Moreover, many kinds of sausage— especially smoked varieties—were desired, but often unavailable in the deficit Soviet economic context.

Accordingly, Russian food stores stock a variety of very popular pork sausages with interesting, even provocative names, in a Jewish religious sense, for example: *Molochnaya* Pork Sausage [milky, Rus.]; *Doktorskaya* Ham [doctoral, Rus.]; *Lubitelskaya* Mortadella Salami [lovely, Rus.]. According to the dream of communist abundance, these were highly desired products during the Soviet period (n.b., but were generally inaccessible due to scarcity). This can be seen in the *On the Tasty and Healthy Food Book* (1952), the well-known recipe book from the period of Stalin or in images of capitalist abundance.[116] Well-known products from the USSR period are available in Russian food stores in Israel and Germany, such as: *Moskovskaya* [Moscovite, Rus.], *Krakovskaya* [Krakowian, Rus.], Servelat (special smoking process) *Polskaya* [Polish, Rus.]. These stores also offer new and different types of pork sausages with product names such as: Governor, Braunschweig, Basturma, Smoked Bacon, Sausage of the First Class, Deli-

---

115 See discussion in Chapter Six.
116 See discussion in Chapter Three.

cacy. All of these products are designed to epitomize different Soviet dreams of abundance and to attract Russian-speaking consumers.[117]

For example, in one case observed during the fieldwork, clerks in a Russian food store in Haifa (Israel) noticed that consumers were asking for special types of sausage: "Do you have Finland salami?" or "I am looking for small Odessa sausages." After a while, they decided to put Soviet names on similar Israeli sausages and if having tasted them consumers said that the sausage tasted different from the original, the clerk answered: "I am afraid that this sausage may be kosher; you know, after all it has been produced here in Israel."

Interestingly, among the investigated group of Russian-speaking Jews, sausages were associated much more with a wealthy life than with unhealthy food or, even less frequently, with being a negative, anti-Jewish symbol.[118] Indeed, on the basis of the fieldwork it seems that the opposite was the case: Pork was perceived to be a healthy food and vital for a wealthy life. Indeed, one pork dish in the restaurant Nest, mentioned above, is called "Viagra"—a humorous reference to the potency of this product.

Another example of the role of pork sausage in migrant perceptions appeared frequently in the Russian-speaking Israeli media in the form of a self-abrogation through use of such an approbation as—*kolbasnaya aliya* [sausage immigration, Rus.]. This phrase is tightly linked with the popular disparaging Hebrew statement about Russian speakers "hem bau bishvil naknik" [They came for sausage, Heb.]. Both phrases refer to those whose main motivation for immigration to Israel was to advance economic interests. Such denotations "work" because they refer to shared knowledge and judgment in Israel in which a clear distinction is made between legitimate (i.e., Zionist) and illegitimate reasons for immigration (i.e., personal economic reasons). Thus, a desire to escape humiliating food lines—where former SU/CIS residents spent most of their free time waiting in hope of

---

117 For example, dreams about communist abundance in Soviet times—*Krakovskaya* sausage [Krakow, Rus.] or Cervelat; later dreams about capitalist abundance—Governor sausage, *Braunschweig* [Delicacy, Ger.]; or, availability of "proletarian" sausages, often referred to by Soviet citizens as "simple sausages" (e.g., *Doktorskaya* [doctoral, Rus.], *Lubitelskaya* [lovely, Rus.]).

118 Certainly, some SU immigrants of the last wave "returned" to the Jewish religion and/or ceased consuming pork, however no such individuals were found among the investigated group in Israel.

receiving a prestigious sausage—via migration is framed negatively for persons who shunt ideological Zionist goals for the sake of sausage.[119]

The dissociation between Jewishness and Judaism and positive pork connotations completely contradict the historic, traditional understanding of pork among Jews in Israel, mentioned above. Indeed, a joke popular in Israel describes a statement supposedly made by an orthodox Jew as he points to meat in the shop and says:

"I would like this beautiful chicken."

The clerk replies: "But it is pork."

The client answers: "I did not ask what it is called. I would like this beautiful chicken."

In the SU, on the other hand, a popular joke describes a Ukrainian's diet:

Russian: "Morning—bacon, afternoon—bacon, in the evening—bacon."

The Ukrainian replies: "It is not true. I wake up in the night too!"

Thus, although Nikolai (in Israel) sees himself as Jew, pork is inseparable from his sense of personal identity. He articulated this perspective by contrasting it to the local Israeli Middle Eastern traditions that he disdains:

"To finish if off with pita [he uses the Hebrew word—'lenagev' referring to the use of pita instead of a fork when eating hummus] is to betray the pork."

Interestingly, pork represents for Nikolai a symbol of Russian (European) cultural affiliation, rather than an indication of Jewish roots that one "betrays" through consumption of pita as embodiment of Oriental food practices, which are in his view barbaric. Acting through the European-Oriental dichotomy, Nikolai's statement is not the opinion of a lone bigot, but rather representative of a common judgment heard among participants in Israel about the "civilized," "cultural," and claimed to be "normal" European traditions of food consumption brought to the "wild" —Oriental

---

119 This humiliating sentence has an obvious association with a type of dog [dachshund], who can be easy attracted with a sausage and whose physical needs are dominant. Moreover, the Hebrew word for sausage, *naknik*, is associated with phallus; and the verb form, derived from the act of making sausage—"l'naknek," means to deceive, to trick somebody, and is linguistically associated with the act of rape. Thus, the Hebrew sentence—"They came for a sausage"—can also be read as a double entendre as they came for a *naknik*, as phallus; or, as, let's deceive/*nenaknek* them (i.e. put them in their place here [in Israel]).

Israel, as personified by eating with one's hands—"to finish it off with pita." A similar logic is intended in the statement by Faina (Israel) concerning food placed in pita: "I don't eat these *falafel*" [as in these inappropriate Israeli-Oriental food habits]. These examples demonstrate how internalized socialization to accusations related to food nationalism has been extended to those who "eat like pigs" (and are accused of being "pigs"); whereas others betray the nationalist (Soviet) practice by refraining from consuming pork (religious Jews) while eating foreign Oriental food using primitive manners.

The large expanse of the Russian speaking population in Israel enables many immigrants to feel that they are part of a big collective that positions itself—sometimes in quite an arrogant manner—as European cultural Others who are proud of their cultural Russian (Soviet) heritage and who aspire to change—that is, to *Europeanize* or *civilize*—the receiving society.

In purchasing non-kosher products in a Russian food store, many immigrants express longing for "proper" (i.e. original) ham/bacon. Indeed, one of the most appreciated of all gifts that a guest from the CIS or from Germany can bring a Russian-speaker in Israel is a "good" ham or package of bacon. Not only does such a present symbolize Russian and European culture, it arouses memories and emotions among Russian speakers in both contexts, for example:

Roman (Germany): "Oh, that tastes exactly like, do you remember, when we went on long train journeys, lasting one or two days, and ate bread with bacon, and tea with sugar cubes ... so relaxed and leisurely."

Felix (Israel): "Now I would really like to have a pork steak with bone. To eat something *normal!*"

Karina (Israel): "I still remember the way we went to school. Every day I had a sandwich with butter, cheese, and bacon."

Interestingly, attachment to eating pork continued many years after migration, even when many of the Israeli participants became interested in traditional Jewish religious practices. And, accordingly, while many in both contexts started to light candles on the Sabbath, as a manifestation of *symbolic Jewish ethnicity*, most continued to consume pork.

Further evidence of attachment to eating pork is reflected in advertisements of Russian food stores, in which the availability of pork (missing, of course, from non-Russian, kosher grocery stores in Israel) is presented as one of the main reasons to visit the store. For example, the advertisement of *Ma'adanei Mania* [Maniya's Delicatessen, Heb.] (picture 5:5) includes a statement about the availability of an abundance of non-kosher meat, accompanied by the following text:

"Such renown, refined a taste. Yes, yes, right here. We prepare and sell such sophisticated meat products, familiar since childhood. No doubt you will be astounded by the shining cleanliness, rich assortment, and exciting smells. Doctoral sausage, cooked ham, drumsticks, raw smoked sausage, liver sausage, blood sausage, sturgeon, fat weeping rose salmon-all only the best freshness [...] special prices in the Meat Department on Saturday" [the Sabbath, when all other stores in the Jewish sector of Israel are closed] [Rus.].

Another advertisement in the Russian language invites patronage at a branch of Tiv Ta'am (picture 5:6):

"At last a branch of Tiv Ta'am has come to the north, close to your home. It will probably be the biggest of all. Just think about all kinds of meat that you can taste. About our gigantic meat department and high quality delicacies—frozen and fresh, low in fat, red and white, smoked and dried [...] Just imagine all this! And that's not all. There is a huge choice of fish, salads, sauces, and breads. Everything tastes good. You can find everything you are looking for in the supermarket, we mean really EVERYTHING [...]. Open all day Saturday." [Rus.]

Of course, such memories stand in complete contradiction to traditional Jewish-Israeli norms of Jewish identity. On the basis of the current research, it appears that pork can embody two diametrically opposed cultural key symbols, representing different collectives. In our case, these collectives represent two diametrically opposed cultural systems making it difficult for them to co-exist and to identify one another as being members of one Jewish collective.

Because of the strong distinction in the Russian language between *yevrei* (Jew) and *iudei* (religious Jew), Jewish immigrants from the Soviet Union—most of whom were avowed atheists—could incorporate the key symbol of the dominant group (Russia as well as the Ukraine) in which they grew up without it affecting their understanding or contradicting their sense of Jewishness. The legitimacy and normativity of consuming pork for the atheistic Soviet Jews did not include the necessity for self-justification in the SU. Furthermore, given their context, Russian-speaking Jews can be differentiated from other Diaspora Jews, where the Jewish tradition carried on despite persecution and outside pressure, and underwent its own ways of development and change (n.b., the major exception is the period of the Spanish Inquisition). For Jews in the European Diaspora, the emancipation process was not automatically accompanied by a decision to consume pork. Indeed, until this very day it continues to be a delicate and problematic issue,

Soviet Jews, in contrast, were exposed to significantly different historical processes. Religious connotations and associations were suppressed in combination with what seemed to be a promise of equality for all citizens in the Soviet Union. Thus, the consumption of pork by Soviet Jews had three additional aspects. First, it corresponds to the trend to secularization of Jews who moved to the big cities after the Revolution. In the post-Revolution period in Moscow, St. Petersburg, Kiev or Kharkov, for example, maintaining any traditional rituals threatened to connect them to their Jewish religious families from the shtetl from whom they were trying to distance themselves (Sleskine 2004). Second, the decision to consume pork cannot be considered to have been a matter of free choice, even for future generations of participants (children of those, who actively participated in the Revolution and building of the new Soviet state). These were the generations exposed to forced Soviet secularization and prohibitions placed on practice of the Jewish tradition, in general, and the consumption of pork, in particular. Indeed, the consumption of pork by the participants' cohort generation cannot be considered to be an "advance," as in conscious emancipation or liberation from religious prejudices, but rather a matter of limitation and deprivation of Jewish cultural attributes and free choice. Third, questions such as—"Do you eat pork?" or "Is it kosher?"—had strong anti-Semitic connotations in the Soviet Union and, hence, can be considered to be a stigmatizations. Such questions seem to be an attempt to stress the non-belonging of Jews to the Soviet collective as well as construct significant Otherness, despite the fact that everybody knew that Jewish rituals were forbidden. And, while such questions were consistent with the normative stress in Russian culture on belonging, they also reinforced many Jews' anti-Semitic experiences, as will be demonstrated in the next chapter. Consequently, from their point of view, the consumption of pork has neither any connection to nor contradicts the Russian-speakers' perceptions of being Jewish.

The data collected in this study on this phenomenon correspond completely with analyses of Russian-speaking Jews in the research of Shternshis (2006) conducted in Russia, Germany, and the USA. Among her many supportive citations, she cited an 82 year old woman who resides in Brooklyn: "This is how to cook kosher pork…because only a Jewish soul can make food kosher" (Shternshis 2006, 13). Here, a perception of being Jewish is evident that is very different from the religious worldview: She stresses essential Jewishness (given by birth, according to the Soviet understanding of nationality) as more significant than laws of the kosher kitchen that are foreign to Soviet Jews, as we will see in the next chapter.

Such views were transported with the immigrants and caused conflicts soon after their arrival in Israel, when some recent arrivals gave their children sandwiches with fat pork/ham/bacon to eat in their mid-day meal school, unconsciously breaking a strong norm—bring only kosher milk products to school (i.e., no meat and definitely no non-kosher meat). Acting through common practices in their home of origin, in Israel, they could not foresee the potential conflict for their child with local pupils and the accompanying threat of exclusion.

Struggle for the right to be Jewish in their own way

A claim could be made that pork has become a symbol of identity for the Russian enclave in Israel. Moreover, different field observations point to the involvement of Russian-speaking Jews in Israel in an active struggle for their right to be Jewish in ways they desire. Furthermore, there are interesting new combinations among what seems to be oxymoronic *Jewish pork* products. For example, a Jewish New Year Greeting—"Shana Tova" [Happy New Year, Heb.]—is written in Hebrew letters along with a picture of a holiday basket containing pork sausages (including one entitled "Soviet"), sheaves of wheat (Soviet symbols for bread, harvesting), apples and wine (traditional Jewish symbols eaten in festive *Rosh Hashana*—New Year) (picture 5:7). Following thousands of years of festive celebrations, the addition of pork is an anathema to traditionalist Jews, and would have been impossible in Israel prior to the Russian-speaking immigration.

Another interesting example that demonstrates a struggle to eat non-kosher and still identify oneself as being Jewish was found tacked on the wall by the of a Russian food store. This artifact consisted of a pseudo-oxymoronic "secular kosher certificate," with the following text:

"The owner of this enterprise maintains high standards of sanitation and hygiene, takes great care in selecting a variety of products, and is proud of the quality of service provided clients. This is done without any control by the rabbinate.

In contrast to his 'kosher' colleagues, the owner promises not to pass along additional fees from the rabbinate so that clients do not have to support [religious] malingerers nor contribute to building religious colleges [yeshivas].

The owner of this enterprise does not need rabbinical certification to declare his right to be considered to be a Jew and an Israeli.

The owner claims that in a democratic state nobody no one has a right to dictate what anyone may or may not be permitted to eat. Signed: *Shinui* [lit. change, trans. Heb.,]"

This document states, directly and unequivocally, a position that is clearly unfriendly to Israeli religious institutions regarding the legitimacy for clients to identify themselves as Jewish and Israeli while still consuming pork; the right to make personal decisions regarding food preferences; as well as, to oppose religious usurpation and control of the public sphere.

The struggle for the right to decide how to be Jewish is, of course, not the preserve solely of Russian speakers in Israel. However, Russians in Israel influenced the scale and pace of change in the nature of the standards, tastes, and symbols used by dominant, non-Russian speaking, local groups. Indeed, despite the controversy over food preferences and the non-kosher Russian-developed chain of grocery markets, Tiv Ta'am, the store continues to be frequented by non Russian speakers. And, while production and consumption of pork continue to be an openly debated issue in the public sphere, it has become part of the new Israeli national cuisine. Indeed, there is evidence of increasing numbers of secular Jewish-Israelis whose everyday consumption incorporates foods perceived to be not only inappropriate, but a taboo if not amoral 20 years ago.[120] In a real sense, the success of Tiv Ta'am stores with their global, multicultural world, open, transnational nature displayed on its shelves was made possible by the last wave of Russian-speaking migration. The direct consequence has been a confrontation with basic key symbols of cultural identity.

Golden wrote that while Israeli falafels and oranges "lost their innocence... and became saturated with national connotation" (Golden 2005, 187) the growth vector of pork is headed in the opposite direction—from a national anti-symbol of Israeli-Jewish collective to a regularly consumed food. Through introducing a broad spectrum of non-kosher small stores, Russian-speaking Jewish entrepreneurs (together with the owners of Tiv

---

120 Products include pork and various non-kosher products (e.g., seafood and semi-prepared dishes).

Ta'am who survived pressure on the market thanks primarily to Russian-speaking clients) realized the latent desire of many secular Israelis of different origins. Introducing numerous new non-kosher products (from rabbit and ostrich to shrimp and lobster) from different countries gave legitimization to evolving Israeli culinary habits. Russian stores and Tiv Ta'am brought to Israel the limitless, desired abundance of which ex-Soviet citizens as well as many secular resident Israelis had dreamed and that had not been possible before in Israel and the SU, albeit for very different reasons. And, thus, while conflicts raged about different ways of *being Jewish*, which challenged a common national symbol, cultural heterogeneity grew in legitimacy and became more visible.

Pork consumption in Germany: "I still keep eating [pork], but feel bad about it"

Since pork is generally consumed by the host population in Germany, it could hardly signal the distinctiveness of the Russian-speaking Jewish group or become a key symbol of Russian food stores. Accordingly, the sale and consumption of pork cannot be seen in this context neither as provocation nor as an indicator of the absence of belonging (as in the case of Israel), but rather as the normal case. In Russia and Ukraine, as well as in Germany, pork has culturally positive connotations. For example, in the German language the word "pork" and "pig" (*Schwein*) are used in diverse metaphors, among others, such positive ones as: "to have a pig" means to be lucky (n. b., an unthinkable metaphor in the Israeli context).

In addition, there are special pork delicatessens which offer foods that definitively cross culinary limits of what is considered to be edible foods in some countries; even what might be labeled "disgusting food" in many countries, not only among Jewish Israelis. For example, new delicacies bacon/speck in skin made of chocolate or *Schweinskopfsülze* ["pig's heads aspic/jellied", Ger.] made by the Dreistern firm, *Schweinsrüsselscheibensülze* [pig's snouts aspic/jellied, Ger.], *Pfälzer Saumagen* [pig's stuffed stomach, Ger.] or even bacon chocolates made by Zotter. These exceptional foods notwithstanding, there remains a great choice of Russian-Ukrainian produced pork meat, sausages, and bacon in Russian food stores in Germany. Their consumption is frequently accompanied by the claim that the product has more fat and is more delicious than the local one. Similarly, *salo* [bacon, Rus.] produced in the Ukraine is brought to Germany as a present.

And, Russian speakers in Germany bring German pork sausages and bacon to relatives and friends living in Israel, where they are highly desired and appreciated gifts.

This having been noted, my participant observation in the field led me to conclude that the topic of pork has become a delicate theme for some Jewish migrants in Germany. This is particularly the case for Jews who are confronted with local German ideas about the question: "What does it mean to be Jewish?" In their interactions with the local population, they are likely to have to confront the assumption that Jewishness is viewed as an affiliation with a religion that prohibits eating pork. Some participants cited their confusion and the necessity imposed on them to cope with discrepancies between different local ideas and their perceptions transported from the SU. For example, Tamara (60 years old), who has a German boyfriend, described having a bad conscience when she admitted to eating pork while being Jewish:

"Earlier [in the SU] I ate pork, you know, normally, just like all everybody did. Now [in Germany] I continue to do so, but I have a bad conscience about it. I keep eating, but feel badly [laughing], for example, when I prepare rissoles with mixed meat [half pork, half beef]. My German friends know that I am Jewish and they ask me, in astonishment: 'So, are you eating pork?'"

Identification of the consumption of pork as a key symbol of non-Jewish affiliation is articulated not only in interactions between Jews and other groups, but it has also become an issue discussed in inner group dialogue among Russian-speaking Jews. First, their understanding of the question—*What does it mean to be a Jew?*—is permanently challenged through transnational praxis (e.g., when Russian-speaking Jews in Germany visit their families and friends in Israel or when their relatives visit them in Germany). This is especially the case among young Russian-speaking Israelis (children of friends of participants in Germany) who do not eat pork. On some occasions, reported to me during the field research, these children created a "distasteful" scene and harsh feelings when during a visit to Germany they asked repeatedly whether pork was used in preparing this or another dish. Katia's statement recalls such an incident:

"I feel bad about this especially when Israelis come [Russian-speaking Israelis]. My cousin visited us with her 18 year old son. He kept asking what this was or what it was made from. They [probably Israelis] have a problem with pork, you know. And they give you a bad feeling that [pause], that, we are eating something wrong here [in Germany], and something is not okay with you."

Inner-group discussions also take place between different generations of Russian-speaking Jews in Germany, who understand their Jewishness in different ways. In such exchanges, the younger generation challenges the Soviet-grounded concepts of their parents about Jewishness transported to Germany, such as the following account of a family conflict: Lisa (62) shared her concern about an ongoing quarrel taking place in her family between her son Vladik (38) and his son Lev (11). As a result of the conflict, she claimed that Vladik was losing his authority as he is continually forced to justify his behavior and is criticized by their son for "betraying" his Jewishness. She related the following example:

Lev: "Tell me, why do you still eat pork?"

Vladik: "Because I think it is delicious!"

Lev: "How could you. We are still Jews!"

Vladik remains silent.

Especially interesting is Lev's use of "still" (lines one and three) in relating two different stances toward his father. The first usage of "still" referred to a temporal and transformation process that Lev expected his father would undergo. With the question, "Why do you still…," he expressed his desire that his father should refrain from eating pork (in the sense that it is a harmful habit like smoking) and his belief that Jews are not supposed to eat pork. In doing so, he transmitted the message that he does not feel his father is Jewish enough and wanted him to become more Jewish by not eating pork anymore. Through the second usage of "still," he emphasized explicitly to his father the contradiction between being Jewish and consuming pork by stating them as polar opposites, as seemingly unbridgeable chasms, stressing that consuming pork is inappropriate for Jews.

The perception of *not being Jewish enough* appears often in the German media where it is constructed through the references to "inappropriate" pork consumption as characteristic of Russian-speaking Jews (Elias and Bernstein 2007). In articles entitled, for example, "Russischer Wodka und unkosheres Schweinefleisch,"[121] [Russian Vodka and non-kosher pork, Ger.], the Jewishness of Russian speakers is questioned due to their consumption of pork. This claim is supported by quotes from migrants who admitted their own non-Jewish habits and consequently *de facto* agreement

---

121 Wengert, V. (2006) "Russischer Wodka und unkosheres Schweinefleisch," *Deutsche Allgemeine Zeitung*, 2 June 2006.

with doubts raised about their *Jewishness*, again according to the German cultural prescription of a religious-driven definition of Jewish identity. For example, this is the argument made by the author of a newspaper article whose headline read—*"Wie soll ich noch ein guter Jude werden?"* [How should I, after all, become a good Jew? Ger.]. The article quoted a Russian-speaking migrant who "revealed a secret by winking"[122] at the author, when he said: "We [Jews from the SU in Germany] prepare borscht with pork [...] should I, after all, become a good Jew in my old age" (ibid)?

Similarly, an article in the German magazine *Stern*,[123] entitled—"Jews in Germany: Now they speak *tacheles* [to talk turkey with s.o., Ger., Heb.];" and sub-titled— "came as Jew, stays as Russian"—includes an interview with an 80 year old Russian-speaking Jew living on social welfare in a "20 square meter Ukraine" (ibid) that he made for himself in his room in a old-age-home. According to the author, this room is "paradise on earth" (ibid) in comparison with the surroundings amidst the old walls of the home for the aged with dusty plastic palm trees on the floor and the smell of the old people (ibid). The author writes in a condescending tone about his conversation with the migrant. The interview took place alongside a table filled with different products, including a

"massive Embassy brand salami. He keeps cutting salami slices for himself. It is not kosher, but tastes especially good to him. 'Please don't tell anyone in the community what we are eating here.'" (ibid) [124]

Besides the ethics of mocking an old person who received the journalist by preparing for him a fare rich with food and drink, the message alluded to by noting the consumption of "Empire Salami" is—given the religious-oriented assumptions of the German speaking reader—one of suspicion of the cultural baggage and questionable *Jewishness* of migrants from Russia.

In summary, the common, taken for granted understanding in Germany about being Jewish is that it is above all an attachment to and practice of a religious orientation (e.g., including keeping a kosher Jewish kitchen and "of course" refraining from consuming pork—an anti-Jewish symbol, par excellence.

---

122 Tichomirova, K. (1997). "Wie soll ich noch ein guter Jude werden?" *Die Zeit,* 25 July 1997. Online: http://www.zeit.de/1997/31/Wie_soll_ich_noch_ein_guter_Jude_werden

123 Braun, S. (2007). "Juden in Deutschland. Jetzt reden sie Tacheles," *Stern,* 4 May 2007. Online: http://www.stern.de/politik/deutschland/587598.html?nv=ct_cb

124 Ibid.

Comparative analysis: Germany—Israel

It is interesting to note that in the immigration from one (Soviet Union) Diaspora context to another (Germany or Israel), the consumption or non-consumption of pork is a normative part of the local food tradition, but reflects differently on the Jewish minority in each context. In the SU, dominant atheist policy and norms did not approve of any expression of religious tradition, and consequently any restrictions on food practices on the basis of religion. As a result, Jews were expected to consume pork in a manner similar to dominant Russian or Ukrainian groups, for example. In contrast, in Germany, migrants lived in a context where there were huge numbers of secular members of the Jewish community, yet the German religiously-determined view of Jews, based upon the orthodox version of Judaism, was used to judge all Jews. Also Israeli ideas about the immigrants' position in Israel, as people who have to be taught to become "properly Jewish" (Golden 2002) influenced the way in which not only religious but also many secular Israeli residents spoke with suspicion and doubt about the Jewish identity of Russian speakers. For example, Reuven, the observant Jewish Israeli-born spouse of the daughter of a participant, precisely formulated this situation as an indicator of power relationships and tensions in Israel:

"If you dress in a short skirt and eat pork in Israel and you are an Israeli [meaning Jew born in Israel], it is normal. But, if you are Russian, then you are a prostitute and are not Jewish."

Thus, participants in both contexts were exposed to the pressure—albeit very different in nature—to explain and to justify their non-kosher food habits as evidence of their suspected Jewishness. While consumption of pork in Israel was often seen by religious and observant groups as a disturbing form of Otherness, non-consumption of such foods in Germany was often seen as *desired Jewish Otherness*. Whereas in Germany consumption of pork by Russian-speaking Jews remained characteristic of "their" habits, in Israel non-kosher habits of Russian-speaking Jews significantly influenced new consumption practices of other groups. And, the latter, also demonstrates and reflects the collision of two national narratives. Additionally, pork consumption of Russian-speakers in Israel turned out to be a key symbol of their resistance to religious indoctrination, as well as, their desire for and involvement in developing an independent collective identity and self-sufficient community.

In comparing how pork products are presented in advertisements in Russian food stores in Israel and Germany, for example, one can see significant differences that correspond to dominant national narratives in both contexts. In the Israeli case, advertisements for Russian food stores portray an abundance of different kinds of sausages, with very few references to or images of pigs. The presumption in advertisements by Tiv Ta'am and Ma'adanei Mizra seems to be that consumers know sausages are made from pork. And, when reference is made to a pig, it is through allusion and is very restrained; such as the advertisement for Ma'adanei Mizra Smoked Bacon (picture 5:4). This advertisement displays a package of *Kopchenoe Salo* [smoked speck/bacon, Rus.]. The product's name is written in Russian letters translated into Hebrew in a very interesting manner. the marketing designer translated only the word "smoked" into Hebrew— "meu'shenet," while using the Russian word *salo* written in Hebrew letters instead of bacon [katlei hazir in Hebrew]; hence, using a word not understandable to anyone who does not know Russian. On the right side of the package, three very small, inconspicuous images of pigs are drawn using thin, fine, black lines. Presumably, the package's graphic design was taken in this order to avoid irritating potential Israeli consumers with use of negatively loaded concepts in the Hebrew language.

In contrast, in Germany, the image of the pig is assigned an important place in the design of product packaging and advertisements published by Russian food stores. This may be due, as well, to the fact that they are frequented not only by Jews but also by *Spätaussiedler* [Russian speaking resettled ethnic Germans, Ger.]. Here, advertisers appeal to potential consumers from both groups via positively loaded images of the pig adopted from the SU as well as positively interpreted images in Germany. Exemplary pictures (pictures 5:8—13) display a fat pig and her piglets in colorful pink images, and with hoofs visible to all—an image presumably irritating in the Israeli context.

5.3 Caviar

Meaning and consumption pre- and post-migration to Israel and Germany

Caviar can appear to be one of the most powerful key symbols of Russian wealth to foreign groups. So well-known as "Russian" abroad, caviar is often mobilized as a symbol of a *cultural food treasure*. Kaufmann claims that "only when one is convinced, that caviar and dry Martini are something delicious, one can develop a taste for it."[125] (Kaufmann 2005, 42 based on Becker 1981). During the Soviet period caviar was one of the most expensive, desirable, and unattainable delicacies, internalised as common shared *taste value*. It may well have led the list of products that were indicators of an economic and political status, as well as, of proximity to state power and authority. Glants, an art historian who writes about the ideas and symbolic meanings of food in art during the Soviet regime, wrote: "Caviar, ripe fruit, gourmet meals, and expensive wines exist only in the houses of the rich and powerful" (Glants 1997, 230).

When they lived in the SU, the participants recalled that caviar only appeared on the table on rare occasions, usually for special occasions, such as the birth of a child, a wedding, or during New Year's celebrations. For example, a picture that "eternalized" the wedding of a participant's daughter in Israel shows a smiling bride and groom sitting at a table decorated with a vase of flowers along with a huge plate containing slices of bread spread generously with red caviar, marking this very important moment in life with the wish for a future life of prosperity for the young family.

Believing that it was especially healthy and having healing power, caviar was also used as an appetite stimulant for pregnant women or sick family members. Such culturally constructed and highly contextual-dependent beliefs about rare, expensive, and desired food products with especially healthy effects are widespread in different cultures. In the very popular *On the Healthy and Tasty Food Book*, first published during Stalin's time and discussed in Chapter 3, red and black caviar were portrayed on the inner cover in the middle of the table, as one of the few color pictures in the book (picture 3:1). Clearly politically loaded, caviar served here as a symbol of the wealth and prosperity to be achieved in the socialist life of the Soviet people. According to the Soviet myth, in addition to being (an illusionary) symbol of the flourishing lifestyle of Soviet citizens, it was an embodiment of generous Mother Russia, evident by the presence of an abundance of

---

[125] "erst wenn man davon überzeugt ist, dass Kaviar und trockener Martini etwas Köstliches sind, kann man Geschmack daran finden" (Kaufmann 2005, 42 based on Becker 1981)

caviar as an indispensable part of the meal offered to *Inostrantsi* [visitors from abroad, Rus.].[126]

Another color picture in the *On the Tasty and Healthy Food Book* (picture 5:14) displayed a jar with red caviar and the even more expensive black caviar. The shot was made from far above the top of the jar as if to suggest to Soviet readers that the communist era of abundance was approaching. The idea of wealth and the beautiful life are commonly portrayed in Russian advertisements as well as in well-known films by showing an exaggerated quantity of caviar being consumed with a big spoon (!), while the actor looks weary and stuffed from eating an abundance of caviar. Yet, since consuming caviar in small amounts is considered to be healthy, especially at important festivities and ritual events, the norm for eating this expensive delicacy, is rarely and only then by spreading it thinly on a piece of white bread with butter. Thus, an advertisement that displays waste of the most expensive of products transgresses the Soviet cultural code. Such a presentation of course strengthens the meaning of this exclusive symbol.

Though the participants continued, post-migration, to use conceptions about caviar brought with them from the SU, a blurring of the boundaries between the practical consumption of caviar and ideal ideas about the elitist symbol of unaffordable and unavailable caviar are detectable. That is, there seems to be evidence of individual experimental play in which old and new ideas are interwoven with one another. For example, I noticed in my fieldwork in Israel that there are cultural ideas about the legitimacy for transforming the festive consumption of caviar into an everyday act. In one of the observed situations, a 10-year old girl and her mother were visiting friends. When she saw there was caviar, she asked if she could have some. As the hostess took a slice of bread, in order to spread caviar on it, the girl said: "No, thanks, I will eat it with the spoon." This seemed to confuse all the adults present and aroused discussions about an indulgent, spoilt young girl. Her mother claimed that things were changing and whereas caviar had once been an unaffordable product when she was growing up, it had become an enjoyable and almost normal practice for her daughter to eat since migration to Israel. Note, however, that cases of the transgression of ideas about "normal" practices point to the continued existence of old cultural patterns of meaning-making.

---

126 It is important to note that frequently this word meant visitors from capitalist countries, had a connotation of superiority, and meant great efforts were expended in hosting such visitors.

Pic. 5:14 Jars with red caviar and black caviar displayed in the On the Tasty and Healthy Food Book

Pic. 5:15 Advertisement of red caviar by "Caviar House Lemberg:" "Special price—30€/kilo" and "With our prices you can eat caviar with a spoon!" (G)

Pic. 5:16 'Tsars' Caviar" sold in Russian food stores in Israel

Pic. 5:17 Cardboard packaging of red caviar sold in Russian food stores in Israel

Pic. 5:18 Croutons with black caviar flavour "Max" (G)

Pic. 5:19 Advertisement for "Zarendom" red caviar [Tsar palace, Ger.]: "So delicious you can eat a pail!" (G)

Pic. 5:20 Herring salad, called in Hebrew "Íkra,"—sounds very similar to Russian word for caviar—Ikrá" (I)

Caviar occupies a central place in Russian food stores in Israel and Germany, where the quantities desired are ladled out of a big pot (sometimes even a pail) with a big spoon. The signs and advertising used by these stores to publicize the sale of caviar employ a variety of strategies, including use of familiar Soviet ideas from books, advertisements, and films, discussed earlier. These advertisements manifest the new availability, abundance, and affordability of the popular consumption of caviar. For example, the advertisement of a Russian food store in Germany named the Caviar House Lemberg displayed a big bowl of red caviar along with the statements: "Special price— Euro 30/kilo" and "With our prices you can eat caviar with a spoon!" (picture 5:15). Another advertisement of the Russian business Zarendom (G) used the statement "Tzar Caviar at proletarian prices." And, the cardboard of the red caviar of Tzars' Caviar sold in Israel (picture 5:16) displays a big plate filled with caviar (picture 5:17). An advertisement of Caviar House Lemberg displayed cans of red caviar in the shape of a barrel. The title in Russian seems at first glance to be strange— "Salmon Caviar—500 gram barrel," until one recalls that a barrel is commonly associated with large wooden containers containing large quantities of sauerkraut, marinated gherkins, or wine; that is, a barrel is not normally used for products issued in such a small quantity as half a kilo. "Croutons Max," flavored to taste like black caviar, available at another Russian food store in Germany is advertised with a picture on the product's package along with a portrayal of a plate filled with black caviar with a big spoon inside (picture 5:18). And, the advertisement of the Russian food store Zarendom [Tsar temple, Ger.] (picture 5:19) echoes scenes from a very well-known Soviet film: A person is picturegraphed seated in front of mountains of red caviar, eating from a huge bowl filled with red caviar with a soup spoon. The caption reads: "It's so delicious you can eat a pail!"

Comparative analysis: Germany—Israel

By employing the ideal images of unlimited, exaggerated consumption of elitist (even Tsarist) caviar, all these examples correspond with the content/message of the picture (5:3) mentioned at the beginning of the chapter. There we see with a sentence written in letters composed of small black caviar against the background of red caviar roes that states: "Life has been a success!" Despite an initial impression of the one-dimensional nature of the statement about life's success by means of caviar, this picture (as well as all the others presented above) is especially significant when connected to the experience of immigration and the transformations it has entailed. There seems to be a symbolic contradiction in framing success as the realization of the ideal Soviet dream of material richness and a shouting for joy about "falling greedily" into the arms of the long-desired but now "real" unlimited material abundance in the land of capitalism. Equally important is the hidden message of this picture: The controversy over achieving "life success" in a state of migration and the problematic socio-economic position of migrants in the new receiving societies, where the absolute majority of them do not work in their original professions, do not receive appropriate social recognition, and have very limited material resources. This seems to be addressing the issue of contested measures of life success and missed actual richness that contribute to the use of a compensation mechanism of ideal ideas about caviar and its practical consumption. Thus, ironically, this picture is a mirror image of the Soviet promise of future abundance, and caviar stands as a *delectable token* for all that has been and is still missed after migration.

According to sales clerks in the small Russian food stores in Haifa, the shop sells an average a kilo of caviar every day. This is an enormous amount of this product considering that a kilo of caviar is expensive, costing at the time of the field study 200 NIS. Hence it is not a basic food, but a delicacy. Yet, it is being consumed by an immigrant population whose income is very low in comparison with the local population (Kogan and Cohen 2005). Also worth bearing in mind is that there were at least 30 similar Russian food stores in Haifa at the time of the fieldwork, where caviar was a "stable" product presumably sold daily. In comparison, in Germany, one kilo of caviar costs an average of 35—40 Euros in Russian food stores and here too it is very popular among Russian-speaking migrants.

From my fieldwork in Israel and Germany, I was able to establish that post-migration consumption of caviar increased noticeably, even though most migrants have low incomes in their new country of residence. Indeed, the high price of this delicacy did not inhibit purchase, even by participants supported by the social welfare system—the majority in the German case study. Caviar is frequently consumed not only at New Year's or special celebrations, but admittedly for the first time as part of a weekend breakfast by most participants. And, it may also be offered in meals offered to guests at meals, something that was never the case in the SU.

Nonetheless, the original status of this symbol remains unchanged, according to my field work. At one birthday party (in Israel), for example, all the dishes were arranged in a self–service buffet, except for the bread with caviar that was served by the hostess directly onto the plates of every guest without asking whether he or she wanted it (i.e. she assumed that everyone always likes and wants caviar, but decided that there would only be one serving per guest). The last slice of bread with caviar was given to the smallest child (a second piece) reinforcing the logic with which every guest could agree—"give children the best."

On the other hand, caviar acquired new symbolic signifying elements in the praxis of immigrants (in addition to richness, prosperity, higher standard of living, and power). As a compensative, empowering mechanism, caviar symbolizes the struggle against the low social and economic position of immigrants as a group, who are in comparison with the settled dominant groups deprived of power to a certain degree in the new society (in Israel but especially in Germany). As an illusory image of a life without worries, caviar disguises to an extent numerous, diverse difficulties that newly arrived immigrants[127] experience as outsiders or to some extent as "marginal men" (Stonequist 1935) and women.

Two episodes support the claim that caviar consumption served as a compensation mechanism. The first episode took place during my fieldwork in Israel. In referring to Israeli herring salad (called in Hebrew Íkra—picture 5:20—which sounds very similar to the Russian word for caviar—Ikrá) Nikolai said: "This Íkra is *their* [resident Israeli] Ikrá." Meaning: This herring salad is what "they" eat as poor substitute for "our" cultivated tradition of caviar.

The second episode occurred during one of my home visits in the German participant observation study. Olga told me that she orders caviar from Hamburg when she finds nine friends [who split the cost], as there one kilo costs only Euro30 and delivery is free.

JB: "Is that a Russian food store there in Hamburg?"

Olga: "Sure, Germans do not buy caviar."

JB: "Why not?"

---

127 Also, after several years of the living in the new country, in comparison with the time they have spent in the land of origin.

Olga: "Because they don't know their way around in this [matter] and cannot afford it themselves. It is too expensive for them. They save money for their pension."

Designated to occupy non-qualified, low-paying positions in Israel and as qualified candidates for social service support in the German case, the low income of participants obviously contradicts purchasing such an expensive delicacy. Hence, consumption of caviar by this population shows that cost does not play the most important role in the consumption process. In purchasing "their" (Russian) caviar, immigrants not only affirm their special claim to living a refined cultural-elitist cuisine, they join—if only symbolically—the elite group of the powerful.

Furthermore, to be able to demonstrate the capability to afford consumption of the most powerful symbol of wealth seems to be a particularly illustrative way of demonstrating—above all to themselves and to those who share and participate in this symbolic system—the improvement in their economic situation in comparison to their pre-migration lives in the SU. This attempt can be seen in an especially clear manner when immigrants host relatives and friends from the CIS to whom they can demonstrate that they have successfully settled into the capitalist society of abundance by offering them the most desired delicacies, such as caviar, anchovy, salmon, smoked bacon, or sturgeon. Caviar above all seems to project the most powerful of symbolic images as this is a product "which they [the Israelis or Germans] don't know their way around" or that "'they' cannot afford themselves." This is a decisive reason for purchasing this product, alongside other arguments like pleasure, price, habit, health or taste.

Given such a context, I disagree with the assumption adopted in the research conducted by Fishler that a person [not necessary in regard to migrants but in general] will attempt to uphold the tradition of dietary habits and maintain "normative rationality in food consumption" (Fischler 1980, 290—1). Alternatively, one could assume that there are different levels of "normative rationality;" *normative economic rationality* as well as *cultural normative rationality.* Indeed, the second option may have a more significant function in some special contexts—for example in migration—as it retrieves—if only symbolically—their past respectable social status and struggles symbolically against their current problematic economic status. Thus, paradoxical as it may seem, migrants may be habitual consumers at open-air markets where fruits and vegetables are less expensive, but they will pay Euro30 per kilo for caviar in a Russian shop (costing them one fifth of their monthly social support) or prepare a festive table laden with a vast array of foods, yet represent themselves as ascetics who contrast their own spirituality with the hedonistic celebrations of their hosts.

5.4 Mixed national identities in Russian food stores in Israel and Germany

Thus far, two directions within transnational praxis have been addressed. First, the meaning of two food key symbols—pork and caviar—has been analyzed through their changing role in transnational praxis after crossing national borders through the act of immigration from the SU to Israel and Germany. Second, a visual reflection of the Russian national revival has been presented, as it has appeared on the shelves of Russian food stores in Israel and Germany, where Russian products receive different meanings that sometimes contradict other national narratives.

This leads us to ask—in what degree are "Russian food stores" in Israel or Germany "Russian?" That is, apart from the simplified ascription "Russian," as different ex-Soviet groups and enclaves are often labeled by non-Russian speakers, this analysis makes it incumbent to consider the meaning of the content of the word *Russian* in the framework of Russian food stores: What meanings do Russian food stores have in the sense of ethnicity? Is it legitimate to consider this framework as the traditional ethnic business of migrants?

Fundamentally, by satisfying the needs and habits of its population, the Russian-speaking enclave in general and Russian food stores in particular are a form of transnational self-positioning and means of coping with a number of challenges: the new socio-cultural environment, the new economic system with its various forms of abundance and transformations in their society of origin. Accordingly, it would be a mistake to assume that Russian food stores only sell Russian food. Looking more closely, one can see that within this framework consumers are exposed to a wide variety of symbols from different cultures and even nations, incorporated in this framework. Accordingly, the combination of different worlds within the food store presents what I have identified as seven possible *worlds of meaning* observed in these settings:

First, the *Jewish Diaspora meal*—including ingredients as well as prepared dishes, for example: gefillte fish, *farshmak* herring salad, *pashtet* liver cream, *roglach*—sweet rolls with chocolate and raisins, *kneidlach* [dumplings] were present especially in Israeli Russian food stores, but also in certain German Russian food stores.

Second, in the case of the Israeli national Zionist Jewish state, there was an expectation that Russian speakers would become members of the dominant Jewish group, at least on the level of the official nation-building policy. And, indeed, Russian stores incorporated many different Israeli food articles—such as hummus, eggplant salad, *tehina* [sesame paste], *burekas* [puff pastry with cheese or vegetable filling], couscous grains [rolled semolina] and *ikra* salad—that have come to symbolize a multicultural culinary integration that has been evolving over 60 years of immigration into an emerging national cuisine. Also, many of the products consumed by the general Israeli population were available in Russian food stores with labels translated into the Russian language.

Third, different products produced in Israel or imported from Russia that employ symbols of Zionism or the Jewish religion and that are oriented to Russian-speaking consumers were found in both contexts but especially in Israel, such as: the Israeli flag on a package of coffee (picture 4:94); depiction of Jews praying at the Western Wall on a box of chocolates (picture 4:19); a street scene from the Jewish Quarter in the Old City of Jerusalem on a bread label (picture 4:13); or subtle references to the Zionist settlement in Israel through depictions of Jewish Israelis harvesting wheat on a bread package (picture 4:11). In the German case study, there were few Jewish religious symbols associated with foods in Russian food stores and no Zionist symbols.

Two examples of vodkas with Russian labels found in Russian food stores are illuminating this third point. One is a bottle of vodka (picture 5:21) produced in Russia that portrays an elderly orthodox Jew with wide-brimmed hat, *peyot* [sidelocks, Heb.] with a blue Star of David drawn above his head. The accompanying text is written in Revolutionary font style letters, formerly used in SU media to report about communist activities: "*Star of David* (in red), *Luxury Vodka, product of Russia.*" Another Jewish vodka, also produced in Russia (picture 5:22—23), portrays a synagogue, a menorah, two stamps of kosher approval (one by the main Israeli Rabbi Avraham Kahan Shapiro). The label on the back of the bottle is written in Russian and displays—to my surprise—a picture of the late Lubavich

Rabbi identified as belonging to the "Brooklyn Diaspora Foundation of New York headed by Rabbi Yehuda Laib Groner" (the late Lubavitch Rebbe's assistant for many years). At the bottom of the label is the Hebrew signature of Rabbi Yehuda Laib Groner and the producers' Russian harvest logo printed in red letters, accompanied by a Soviet symbol of wheat sheaves.

Fourth, many products from different republics of the former Soviet Union were found in both contexts. Being no longer part of a big empire, these independent countries are appropriating new images as they undergo their own nationalistic processes. Symbols involved in these processes became part of the immigrants' transnational praxis. For example, there is hot sauce, brandy, and wine produced in Georgia (previously mentioned, picture 3:2; 5:24) (I and G); Armenian brandy including the country's national symbol—Mt. Ararat on the label (picture 5:25) (I and G); Latvian sweets—Melodies of old Riga (picture 5:26) (I); sunflower oil and pepper vodka from the Ukraine with the national symbol—a bison (picture 5:27) (I); Ukrainian national vodka *Horilka* (picture 5:28) (I and G) Ukrainian buckwheat "The best national product" (picture 5:29—30) (I and G); Spartak chocolates with national Belarus symbols—Belarus forest and Belarus bison (picture 5:31) (I); different Moldavian wines "All the best from Moldavia" (picture 5:32) and cherry chocolates (I and G); Lithaunian sweetened condensed milk (picture 5:33) (I); Kazakhstani chocolates The Songs of Abai (Kazakhstan national poet) with his portrait or Kazakhstani sausage (pictures 5:34—35) (G); and *Manty* [dumplings] from Uzbekistan and Kazakhstan. Especially interesting is the example of hot sauce *Dzhigit* [image of a Georgian horseman and hothead] made in Bulgaria and sold in Israel and Germany (picture 5:36) (I and G).

Fifth, Russian food stores sell products from different countries throughout the world, such as: French white cheese (picture 5:37) (I): American Star mayonnaise (picture 5:38) (I); Italian spaghetti, English or Indian tea (pictures 5:39—40) (I and G); Scottish breakfast tea prepared in Sri Lanka and imported from the Ukraine (picture 5:41) (I); Bulgarian sauce, Hungarian salami, Ukrainian Japanese pear juice (5:42) (I); Slavic beer from the Czech Republic (picture 5:43) (G); Bulgarian and Hungarian marinated vegetables (pictures 5:44—45) (I and G); Polish bonbons, chocolates, and marmalades (pictures 5:46—7) (I and G); Dutch sweetened condensed milk (picture 5:48) (I and G); and so forth. Usually, these are not arbitrarily selected products, but rather a kind of mixture consisting of

Pic. 5:21 "Star of David" (in red), luxury vodka, product of Russia (G)

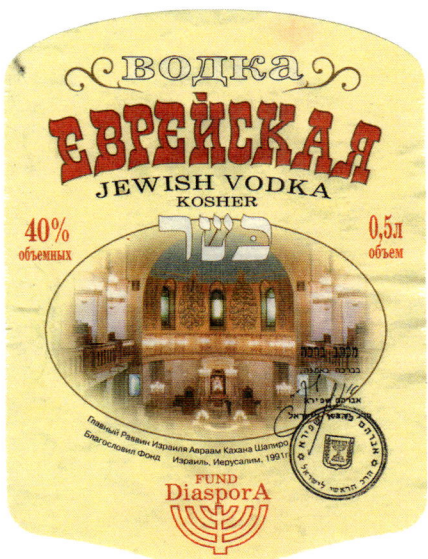

Pic. 5:22 Jewish vodka (G)

Pic. 5:23 Back side of Jewish vodka bottle with a photo of the late Lubavich Rabbi, issued by the Diaspora Foundation Brooklyn New York presented to Rabbi Yehuda Laib Groner (G)

Pic. 5:25 Armenian brandy displaying Mt. Ararat (I, G)

Pic. 5:24 Georgian brandy "Tbilisi" (I)

Pic. 5:26 Latvian sweets "Melodies of old Riga" (I)

Pic. 5:27 Pepper vodka from the Ukraine with national Ukrainian symbol—a bison (I)

Pic. 5:28 Ukrainian national vodka "Horilka" (I, G)

Pic. 5:29 Ukrainian buckwheat (I, G)

Pic. 5:30 Ukrainian buckwheat "The best national product" (I, G)

Pic. 5:31 "Spartak" chocolate with national Belarus symbols—Belarus forest and Belarus bison (I)

Pic. 5:32 Moldavian wines from the series "All the best from Moldavia" (I, G)

Pic. 5:33 Lithuanian sweetened condensed milk (I)

Pic. 5:34 Kazakhstan chocolates "The songs of Abai" with the portrait of national Kazakhstan poet (G)

Pic. 5:35 Kazakhstan sausage (G)

Pic. 5:36 Hot sauce „Dzhigit" [image of Georgian horseman and hothead] produced in Bulgaria (I, G)

Pic. 5:38 "American star" mayonnaise (I)

Pic. 5:37 French white cheese "Paris Cow" (I)

Pic. 5:39 "English Royal Tea" (I, G)

Pic. 5:40 Indian tea "Safari" (I, G)

Pic. 5:41 Scottish breakfast tea produced in Sri Lanka and imported from the Ukraine (I)

Pic. 5:42 "Japanese pear" juice produced in the Ukraine (I)

Pic. 5:43 "Slavic" beer from the Czech Republic (G)

Pic. 5:44 Bulgarian marinated vegetables (I, G)

Pic. 5:46 Polish bonbons "Cow" (I, G)

Pic. 5:45 Hungarian marinated vegetables (I, G)

Pic. 5:47 Polish jam "Konfitura" (I)

Pic. 5:48 Sweetened condensed Dutch milk "Varya" (I, G)

what for Russian speakers are new foods that have globally received a status as recognizable national signifiers (Welz 2000) and those that attained popularity and were sought earlier in the SU (e.g., Bulgarian sauce, Bulgarian marinated tomatoes, Polish bonbons, Hungarian salami, or Indian tea). Such globalized and national signifiers (ibid) that embody "positive ethnic stereotypes" (Appadurai 1988, 18) represent the myth of the melting pot. This is especially evident in culinary matters (ibid., 20). Still, for the participants, symbolic participation in the globalized world through consumption was very meaningful as it epitomizes their liberation from the closed totalitarian Soviet system through the act of migration which enabled this participation.

Sixth, these stores also sell products from contemporary, nationalized Russia as well as products from the CIS advertised in Russian-speaking programs broadcasted from these countries. These are products that their friends and relatives who have not emigrated often cannot afford for themselves. Consequently, in these cases, they represent a reference group that enables participants to assess who has greater economic resources and enjoys a better standard of life. Labels from the products available in both contexts reveal that some refer to popular Russian cooking programs, such as *Tasty Hysterias, Women's City, From a Woman's Life,* or *Smak* [Passion Food, Rus.] including pictures of presenter Andrei Makarevich (picture 5:49) (I and G). A juice has a picture from another popular entertainment program *Moya Semya* [My Family] (picture 5:50) (I and G); Pole Tchudes Chocolate [Magic field, named after the popular entertainment program Pole Tchudes with its presenter Leonid Yakubovitch] (picture 5:51) (I); a bottle of chili sauce with a picture on the label of the prominent standup comedian Vladimir Vinokur (picture 5:52) (I); and, *Verka* Mayonnaise displays Andrei Danilko in his well-known role dressed as an Ukrainian women named Verka Serduchka (picture 5:53) (I). These products also illustrate a form of transnational, border-crossing life purchasing and consuming that enables immigrants to participate in contemporary Russian cultural life at a distance. This category includes all manners of nationalizing processes taking place in contemporary Russia, mentioned in the previous chapter, when people *taste nationalism* from abroad, after the voluntary act of immigration. This group of products gives consumption a different meaning in terms of being a symbolic marker of cultural Russianness and virtual participation in ongoing processes in Russia.

Pic. 5:49 Advertisement of food products with a label of the popular entertainment program "Smak" [Passion Food, Rus.] with its presenter Andrei Makarevich (I)

Pic. 5:50 Juice with a photo from the popular entertainment program "Moya Semya" [My Family, Rus.] (I, G)

Pic. 5:52 Label on bottle of chili sauce with a photo of prominent stand-up comedian Vladimir Vinokur (I)

Pic. 5:53 "Verka Mayonnaise" with photo of Andrei Danilko in his well-known role dressed as an Ukrainian women named Verka Serduchka (I)

Pic. 5:51 Chocolate "Pole Tchudes" [Magic Field, Rus.]. named after the popular entertainment program "Pole Tchudes" with its presenter Leonid Yakubovitch (I)

Pic. 5:55 Advertisement of foods available for New Year's festivities in the Russian food store "Laguna" (I)

Pic. 5:54 "Russian" shelves in the regular German supermarket "Rewe"

Seventh, there is an abundance of the most sought for and prestigious products in the Soviet empire, which no longer exists, as well as so-called Soviet "proletarian" foods, both discussed in the previous chapter. This last point can be treated as a kind of creation of an "imaginary space" (Dolve-Gandelman 1990) and life in the symbolically realized terms of the promised wealthy communist society abroad.

Simultaneously, some products popular among the Russian-speaking population and marketed, initially, in Russian food stores exclusively have spread to regular Israeli and German supermarkets where they are shelved together with other products (e.g., Kefir Malinka in Germany or *Tvorog* [white cheese, Rus. in Israel] and sometimes on a special shelf as Russian products within a multicultural range of food articles from different countries symbolizing the global expanse of taste tendencies. The latter tends to be the case in Israel, where the Tiv Ta'am supermarket chain realizes its logo—"taste from around the world"—by having the richest selection of global foods. The tendency in Germany is to display global products on shelves dedicated to different cultures in the Wall Markt, Rewe and Kaufhof supermarkets. These *Russian shelves* usually display such products as: sweet concentrated milk, chocolates, and other sweet articles—*sefir* and *pryaniki*, marmalade, fruit juices, fish and vegetable products, buckwheat, *pel'meni* [pasta squares filled with meat, Rus.], wines, and of course vodka (picture 5:54).

The variety of products available in Russian stores does not stress, explicitly, the exotic nature of foreign food products from far away countries as is usually the case in regular supermarkets and delicatessen shops in Israel and Germany. Rather, Russian food stores embody the interplay of what is desired and prized by former Soviet residents—namely an accessible, open, and globalized world with an abundance of reliable products.

Numerous advertisements by Russian food stores (in Israel and Germany) epitomize the mix of all seven trends elicited above, so that they cannot be separated from each other or reduced to the oversimplified label "Russian." The following list of products in an advertisement of foods available for New Year festivities in the Russian food store Laguna in Jerusalem (picture 5:55) is exemplary of different examples of multicultural, global fare found in the field study, listed by product, quantity, and price in Israeli shekels (NIS):

– red caviar, 100 grams, 15—90 NIS
– schnitzel [Hebrew word written in Russian letters] 16.90 NIS/kg

- French champagne—Paul Remit, 2 bottles for 50 NIS
- Odessa champagne, 1 bottle—29.90 NIS, 2 bottles—50 NIS
- Hungarian champagne, 2 bottles, 50 NIS
- Soviet champagne, 1 bottle—20 NIS, 2 bottles—35 NIS (if total purchase of foods is over 200 NIS
- Finland vodka—54.90 NIS

In summary, the different images mentioned in the present and previous chapter demonstrate the multiple, hybrid, and sometimes fragmented identities and transnational frontier-crossing character of the Russian food store in Israel and Germany. The range and variety of dishes and food products available confirms, in my view, the general tendency analyzed in the literature on "transnational living" (Guarnizo 2003; Olwig and Nyberg Sorensen 2002; Smith 2001); "mobile livelihoods or fluid fields" (Olwig and Sorensen 2002); and "transnationalism from below."[128] Indeed, this is the case even if constructed within the Russian-speaking enclave, which may appear at first glance to be a closed space. In this case, the Russian language not only becomes the "collective marker of identification in forming social networks" (Darieva 2000, 2) but its use also supports the illusion of a homogeneous Russian (ethnic) identity that does not really exist. Accommodation of immigrant demands for familiar, desired goods and the increasing geographic expansion of circles of Russian food consumers abroad entice entrepreneurs in CIS countries to export to a new transnational global market that presupposes extensive social networks. However, rather than consider immigrant entrepreneurship solely as a form of economic adaptation (e.g., Portes, Haller and Guarnizo 2001) or participation of migrants in the receiving society via consumption, we can chose to view Russian enclaves as a 'transnational space' in which identities are constructed, reconstructed, presented, and negotiated through social interaction of immigrants as consumers and entrepreneurs, and where transnational symbols are acquired via these articles.

Today most immigrants are involved in some kind of transnational space and transnational activity.[129] Indeed, transnational practices can be seen as a kind of active coping with economic and political globalization.[130] In fact, the regular consumption practices that take place in Russian food

---

128 See Guarnizo and Smith (1998); Portes (1999); Smith (1998).
129 See Appadurai (1990, 1993); Basch et al (1994); Portes (2001).
130 See Appadurai (1996); Morawska (2003).

stores, as well as, in watching Russian TV broadcasts and reading the Russian press engage most immigrants as active everyday participants in the practice of a transnational lifestyle in transnational space via a transnational enterprise. In doing so, they are participants in the design of this space without necessarily being entrepreneurs themselves. Thus, transnational stores not only play an important role in the process of the circulation of images between the country of origin and the receiving country,[131] they are also significant in the further development of the multicultural transnational societal design.

5.5 Reconsidering the immigrant enterprise: From traditional, closed ethnic business toward a *virtual transnational enclave*

As noted at the beginning of this chapter, the concept of *transnational entrepreneurship* usually refers to transnational economic action, which is a special form of immigrant remittances to the sending society or investment by emigrants in the original country. Immigrant enterprise in the reception country is usually referred to as "ethnic business" or "ethnic entrepreneurship;"[132] that is, one representing a larger phenomenon of a language conditioned "ethnic enclave" of migrant group in the receiving society. In contrast, I claim that, in the case of Russian stores in Israel and Germany, we are dealing with a form of transnational enterprise in the respective receiving country, that is, one that is not solely ethnic Russian.

Russian-speaking entrepreneurship differs in a number of key characteristics from the conventional ethnic entrepreneurial niche (Razin and Schlinberg 2001). First, demographically, entrepreneurs are usually not older than 40 and do not have extensive kinship networks (ibid). They have also been found to have small families and limited economic resources, but do have a high level of educational and human capital stock (ibid). This is especially evident in situations noted in the fieldwork when some clerks in Russian food stores in Israel and Germany addressed one another patronymically (i.e., not by first name only but combined with the father's personal name). This is a common form of polite address in Rus-

---

131 According to Mankekar (2005).
132 For this differentiation see for example Guarnizo (2003).

sian that was not characteristic in usual communication between clerks in SU food stores. This may point to a hierarchical work relationship otherwise absent between two clerks or be a way of speaking among intelligent, educated Russian speaking stratum. This is an interesting strategy, one that manifested and stressed an actual societal attachment of migrants who were unemployed in their original profession.

In the Israeli case, Russian speakers make up 20 percent of the Jewish Israeli population and, therefore, do not consider themselves to be a weak minority group. All these factors distinguish them from the usual ethnic entrepreneurship of immigrants, who are normally men over 40 (by which age they have saved resources for their own business) with extensive kinship and social networks and without higher educational qualifications brought from the original country (ibid).

Second, collectively, Russian food stores create a kind of *transnational field*, in which individuals cope with a new national local reality as well as with the globalization phenomenon, and reconstruct and negotiate collective identities. This complex process takes place through familiar and shared social codes and cultural symbolic means. Thus, simultaneously, consumers purchase many products produced in the CIS and in doing so they influence to a certain degree economic and social developments in their country of origin. Thus, although they are not physically in the country of origin, many (especially in the German context) are closely connected to present-day Russia (Ukraine or any other CIS country) through the purchase of new articles, which they become aware of through advertisements in translated programs.

The tendency in the modern Western society to long for a confidential community, for isolated "safety spaces with control,"[133] and for closed homogeneous groups, even if illusionary (Schroer 2004) is special, actual, and necessary for newcomers exposed to a completely new, heterogeneous and anonymous society. In this process, food stores appear to be a familiar world to Russian-speaking consumers. Russian food stores serve as a kind of small, apparently safe Russian-speaking community-oriented space, within which transnational identities are created and references to different "social worlds" (Schütze 2002) and images are possible. Within this framework they are not forced to define themselves, to resist their image as

---

133 See Goffman (1963).

foreigners, or to challenge stereotypes about Russians in Israel or Germany.

Third, my empirical work confirms the recently emphasized possibility of simultaneity, coexistence, and incorporation of immigrant transnationalism and certain assimilation (Morawska 2003, 2004; Levitt 2001) in the receiving society. In the Israeli and German contexts, cultural symbols penetrate the Russian store and people internalize these "social worlds" through their physical presence and active participation in the new society. Compared with those who stay 'behind' in the society of origin, we are dealing with a transformed group of immigrants who are constantly changing, including seeing events in the CIS from their present position as Israeli or German citizens. In doing so, they also influence globalization and economic transformations that are evolving in their society of origin.[134]

Fourth, the term "transnational livelihoods" (Olwig and Sorensen 2002) or "transnational living" or "space" (Guarnizo 2003; Olwig and Nyberg Sorensen 2002; Smith 2001) may also reflect active but only partial membership in two or more societies, as in the case of immigrants in Germany who are confronted with three reference nations—the CIS, Israel, and Germany—and who do not feel fully part of the collective identity of any nation, be it in the CIS, in Israel, and certainly not in Germany. In that sense the transnational space may be, simultaneously, a form of *in-between state-of-mind*, space, or a permanent "liminal state" (Turner 1986) in which multiple social worlds are reproduced. The simultaneous process of transnational practices and assimilation or cultural and social involvement in every context crystallizes the degree of foreignness in every space ("There we were Jews, here we are Russians") and distinguishes their collective national identity from local identity in Israel, Germany, and the CIS. The enclave marks them as noticeably different from local groups. At the same time, frequently, they express strikingly different perceptions, positions, and problems from those of their friends who remained in the CIS and with whom they remain in contact, often in intensive contact. It seems that this particular form of transnational entrepreneurship is neither an isolated phenomenon nor an "ephemeral activity" (Guarnizo 2003) of an individual enterprise. Rather, it can be located and analyzed via globaliza-

---

134 For the transnationalism of those who remain, see especially Golberg (2001); Levitt (2004).

tion and a boundary-crossing discourse that relates to immigrant livelihoods in different countries of the world.

Fifth, with respect to political myths about national collective identity
(especially Jewish identity as a part of nation-building processes in Israel),
transnational activities initiated and practiced by immigrants can be seen by
the dominant group (which actually controls the key positions in the society) as undesirable and even hostile, even when the official policy legitimates multicultural lifestyles.

Finally, before concluding, I would like to point out two main differences between Russian food stores as transnational enclaves in Israel and
Germany. First, as discussed in the previous chapter, the "Russian street"
(as it is referred to in the Russian-speaking media) has significantly different visibility in Israel in comparison with Germany. Whereas in Israel,
stickers, labels, and signs in Russian have become an inevitable part of the
local public landscape, they are still rare in Germany. In Israel, boundaries
between dominant groups and Russian speakers are symbolically blurred
through the mixing of Russian and Hebrew letters on the store signs.
However, Russian food stores in Germany are invisible; that is they are
undistinguishable from their German counterparts from the outside. In
this regard they seem to have an additional role as a secure asylum for
Russian-speaking immigrants. Additionally, whereas Russian food stores in
Israel can serve as a public forum open to social participation (even given
the own terms of the group that may seem to be illegitimate to resident
Israelis), in Germany Russian food store serves various groups—Russian-
speaking Jews as well as Russian-speaking resettled ethnic Germans who
have a status of marginalized minority.

Second, especially in the Israeli case, a physical pendulum between CIS
and Israel is absent in transnational practice. From a distance, the virtuality
of the transnational character of this framework is more evident in the
Israeli context as participants in the German case visit their relatives and
friends in CIS more frequently than their Israeli compatriots, who usually
prefer to use their holidays for vacationing in Europe rather than in Russia
or the Ukraine. Moreover, many Israeli participants no longer possess
Russian citizenship. This makes the virtual nature of transnational action
undertaken in Russian food stores all the more important. Still, the consumption process within Russian stores in both contexts represents forms
of participation from a physical distance that relativizes the national Rus-

sian patriotism of ex-citizens who voluntary emigrated to Israel or Germany.

Thus, *virtual transnationalism* seems to be an alternative kind of transnational activity, one that makes it unnecessary to visit Russia. These stores offer consumers an opportunity to touch, experience, and even participate in changes in current Russia despite the physical distance. This *virtual transnational enclave* seems to include the contradictions that exist within this framework: On the one hand, openness and incorporation of new and multiple national, multicultural, and globalized elements; and, on the other hand, simultaneously, the enclaves are strongly conditioned and influenced by the Russian language and Soviet cultural baggage. Rather than encapsulating people in the cultural "ghetto" in the "Russian street," Russian food stores serve as a virtual transnational enclave that combine the intimate with pervasive globalized elements; when entrepreneurs and consumers make their own way by choosing their own path for settling-in and struggling for recognition through their own cultural and educational resources.

6 Transjewish affiliation: The construction of ethnicity by Russian-speaking Jews in Israel and Germany

The primary goal of this chapter is to examine the different contents of Soviet Jewishness as transported, reconstructed, and performed by the participants in their narrative descriptions, in different conversations during participant observations, as well as, in the interviews. The substance of such Jewishness is of special interest given the complex reality faced while living in the SU: On the one hand, they could not escape, reject, or hide their Jewish attachment because their passport stamp identified them as Jews. And, at the same time, for almost 70 years, Soviet policies placed strict limits on the practice of the Jewish culture, languages, traditions, or religion.

A combination of diverse factors created a unique situation that shaped the content of Soviet Jewish identity, such that it differs in significant ways from Jewish identities that developed in Israel and other Diaspora countries. In order to understand their views, the investigation focused on the participants' concept of *Jewish ethnicity* and sought to attain two primary goals. First, to understand the participants' perceptions as well as ways of active living; as in "how do people live their ethnicity?"(Lenz 2007) or how people accomplish "doing of being Jewish?" (Inowlocki 2000). This analysis was based on Inowlocki's assumption who claimed, in analyzing anti-Semitism, racism, and the reaction to immigration, that "the reconstruction of individual cases demonstrate social and political dimensions as structural conditions of action and suffering" [Ger.].[135]

Accordingly, this investigation analyzed how constructions of Jewish ethnicity relate to local ideas about ethnicity and Jewishness in Israel and Germany, as well as, traced the changes in the "doing of being Jewish" (Inowlocki 2000) that evolved in new and different societal contexts.

---

135 "… dass gerade die Rekonstruktion von Einzelfällen gesellschaftliche und politische Dimensionen als strukturelle Bedingungen von Handeln und Erleiden aufsteigen kann" Inowlocki (2003, 226).

The second primary goal of the analysis presented in this chapter is to understand how constructions of Jewish ethnicity, as described and activated by participants in different ways, correspond with local ideas about Jewishness in the two new contexts of Israel and Germany. In doing so, the investigation answers a broader question: How, after transversing the national borders of the CIS to Israel or Germany, are the different, taken for granted, personal ideas and common knowledge of Soviet, Israeli, or German Jews used to answer the question—What does it mean to be Jewish?

This chapter begins with the presentation of the key assumptions regarding ethnicity that guided this research. This is followed by a description of the concept *ethnicity* as related to Russian-speaking Jews. The primary findings are presented in the form of four central components involved in construction of *Jewishness* that were transported and developed in the new context: First, the Soviet ideas of *innate Jewishness* and *visible Otherness*, including their construction and contradiction in comparison with local Israeli and German ideas about ethnicity that migrants confronted following migration. Second, construction and stigmatization of *significant Jewish Otherness* that utilizes different anti-Semitic strategies (e.g., ascription of negative features to Jews, being Jewish as a form of pollution, the stigmatization of Jewish names, guttural "r" associated with Jews, and creation of swearwords in Russian language related to Jews), and "complimentary" coping strategies developed by Jews while living in the SU and after migration to Israel and Germany. The ethnization process analyzed includes participants' descriptions of "stigmatized" Jewish identity and its modification in Israel and Germany. *Emotional attachment to the State of Israel*, the third component of Russian speaking Jewish identity, functioned as an exclusion mechanism during the participants' lives in the SU and assumed different dimensions and directions following migration to Germany. The final component of Russian-speaking Jewishness—a paradoxical form of *being Jewish through affiliation with the Soviet Russian cultural elite*—underwent transformation following the migration to Israel and Germany. The summary discussion of these four components, as they developed in two different contexts—in Israel and Germany, focuses Russian-speaking Jews' *triple transjewish affiliation*.

6.1 The "ethnicity" and ethnization processes of Russian-speaking Jews

A vast literature on ethnicity and ethnization has developed over the last 15 years. Among the central issues studied are the discrimination of minorities by majority groups and receiving societies' responses to migrant groups. Drawing upon this literature, the central concern of this study is the identification of nationalism with ethnicity, in general, and its special role in ex-socialist states, in particular; including crucial reorientation processes as well as the frequent neo-traditionalist and ethno-religious connections that emerge in this process (Calloni 1999). Furthermore, we examine how the concept of ethnicity assists us to understand the investigated group, in particular from the *emic* perspective (i.e. what meaning Jewish ethnicity has for participants) and how their views can be compared *etically* (i.e. the theoretical view of this topic)? For example, if the participants feel they are part of the Jewish ethnic minority, they might also experience the surrounding society's conceptualization of ethnicity as "the affirmation of the 'great Slavic-orthodox nation'" (Calloni 1999, 121) or ethnization as "reinforcement of the imperial regime" (Lerner 2006, 16) as is the case for Russia today.

This study adopted Weber's perspective, developed in 1922, that stressed the subjective belief which lies at the core of ethnicity in reference to the original common reference community left in the past. In this regard, Weber stressed the cultural constructive nature of the concept of ethnicity: "einerlei, ob eine Blutsgemeinsamkeit objektiv vorliegt oder nicht" [lit: all the same, if there is objective evidence of common blood connection or not, Ger.].[136] In doing so, he developed a derivative subjective question: Does such a connection serve to establish one's *own we-feeling* and feeling of being *different* or *the Other they-feeling*? In other words, ethnicity serves as a strong resource of demarcation or categorization (Zurawski 2000) [i.e., one affiliates oneself to a certain ethnic group]

---

136 "Wir wollen solche Menschengruppen, welche auf Grund von Ähnlichkeiten des äußeren Habitus oder der Sitten oder beider oder von Erinnerungen an Kolonisation und Wanderung einen subjektiven Glauben an eine Abstammungsgemeinsamkeit hegen, derart, dass dieser für die Propagierung von Vergemeinschaftungen wichtig wird, dann, wenn sie nicht ,Sippen' darstellen, ,ethnische' Gruppen nennen, ganz einerlei, ob eine Blutsgemeinsamkeit objektiv vorliegt oder nicht" (Weber 1922, 237).

"through birth. Nothing has to be done, as one cannot acquire affiliation with this group, and the collective uniqueness of the great past and future can be enjoyed, as guaranteed through the ethnic myth" [Ger.].[137]

One of the fundamental assumptions of this study is that ethnicity is constructed. Accordingly, even though ethnic attachment is usually assumed by the participants to be *natural, immanent, self-evident, omnipresent,* and *taken for granted,* all beliefs are the result of social and political processes, constructed through ascriptions that over time are internalized by the dominant group as well as by the ethnicized minority.[138]

Of particular importance in this study is the link between the concept of *foreigner* and ethnicity; that is, the case when Others are perceived and presented as being "different by nature" (Colloni 1999). In many such cases, they are also perceived as threatening a given social order whose interests, too, are also politically constructed as objective and absolute (Schäffter 1991). Consequently, there may be cases in which the conceptualization of *foreign* can be interpreted as repressive "politically effective subliminal order performances" [Ger.].[139]

What are the components that comprise a sense of ethnic attachment? According to Zurawski, *ethnicity* consists of four factors: culture and language, self-description, personal experience, and foreign description (Zurawski 2000). As will be shown later, Russian-speaking Jews meet all of these criteria except culture and language. The majority of emigrants accepted their Jewish affiliation, but at the same time do not believe that it should necessarily be accompanied by their observance of traditions, culture, restrictions on food practices, or religious practices. They cultivate the Russian culture, but feel offended when perceived and/or presented in the media—overtly or implicitly—as Russians who are "not Jewish enough."[140]

Moreover, according to the findings in my study, a *new ethnicity* can be formed through transformative processes such as migration. Thus, what Others may refer to as *Russian-speaking Jewish ethnicity* may not correspond

---

137 "qua Geburt, man braucht nichts dafür zu tun, muß die Zugehörigkeit zur Gruppe nicht erwerben, kann die kollektive Einzigartigkeit einer großartigen Vergangenheit und Zukunft, die der ethnische Mythos garantieret, genießen" [Ger.] Stender (2000, 76).

138 For presentations of politically constructed concepts related to features of minorities, presented as natural, see—Calloni (1999); Gilman (1986); Inowlocki (2003); Welz (1994); Yuval Davis (2006).

139 "politisch wirksame *unterschwellige* Ordungsleistungen," (Schäffter, 1991, 15).

140 Regarding Israel, see Avraham et al (2004); Golden (2002). For Germany, see Becker (2003); Becker and Körber (2001); Darieva (2004); Körber (2005); Ostow (2003).

to, and may well contradict, the members own vision of their ethnic affiliation. Hence, ethnicity can be considered to be dynamic: part of a permanent redefinition and reconfirmation process that is a significant part of self-identity. As such, it is connected to what Anderson referred to as attachment to an "imagined community" (Anderson 1991). Surprisingly, in the case of ethnic affiliations, the secondary group's features are close to those usually held by the primary group (Heckman 1997 quoted by Stender 2000). That is, ethnic groups are characterized by having a

"strong 'we'-feeling; that is, a strong identification with the group, sense of emotionality and centrality of personal affiliation with the group, feelings of nearness, familiarity, along with close and durable relationships" [Ger.].[141]

Thus, in confirming the assumption that there is no one inclusive, contemporary form of Jewish identity (e.g., a presumed solely religious identity) (Webber 1994), the study elucidates different components of Russian-speaking Jewish ethnicity as it is constructed and presented by participants in two contexts.

Turning to historical-political developments that took place during the Soviet regime, the study traced the unique ways participants preserved and reconstructed their ethnic affiliations; despite, and perhaps in reaction to, strong Russification forced by the Soviet policy that was deeply internalized by many minorities, especially Soviet Jews. Given that there are approximately 150 million people in the world who speak Russian, this does not mean, necessarily, that all these people see themselves as part of a Russian ethnic group. During the Soviet period, many minority groups (and actually majorities in all republics apart from Russia) were forced to confront the Russification forced upon them that sought to achieve a "common Soviet ethnicity" (Voronkov 2000); or as Malachov stated—"their 'ethnicity' is Soviet" (Vladimir Malachov, cited by Lerner 2006, 15). Following Perestroika, Russificiation was often viewed as unpopular and all associations with Russia were rejected by many ex-Soviet minority groups.[142] Accordingly, many people whose mother language is Russian,

---

141 "starkes"Wir"-Gefühl und hohe Identifikation mit der Gruppe, Emotionalität und starke Zentralität der Einstellung zur Gruppe, Empfindungen von Nähe und Vertrautheit in den Beziehungen, Dauerhaftigkeit der Beziehungen" Heckman (1997, 47) quoted by Stender (2000, 74).
142 This strong reaction against the long period of forced Russian ethnicity followed Perestroika and the establishment of the independent states, accompanied by national conflicts within the former Soviet republics with Russians. As a result, after the Perestroika,

who actively practice Russian culture, and who view Russia (or CIS) as their primary home country would never identify themselves as *ethnic Russians*.[143] Indeed, in this sense, the findings of this study, achieved through the *emic* approach, suggest that Jews from the SU would never describe themselves as *ethnic Russians*, but rather as *ethnic Jews* who feel a strong sense of attachment to Russian culture.

Given that this concept had been completely deprived of its original cultural, traditional, religious content, what did Jewish ethnicity mean for Soviet Jews? That is, what other cultural, social and political meanings did this concept acquire? Scrutinizing their special case, it appears that a unique understanding of Jewish ethnic attachment developed. The four main components of this understanding are discussed in this chapter. Overall, the claim advanced is that the special case of Jews of Russian origin who migrated to Israel and Germany can be represented by a new concept to be explained in this chapter, namely, *Russian-speaking Jewish ethnicity*, or what will be referred to as *Russian speaking trans-Jewish ethnicity*. These terms are designed and confirmed through new reception contexts that build upon a transnational cross-border space that is connected to and corresponds with processes taking place in today's CIS, along with ethnic concepts that connect to relatives and friends still residing there with whom the migrants share intensive participation in social networks.

6.2 Component One: *Innate ethnicity* and *visible Otherness* and its fate abroad

Two different concepts of Jewishness developed in the Russian language: *Iudei* means religious Jew and *Yevrei* refers to *nationalnost'* Jew [nationality in the Soviet sense, analyzed below, Rus.]. At first glance, it may seem that the meanings of these terms extend those developed during Jewish eman-

---

Russians were assigned a new status within these republics (independent states) as an ethnic minority who were not only seriously oppressed but also frequently deprived of local citizenship (e.g., in the Baltic states).

143 This corresponds with findings of Chervyakov, Gitelman, and Shapiro (1997) about the ethnic consciousness of Jews in contemporary Russia, as well as, Ritterband (1997) who found that Russian-speaking Jews in the USA retain a strong affiliation to Russian culture but reject categorization as "Outsider" Russians.

cipation in 18th century Western Europe (i.e. religious affiliation to Judaism and ethnic affiliation to Jewishness) (Chervyakov, Gitelman and Shapiro 1997). However, in contrast to references to other Jews in the West, the ethnic affiliation of Jews in Russia was exclusively primordial in nature and lacked any cultural content. Thus, whereas the first concept (*Iudei*) was never used by Russian-speaking Jews self-descriptively, there was widespread use of *Yevrei* as the Soviet understanding of nationality and therefore did not assume any religious or traditional cultural praxis.[144]

Fundamentally, then, ex-Soviet Jewish migrants perceive their Jewishness as *vrozhdennaya nationalnost* [innate nationality, Rus.]. This self-referential concept assumes an innate primordial characteristic based on the idea of blood relations and accordingly is perceived as a subcategory of race. "[Being] a unique Soviet category established as a crucial category of ethnic classification" (Lerner 2006, 5), *nationalnost'* represents a special construction of "biological nationality" (Slezkine 2004), "biologic ancestry" (Oswald 2000) or "primordial ethnic consciousness" (Lerner 2006, 16) that migrants internalized early in their life in the SU.[145] As noted, during the atheistic period in the SU, Jewish affiliation was considered to be *nationalnost'* (in the framework of socialist national policy) rather than religious affiliation, as is the case in Germany. Independent of individual will, *nationalnost'* played an important role in the life of every citizen. This was especially the case in the lives of members of minorities, as their identity was easily recognized and identifiable due to legally required declarations found in state-issued identity cards. Accordingly, there was an ever-present potential that minorities could be excluded, limited, or discriminated against—as happened in the case of Jews. Slezkine captured this situation as follows:

'Every Soviet citizen was born into a certain nationality, carried it with him from daycare and through high school, had it officially confirmed at the age of sixteen, and then carried it to the grave through thousands of application forms, certificates, questionnaires, and reception desks" (Slezkine 1994, 450).

---

144 For disassociation of Jewishness from Judaism during the Soviet period, see among others: Chervyakov, Gitelman and Shapiro (1997) and Shternshis (2006).

145 This only corresponds partially with the *halachic* matrilineal understanding of Jewishness, according to which a person is defined as a Jew when his/her mother is a Jew. In Soviet terminology (including the scientific), such a person would be recognized as a half Jew and called *nechistokrovnyi. yevrei* [non-pure blooded Jew", Rus.; meaning only one parent is Jewish] as opposed to *chistokrovnye yevrei* [pure blooded Jews, meaning both parents are Jewish, Rus.].

While some Russian speaking researchers assume *nationalnost'* to be a taken for granted referential category,[146] other researchers—whose views are supported by this researcher—claim that it is racist, as it can be associated with Nazi forms of nationality construction and is an inescapable, imposed identity stamped in the citizen's passport (e.g., Lerner 2006; Malachov 2001, 2004). Yet, paradoxically, one can claim that such practices along with anti-Semitism preserved formal Soviet Jewishness (Slezkine 2004) and forced Jews to cope constantly with this concept, leading in turn to the invention of new contents.[147]

The difficulties encountered at various levels and in different spheres connected with not being of the *right* nationality (i.e. being part of Jewish minority) or with so called *pyatyi punkt* [lit. point five, Rus; reference to the fifth line of the passport identification information] was part of a shared common Soviet knowledge and the everyday experiences of the participants. Thus, both strong everyday *bytovoi* [lit. domestic, Rus; a Soviet term] forms of discriminations, as well as, institutional anti-Semitism were stigmatizations associated with *yevrei* in the SU.

The following examples demonstrate participants' ethnization and self-ethnization; that is, how Soviet ideas of innate, inevitable, and engraved (imbodied) ethnicity or, according to Calswell, how "racialized Othering" (Caldwell 2003, 255) was articulated as a taken for granted, true, "essentializing stigma" (Rapoport, Lomsky-Feder, and Heider 2002) (i.e. physical characteristics of their Jewishness, ascribed to them by birth). According to the views of most participants, in both contexts, these physical characteristics distinguished them from members of the dominant group as one could hardly hide or abandon them. Furthermore, these examples demonstrate how the Soviet idea of innate nationality is tightly interlaced with anti-Semitic experiences:

---

146 Refers to blood and is associated in Western thought with Nazi theory about "pure" blood. These terms are still popular in Russia and continue to be used in sociological research of the national identity of Russian Jews. For example, the concept of "nechistokrovnye yevrei" identified by Gitelman, Chervyakov, Shapiro (2000, 2001); or, "quite Arian appearance" which does not fit neither inner identity nor "the official status" of Jews (meaning *nationalnost'* stamped in the passport) according to Nosenko (2004, 5), who stated: "To be or to feel? Main patterns of Jewish self-identity among theoffspring of mixed marriages in today's Russia."

147 *Nationalnost'* was eliminated as a stamp in the Russian passport in 1999; see Darieva (2004, 71).

Olga (painter, 55 years old, Germany): "I could not hide my Jewishness, because it is written on my face. It is hereditary and cannot be changed, a kind of innate sign. There are Jewish physical features and also some national traits. Like, many have exaggerated worries and concerns, such as those of 'Jewish mothers.' You know, there is nobody [among the Jews] who feels himself completely safe."

Naum (Germany) signaled to me a kind of trust at the beginning of the first interview, when greeting me at the door he stated, following my introduction by an informant:

"Yes, finally one normal, authentic, Jewish face in Germany! That is *nash chelovek* [one of our kind, Rus. meaning Jewish]. You can see it immediately!" [148]

Pasha (doctor, 45 years old, Germany): "Once I got into the subway. There was a free seat, so I sat down. A woman sitting beside me said to her friend: I just wanted to sit here, but a man with *pyatyi punkt* [point five; Yevrei] already occupied it. You know, *b'yut po lizu* and not your passport [lit. one slaps your face, physically beat you as Jew. Rus. Pasha uses a popular Russian expression meaning one will discriminate—literally—due to your looks, not according to your passport]."

All three of the participants cited here presumed that innate Jewish physical traits are *engraved* on their faces and that they are neither immutable nor avoidable in interpersonal relations. Further, their experiences of anti-Semitism are mixed with the Soviet perception of nationality.

When Pasha used the popular Soviet phrase—*"b'yut po lizu,"* he means that it is impossible to hide your Jewish features. That is, even if the nationality identification in the passport is changed, a person will still be recognized and stigmatized due to his/her physical appearance. Indeed, Pasha revealed in the interview that because his father is Russian he was able to register *Russian* in his passport. However, this did not enable him to escape anti-Semitic experiences in his everyday life in the SU.

The following discussion provides a more detailed analysis and examples of this phenomenon in an attempt to answer the question frequently asked by non-Russian speaking persons: How did she know that he was Jew?

---

148 See Chapter Eight for further discussion of the multiple meanings of the construction of *nash*.

Contradictions between migrant and local resident perceptions

The Soviet perception of *innate nationality* as ethnic affiliation and its rup-turing as a sub-category of race causes many misunderstandings in interactions with other groups both in Israel and especially in Germany. It is assumed in both countries that ethnic affiliation, in general, and Jewish affiliation, in particular, require or presume cultural praxis. In contrast, participants in this study perceive their Jewishness as an *a priori*, essentialist category. This perception corresponds with the findings of other studies; for example, Markowitz's study of Russian speaking Jews in the USA (Markowitz 1988) or the findings of Chervyakov, Gitelman, and Shapiro (1997) who studied how Judaism is perceived in the ethnic consciousness of contemporary Russian Jews:

> "Only one percent (!) of Russian Jews considered practicing Judaism and only three percent name observance of national traditions (that is mostly religious practices) as the defining characteristics of Jewish identity [...] Finally not a single person mentioned such items as observing the Sabbath or the dietary laws (kashrut) or attending synagogue services" (Chervyakov, Gitelman, and Shapiro 1997, 293).

In this regard, we recall that Russian speaking Jews were deprived of any Jewish institutions or formal Jewish cultural life in the SU. As a result, it was only following emigration to Israel, Germany, and other countries that they were challenged to explain their different cultural and religious Jewish *habitus*. Engaging in this debate actually enabled many migrants to learn about these rituals and traditions for the first time. This process and use of the Soviet grounded logic of innate, immanent, essentialist Jewishness explains why migrant arguments were often perceived by both Jewish and non-Jewish non-Russian speakers encountered during the fieldwork in the two new contexts not only as unconvincing, but as strange, inappropriate, and even disturbing.

The clash between different bodies of knowledge and understandings of Jewish affiliation were evident almost immediately upon arrival in the initial interactions between newcomers and non-Russian speakers in both receiving societies. Often these interactions produced sharp misunderstandings and irritations. This was especially the case in Germany where Jewishness is assumed to be a religious affiliation. This explains why the Jewishness of recent arrivals was doubted: On the one hand, they immigrated to both countries through their Jewish affiliation.[149] Yet, on the other hand, they fit neither the Jewish cultural or traditional *habitus* nor did they demonstrate any religious knowledge or forms of participation.

Expressions of doubt as well as negative framing of Russian-speaking Jews as Russians or fake Jews were expressed extensively in the media in Israel and Germany.[150] Attempts to patronize their Jewishness are often formulated as "the community must make them into real Jews."[151]

This assertion by dominant groups that Jews from the SU prove their Jewishness forced migrants to explain, as well as, to justify themselves. On the one hand, such assertions helped dominant, resident groups to redefine values expressed in the encounter with Russian-speaking immigrants.[152] On the other hand, these statements contained an implicit challenge to the migrants' legitimacy and right to live in Israel or in Germany. And, indeed, such assertions were perceived by participants in both contexts as abusive, humiliating, painful, and inappropriate—for two reasons: First, because they establish a hierarchy of power relationship between groups, enabling those who demand that there be a homogeneous nature to *Israelis* or *Germans* to assert their status as "master in their own house." Inowlocki captured the essence of this situation: "[they] have a right to put questions to minorities, therefore forcing normative answers" [Ger.] (Inowlocki 2007). Thus, under these conditions, Others who sought to carve out a place for themselves in these *new* societies were expected to explain and to justify their views and identities.

Given this normative view of power sharing and reproduction of hierarchic relations, questions put to émigrés were not only one-sided, but also redefined the *nativeness* of those pretending to be native.[153] Second, these

---

149 A popular Russian Perestroika joke states: "[to] be Jewish is no Luxus, but a means of transport;" meaning the possibility to instrumentalize Jewish affiliation for emigration from the SU.

150 For Israel, see Avraham et al.(2004); Elias and Bernstein (2007); Golden (2002). For Germany, see Becker (2003); Becker and Körber (2001); Darieva (2004); Elias and Bernstein (2007); Ostow (2003).

151 „Die Gemeinde muss sie vor allem zu echten Juden machen?" As one journalist, Hans Riebsamen, wrote in "Kleines Jüdische Wunder" [small Jewish wonder, Ger.] in one of the leading German newspapers *FAZ*,.(November 11, 2006, 1).

152 Golden (2002) claimed this was true for the Israeli case.

153 As is the case not only in interaction with people from dominant Israeli or German groups, but also in interaction between newcomers in Germany and resident Jews in Germany. The later are a numerical minority but still occupy almost all key administrative positions in Jewish German communities.

assertions were perceived by participants as discouraging, because they glossed and implicitly doubted, even rejected, the very significant, frequent, and painful experiences (e.g., anti-Semitism), the long ethnization process, as well as, exclusion as Jews in the SU. This seemed to involve participants in inner self-ethnization as Jews to a certain degree.

The participants viewed the doubts expressed about their Jewishness as a means to disavow or to deny recognition of their innate traits, which according to their everyday life experiences in the SU could not be dispelled. Felix (Israel) spoke harshly about what he considered to be inappropriate Israeli questions when they demanded an explanation of what is exactly Jewish about the group referred to in Israel as *Russim* [Russians]: "I was born a Jew and I do not have to prove my Jewishness to anyone. Why, why do I have to justify myself?"

Similarly, Valentin (Germany) related an incident in which he had to confront a resident worker's suspicious attitudes, within the Jewish community, who did not want to recognize him as a Jew, irrespective of the fact that his SU documents state that he was registered as Jewish:

"Being Jewish is defined here according to Judaism, as an innate inheritance from your mother, but not so if you are born in Russia; because then people suspect that you forged your documents."

Participants reported that such confrontations frequently led to conflicts, especially in the German context where Jewish newcomers were dependent upon on receiving assistance from local Jewish communities.[154] As discussed in Chapter One, clearly these conflicts derive from the significantly different views held regarding the issue of "who is considered to be Jewish?" and "what it means to be Jewish?". Naum described his first visit to the Jewish community as frustrating because he was unable to realize his feeling of being associated with the Jewish collective:

"We didn't have anything [culturally] Jewish apart from the synagogue. I thought I would come to be with *svoimi* [lit. Ours, soul mates, Rus.],[155] but I did not find *svoich* [Ours, my soul mates, Rus.]."

Conditioned by different societal contexts within which Russian speaking and resident Jews were socialized, culturally different ideas about being

---

154 For more about tensions of Russian-speaking Jews with settled Jewish communities, see Dietz (2000); Schoeps et al.(1999); Tress (1995).

155 A Russian concept that describes collective affiliations that is close in meaning to the concept of *Nashi*, mentioned above.

Jewish were not the sole source of clashes between members of these two communities. Another reason for confrontation and participants' dissatisfaction with the Jewish community in Germany was the religious-based criterion of Jewish maternal lineage applied to determine the legitimacy of their claim that they were Jewish. According to the traditional rabbinic *halachic* [legal] regulation, only children born of a Jewish mother are accorded the right to be members of the Jewish community. This intracommunal ruling stands in dramatic contrast to the German legal regulation that permits immigration to Germany if either parent is/was Jewish. Interestingly, similar reasons were used to determine Jewish identity by the SU state and were the source of migrant suffering of discrimination as Jews in the SU. Thus, in spite of the German state's legal determinations, in some cases only one member of the immigrant family was allowed to participate, officially, in communal Jewish life. For example, children born to a Jewish father and non-Jewish mother were not considered to have equal rights to participate in different events (e.g., they were not accepted for participation in community sponsored trips to Israel reserved solely for 'real' Jewish children).

Although legitimated by the Jewish religious laws, such exclusion was perceived by participants as a direct discrimination by the Jewish community. Given the background of Soviet discrimination and their own sense of Jewish identity, they were very dissatisfied with being considered to be *just* family members who accompanied the *real* Jews who migrated and not being allowed to participate in communal life. Some families with officially sanctioned Jewish members broke off any connection to the community in protest and solidarity with other *non*-Jewish family members.

Thus, the *real* nature of Jewishness in Germany must meet two contradictory formal conditions: First, accordance with Jewish, *halachic* matrilineal law, and, second, the presumed homogeneous cultural Jewish heritage. Thus, formally, even if one could demonstrate the first condition, only very few the migrants could demonstrate the second. Given that participants had been socialized as atheists in the SU and encountered difficulties adjusting to life in a Jewish community driven, formally, by primarily religious institutions, many Russian-speaking Jews complained that activities and services offered within the local Jewish community did not meet their needs and expectations. What they wanted was to be granted entrée into an informal social and intellectual communal association that would, first and foremost, recognize their Jewish identity, as well as their Russian cultural baggage, and be a source of support. Instead, the receiving community functioned as a religious institution, since it assumed Russian speakers should be involved, primarily, in preserving a ritual heritage.

In summary, as traced in the fieldwork and confirmed by the presentations of Russian speaking Jews in the media, the general tendency of both sides was a polarization of seemingly unbridgeable differences between Russian and non-Russian speakers that focused on the Otherness of *Homo sovieticus*. This stands in dramatic contrast to the many similarities shared by Russian speaking Jews and resident members of the Jewish community in Germany[156] (e.g., living as Jewish minority in Germany; their approach to the State of Israel; sensitivity to various forms of anti-Semitism; and similar personal stories of discrimination, exclusion, or a history of family members exterminated in the Holocaust).

For their part, Russian-speaking Jewish migrants in Israel and Germany frequently used familiar and inclusive Soviet terms when speaking about their Jewishness. For example, they referred to their "Jewish blood," "Jewish face," "half" or "three quarter Jewishness. All of these terms irritate those who do not share their Soviet experience and Soviet *nationalnost'* rhetoric.

Svetlana, for example, speculated about the obvious irritation of a potential employer when during a job interview in Germany she responded to a question about her origins by stating: "Actually I am Russian, even though there is at least 75 percent Jewish blood flowing in me." Here, Svetlana stressed her Russian cultural affiliation. However, she did so in Soviet *nationalnost'* terms that relate to her Jewish hereditary and blood lineage; an approach entirely inappropriate in Germany. From the employer's point of view, her use of Nazi terminology might have been understood to be a provocation. On the other hand, she was responding to a question posed by a potential employer regarding a position in an art gallery. His question could be challenged as unrelated to her professional skills. Although he knew from her curriculum vitae that she had immigrated from the SU, he asked her about her "actual origins." Svetlana explained that she understood that the employer was not referring to her city of birth, but rather to her *nationalnost*. Svetlana was not selected for this position. In reflecting on her initial attempt to find work in the local job market, she remembered only one obvious negative sign of the employer's

---

156 See detailed comparative discussion in concluding chapter of this monograph.

irritation about her reference to Jewish blood and argued that it was the only obvious reason she was rejected for the job. However, her overall conclusion was "that it is better not to mention your Jewishness with Germans."

Another interviewee, Anatolii (I), described how he was misunderstood during a hearing at the *Rabanut* [Israeli religious court, Heb.]. In inquiring about his Jewishness, his friend Andrei was called as a witness to give evidence regarding Anatolii's Jewish way of life, his praxis, in Russia. Anatolii thought that Andrei used an argument that according to his way of thinking had to be accepted as absolutely convincing.

Andrei stated: "Just look at him! His nose and his face look Jewish and there [in Russia] everybody knew it. He did not have to prove it to anybody…"

Although he produced his original birth certificate, in which his mother was registered as a Jew, Anatolii's claim to Jewishness was rejected by the rabbinical court. This case demonstrates not only the collision of different terms of reference, but also the immutable criteria used by Israeli religious courts in determining petitions to be recognized as being Jewish. These criteria and judgments do not take into consideration the real life experiences of people, ignoring the fact that the practice of Judaism was forbidden in the SU. Thus, given the circumstances in which they grew up and lived during the Soviet regime, migrants in Israel face a nearly impossible task of providing proof that satisfies the rabbinical judges. Visible gaps in cultural-symbolic code systems were often inter-preted as a rejection of meaningful experiences migrants experienced as Jews in the SU, as in the case of Anatolii.

From the perspective of non-Russian speakers, especially in Germany, statements such as those quoted above, referring to immutable, innate, genetic Jewishness may well be interpreted as a disturbing reference to race, physiognomy, or blood relations associated with Nazi ideologies and policies, and hence may even have been viewed as a provocation. Thus, the common shared knowledge used by ex-Soviet Jews in relating to genetically inherited characteristics obviously contradicts local symbolical codes and residents' experience in the "social worlds" (Schütze 2002). Such miscommunication may well create a permanent gap in perception that can only be bridged through intensive efforts.

It is only after migration that migrants come to confront these significantly different, commonly held ideas. This process seems to lead them to realize that their assumptions about innate Jewishness are not shared universally. The following excerpt from the interview with Tamara is an example of such a process:

"They [Germans] have no idea about the nationalnost'. They think it is citizenship. You have to explain what it means every time, but still they do not understand *yevreiskaya liniya* [Jewish lineage, Rus.]. When they learn you are Jewish, they want to take you to a Klezmer concert and are disappointed that you are not a religious Jew. Other friends of mine asked if I could show them how we celebrate Jewish holidays. I was so ashamed that I knew nothing about how to celebrate them. I kept delaying and delaying…"

Even when participants come to recognize the existence of different cultural-symbolic code systems and shared knowledge, some doubt the legitimacy of such a difference. In the following example, Pasha claimed that Germans actually share similar terms (of innate, immutable, visible Jewishness), but refuse to express these understandings in the public sphere because they know that they are inappropriate according to the codes of political correctness and can induce conflict.

Pasha (Germany): "I immediately recognize if a person is Jewish or not on the street. With such looks [referring to himself], you can't hide a thing. You don't have to tell them that you are a Jew, but still they all know it. We all know this is the way it is and I am sure Germans also recognize and make such distinctions, but they won't tell you because it's not politically correct here."

These examples are representative of an ascribed manner of identification, *tipichnaya yevreiskaya vneshnost'* [typical Jewish looks, Rus.], asserted to exist among Jews from the SU that continues to be applied in new contexts. These "polemically used ideas about body" (Diemling 2005, 78) do not refer to a new phenomenon, as amazingly similar claims were made in Middle Ages and Enlightenment Europe:

"One can recognize Jews immediately among thousands of people. God assigned them special features such that from the first glance one knows they are Jews, even though they try very hard to hide themselves" [Ger.].[157]

---

157 "daß man unter viel tausend Menschen sofort einen Juden erkennen kan." Gott habe sie mit besonderem "Charactere oder Merkmal" gezeichnet, "daß man sie bald im ersten Anblick für Juden ansieht/ ob sie sich auch noch so sehr zu verbergen suchen," Maria Diemling, citing ethnographic study of Johann Jacob Schudts *Jüdische Merckwürdigkeiten* ["Jewish oddities", Ger.], from 1717 about Jews in Frankfurt, (Diemling 2005, 79).

Analyzing constructed concepts of the *Jewish body*, Gilman claimed that the concept of constructed Jewish body was inseparable from its stigmatization, as he pointed out in regard to the purpose of creating Otherness:

"This is still true even in the case of the new 'ethnic-specific' aesthetic surgeries of the 1980s—for the fear is not in looking Jewish but looking 'too Jewish'. […] For being too visible means being seen not as an individual, but as an Other, one of the 'ugly' races" (Gilman 1994, 394).

The somatic image of the Jew was stigmatized in the SU as an *ugly* Other. This image of *innate Jewishness* and *visible Otherness* developed as a result of anti-Semitic and racist Soviet politics as well through various forms of everyday anti-Semitism. The following key elements of this image were identified by participants in both contexts: dark, curly haired, pale people with long, sometimes bent noses; large, dark, protruding eyes; thick lips; full women with x-shaped legs, often referred to in Russian as "Jewish legs."

This racist image of the typical Jew continues to be widespread, not only in the SU. It is not only the Jewish nose that was the typical anti-Semitic symbol of Jews (Gilman 1994). Gilman, for example, cited the 1857 memoirs of Polish noble Adam Gurowky: "sallow rose-like complexion, thick lips, crisply-cut black hair" (Gilman 1986, 8). Furthermore, in a nearly exact description to that provided by former Soviet Jews interviewed in this study, Diemling cited a portrayal by Schudt (1717)[158] of Jews in Frankfurt:

"Among several hundred of their kind, he had not encountered a single person without a blemish or other repulsive feature. For they are either pale and yellow or swarthy; in general they have big heads and mouths, pouting lips, protruding eyes and eyelashes like bristles, large ears, crooked feet; hands that hang below their knees, [scattered] big shapeless warts, or are their otherwise asymmetrical and malapportioned limbs." [159]

These images of the Jewish body, what Diemling referred to as "physiognomic speculations" (Diemling 2005, 81), which also evoke the Nazi image of the "ugly Jewish body," were internalized and transported by Russian-

---

158 Schudt 1717—„Jüdische Merkwürdigkeiten" [Jewish oddities, Germ.] by Diemling (forthcoming, 6).

159 Diemling (2005, 6); The original German version of the citation: "dann sie sind entweder blaß und gelb/ oder schwarztlich/sie haben insgemein große Köpffe/ große Mäule/und auwgeworffene Lippen/ herfürstehende Augen/und Augen-Wimmer als Borsten/große Ohren/ krumme Füße/und Hände."

speaking Jews to Israel and Germany, where they continue to be taken for granted until today as a given biological/genetic reality. Though in Israel biological/genetic components have been preserved without their hideous inferences, no evidence of change in views was evident in this study among Jews of Russian origins in Germany.

The internalized anti-Semitic ideas about Jews as well as the fixed racist Soviet nationalnost' ideas about biologic features of being Jewish made it impossible for some participants to accept black or dark-skinned Jews, as it is evident in the next citation. Naum (Germany), who perceived me to be an Israeli, abruptly presented me with a rhetorical question that referred to Jews in Israel:

"I just don't understand. Why do you [Israelis] accept Ethiopians into the state? Just look at them. They are black and don't look like Jews at all! They can wear three kipas [skullcaps], but they still will not be Jews!"

This example demonstrates the essentialist nature of assumed to be innate Jewish traits juxtaposed to acquired religious and cultural ones. In Naum's view, one cannot become Jewish through religious conversion, for example. That is, even if a person becomes *iudei* [religious Jew, Rus.], he/she cannot become *yevrei* [Jewishness, perceived as innate, Rus.].

Different bodies of knowledge and their development

The empirical findings revealed a gap between former Soviet Jews' perspectives about Jewishness in their interactions with non-Russian speakers in Israel and Germany. Here, the theoretical challenge confronted in the field work is, on the one hand, to respect participants' claims that they are recognizable as Jews and can recognize other Jews according to their physical appearance; and, on the other hand, our understanding as social scientists based on nearly worldwide academic consensus that there is an absence of scientific basis for the claim that it is possible to divide humans into biological types—*races*, or point to a particular group's exclusive, typical physiognomic features (Cavalli-Sforza 1994; Haney Lopez 1994; Kattmann 1982, 2003; Kaupen-Haas 1999; Levontin, Rose and Kamin 1984; Miles 2002; Smedley and Smedley 2005; Weingart, Kroll and Bayertz 1992).

Yet, coming from large cities in Russia and Ukraine, ex-Soviet Jews bring with them uncontestable experiences in which they were in fact often recognized on the street and stigmatized as Jews. How, then, can we explain the participants' conviction of the existence of clear physiognomic national characteristics so zealously refuted by many German and European researchers? First, we recall that participants' ideas are the product of socialization processes undergone throughout their life in the SU and are not based on scientifically-based physiognomic characteristics. Different from other Soviet ethnic groups, who for the most part reside in their own republics or autonomous units, ex-Soviet Jews lived throughout the SU where they were well-integrated, identified with their Russian cultural affiliation, and spoke the Russian language as their mother tongue (Chervyakov, Gitelman and Shapiro 1997, Kandel 2002; Slezkine 2004). Generally speaking, apart from ascribed physical traits, there were no cultural or material symbols, such as clothing or accessories that marked them as differing from local dominant groups in European republics of the SU, particularly Russia and Ukraine where most participants lived prior to migration.

In contrast, the participants who migrated from other regions in the SU claimed they were one of the few non-Slavic groups living permanently in the non-European republics and were culturally integrated there. The anti-Semitic image of Jewish appearance led to a stigmatization of those who looked darker than others. Therefore, the physical appearance of participants with dark hair and eyes, in particular, were frequently perceived to be different from Slavic traits. The reason was not only that they *looked like Jews*, but there was also an absence of comparative reference groups (e.g., other groups of Mediterranean origin) who at the time were living within tightly closed republics. Moreover, the strict Soviet system of passport identification by address made it difficult for a person to change the city or republic where he or she lived. As a result, there were relatively few people from the so-called Caucasian or Asiatic republics living in big cities of Russia and the Ukraine. Thus, participants with blond hair who would not necessarily be identified as Jews reported stigmatizing comments made by members of dominant groups when they were revealed to be Jews, such as reported by Nikolai (Israel):

"Really? I would never think that about you [meaning that you are Jewish, without mentioning stigmatizing Russian word *yevrei*, Jew]. You don't look Jewish at all."

Participants living in these regions who possessed the attributed traits (i.e. they fitted the Jewish stereotype) reported being frequently "recognized" (stigmatized) throughout their life in the SU. That is to say, the *social intuition* of citizens in the *closed* republics of the SU mixed with widespread anti-

Semitic images led to their being *recognized* as Jews, since they were slightly different looking Others from the Soviet Russian *habitus*. Asya (Germany; of Greek origin, married to Boris) added the following comment to Boris's account of his anti-Semitic experiences as Jew: "You know, on the street, I was always thought to be Jewish, as well. It is clear because nobody could imagine that I am Greek."

Asya's experiences fit the general *habitus* and in particular the experiences of blond migrants to Israel and Germany who noted that, minimally, they were "saved" from everyday forms of discrimination on the street. On occasion, the racist schema would be recalled by a non-Jew stating that "you are blacker than you are supposed to be." However, they reported that they continued to suffer from institutional anti-Semitism because of their formal definition as Jews or other anti-Semitic mechanisms that were applied, when some act was interpreted by colleagues as being of a Jewish nature. Also, other appearances—for example Mediterranean—were associated with the Jewish one.

Participants considered Soviet anti-Semitism to be an all-embracing, omnipresent, taken for granted category, even an innately genetic phenomenon.

For example, Lisa (Germany) observed: "Many did not know what a Jew is, but knew that it is bad. It was already innate anti-Semitism. There is anti-Semitism in their [generalized Russian or Ukraine] blood."

Participants described how persons from Caucasian or Asiatic republics (e.g., from Georgian, Armenian, or Azerbaijan), who worked in Russia or Ukraine as entrepreneurs in local markets, differed from the Jews in a number of ways. First, their occupation was ethnically designated and limited. Second, their cultural artifacts (e.g., clothing, caps, or Christian cross) made their non-Jewishness visible. Additionally, unlike other different looking minorities, the participants spoke without an accent in Russian, but in many cases still had Jewish names. This contributed further to ethnization and stigmatization.

In this sense, the social construction of biological Others corresponds to the claim made by Miles that it is necessary to consider the designation of race or biological groups as a "descriptive category imposed on individuals and groups" (Miles 2002, 82). Hence, verbal recognition (i.e., stigmatization on the street) signifies obvious differences that assign public, social exclusion; a frequent phenomenon reported by participants. Initiation of stigmatizations of visible Others recreates and reconfirms collective identity as personal attachment. Interestingly, participants cited that anti-Semitic, racist "recognitions" always took place through aggressive use of the word *yevrei* as a swear word applied to any type of Other in order to stress his foreignness or to reconfirm one's own belonging through use of means of exclusion. Thus, if there is no obvious marker of foreignness, it can be socially constructed, artificially, as a mean of exclusion in the form of cultural myths, such as the fantasy of the Other or "enacted daydreams" (Gilman 1986, 19). Indeed, in this regard, we recall Horkheimer's and Adorno's claim, made in 1947, in regard to fascist anti-Semitism in nationalsocialist Germany: "To a certain extent fascist anti-Semitism first had to contrive its object" [Ger.].[160]

6.3 Component Two: *Significant Others* in the SU and abroad

Anti-Semitism and *domestic foreigners*

In addition to the belief in innate biologic *nationalnost'*, or "racialized Othering" (Caldwell 2003, 255), Russian-speaking Jews confronted various other obstacles, difficulties, as well as direct and indirect forms of personal discrimination and disenfranchisement. Almost all participants in both contexts described or at least mentioned having anti-Semitic experiences. For example, there were institutional obstacles such as *numerus clausus* that limited access of Jews to universities and jobs in prestigious professions. And, there were forms of what is referred to as *bytovoi anti-Semitism* [everyday or domestic anti–Semitism, Rus.], such as verbal insults, abuse, anti-Semitic jokes, and physical violence. Transported with the migrants, these experiences are representative of research findings about anti-Semitism in the SU (Dietz 2000; Gitelman 1994, 1995, 2000; Shternshis 2006; Slezkine 2004; Tress 1995). As well as, the results of a 1994 public opinion survey conducted in CIS: "93 percent of the respondents [reported to] have 'negative stereotypes of Jews' and 44 percent showed unambiguous anti-Semitic attitudes."[161]

---

160 "Der faschistische Antisemitismus muss sein Objekt gewissenmassen erst erfinden" (Horkheimer and Adorno 1997 [1947, 237]).
161 Wolffsohn and Bokovoy (2003 cited Salpter, *Ha'aretz* September 28, 1999).

Beliefs about innate and visible Jewishness projected negative connotations of an unavoidable "bad destiny" (Shternshis 2006) and the stigmatized identity discussed in this chapter. The evidence collected suggests that socialization to ingrained innate Jewishness and significant Otherness (the first two components of the chapter) are essential constructions in this traumatized, negative Soviet Jewish identity. These stigmatizing labels "represent the privileged group's myth that these categories are immutable" (Gilman 1986, 4). These elements personify cultural anti-Semitic constructions that ascribe negative Jewish features in combination with parallel cultural linguistic constructions which are embedded in the Russian language and that stigmatize Jewish names. Thus, a special Jewish accent is ascribed to Russian-speaking Jews pronunciation of certain Russian words; for example, words with guttural or what is referred to as the Jewish "r." Or, Russian curse words created from stigmatized Russian words connected with Jews. This image of Other as significantly different by nature is not a unique Soviet phenomenon, indeed it resembles strongly anti-Semitic European narratives that date back to the Middle Ages (Diemling 2005; Gilman 1986; Kandel 2002).

Thus, the strong ethnization process of Soviet Jews that included negative stereotypes and their stigmatization functioned as clear mechanisms of general exclusion and disenfranchisement.[162] Migrants recalled being permanently reminded of their Jewishness as both *visible* and *significant Other*. This was a kind of suspicious foreignness that was permanently reconstructed outside, in the public sphere, and discussed in the intimacy of the family at home. Participants shared numerous examples of traumatic anti-Semitic experiences in the interviews. Indeed, individual anti-Semitic experiences and collective familial memories about it played a very important, formative role in determining the *subjective sense of personal Jewishness*. This element alone is sufficient, I submit, to refute statements heard frequently in Israel and in Germany about Russian-speaking Jews suspicious or fictitious Jewishness. Further, it counters the claim often made that since there was no voluntary identification with Jewish culture and praxis, the anti-Semitic experiences as excluded and different forced them to feel Jewish. And, hence these experiences are insufficient to be "really Jew-

---

162 This finding corresponds with the study conducted by Lewin-Epstein, Roi, and Ritterband (1997).

ish."[163] On the contrary, I claim that the obligatory ethnization process forced on Soviet Jews, over an extended period of time, significantly affected and manifested itself in their identity as a Jew and as a member of the Jewish minority; in their way of acting as social agents; and in their coping with stigmatized Jewish affiliation until today. If so, it would be a mistake to neglect the role of anti-Semitic exclusionary mechanisms in their ethnization and Jewish identity.

Misha (Germany) stated this most clearly in sharing his present views of his Soviet Jewishness:

"Our family did not differ in anyway from other intelligent Soviet families, but the element of Jewishness was always there. I was different because of discrimination [I experienced]. To be Jewish meant to overcome these difficulties [pause]. Yes, such *strange Jewishness* [...]."

Independent from individual coping strategies that each person developed as a result of living as Jews in the SU, all participants demonstrated the collective self-consciousness of Jews as an oppressed, stigmatized, excluded group. These feelings parallel what researchers have referred to as "domestic foreigners" (Levinson 1997, 12), "internal strangers," or being "abroad at home."[164] The following three examples from the fieldwork demonstrate this feeling.

Sergey (Germany) formulated his being a stranger through his sense that he is a potential victim:

"Of course, I felt at home there, everything around was actually part of me—the language, streets, people, nature [...] but you knew that if something would happen, we [Jews] would immediately be made scapegoats."

Tania (Germany) attributed her feeling of foreignness to the complex of Jewish exclusion by dominant groups and self-distancing by Jews from other groups via the religious idea of the *chosen people*. However, her personal reference to Jewish collectivity does not absolve her from feelings of isolation and inner strangeness:

---

163 Moreover, these doubts are also often stressed in the media through refutation of the assumption about anti-Semitism as a main reason for emigration to Germany. See for example Kanis, "Voller Hoffnung. 15 Jahre Zuwanderung: Eine Tagung des Zentralrats in Köln", *Allgemeine Jüdische Zeitung*, May 26, 2006, 19.

164 Slezkine (2004); Gitelman found that 75 percent of the immigrants felt at home in the Soviet Union, all or almost all of their lives (see Gilman 1995, 26).

"I only had a nebulous idea about Jewishness, in part its limitations [that she actually experienced], of course, but certainly there were feelings of the chosen people, isolation, and of inner strangeness [unusual expression in Russian; also inner self-feeling/self identity of stranger]."

Tamara's description (Germany) reflects the general view repeated by many participants in both contexts about their Jewishness in the SU:

"I never chose my friends according to their nationalnost', but rather it was instinctive. And, it usually turned out that they were Jews or from mixed families. There were few "pure" Russians, rather always some with strannostyami [lit. strangeness, oddities, strange attributes, Rus; meaning not those who belonged to the normative majority] [smiles], from minorities. And, with pure Russians, I always felt fear and constraint."

Like Tamara, almost all participants in Germany and Israel stressed that in most cases their friends had a Jewish background, even if they did not choose them consciously because of their Jewishness. Only a few participants reported being friends with members of dominant groups. Also characteristic is the distinction Tamara made between "normative" (i.e. pure ethnic Russians) and Others (i.e. an inclusive category referring to minorities, including Jews; she juxtaposed them to the "normal" majority with the word "those with *strangeness, oddities, strange attributes*"). In doing so, Tamara claimed that Soviet Jews as Others were part of the narrative about people with certain biographic deviances from normative biographies of ethnic Russians. Here, her inner feeling of being a domestic foreigner made it easier for her to communicate with similar Others.

This view was inconvenient and restricted social interaction as it did not include those who did not share her life-experiences among the minority in the SU. Within the Soviet context this collective identification of domestic but foreign (i.e., "scientifically contrasted" (Schäffter 1991, 23), different from the normative mainstream or "different by nature" (Calloni 1999, 12) was manifest in experiences of discrimination. This is to what Calloni referred to as "racial categorization" (ibid), and Caldwell "racialized Othering" (Caldwell 2003, 255). Generally speaking, the participants' understanding of their own Jewishness conforms to a type of ethnicity that Calloni defined as a

"restrictive and reductive framework for the definition of the self and the collective identity [that] he/she refers to when the individual as a social actor has to define strictly his/her attachment, or worse, when he/she has to assume the stereotypes given by a dominant group."[165]

Thus, on the basis of my fieldwork, I can claim that the personal experiences of exclusion and Soviet social construction of Jews as *ultimate or significant Others* played a much stronger formative role in the participants' self-perception as Soviet, atheistically oriented, culturally Russified, educated Jews from the big cities of Russia and Ukraine, than did the central precept of Judaism that Jews are the Chosen People who have a special mission and seek to separate themselves from non-Jewish persons.

Knowledge transformations: Images of "polluted" Otherness

The parallel between being Jewish and disease was noted several times during the interviews. In general, the repugnant images of Soviet *Jewish Other*, detailed below, echo the long tradition of anti-Semitic European history. For example, Diemling's analysis of 18th century Christian-Jewish relations in Frankfurt found that the description of Jews as "unerfreuliches, schmutziges, unharmonisches Ganzes," [coherent, dirty, rather unpleasant, total, Ger.][166] employs terms of reference that correspond strongly with reductive ascriptions found in the current research.

The multiple dimensions of these negative stereotypes and ascriptions are exemplified in statements by Leonia (Germany) and Nikolai (Israel). Leonia (Germany) recalled that no one was willing to rent a flat for his father in a small city:

"People said to the owner of the flat where my father lived: 'It is not good that a Jew is living near you.' As if to say, he would be stricken by the plague."

Nikolai (Israel) articulated the image of the "polluted" Jew in more detailed way:

"Like Iosif Brodsky,[167] I was ashamed to say the word *yevrei* as a boy and even as a

---

165 Calloni (1999, 118) referred to the chapter on anti-Semitism in Horkheimer and Adorno (1986).

166 Diemling (2005, 80); see the English version of the article: Diemling (forthcoming, 5).

167 Joseph Brodsky was one of the most popular Soviet dissident writers and poets who immigrated to the USA, won a Nobel Prize, and worked as professor at the University of Cambridge. Describing his own memories and thoughts about being Jewish, he wrote: "I was ashamed of the very word 'Jew'—without the nuances of its content. The destiny of this word depends on the diversity of the contexts, and on the frequency of

teenager,[168] because it was always negative, just as he wrote. Do you remember? Like a venereal disease with all its associations. It always meant something negative. You knew something was wrong with you just because you are Jew. This is terrible, but it was actually like that. In some places there were people who did not say Jew, but 'French' when they saw a Jew. They would say: 'Look, French is going.'[169]

To mention the word Jew, and all that was connected with it was always at the wrong moment [i.e., there was no social space for Jews]. It is clear that in such an atmosphere you try to hide your Jewishness.

When I was small, I always dreamt about becoming Russian or at least Ukrainian. I wanted to be equal in all respects, to be as Russian as possible, so that nobody would 'suspect' me. Also, I do not look like a Jew, and when people learn that I am they said: 'Really? I would not say you look like...'

And you always wait for something bad [to happen]: You will not be accepted by the university; you fear you will not get the job you want; you are not allowed to go abroad with a delegation, because you are in the category of *neblagonadezhnye elementy* [untrustworthy elements, Rus.] for fear you will go and, as a Jew, stay in the west and betray your motherland."

This explanation was repeated in different variations in my interviews in Israel and Germany and has been confirmed by other investigators of this topic (Gitelman 1994; Krupnik 1994; Schweid 1994; Slezkin 2004). Altogether these views demonstrate the clear negative connotation of the word Jew as well as all associations with Jewishness that existed at different levels of society there. We see in Nikolai and Leonia's descriptions different negative aspects of the traumatic self-perception as Jews in the SU. Nikolai articulated explicitly his memories of difficulties he had in accepting Jewishness as a part of his self-identity, because it meant "something is wrong with you."

---

its use. The word Jew appeared extremely rarely in the Russian written language. Its status is approximate to a swearword or to a venereal disease. A seven year old child knows his way around the language in order to feel the coarseness and sharpness of this word and it is especially unpleasant to apply this word to oneself [...] I had fewer problems with the word '*Zhid*' ['Yid', Rus.], because it is clearly abusive and without content [...] I am describing all this not because I suffered from my Jewishness, but because my first lies were connected with my identity." (Brodsky 1986: 11—12) [Rus.]

168 Since there is no Russian equivalent to the adjective "Jewish," it is difficult for Russian Jews to describe themselves without using the negatively loaded word *yevrei* [Jew].

169 In another interview, Leon [G] explained that he felt discriminated against when he was abused with the popular word "Engineer" or "Engineer in glasses," meaning "Jew;" and when institutions in which Jews were accepted to study were called "synagogues."

Feelings of inferiority as well as vulnerability and oversensitivity because of their Jewishness were repeated by many interviewees during the fieldwork. Nikolai's emphasis on his non-Jewish outlook, stressed the dream of equality, to being as Russian as possible, and hopes that his dream would be realized. However, such self-perception extends beyond *visible Otherness*. Nikolai mentioned the narrative of Joseph Brodsky who drew the parallel between Jewishness and a venereal disease. In doing so, Brodsky and Nikolai suggested that being Jewish is like an infectious disease; initially invisible, but forever present, unless cured, bringing no good of any kind. Additional difficulties associated with *nationalnost' Yevrei* include *numerus clausus* in which case Jews were restricted, limited, or prohibited from admission to the university or from being hired for certain jobs.

The connection between Jewish impurity and ill-repute, so well-documented in research about relations between Christians and Jews since the Enlightenment in Europe (e.g., Diemling 2005) is present in Nikolai's account and recalls Douglas' analysis of social status (Douglas 1966). Ethnization as a politically institutionalized exclusion mechanism can be found, as well, in the Soviet myth of the "untrustworthy element," formulated by Slezkine as "Jews intrinsic political unreliability" (Slezkine 2004, 341).

Nikolai's comment about ongoing and inappropriate mention of the word *Jew* ["Mention of the word Jew… was always at the wrong moment") relates to the special feeling of exclusion where there is no right moment in normal everyday or place (social space) in reality for Jews. The inter-exchange of *yevrei* with "French" in the context of insular SU is a sophisticated way to exaggerate the strangeness of Others who can never belong (i.e., French cannot be Russian).[170]

Nikolai reflected on his Jewishness in the SU from the point of view of his current perspective living in Israel. He described himself as "well integrated into the Jewish state." There all of his family became religious except his youngest child, a 19-year-old son. In contrast, migrants to Germany, like Leonia, often continued to "bear" negative self-perceptions of being Jewish that dissipated very slowly and only partially. Indeed. Leonia

---

170 Hidden in this mockery is another aspect, namely an anti-Semitic image about "kartavye evrei" [Jew pronouncing guttural "r", Rus.]. This is expressed through the image of the French, since they pronounce the guttural 'r' in a significantly differently manner than the hard Russian "r."

remained indignant about his father's treatment in a small Russian city as a *plague-stricken* Jew.

Pasha (45 years old, Germany), a medical doctor, is another interesting example, as he presented one of the most extreme cases of internalized anti-Semitic perceptions found in either field study. Pathologizing his Jewishness, Pasha claimed that Jewishness alone is "responsible" for his psoriasis:

"I think all my problems are from my Jewishness, not from my father [his father is a Russian Christian]. For example, my skin problems are from my Jewishness. That is for sure. Because my skin starts to itch every time I am in a room with Jews. They have a different aura than Russians."

Pasha's description of the eruption of a skin irritation when interacting or being in a space with other Jews is not a unique, indeed his account reproduces traces found in many historical contexts. Embedded in his account are his split loyalties between Russia [where his Christian father remained] and Germany [where his Jewish mother has resided with him since their emigration]. Thus, his itching reflects or even repeats precisely the old idea of "fear of impurity through contact between Christian and Jewish bodies" [Ger.].[171]

Filth and skin disease are obvious similarities between the description of Jews having venereal disease and psoriasis. The latter stands in contrast to everyday grime as it cannot be removed easily from the body with soap and water. Hence, feelings of impurity, expressions of disgust with one's own body, and consequently of self-identity have deep somatic roots. By repeating the ancient anti-Semitic image of pollution or Jewish impurity, used as well by Nazis, this citation clearly states Pasha's desire not to be Jewish. Yet, given his understanding of innate, genetic Jewishness engraved in his body, this desire can never be realized. Consequently, an undesired, inevitable visibility has been transformed by Pasha into a physical feeling of itching upon encountering Jews. This situation echoes Gilman's idea of undesired Jewish visibility, based on Jean-Paul Sartre: "It is being visible in a 'body that betrays' that the Jew is most uncomfortable" (Gilman 1994, 394)

Of course, Jewishness that includes such deep internalized self-hatred cannot be transformed easily, especially through emigration to the German

---

171 "Angst vor Verunreinigung durch den Kontakt zwischen dem christlichen und dem jüdischen Körper," Diemling (2005, 85).

context, which hardly represents a harmonic historic environment for treating the topic of painful Jewishness. In this regard it is interesting to note that Pasha visited Israel three years after this interview. In talking with him after his return to Germany, he related having an exciting trip. And, recalling his statement three years before, said that for the first time his skin does not itch anymore when he sees Jews.

Stigmatized Jewish names: before and after migration

Exclusion through ethnization processes can be achieved in different indirect ways. In addition to the perception of Jewishness as pollution, participants reported anti–Semitic experiences connected to the rhetoric of stigmatized Jewish names. Igor (Israel), for example, remembered the special way he called his wife in public without mentioning her Jewish name since he was embarrassed by it. He smiled as he elaborated on this experience:

"If I was outside and wanted to ask my wife something, I would stand near our window and said—'Lena, please call Mom'—because I was ashamed to say Sarah. I just could not do it. It sounded so Jewish, and everybody would hear it and laugh. There were a lot of jokes about Abraham and Sarah, you know…"

After living in Israel for almost 20 years, Igor reflected on his past experiences through his current perspective; that is, through his positive Israeli Jewish identity. In contrast, participants in Germany did not smile when discussing this subject, as all indicated that it remains a painful topic, even shameful for some. Sveta (Germany) recalled that: "I always turned red in the school when my family name, Abramovich, was called."

Indeed, German participants were quite surprised when they noticed that many resident Germans (not necessary Jewish) named their daughters with what they considered to be negatively loaded names such as Sarah. Sergey, who retained his obviously Jewish family name, Abramson, and is someone who claimed that he never removes his Star of David neck chain, expressed shock about this phenomenon:

"[there are] numerous anti-Semitic jokes about Sarah and Abraham in the Russian language. How can they [Germans] name *their own* (!) children like that?! I just cannot understand it. You know they [Germans] are generally very strange. Just imagine calling your daughter Sarah?! Well, I don't know [shakes his head seemingly confused]."

While similar statements were made by participants in Israel, it was in the German Diaspora context that anti-Semitic Soviet clichés attained a very different meaning for many Jewish participants, as they remained negatively loaded. Given views that were developed through atheistic socialization, Sergey regarded use of the name Sarah as an ill advised selection, one should preferably avoid. In his view, such a name lacks any positive religious connotations and thus it is unclear how a rational, sober-minded person would voluntary choose a stigmatized name for his own child. Sergey does not understand how parents, who can shape their child's social future, would act in such a manner. Consequently, he cannot fathom that the situation would be different in another society, nor has he found an appropriate explanation according to this logic that resolves his lack of understanding. Confused, but still questioning what he considers to be an incomprehensive act, he repeats another cliché, when he concludes that "Germans are generally very strange." In seems that an accumulation of different images and significantly different ideas about "normative action" led to his feeling self-alienation from, as well as, reproducing mutual foreignness.

According to Schäffter's analysis of different types of foreignness, Sergey's irritated and confused reaction could be categorized both as "Das Fremde als das Unheimliche"[172] [foreign as uncanny, Ger.] mixed with the type "Das Fremde als Fremdartiges" [foreignness as outlandish, alien, Ger.] (Schäffter 1991, 14) also as abnormal, anomalous, not belonging and inappropriate (ibid). This is an "oppressive experience," ("beklemmende Erfahrung," ibid) and obviously in contradiction to feeling safe. However, instead of reflecting about the absoluteness of trusted concepts and the "blurring" of conceptual boundaries (as would be the case according to the ideal first type of Schäffter), this strange information is judged to be in contrast to his existing, stable understanding. Further, it is seen as an anomaly or as something unbridgeable (corresponding with Schäffter's second ideal type), and consequently is rejected.

---

172 This term "das Unheimliche" (the Uncanny) was originally invented by Freud to address the ambivalence and ambiguity related to different meanings implied in this word in German language. Heimlich can mean homely, but also familiar, intimate, and cherished since it is related to *heimisch*- native. Consequently *unheimlich* (unhomely) relates to the opposite of the familiar and intimate, cherished, and native; that is, to the foreign, weird, concealed, secret (Brewster 2002).

Stigmatization of Jews through the Russian language

Another linguistic-cultural stigmatizing strategy has two modes that are relevant to be discussed here. First, although former Soviet Jews speak Russian without any accent, they are very self-conscious about stigmatized connotations often ascribed to Jews. In particular, the use of the guttural "R," referred to as the "Jewish R," as juxtaposed to the normative hard "r" pronunciation more commonly pronounced in the Russian language. Once again, the phenomenon of ascribing special pronunciations and/or an accent to Jews is not an exclusive Soviet phenomenon.[173] Second, Nikolai's example of the synonymous "Jew" and the anti-Semitic French, as in "French is going," too, hints at the pronunciation stigmatization.

Many more direct statements were recalled that stress Otherness through ascription of stigmatized "Jewish" guttural pronunciation of the letter "r" to Russian-speaking Jews. Naum (Germany), who was the only participant who in fact pronounced the guttural "r," described a very unpleasant experience related to his use of guttural "r" in Russian. The incident took place many years after emigration during a phone call to a friend in Russia:

"We called our friends there [in a so-called communal flat in Russia where several flatmates share one phone number]. A woman answered and called out in response to our greeting: 'Vera Michailovna [their friend]! Pick up the phone, some Jew is calling you.' You know, all the nostalgia disappeared immediately."

Misha (Germany) recalled memories of times when claims were made that he was using the guttural "r," whereas in fact he was not. He claimed that the guttural German "r" is not necessarily Jewish, but can also be "normal" and even desired. Yet, he only realized this following migration to Germany; that is, after 50 years of believing and feeling shame about the acclaimed incapability of Jews to pronounce the regular Russian "r." In Germany he discovered that guttural "r" is derivative from its German origin. As in Yiddish, it evolved from Russian speaking Jews who presumably wandered into Russia and the Ukraine speaking Yiddish. Reflecting on this process, he realized that it was above all a means of creating exclusion and stigmatization:

---

173 See, for example, the work by Diemling (2005) about the perception of Jews in 18th century Frankfurt.

"My parents lived in the Jewish quarter in Kishinev [Moldova] and did not speak Russian very well. Anti-Semites called out '*kurrochka*' [the diminutive form that references the Russian word for chicken; Misha pronounces it with extra rolling of the guttural—"r"] not only referring to them but also to me. I was ashamed of myself. How can it be that they [other Jews] are so inferior and cannot say the [normal] "r" [pronounces the hard Russian "r"]? 50 years later I came to Germany and heard this guttural "r" again but here it is normal. Probably the Yiddish guttural "r" originates from German."

In addition to the stigmatized guttural letter "r," participants mentioned several swear words in Russian created from words related to Jews or abusive Russian words that refer to Jews. Many other disparaging, hurtful Russian slang words describing or referring to Jews were cited, such as: "*zhidi*" [Yids], "*zhidyary*" [exaggerated form of Yids, such as biggest or most]; "*yevreichata*" or "*zhidki*" [condemnation or belittlement of Yids]; "*zhido-massony*" [Yids who were Masons]; combination, "*chitroumnye yevrei*" [cunning Jews]; "*gorbonosyi*" [crooked or hunch-nosed, Rus.]; "*haika*" [contemptuous, recalling the Jewish name Haya; meaning Jewish women in general, Rus.]. All these words were well known and often experienced by most of the participants directly, but especially by those whose looks matched common stereotypes about Jews. Particularly striking was the use by participants in Germany of *zhidi*, *zhidyary*, *chitroumnye yevrei*, *gorbonosyi* and *haika* in referring to Other Jews, when criticizing their negative features, and stressing their own attempts to distance themselves from *such* people.

These descriptions of the participants' experiences and references collected during the study correspond completely with the general claim made by Slezkine about the pejorative, often diminutive nature of all Russian words describing Jews: "permanently associated with particular modifiers (cunning, mangy) and used productively to coin new forms (such as Russian *zhidit'sa*, to be greedy)" (Slezkine 2004, 108) [created from the Russian *zhid*, an abusive word for Jews]. Furthermore, according to Malachov, the Russian language can be seen to be an "exact indicator of the intellectual and psychological climate in the society" [Rus.] (Malachov 2001, 106).

During the fieldwork in Germany, the uses documented of the Russian stigmatized word "Jew" seem to reveal the participants' inner conflicts as it was primarily associated with a social stigma in the SU. Hence, it was a word that many participants in Germany would rarely apply voluntarily in referring to themselves, voluntarily. Slezkine formulated a precise formulation of the difficulty encountered in admitting one's Jewishness in the public sphere in the SU: "The public statement 'I am a Jew' was either a confession of guilt or a gesture of defiance" (Slezkine 2004, 339).

Deprived of any cultural content, *stigmatization* was the main signifier of their Jewishness in the SU. As stated by Bella (Germany):

"To be Jewish implies a terrible history and a difficult life. It is a *kleimo* [like a brand engraved on the body] on you as a characteristic that follows your entire life."[174]

Thus, in summarizing the results, participants in the SU developed different coping strategies throughout their lives that produced a wide variety of actions: Avoiding articulation of the word 'Jew' or words connected with Jewishness, repression, or rejection of Jewish affiliation. Many rejected references to themselves as "*yevrei po pasportu*" [passport Jews, Rus.]. Thus, many sought to distance themselves from this group by attempting to avoid it, by expressing hostility to it, or refusing to give the "label" a positive content.[175]

Modifications of "engraved" Jewish identity in Israel and Germany

Generally speaking it would not be entirely correct to claim that the obligatory character of Jewish Soviet identity changed to an optional one with emigration. In Israel, Jewish attachment was once again registered on identity cards and, in Germany, too, Jews are easily recognizable as a unique group in their state-issued documentation as they alone have been awarded the special immigration status of *Kontingentflüchtlinge* [contingent refugees, Ger.]. Nonetheless, registration of Jewish attachment has significantly different meanings in the two countries.

Immigration to two very different countries—Israel and Germany—determined to a large extent the ways in which immigrants considered, experienced, and reflected their Jewishness in each of the new contexts. Although they came from the same socio-cultural Diaspora context of the Soviet Union, different memories of their former home were reactivated in

---

174 This vision does not mean that people necessary try to distance themselves from all Jewish rituals and Jewish culture today. Bella, for example, works in the Jewish community in Germany. Rather it deals here with an Outsider ascription of the dominant groups in the Diaspora and ideas about the contacts and interactions with non-Jewish Others.

175 See discussion below under Components Three and Four.

accordance with the situations in which they found themselves in the new context. Whereas to come to Israel as a Jew meant to be awarded the privileged status of citizenship, the expectation advanced by means of ideologically driven policies was that immigrants would "melt" into the Jewish national collective and inevitably become part of it, at least symbolically. In contrast, to come to Germany as a Jew meant endless confrontation with a painful chapter in history of Jews in Germany and to become part of other Diaspora minorities than in the SU.

In Israel, national politics and policies advanced, with fervor, the transformation of the Jewish self-image from its former stigmatized, traumatized Diasporic status to the powerful, dominant one, embellished with emotionally positive elements of Jewish identity. In contrast, in Germany, all the painful experiences, negative minority images, "engraved" identities, and even elements of self-hatred of personal Jewish identity seem to be preserved by the Jews interviewed. Tania, for example, stressed the *burdensome nature* of her being Jewish in Germany, describing it as a permanent process: "There is nothing easier than to be Jewish in Israel, whereas here [Germany] it is a permanent process of overcoming."

During my interviews in Israel, memories about the Jewishness of immigrants in the SU were reconstructed above all else through comparisons with the current transformation experienced there that stressed the positive and important aspects of their self-identity. These memories seem to override, even repress in some degree, the painful anti-Semitic experiences of their life in the SU. Elements from Jewish symbolic rituals such as Jewish food (e.g., gefillte fish, tzimes, roglach, teiglach, farschmack, kneidlach, or matza) were well known to participants (Israel) and their relations with traditionally oriented grandparents were mentioned frequently and accentuated in descriptions of their Jewish life in the SU. This seemed to be an effort to create a symbolic continuation with the dominant Jewish Israeli culture. Often the unpleasant anti-Semitic experiences of life in the SU were articulated as the common experiences shared by all Soviet Jews[176] and were referred to humorously or as a rationale supporting their right decision to choose Israel as a migration destination.

The Jewishness of participants (Israel) was presented as an innate, given, genetic fact that for the first time was part of a desired personal

---

176 This corresponds with findings of Rapoport, Lomsky-Feder and Heider (2002) about the normalization of Soviet anti-Semitic phenomena experienced by Russian-speaking migrants in Israel and Germany.

identity that was visible and in some situations demonstrated as a part of the normative dominant identity. Nonetheless, while these migrants tried to demonstrate their Jewishness by adopting the official, national Jewish narrative, such attachment continues to be doubted by many non-Russian Israelis in public discourse. Indeed, internally held *innate visibility* has been accompanied by a new kind of *Significant Otherness* constructed from outside in which the migrants are portrayed as foreign and often stigmatized as Russians. Thus, variations of Significant Otherness are present in both contexts of Israel and Germany.

This finding is demonstrated in the following incident recounted by Ella during an interview conducted during the final stage of the fieldwork in Israel (2008; i.e., 17—18 years after most participants' migration). First, by way of background, Ella's comments relate to a terrorist attack that took place in Jerusalem on July 2, 2008 when an Arab construction worker killed several people by driving a bulldozer that rammed, smashed, and drove over cars. Ella recalled watching TV news accounts almost every hour and speaking with her friends about the Jewish-Arab conflict and how it could be resolved. In doing so, she used the terms "we" (Jews) and "they" (Arabs). During a program that was telecasted following the evening news, she recounted being astounded and extremely upset by the comments made by a stand-up comedian who joked about Russians while pretending to present the weather forecast at the end of the daily news.[177]

"I couldn't fall asleep at all that night. What happened was so terrible. [I mean] what this terrorist Arab construction worker did. And then I turned on the TV that evening and heard the reports of a mother who tried to save her baby by throwing her out of the car window before she [the mother] died. After all of that [these reports] comes an idiot [on another program] who says: 'Tomorrow it's going to be warmer. This is bad news for Russian *meav'tech'im haRussim* [Russian security guards; she included the Hebrew phrase while speaking Russian]. But we have a solution for you. [holds up deodorant]. It is cold at first, but then fresh.'

Can you imagine? All Jews were shocked by the terrorist act while he spoke about *harussim hamasrichim* [lit. stinking Russians, Heb; again Ella used a well-known Hebrew phrase amidst her Russian speech]. Such a racist! How can anyone do something like this? And the entire country heard this and many people probably laughed at us [ex-Soviet migrants]. So we [with her daughter] sent a letter of protest, but it did not help. Nobody apologized…"

---

177 The statement can be seen in the last five minutes of the Hebrew newsreport broadcast on theInternet: http://news.nana10.co.il/Article/?ArticleID=564036&TypeID=1&sid=126, 21.06.2010.

Clearly Ella was disturbed by the timing of such humor, the day of a terrorist act, as well as, the fact that jokes are made about Russian-speaking Jewish migrants who risk their lives in return for minimal wages working as security guards at shop entrances. However, in my opinion, this citation also reveals the contradictions in her everyday identity performance of "being Jewish" (Inowlocki 2000). Whereas terror acts gave Ella a particularly tragic opportunity to identify herself with the Israeli-Jewish collective, citing the comedian's jokes about the news stresses the status of former Soviet migrants as stigmatized Russian Others, who are marginalized if not excluded by the dominant group, all the while performing the fictitious, illusory claim that a homogeneous Jewish collective exists. All of this challenges Ella's capability to cope.

This interpretation is reaffirmed in the views of non-Jewish spouses who attempt to construct their Jewishness; again, the most desired identity while living in Israel. Especially interesting was the example of Olga, a 47-year old Russian woman who is divorced from her Jewish spouse and lives with her 16 year old daughter in Israel. Olga related her feeling of being Jewish by means of a dream in which she dreamt that her parents were Jewish and purposively lost their documents in order to escape their Jewishness in the SU. This mystified construction of Olga's sense of illegitimacy imparted in social life to ethnic Russians in the Jewish national state corresponds to the findings of Zaslavskaya and Horowitz who interpreted such tactics as one of the strategies of attachment to Israel undertaken by young, non-Jewish, Russian speakers in their attempts to perform being Jewish (Zaslavskaya and Horowitz 2007).

Jews in Germany develop and perform "being Jewish" in a different manner (ibid). As will be discussed in the next chapter, the painful and traumatized Jewishness born by migrants from the SU to Germany was not only preserved, but became even more complicated due to the legacy of the Holocaust. Thus, different from the aspiration to be Jewish in Israel, Russian-speaking Jews in Germany partially reproduced and implemented different strategies for dealing with rejection or distancing themselves from the stigmatized images of Jews. Even participants who started to be interested in Jewish culture and traditions upon immigrating to Germany sensed the negative connotations associated with the concept *Jew*. Consequently, they were ashamed to use the Russian word *Yevrei* and, as in the SU, avoided using it or at most whispered it.

However, nearly every interviewee in Germany started by repeating a similar clearly formulated statement: "Actually there is nothing Jewish about me." Yet, throughout the interview, it was clear that being Jewish was a significant albeit controversial and painful part of their personal identities.

Elionora (Germany) is a representative of this phenomenon. In our interview, she started with the claim that there is nothing Jewish about her, followed by two sentences in which she listed things she knew about Judaism and traditional Jewish life. The following citation reveals the controversial nature of this essential but undesired sense of attachment with which she has been coping throughout her life:

> "It is not very lucky to be born a Jew. Actually I'm not Jew in any sense. I am my mother and father's daughter and I too wanted to save my daughter from Jewishness, but she married a religious Jew [...] Yes, I know about Pesach [Passover, Heb.] and Yom Kippur, and I did understand Yiddish but always answered in Russian. I did not want to have anything in common with it. But I could not hide that I am a Jew…"

Most participants in Germany indicated that they preferred to hide their Jewish identity in interactions with non-Jews in Germany in the public sphere. This seems to be a strategy both to protect themselves from potential anti-Semitism as well as to avoid unpleasant confrontations within two possible narratives: First, the Holocaust and collective German history; second, at the micro level, different personal German and Jewish biographies. Participants usually presented themselves as Russians; that is, as non-Jewish, non-Russian speakers.[178] Participants related that on several occasions Germans, with whom they shared their Jewish identity, advised them not to tell "other Germans" of their being Jewish, because "there are many anti-Semites in Germany." As a result, in order to avoid the complexities of Jewish related topics in Germany, most participants chose what seemed to be a better or less harmful of two stigmatized labels—as Russians or Jews. Here, in this context, they believed that being considered to be Russian was better than being a Jew.

This action by participants (Germany) may also be an alternative strategy for coping with stigmatized identities. In order to escape negatively laden Russian and Jewish labels or controversial identities in national terms

---

178 In one case a woman had to impersonate being an ethnic German, as discussed in Chapter Nine.

within local German contexts, some participants preferred to present themselves as *chelovek mira* [world citizen, Rus.]. Rather than Hannerz's (1990) concept of "voluntary elitist cosmopolitan," such a construction may be an attempt to shield themselves from the painful history associated with such an impossible attachment (i.e. as Jews, as well as, Russians in situ with the national German collective) that provides an interim cover while searching for a dignified alternative. In this sense, self-presentation as world citizens differs also from Pécoud's idea of "cosmopolitanism from below" (Pécoud 2000). Contradicting the view of Hannerz, Pécoud argued that as a result of constraints people seek to improve the conditions of their lives and to advance their own transnational entrepreneurships by developing cosmopolitan competencies as a necessary part of their economic praxis.

Yet, self-presentation by ex-Soviet Jewish migrants in Germany by means of the concept of *chelovek mira* may be seen as a defense mechanism deprived of content. World citizenry, as understood today, would include positive experiences in mobility, the command of a language or at least the capability to speak English as a necessary means of communication in different societies, as well as, global thinking (non-national). Yet, all such components of cultural *habitus* are absent among Russian-speaking Jewish citizens in Germany: They immigrated from the closed Russian-speaking empire and in most cases had not visited any other country prior to emigration. Rather than being polyglots, many participants in the German case complained that unfortunately they did not know any other language except Russian. And, during the interviews they demonstrated nationalist thoughts using a nationalist terminology in everyday speech, as will be demonstrated in the next chapter. Indeed, all stressed attachment to the Jewish nation and many expounded nationalistic right-wing political views ground in nationalist values. The fact that none of the participants in Israel claimed identity as a world citizen, too, supports my claim that *chelovek mira* was used as a strategy to shield themselves from both a painful, contested identity and missing sense of attachment.

Also striking was the discovery that the same persons who declared themselves to be world citizens in one interview expressed internalized anti-Semitic sentiments in another interview. Perhaps this is due to a desire to be an inconspicuous part of the majority's normal collective identity, as in doing so they perform strong aspirations to belong and a willingness to expend enormous efforts to look, live, think and act like members of this majority group. Whether or not this is their motivation, such statements reveal an internalization of various dominant values and acting, some of which are anti-Semitic. However, as Gilman pointed out in his analysis of the phenomenon of Jewish self-hatred, such attempts usually do not lead to acceptance by Others, they rather cause conflicts within the inner identity:

"But the more one attempts to identify with those who have labeled one as different, the more one accepts the values, social structures, and attitudes of this determining group, the farther away from true acceptability one seems to be" (Gitelman 1986, 3).

Anti-Semitic Jewish expressions applied by some participants in Germany to describe Other Jews can also be seen as a dramatic form of coping with self-hatred as Jews and as an aspiration for an unattainable, normative identity. This phenomenon includes the use of clichéd sentences about Jews as those responsible and guilty for being hated in the world; canny, spendthrift Jews; or references to *zhidi* to describe Other Jews. At least seven interviewees employed anti-Semitic references internalized in the SU and then reproduced in Germany. In doing so, participants may be trying to distance themselves from a self-perception of Jewish identity that is *engraved* upon them. For example, at least five interviewees formulated the reason for not emigrating to Israel through use of humor, such as the following statement by Alexii (Germany):

"You know, there are too many Jews. Somebody, I think Einstein, said that good only comes in small quantities—and even they should be spread like fertilizer, because when they are all in one small place, well, you know [laughs, pause]… It would be quite difficult for me to stand them in large numbers."

Alexii was happy he did "not look Jewish" because he escaped at least direct *bytovoi* [lit. domestic; meaning, everyday, Rus.] anti-Semitism in the SU. To immigrate to Israel would mean to choose, voluntarily, something that he tried to escape from his entire life; that is, to admit to and to perform publicly his stigmatized Jewish identity. This would be achieved even by simply being among other Jews, instead of his usual praxis of hiding his passive Jewish identity (registered in his passport) and trying to assimilate as much as possible. Gilman observed that this form of Jewish self-anti-Semitism was "valid as a label for a specific mode of self-abnegation that has existed among Jews throughout their history" (Gilman 1986, 1).

Independent of the question whether or not these participants realized the anti-Semitic nature of their statements, this strategy represents one way of coping with an *engraved*, essential, given, and inescapable Jewish identity that did not include a praxis of any kind by Soviet Jews. This interpretation explains Russian-speaking Jews' confusion when Germans who knew they were Jews would ask: "Do you work on Saturday?" "Do you eat kosher?" "Do you speak Yiddish at home?" or "How is it in your motherland?" [meaning, Israel]. Seemingly neutral, naïve, or the result of *pure* curiosity, such questions often produced among Jewish counter-parts strong associations and memories from the SU of having been "spotted" and stigmatized as Other; that is, as being of a different nature, one not attached to the dominant Soviet collective. Indeed, despite the fact that they possessed the same Russified, Soviet cultural *habitus* as that of ethnic Russian citizens, such questions evoked memories of their unsuccessful attempts to be Russians, including their unbridled zeal for many decades to distance themselves from the image of *mestechkovye yevrei* [shtetl Jews, Rus.] reflective of their religious grandparents.[179] Mila (Germany), for example, recalled:

"I brought a dish to work [in the SU] and colleagues asked jokingly: 'Is it kosher?' Of course I was embarrassed. I replied by saying: 'What is that to you?' Ahhh [waves her hand with a gesture as if to say 'there is nothing more to add' or 'it is obviously clear'], all this Jewish stuff [pause] was sickening."[180]

Although the same questions about Jewish traditions, religion, or Yiddish had very different meanings when asked in Israel and Germany, they were perceived by participants in both contexts as stressing differences and group boundaries that conjured up unpleasant experiences rather than interactions based on curiosity. However, it is important to stress that the confusion and irritation about Outsiders' questions do not contradict some interviewees' interest in the Jewish tradition or participation in local Jewish communal life. For example, Mila (cited above as somebody who bore the branding of *engraved* Jewish identity her entire life) began to read about the Jewish tradition and to observe Jewish holidays following migration to

---

179 Slezkine (2004) noted that after the Revolution Jews denied all Jewish attributes and tried to be more Russian than the Russians themselves.

180 In order to contextualize the discriminating situation described by Mila, one has to realize that in the socialistic societies the place of work was "not only the center of everyday social gathering, but also the symbolic space of community and national affiliation" (Berdahl 2002, 478).

Germany. Thus, this analysis indicates how participants decoded and interpreted inexplicit intentions of non-Russian Outsiders who asked questions connected with affiliation and its practice.

6.4 Component Three: Suspect loyalty: Soviet Jewish Otherness through affiliation with Israel

In addition to the exclusionary practices and negatively loaded connotations of Soviet Jewishness, positively loaded constructions of Jewishness that influenced everyday praxis of this group, too, should be discussed. Two positive aspects that constitute Jewish Soviet ethnicity were identified in the study: the connection to Israel (Component 3) and pride in the achievements of Soviet Jews in different cultural-societal domains (Component 4).

In describing their life in the Soviet Union, participants recalled their deep interest and emotional involvement in events related to Israel that were generally reported negatively in the Soviet press. Israel's important role in constructing Jewish identity is shared with Jews in other Diaspora countries.[181] Although Soviet Jews only possessed general often incomplete understandings of life in Israel and/or never imagined they would be allowed to visit Israel, nonetheless they reported having felt a strong identification with everything that happened there. Accordingly, many reported that they opposed successive Soviet government polices that condemned Israeli military policies and domestic treatment of Arab minorities. Such opposition distinguished the Jewish collective from dominant groups of Soviet citizens. The following two examples from the German fieldwork exemplify this finding:

Leon (Germany): "My mother met Golda Meir in Riga [...] We were undeclared Zionists and believed in Israel's real right to exist. When anyone spoke about problems in Israel, I could not feel that I was a Russian or when there was a war [in Israel], it was clear with whom I sympathized."

Naum (Germany): "Once, there [while he was living in the SU], money was collected for Palestinians at my Institute. I said: 'I will not contribute. They are killing my people there [in Israel].' [I was told] 'You must do so;' and later, 'You are not

---

181 See, for example, studies about American Jews in Feingold (1991) and Meyer (1990).

worthy to be a Soviet engineer.' And then I had to pay in order *not* to retire from my job. And, just think, this was in the 80's! "

Israel was not the only place in the world where the participants' relatives resided. Yet, Israel and its capital, Jerusalem, epitomized, metaphorically, the idea of their own home and historic *motherland*, even if Israel was far away and they had never visited it. Everyday experiences of anti-Semitism and suspicion of Soviet Jews as disloyal, untrustworthy elements were expressed in the society by institutional representatives who played their role in distancing Jews from a total identification with the Soviet Union as their motherland.[182] Furthermore, most participants living in Israel and in Germany reported having feelings of permanent insecurity about the Soviet policy concerning Jews and the potential affects of such policies on their own life and the lives of their children.

The sharpest feelings of Otherness were felt during waves of Jewish emigration, for example during the 1970's. Thus, although they chose to remain in the SU, they were permanently exposed to expectations to prove their loyalty to the state and to explain their attitudes about those who emigrated. There was enormous pressure exerted on them by the surrounding social environment that identified them with the émigrés [Jews] who "betrayed the state" (in the political language at that time) through emigration to the West. Then, to have relatives or closed friends abroad was considered to be a personal participation in the "crime" and had many consequences including sanctions that affected their lives. The humiliation suffered by having to renounce or to condemn their own relatives in public did not instill more trust in them. Paradoxically, by deciding to stay in the SU, they were considered to be even more suspect, as *different Others*.

Finally, as detailed in Chapter Eight, following migration to Germany, Russian-speaking Jews did not lose their closed emotional affiliation with the state Israel, even if they were critical of it, rather they developed even stronger support.

---

182 Such positions were stressed and reinforced by Soviet authorities who suspected Jews of being "untrustworthy elements" and potential "betrayers" of the motherland through the act of emigration.

6.5 Component Four: Affiliation with Soviet Russian cultural elite

The final component of the concept of former Soviet Russian-speaking Jews' *Jewishness* is the attachment to the socio-cultural values of this group. Such attachment can be seen, for example, in the Jewish cultural tradition that places a high value on education, especially on the study of religious texts (Slezkine 2004; Kessler 1996), which in the Soviet case was combined with the socialist cultivation of education. As Lida (Germany) formulated it in our interview: "Our [Soviet Jews] religion was education." The value of learning survived despite all sorts of limits and obstacles placed on entrance to universities or appointment to prestigious jobs.

Paradoxically, for many of the Soviet Jews, Jewishness meant completing an academic (Soviet) education and embodying, as well as, being accepted into the stratum of the Russian intelligentsia (Ritterband 1997; Slezkine 2004). In doing so, Jews sought to realize a central precept of Russian culture, one that demonstrates achievement of a high level of education combined with a commitment to certain moral and social values. This precept is exemplified in the following statement by Misha (Germany):

"I was always proud to recognize a lot of *nashich* [Ours, Rus.; here meaning Jews] among the Russian intelligentsia [meaning Soviet Russian intelligentsia]. My wife and I viewed movies or performances in the theatre and knew that he, or he and she, are great and they are Jews, but among the Russian elite. At that time to be a Jew in Moscow obligated you to be well-educated, to speak good literary Russian, to have read this and other books, to know your way in history, to have studied piano as a child, to play piano or the violin, which we have all done, and yes, to criticize Soviet policy in private. Maybe among Jews in the Soviet peripheries, in Chernovzy or Zhitomer [small cities where many Jews lived in the Ukraine that were referred to as the 'pale of settlement' before the Revolution] it was different. They knew Yiddish and more about Jewish traditions than did people in the big cities."

Ella (Israel) offered similar observations: "Of course, all our culture was Russian. Actually it has remained Russian until today. The language, books, and authors I love are Russian authors: Babel, Brodski, Erenburg, Grossman, Mandelstam, Pasternak, Gorin…[pause]."

JB: "All the authors you mentioned were Jews."

Ella: "Yes, mostly Jewish Russian authors. We have always distinguished between Jewish and non-Jewish actors, authors, producers, poets. It was pleasant to see a

Russian genius who was a Jew. Do you remember what happened when Kasparov [a Jew] played chess against Karpov? Karpov [a non-Jewish Russian chess player] was supported by the authorities. You know sport was a very political matter at that time [in the SU]. We were scared that play would be interrupted if they saw that Kasparov was going to win. All Jews [Soviet Jews] were worried. It was really an event! [pause]"

JB: "So you mean Jews in the Russian culture?"

Ella: "No, I identify myself with Russian culture, and there were a lot of famous Jews within Russian culture. Jewish families usually hold Russian culture in high esteem and have contributed much to its development. That is why they were blamed so often for 'usurping' Russian culture. You know speech about '*zasilie evreev v russkoi culture*' [lit. the Jews' strangle hold over Russian culture, Rus.]. There were many educated people among Jews and you always saw many books in their homes and also here [in Israel] you see how many books they brought and buy in Russian bookstores. "

These two examples display the characteristics of Jewish ethnicity practiced in the private family sphere in the SU—a private, enclosed, isolated space that is safe from the *outside* world. This finding corresponds, in general, with other research findings (Chervyakov, Gitelman and Shapiro 1997; Slezkine 2004). Both Misha and Ella are proud to belong to the Jewish group that they feel contributed to the entire Russian Soviet culture. They emphasize in explicit ways the important role of education and acquiring elements of high culture as an inextricable part of being Jewish.

Furthermore, both participants assumed that to be Jewish is to be associated with the educated Russian (meaning Russified Soviet) intelligentsia community. In her response to my question, Ella made it clear that she refused to think categorically and to distinguish between "Jews" and "Russian culture." For her, as was the case for all participants in the two fieldwork studies, both are inseparable parts of her personal identity. She stressed that she did distinguish between *ethnic Russian* and *ethnic Jewish* agents of Soviet culture (in the Soviet meaning of *nationalnost'*), but the only culture she had internalized and knows is the Soviet Russian one. It is the cultivated, elitist, legitimate culture within which Soviet Jews participate. And, she acknowledged that they did so as Jews, hence compensating, symbolically for the stigmatized nature of the concept "Soviet Jew." Their pride in Jews who contributed and co-created to the Soviet-Russian elite culture is supported by awareness of the overrepresentation of Jews among the Russian cultural elite (n. b., Although Jews made up 0.7 percent of the population, their representation in highly qualified professions as well as in cultural and political areas was 10—20 percent; thus, they were clearly overrepresented: i.e. 10.8 percent of all scientists, 14.7 percent of all medical doctors, 10 percent of all lawyers, and 10 percent of writers (Kessler 1996; Schoeps 1992; Slezkine 2004; Weinerman 1997)).

Both Misha's and Ella's descriptions reveal the tendency to use the phrases "cultural Russian intelligentsia" and "Soviet Jewish" interchangeably. When the topic of the Jews' cultivation of the Russian culture is discussed in both citations it is impossible for either participant to consider Jewish and Soviet Russian as two different discourses. Interestingly, they do make a clear distinction in many other discussions between Soviet-Russian and Jewish discourses, especially in regard to socio-political issues. These findings of realizing and feeling themselves as Jews through Russian culture confirms the research of this topic presented earlier (Chapter One).

Thus, we can say that the group of Jews investigated possesses the cultural capital of an "upper class group." They are a highly qualified, well-educated group who grew up in the large cities of Russia and the Ukraine. As such, they adopted habits characteristic of the cultural milieu, such as visiting theaters and concerts given by artists visiting from the CIS, attending exhibitions, classical music concerts and operas, as well as, avidly reading of new publications of Russian literature and poetry.

Interestingly, in the Israeli and Germany cases, we can trace different ways in which participants drew group borders, as an effort to distinguish themselves from certain resident populations. In the Israeli case study, they distinguished themselves especially from those populations that embodied the image of Middle Eastern groups, stressing their European origin. Their collective positioning and preserving of the European Diaspora culture recalls similar actions by other Jewish-European immigrants in Israel, especially German Jews who had preserved their cultural *habitus* throughout 50 years of living in Israel, prior to the period when the acclaimed multicultural model of society was advanced.[183] In the German case, Jews sought to distinguish themselves primarily from other immigrant labor groups in Germany, especially from other Russian speakers (e. g., *Spätaussiedler*, resettled ethnic Germans mostly from Kazakhstan, Ger.), with whom they are

---

183 There are additional inner differentiations concerning the concept of Jewishness, as for example between Soviet European and Soviet Asiatic Jews, between rural Jews and Jews in the cities, or between educated and uneducated Jews. This differentiation will not be elaborated here as this research project deals with a specific group of Jews from Russia and the Ukraine.

often presented in the public sphere under the reductive label as "Russians."

Thus, a close comparison reveals a significant difference in tracing the groups' self-drawn borders between the collective's image making in Israel and Germany: Given their self-identify as members of the Russian cultural elite, former Soviet Jews sought to continue to live according to this life style in both Germany and Israel. In Israel, participants performed as well-educated, qualified professionals. They stressed that they were representatives of the European culture in the "Orient." Furthermore, despite economic difficulties sustained by migrants in the Israeli economic market over the last 15 years, a flourishing Russian cultural enclave developed that facilitated and advanced cultural self-realization that is a source of pride, rather than "a sign of shameful otherness" (Mittelberg and Borshevsky 2004, 89; see also, Zilberg 2002). This enclave includes such cultural and educational institutions as the *Gesher Theater Company* and *Mofet* school network, both well-known and considered to be prestigious far beyond the Russian speaking enclave in Israel in the wider Israeli cultural scene. Consequently, participants were conscious that the Soviet-Russian culture of one million ex-Soviet Jews in Israel succeeded in being influential in almost all areas of Israeli life and continues to make significant contributions to developing the controversial, multicultural image of Israeli Jewish collective.

In Germany, however, the low number of Russian speakers, in proportion to the entire German population, as well as, controversies over the image of the ex-Soviet enemy has made it difficult for the migrants to realize their potential to contribute to or to integrate Soviet-Russian culture into the dominant, resident cultural collectives. In addition, the participants' potential cultural-social contribution to local Jewish communities was made difficult because of two longstanding traditions of deeply ingrained dichotomized stereotypes in Germany between civilized, modern, West Europeans versus the barbaric, backward, Eastern Europeans; and, second, because of the stereotypes about Soviet Russians preserved since the Cold War period. Moreover, it was not the Russian culture but more precisely the cultural-religious Jewishness that was expected as the migrants' symbolical contribution to the new image of Germany as Jewish communities expanded after the Holocaust. However, such an image could not be realized by ex-Soviet Jews. Thus, the idea of Jewish being associated with the Russian cultural upper-class served only as an object of pride within the Russian enclave and in private discussions and, furthermore, it remains a permanent misunderstanding between Russian and non-Russian outsiders by resident Jewish as well as different German groups.

6.6 Conclusion

By way of summarizing this general portrayal of Russian-speaking Jewish ethnicity that is characteristic of migrants who immigrated to Israel and Germany, we can say that due to historical circumstances and structural constraints the Russian-speaking Jewish ethnicity was a unique kind of identity in comparison with Jewish identities that exist in settlement countries of Israel and throughout the Western Ashkenasim Diaspora. One might conclude at first glance that the negative orientation of the first two components of Russian speaking Jewish ethnicity—*innate visibility* and *significant Otherness*—was offset by the last two components—*pride in Israel and Jewish representation in* and *contribution to the Soviet-Russian culture*. However, the conclusion posited here claims that all four components represent different elements of an exclusion mechanism applied to Soviet Jews in Israel and in Germany that are inseparable from experiences of discrimination described in the interviews.

Innate, visible and significant Otherness, stigmatized through somatic conceptions of the Jewish body, are claims that associate Jews with pollution and impurity, a special *Jewish* accent, and negative character features that suggest that Jews are a disloyal and untrustworthy group. Continuing in the tradition of anti-Semitism, these features easily incorporate other ideas connected with Jews. For example, pride in the accomplishments of the State of Israel that was "built by [other] Jews out of the desert" (reproducing an acclaimed national Israeli myth endlessly repeated by Soviet Jews). Yet, this claim was perceived by many non-Jewish residents, as well as, officially in the public sphere as treason to the Soviet motherland and betrayal through potential emigration. In turn, numerous contributions by Russian-speaking Jews in shaping Soviet Russian culture, too, received an anti-Semitic interpretation, as they were not perceived to be real Russians. For example, they usurped the place of real Russians in the cultural production and projected the provocative pretension of Jewish cultural superiority based not on "their own Jewish" but rather through "our Russian" culture that they have no right to possess. Thus, on the basis of the interviews, Russian-speaking Jewish ethnicity has to be viewed in conjunction with strong traumatic stigmatizations as well as with the events and conditions of exclusion and discrimination experienced by Soviet Jews.

Russian-speaking Jews who immigrated to Israel learned the collective narrative that explains these experiences as the painful destiny of Jews in the Diaspora, which they left behind, if only symbolically, until joining the unification and empowerment efforts of Jews in Israel. In preserving Soviet-Russian culture and the idea of *innate Jewishness*, participants in Israel recalled fragmented memories of Jewish cultural rituals practiced by grandparents who spoke Yiddish, practiced Jewish religious life, and had lived in shtetls. Such performances can be seen as a way to create continuity with their Jewish cultural past, in the present. In doing so, the idea of *significant Otherness* is transformed at the macro level into *significant Otherness* as a chosen folk. However, the other transformation of *significant Otherness*, found in the Israeli case was their frequent exclusion from the illusionary homogenous Israeli collective, given their significant difference as *"Russim"* [Russians, Heb.].

Russian-speaking Jews who immigrated to Germany found themselves in a much more controversial and conflict-laden situation of *significant Otherness*. Their unique understanding of being Soviet-Jewish alienates them in a number of ways: Group members included Holocaust victims and ex-Soviet winners who immigrated to their former enemy's and perpetuators' country. And, while life within the Jewish community in Germany is guided by the precept to act as one common Jewish culture, in practice the migrants' own vision of their Jewishness was ignored or rejected, while they were patronized by members of the local Jewish community who sought to transform them into "real Jews."[184]

While the Jewish identity of participants differed in both contexts, overall it can be characterized as a subjective feeling of being Jewish that was continuously challenged in the SU, as well as, in Israel and Germany in migrants' everyday experiences. The idea of immanent, innate Jewishness retained together with the subjective feeling of being Jewish often caused

---

184 This is often formulated as such by Jewish members who reside in the community, as well as, abroad, and is also cited in the German media. See for example Riebsamen "kleine jüdische Wunder," *Frankfurter Allgemeine Zeitung* 11 November 2006 or Kanis, "Voller Hoffnung. 15 Jahre Zuwanderung: Eine Tagung des Zentralrats in Köln," *Allgemeine Jüdische Zeitung*, (May 26, 2006, 19).

participants to be confused: for example, when asked: "What is particularly
Jewish about people who do not know the Jewish culture, religion, and
tradition?" or "Are you a practicing Jew?" Such questions were perceived
by participants as absurd, something akin to asking: "Are you a practicing
woman?"; "Are you practicing being an educated person?" or, "Are you
practicing being European." This is due to the perception of *being Jewish*
held by the participants and their feeling that the inescapable, immanent,
innate nature of their Jewishness did not need any proof nor did it presume the need to demonstrate any form of cultural practice. In summary,
as Felix (Israel) formulated it [inveighing an offensive tone]:

"They [Israelis] ask you 'bema bidiyuk atem Yehudim?' [How exactly are you Jewish? Heb.; uses Hebrew sentence in Russian speech] What in the hell should be
particularly Jewish about me if I was already born as a Jew and feel Jewish?"

6.7 Triple Trans-Jewish affiliation

The findings also suggest that following emigration from the SU, the participants' construction, reconstruction, and performance of Jewish identity
involves a *triple transnational affiliation* to Jewish ethnicity: First, to the Jewish
ethnicity practiced in the country of origin; second, to Jewish perceptions
and practices in the new society (Israel or Germany); and, third, to the
Jewish collective in Israel, for those who immigrated to Germany, and to
the Russian-speaking Jewish Diaspora in Germany, for those who immigrated to Israel.

The possibility for Russian-speaking Jewish migrants to have permanent access to these three countries created a special situation that allowed
for prolonged comparisons between life in two Jewish Diasporas (CIS and
Germany) and in Israel, the historic Jewish "motherland." The mass media
were one of the primary sources of information feeding this process and
included Russian-speaking satellite TV channels, Russian language Jewish
periodicals (e.g., the widely read *Vesti* in Israel or *Yevreiskaya Gazeta* in
Germany),[185] and Internet sites.[186] The second primary source was the

---

185 According to Zilberg (2002), there are between 15—20 Russian publishers in Israel that
    publish magazines, journals, and books in the Russian language. For the German Rus-
    sian-speaking Jewish oriented press, see Darieva (2000) and Elias (2005).
186 See for example, www.sem.40.ru; www.evrei.ru.

extended and extensive community that maintained itself through social networks with and visits by migrant friends and relatives in both countries. And, in regard especially to Israel, migrants in Germany preserved a strong emotional tie to Israel via contacts with their many friends and relatives who chose to migrate there. Indeed, all German based participants demonstrated extensive interest in all contemporary Israeli affairs, often referred to as the "historic motherland" (n. b., often accompanied by clichés).

Indeed, as the analysis in Chapter Eight reveals, Israel as a collective reference played a divisive role separating Jews and non-Jews in Germany, especially when Israeli politics are discussed. This phenomenon occurs because Russian-speaking Jews view German non-Jews' critique of Israel as potentially suspect for anti-Semitic reasons, as was usually the case in the SU. Thus, Russian-speaking Jews similar to resident Jews in Germany react in a very sensitive way to German media or non-Jews' positions and approaches to the topic in everyday praxis. In addition, the theme of anti-Semitism as experienced in different countries and throughout history remains an active concern for most participants in Israel and Germany, since it is a very significant category of concern related directly to their living situation and therefore influences their behavior and general thinking about the Jewish collective.

Furthermore, the fieldwork in Germany revealed that the participants share a collective sense of traumatic stress. The active interest and emotional participation of the investigated group in Jewish Israeli life extends and nurtures, in my view, their perception of the traumatically conditioned life of being Jewish. In her research of the Jewish community in Cologne (Köln) Germany, Elias argued that Jewish immigrants in Germany identified themselves with the Jewish rather than the Russian Diaspora (Elias 2005, 177). However, in my fieldwork, I found enduring references and strong attachments to more than one country. Interviewees in Germany follow "every event" in Israel, considered here to be their land of origin, in regard to Jewish life there as well as general cultural-political affairs.

One of the significant characteristics of the current research project was finding active social networks in the transnational space—especially in the German case. Overall, it has to be said that post-migration participants remained in close contact with relatives, friends, and acquaintances living in Israel, CIS, Germany, other countries, and in particular in the United States and Canada. These intensive contacts, as well as, media consumption played important roles in reactivating, refreshing, and modifying concepts related to self-identity, in general, and Jewish identity, in particular. Indeed, there was limited evidence that ex-Soviet Jewish migrants to Germany sought to reject and distance themselves from Jewishness that was experienced as obligatory and traumatic during their lives in the SU. Rather, there is evidence that many participants actually developed an interest in Jewish tradition and culture, even if only at the symbol level in terms of the practice of everyday life, as a kind of "symbolical ethnicity" (Chervyakov, Gitelman and Shapiro 1997). This phenomenon parallels developments among the Jews who remained in the contemporary CIS (ibid).

Especially interesting was the finding that not only the participants in Israel struggled to attain the status of real Jews in comparison with Others [n. b., so confirming—if only symbolically their attachment to the dominant Israeli collective], but some participants in Germany tried to define themselves as *more Jewish* than their Russian-speaking Jewish compatriots in Israel. In both cases one can view these performances as a kind of carrying on an imagined dialogue within the strongly influential Israeli and Germany contexts, in which the realness of their Jewishness is denied or at least is challenged by the surrounding Jewish and non-Jewish communities.

Roman (Germany): "I wonder about our friends from Israel [Russian speaking Jews] when they visit us. They are less Jewish than we are here. They don't go to the synagogue; don't know much about Jewish holidays. They are at home there [in Israel] and don't need to prove that they are still Jews as we do."

Toma (his wife): "And they [Jewish friends who live in Israel] ask: How can you live among fascists?"

Lisa (Germany), on the other hand, represents an alternative stance, distancing herself from Jewishness, as we see in this exchange with Sasha, her husband:

Sasha: "Of course we are Jews, exactly like those who live in Israel. I was born a Jew and could not become somebody else now."

Lisa (born to a Jewish father and Russian mother interrupts in an aggressive tone, looks at their daughter who was listening to the conversation, and says quite loudly):

"What are you talking about? We are Russians. All the Jews left for Israel. We are not real Jews, we are just Russians […]"

Daughter scared: "Mum, ok, ok, calm down, we are Russians, we are Russians! [Sasha shocked by her reaction remains silent.]"

Comparing their life with that of compatriots in other countries, participants in both Israel and Germany often argued that their decision to immigrate was correct. The rationales presented often had a transnational nature. Russian-speaking immigrants in Israel often reminded their friends in Germany about the war and the Holocaust (as in Toma's remark, above), while Russian-speaking migrants in Germany stressed the "oriental," foreign nature of Israel, the economically difficult living conditions, and the harsh climate.

Olga (Germany): "Every time I fly there I see that it was good to come here [Germany]. If I had immigrated to Israel I would have had to share a rented flat with fellow occupants, to work as a cleaner or a geriatric nurse, and would have suffered permanently from the heat and the Orient.[187] And I [already] have heart problems. I am a European person. I suffered enough when I lived in the communal flat in Russia [in a 16 square meter room meant to inhabit four persons,] until I was 35 years old. And I worked hard my entire life [...]"

In turn, Bella, who immigrated to Israel, argued she was right to decide to come to live in Israel. Comparing her decision to that of people who immigrated to Germany, she said [in a judging tone]:

"Everyone made his choice. We came to the Jewish state and they...[pause], well, to economic wealth. I can understand that. It is convenient there, no question, but nevertheless to Germany? For this price?[...]"

Following this statement, Bella showed me an Israeli newspaper article in Russian about the problematic nature of the decision to immigrate to Germany, in support of her decision to participate in the Jewish Israeli collective. The author of this article, Hanan, described a recent visit to Germany as an ex-Soviet, now Israeli author.[188] During the trip, he read his most recent play to Russian-speaking migrant audiences. The plot of the play is about the agonizing reflections of a Jewish family in Germany who immigrated from a small Soviet village, where all the Jews had been murdered by the Nazis. In the newspaper article, Hanan described how he

---

187 The combination of the hot climate and the Orient used in referring to Israel is repeated in many other interviews and, thus, appears to have become a key phrase in describing Israel by ex-Soviet immigrants in Germany.

188 Hanan, "Return to Ashkenaz," *Vesti* (supplement "*Okna*") (February 16, 2006, 30—32 [Russian]).

would look into the audience and see the weeping faces of the immigrants, and how all his books were sold out during the intermission.

On the way "home" (i.e. to the airport to fly to Israel), he described looking at the passing German landscape from the car window and stated that now he is no longer ashamed of these people [i.e. Russian-speaking Jews in Germany], but rather feels

"endless pity that they have chosen Germany—this big Jewish cemetery—as their new homeland, just because they are afraid and because they do not want to be Jews"(Hanan 2006, 32)[Rus.].

Thus, the first characteristic of transnational interaction identified in the fieldwork deals with changing and redefining group identity by distinguishing it from constructed Others. This is one of the principal processes of collective identity creation (Hall 1997; Hedetoft 2003; Schäffter 1991; Simmel 1950; Stonequist 1937). By juxtaposing themselves to Russian-speaking Jewish immigrants in Germany, Russian-speaking Jews in Israel claimed to have made the right moral decision by "coming back to their historical motherland" and to being "more Jewish." In supporting the national myth of Israel as the Jewish state, I claim they redefine themselves as Jews. They are reproachful when asking Russian-speakers in Germany to justify their right decision to immigrate to Germany. Jewish identity, while being contested in both cases, remains controversial and painful only in the German case.

Yet, it would be a mistake to conclude that the two groups are in permanent conflict or that all interactions between them are reduced to only defining self-identity by juxtaposing one to the other (i.e., making Russian speaking compatriots in another land into a kind of "our [Russian speaking] Others"). On the contrary, retaining their enduring contacts—mostly by means of interactions by telephone calls and mutual visits in Israel and in Germany—suggests that there is an intensive inter-relationship between the two groups who share many common elements. Even though they represent different collectives (European–German Jewish and dominant Jewish Israeli), both continue to be perceived in their mutual perceptions as part of one former Soviet/Russian-speaking Jewish group who share a history and socio-cultural codes that are preserved in both cases via a common Soviet-based terminology about the Jewish ethnicity. Thus, the second result of these transnational interactions is the preservation of the authenticity of shared Soviet viewpoints, as well as, active resistance to a prescribed way of being Jewish forced on the participants by dominant groups in Israel and in Germany (by resident Jews as well as non-Jewish Germans); that is, by those who do not share their cultural symbolic habitus and do not understand their vision of Jewishness.

Several elements identified by Woocher (1983, 67—6 quoted by Chervyakov, Gitelman and Shapiro 1997, 300) as central for American Jews seem to be valid, in both case studies; for example, concerns about Jewish survival in a threatening world, the centrality of the State of Israel for Jewish identity, and the sense of mutual responsibility for Jews throughout the world. Transnational interactions as well as the use of various electronic media have enabled the participants in Germany and Israel to be actively engaged in the lives of different Jewish communities throughout the world, especially in relation to world events involving anti-Semitism. However, this study revealed that it is not only anti-Semitism that strengths the common Jewish identity of secular Russian-speaking Jews (Webber 1994); affiliation with the entire Jewish collective, too, is important. For example, participant groups held similar right-wing political positions concerning the Jewish-Palestinian conflict within Israel.

Thus, the participants' different transnational references support my conclusion that their form of Jewish ethnicity can be referred to as *Transjewishness*; that is, a situation in which members continuously compare their Jewishness with that of other Jewish groups living in different countries. Furthermore, considerations of how participants perform "being Jewish" (Inowlocki 2002) suggest that *Transjewishness* can be further elaborated by taking into consideration ongoing discussions and refashioning of answers to the question of what it means to be a Jew in different sociocultural contexts.

Although it was originally thought that oppressed ex-Soviet Jews who found shelter in Israel or Germany would break off any contact with their society of origin, this study found that participants continued to be in intensive contact with their country of origin—through personal contacts, social networks, as well as, the media. This process enabled them to keep up-to-date and engaged as active participants in the development of social networks in the society of origin and in the German case, to maintain the *pendulum phenomenon* between CIS and Germany.

In addition, one can trace different forms of transnational networks in every one of the cases investigated. While migrants living in Israel prefer to visit their friends in Germany, it is rare for them to visit their pre-migration home. However, they do maintain contacts with friends and relatives in the

CIS via *virtual transnational connections* (i.e., via mass media, telephone calls, and Russian institutions in Israel). In contrast, Jewish migrants in Germany do not only maintain a *virtual transnational connection*, they visit both their land of origin, as well as, Israel. This alternative social network may be related to the consensus view among participants: Given that Germany is a national state, it was impossible for them to become Germans, that is, to feel that they belong to more than one national state. Thus, while they live in Germany, they stated that they had more affiliation with Russia and Israel, albeit from a distance. The concrete manifestation of this feeling can be seen in the temporary nature of their lives as they organized living in their "micro-home" in rented apartments, whereas the macro-home was identified with the concept of *homeland* that was only partially realized by attachments and movement between Russia, Israel, and Germany, but still stayed as a matter of major inner concern.

In this regard, the Russian-speaking Jews in Germany stand in dramatic contrast with their compatriots who immigrated to Israel. In Israel, former Soviet Jews are involved, intensively, in buying, building, designing, arranging, and equipping their microcosm; literally, their physical *home* in the new society. And, at the same time, they are very concerned about the macro-home; that is they follow intensely developments related to the political, economic, and social nature of the entire new homeland, with which they feel an intimate connection.

7 Winners once a year? Making sense of WWII and the Holocaust as part of a transnational biographic experience

A unique view of the Holocaust distinguishes ex-Soviet Jews as a demographic group from all other Jews in the Western world, as well as, from the western perception of the Jews. The Holocaust "became the central episode in Jthe ewish and world history and a transcendental religious concept referring to an event described as incomparable, incomprehensible, and unrepresentable" (Slezkine 2004, 365). Yet, significantly, Soviet Jews do not share this view nor do they identify themselves as victims of the Holocaust. Rather, most see themselves as part of a collective of victors whose members include former soldiers of the Soviet army who struggled together with all other Soviet citizens against what is often referred to as the "brown plague of Nazism" during WWII. The migration of this group to Germany accentuates this confusing situation in two primary ways: First, as members of the victorious Soviet state, their rhetoric differs and, indeed, is antagonistic in comparison to the local German rhetoric; second, they are Jews who migrated to the country of the Holocaust.

Accordingly, this chapter examines the coexistence, integration, and contradictions between three narratives that are involved in construction of the collective and personal identities of ex-Soviet Jews living primarily in Germany, compared to those in Israel: The Soviet victory narrative, the Holocaust narrative, and the German narrative about the country's Nazi past. By way of introduction, the discussion begins with a short description of a victory celebration that took place in the Jewish community studied whose approximately 2000 members consist of some German families who converted to Judaism and an overwhelming majority of Russian speakers. With the exception of the few German families, the victory celebration reveals an exceptional case of relatively homogeneous needs felt by a Russian-speaking community whose members share and use the same political narrative.

7.1 Celebration of *Den' Pobedy* Victory Day

The Jewish community investigated is located in Standstadt, a city in North Rhine-Westphalia Germany. There I observed the celebration of the 60th anniversary of the Soviet WWII victory on May 8, 2005. Upon entry into the building, the participants were greeted by large displays that included: pictures of community members as soldiers in the Red Army; relatives who served as civilian workers at the front; postcards of the fireworks display on Victory Day celebrations on the Red Square (held in the presence of prisoners of the German Armed Forces with Nazi flags lowered), pictures of Generals Zhukov and Rybakov; signs in triangular letters from the front with slogans, such as "Headed to Berlin!," "Soviet motherland behind us!," "Congratulations on the 9th of May!," "No victory without them," "No-body is forgotten, nothing is forgotten," and "they did cause our people to kneel." This exhibit of personal pictures and letters from the front, mixed with Soviet patriotic clichés and well-known images of the war, seemed to represent the entire, imagined Soviet nation rather than the background of the specific Jewish community of veterans present in the city. The hall was decorated with carnation bouquets, a tradition in Soviet celebrations of the 9th of May.

An approximately 60-year-old woman played war songs on the accordion; songs every Soviet citizen knows by heart:

"Real joy brought tears to our eyes [...] the Victory Day, the Victory Day, the Victory Day [...]" and "[...] tell us the truth, veterans; believe us, the youth very much needs it!"

The evening program was a tribute to the veterans. There was an emotional atmosphere as participants laughed, cried, sang and danced. Well-known songs and patriotic rhetoric created social intimacy among the participants, even if reproduced in clichéd form.[189] *What constructed truth was conveyed here?*

Hundreds of Russian-speaking community members from four generations attended the celebration. Food was plentiful and included caviar. The program was extensive and conducted exclusively in Russian: Poems were recited and a choir performed; speeches were made by a community leader, a rabbi, the director of the veteran's association; and video recordings were

---

189 This is close to the claim of Sandomirskaya (2004, 125) about the social intimacy created between those who use and share a political clichéd language about the motherland.

shown of veterans awarded the new medal issued in Russia: "60 years of victory in the *Velikoi Otechestvennoi Voine* [Great Patriotic/Fatherland War, Rus.] 1941—1945" and the "Defense of the *Rodina* [motherland, Rus.]" medal, given to Jewish war veterans by consular officers in Bonn, i.e. Mr. Sinkevich, the Russian Consul General; Mr. Ilinksky, the Ukrainian Consul; and Major General Klichko, the Russian military attaché.

After the migration, does the CIS remain *Rodina* [motherland, Rus.]? *Does the personal and collective affiliation with national terms remain as strong as it was before also after emigration?*

An approximately 16 year-old boy, brought to Germany at the age of five by his parents, recited a poem that relates the story of a Red Army soldier killed at the end of the war in one of the last battles in Germany, and who was buried on foreign, German soil. He hears children playing above him, but cannot understand their language. In the German context, from the perspective of a today's young Jewish migrant, the poem's war rhetoric sounds somewhat strange, particularly coming from a Russian-speaking boy who was socialized in Germany and now speaks German better than Russian.

A memorial candle is lit. All in attendance rise when the moderator asks that those who lost a father, mother, brother, or sister during the war to stand. There is a minute of silence to honor 27 million Soviet people who fell during the war. Jewish Holocaust victims were not explicitly mentioned. In fact, the word "Holocaust" was only mentioned once during the entire evening, and only then briefly when a Russian-speaking rabbi led the audience in prayer:

"[…] that we will continue to celebrate the victory in which, unfortunately, six million could not take part and for whom we pray on Holocaust day."

The words *Jew* or *Jewish* were not mentioned during the entire evening. One allusive reference was made by a speaker who spoke about soldiers, civilians who worked at the front, and inhabitants of Leningrad during the blockade. He referred to ghetto prisoners (again, not explicitly Jewish prisoners) when he repeated the well-known Soviet political cliché: "Ghetto residents and Nazi KZ prisoners whose childish faces were lit up by the sun through the barbed wire." The entire evening reproduced, exactly, the official Soviet scenario that has been repeated for decades. An evening filled with the celebration of heroism and valor that delighted and was enjoyed by all in attendance. Clearly, such joy was not to be "spoilt" by mention of the stigmatized concept of the "Jew" or the Holocaust, whose remembrance date is reserved for the 9th of November.[190]

As Katia told me after the event in response to my noting the lack of reference to Jews in the Jewish community on this day:

"Why should we speak about that on 9th of May of all days? It is a celebration of *nashi* [our own, Russ.,] veterans. There is the 9th of November for commemorating and mourning. [pause, then in an offensive, angry tone she said] Must the Holocaust be everywhere?"

By stressing strong collective affiliations, *nashi,* has a special meaning in Russian and is a concept that plays a central role in the process of group construction. It might even be considered to be the key Russian word for collective belonging.[191] Caught up in the spirit of the traditional Soviet celebration, Katia used the word *nashi* in the sense of *veterans,* as in *"our veterans;"* that is, "our Soviet veterans," referring by means of patriotic terminology to those who fulfilled their moral duty [*dolg pered Rodinoi',* duty towards the motherland, Rus.], fought in the Soviet army, and showed their heroism. Thus, according to her perceptions and terms of reference, a clear distinction is made between Jews as victims of the Holocaust and Soviet citizens as victors. The two are distinctly different, emotionally laden categories.

Katia was three years old when her father fell as a soldier in a war in which her mother's family was exterminated because they were Jews. From her response we learn that she demanded the right to celebrate the Soviet victory with others. This interpretation can only be possible if the Holocaust narrative does not penetrate the hermetic, Soviet politically constructed narrative of the victory as a certain way of capturing the past. Her rhetorical question—"Must the Holocaust be everywhere?"—would be an unthinkable statement for Jews in Germany or Israel who neither share nor assume that the victory narrative is taken for granted, common knowledge.

Given this brief introduction, the analyses presented in the remainder of this chapter presents a comparative analysis of the contextualization, re-

---

190 Kristallnacht, or The Night of Broken Glass, refers to a pogrom that took place in Nazi Germany on November 9—10, 1938. During this event, 91 German Jews were murdered, 25,000–30,000 were arrested and deported to concentration camps, more than 200 synagogues were destroyed, and tens of thousands of Jewish businesses and homes were ransacked (Kandel 2005).

191 See Caldwell (2005) for an analysis of the use of the concept of *Nash* as a part of nationalist rhetoric in McDonald's commercial advertising in Moscow.

actualization, and amendment of the perception of the Holocaust and WWII by Russian-speaking Jews in Germany with that constructed by Jews in Israel. The aim of these analyses is to answer three clusters of questions:

– How do people interact in a situation in which different bodies of knowledge, different political narratives, and different constructions of social worlds, usually taken for granted, meet and clash in the inner phenomenological domain as well as in the transnational biographic experiences of migrants? What happens, when through migration and intercultural interactions, the same events are remembered, understood, and interpreted in a completely different manner not only by different groups in the CIS, Israel, and Germany, but also by different Jewish groups in these countries? How do migrants cope with the unique situation in Germany, when as ex-Soviet Jews there is pressure to demonstrate loyalty to narratives that contradict one another in many significant ways?
– Do patterns of interpretation and remembrance change during the migration process? What new meanings of the past appear in the new environment, especially for ex-Soviet Jews in the German discourse context?
– Do the different contexts of Israel and Germany have an impact on individual coping strategies. How do they shape historical memories and affect the process of collective identity construction?

7.2 Conflicting meanings of May 8th and 9th

Nationalistic hegemony dictates the conceptualization and even the dates of WWII observance within the borders of Germany, CIS, and Israel (May 8th or 9th). However, once these boundaries are crossed, three key and significantly different commemorative narratives were questioned and contested as different approaches to "management of the past (Boym 2002, 13):" the nature of the Soviet victory, Germany's relationship with Nazi history, and the nature of the Holocaust. This was especially the case with ex-Soviet Jews who migrated to Germany.

This situation became apparent during my fieldwork in regard to one specific group of persons forced to cope simultaneously with these three commemorational narratives and to demonstrate loyalty to each: namely

Jews who as former Soviets migrated to Germany. In this regard, Golden's observation about the ways a particularistic Israeli historical consciousness is officially imposed on Russian-speaking migrants has broader relevance: "Attachments to place become significant only in relation to the ways a place is constructed as historically meaningful" (Golden 2002, 7).

Based on this formulation, the pertinent question addressed in this chapter is: What attachments develop when migrants cross national borders and have to deal with significantly contradictory historical narratives? Secondary questions that help answer this overarching question include: How do different multiple forms of historical consciousness coexist in the lives of migrants in Germany? Can migrants who are ex-Soviets and Jews sympathize with German soldiers who died during the war? How do they feel about the discussion, emerging since 2005, about the bombardment of German cities as well as the deprivation afflicted upon Germans near the end and immediately after the war? How do they deal with war narratives along with Holocaust narratives regarding the six million victims and personal stories about their own relatives who were exterminated during the Holocaust? Given their dependency on the German social welfare system, how do interviewees make sense of their affiliation with the "victor" collective, living out the heroic defeat of Nazism, and their low social and economic status as immigrants?

Commemoration of the 8th—9th of May can be conceptualized in a number of ways: As a memorial day for all persons who fell during the war; as a "celebration of the defeat of the German Reich"[192] and signing of the unconditional capitulation of the German armed forces; as commemoration of the day the Soviets defeated fascism and ended the National Socialist regime; a time to mark the liberation of prisoners from concentration and extermination camps and a day to remember the Jews who were exterminated; as a day to remember members of the resistance and partisans movements, deserters of the *Wehrmacht* or other opponents of Nazism; as the end of the WWII and renewal of Stalin's tyranny and occupation of East Europe; or, in the German context, as commemoration of the final loss of national German pride—the deeply rooted image of the Nazi as the personification of unprecedented evil in the Western world, as well as, when many Germans begin to dissociate themselves from the national

---

192 "Fest der Befreiung," "Young Communists" (May 3, 2006).

ideas, and to distance themselves from National Socialism, and the image of the "collective evil."[193]

A micro-analysis of the actual date selected for commemoration exemplifies the variance and difficulties confronted by migrants. The 8th of May is observed throughout the Western world as Victory Day in Europe [VE] Day, in celebration of the implementation of the agreement of unconditional surrender signed the previous day. Victory Day is celebrated on the 9th of May in the SU to commemorate the day when General Field Marshal Keitel, General Admiral von Friedeberg, and Colonel-General Stumpff signed the act of unconditional surrender with Chief Marshal Tedder and General Zhukoff in the Soviet headquarters in Berlin-Karlshorst (the night of 8—9 May). While in Germany, there is no official day of remembrance, the federal chancellor traditionally makes a speech on the 8th of May to commemorate the end of the war.

Interestingly, the first official observance of Victory Day in the SU took place in 1965, to mark the 20th anniversary of the Soviet victory. This can be considered to be a public performance of state power and valor. However, it was only at the end of the 1970s that it became an official legal holiday. Also, it was unpopular to display military decorations and medals in public until 1965. Thus, it may well be that 20 years after the war, the victory celebration assumed a political character as the most important signifier and representative of the concept of the *Soviet motherland* advanced by the higher echelons of government. In relation to the population of our case study, this means that the Soviet tradition of the victory celebration was first internalized and rooted in the consciousness of participants late in their socialization, when they were young adults. It was only then that this day started gradually to be seen as especially important and later as a "natural" event that was always there.

The first transnational, post-emigration act undertaken by a new migrant may well be changing this WWII related commemoration date; that is, when migrants start to observe this day according to the local, German custom; that is, on the 8th of May and not the 9th. Yet, while the date had changed, the content and the form of celebration remain unchanged from previous forms of observance in the SU.

However, it is extremely difficult to combine different perspectives, mentioned above, to which migrants are exposed in their transnational

---

193 Expression of sorrow for fate of civilian Germans bombarded, deprived of all, and for the violence involved in ending the war.

praxis and globalization (and denationalization) process. These different interpretations of the 8th—9th of May signify differences that exist among diverse groups and refer to bodies of knowledge that have been institutionalized, politically instrumentalized, and taken for granted. In their normalized form, migrants use these socialized meanings spontaneously and in an unreflective manner in their everyday lives, even in the new context. Yet, upon migrating to the new context, in Germany in the case of Russian-speaking Jews, this emotionally rich, taken for granted knowledge "suddenly" becomes illegitimate.

7.3 Soviet victors' narrative and the theme of the Holocaust in the SU

WWII is usually referred to in the SU as *"Velikaya Otechestvennaya Voina"* [The Great Fatherland War, Rus.]. Contemporary research studies estimate that more than 27 million Soviet citizens died during the war.[194] Glorifications of the victory and the heroization process, which epitomize the triumph of the motherland, have undergone many variations and have become one of the most powerful Soviet national myths, serving as a "total signifier (Sandomirskaya 2004)."

Soviet heroism is eternalized in a number of ways. Each year, on the 9th of May, this myth or commemorational narrative ("unique epiphany of victory" [Roberman 2007]) is re-evoked, revived, and nourished through political demonstrations, commemorative events in schools and institutions, and viewing of emotionally driven films and media reports. Additionally, since the end of the war, many war museums, memorials, and monuments have been erected and have become an integral part of the national landscape throughout the CIS. And, meetings at veterans' clubs as well as visits by veterans with pupils in schools are normal, indeed institutionalized, activities.

The narrative of the Soviet victory includes rich accounts of superhuman efforts and risks, suffering, resistance, persistence and imperturability, unquestioned loyalty, cooperation and courage, patriotism and readiness to

---

194 The estimate frequently mentioned is that 67 million persons died worldwide during WWII.

sacrifice voluntarily on behalf of the *Rodina* [motherland, Rus.], at any
moment, when "it calls upon you."[195] This is the myth of an unprecedented victory that was achieved, in spite of superior German technology
and inadequate Soviet equipment at that time, due to the unique solidarity
of the inter-Soviet collective. All components of this myth affirm and
demonstrate the omnipotence of the Soviet state evident during the war.
These celebrations maintain historical continuity and celebrants are
empowered by reliving the myth. It is one of the most powerful Soviet
narratives that, when recalled, involves reconstructing and reinforcing the
concept of the motherland and the Soviet empire. As such, this myth
consists of "impenetrable bodies of signs, stubbornly resistant interpretation and translation" (Sandomirskaya 2004, 123) usually assumed to
be "natural," even "native"[196] by insiders (i.e., Soviet citizens) who share
and use them.

Yearly celebrations of the victory reaffirm and preserve a certain version of the "native" history and Stalin's patriotic canon of *Rodina* "merged
with hardcore Russian chauvinism from above" (Sandomirskaya 2004,
124). These practices continued until the very end of the SU. This perception of historical continuity and feeling of empowerment achieved by re-
connection with the Soviet victory in the WWII, created and strengthened
every year through official celebrations, is significantly different from
Western perceptions of the war, and especially the Holocaust, as marking
different epochs before and after the unprecedented evil. Or, stated differently, while Soviet rhetoric stresses absolute victory over evil, the Western
conception stresses the fact that the Holocaust took place and consequently demands reflection on modernity, political regimes, and cultural
values.

Zwi Gitelman referred to the reproduction of the "victorious fight" as
the legitimating myth for the Soviet system and the deprivations incurred
by its citizens (Gitelman 1994, 18). Since the Perestroika, this political
narrative has been reinforced, mystified by a national (often nationalistic)

---

195 Translation of one of the principal sentences of the war rhetoric: "*Rodina mat' zovet'!*"
[The motherland is calling you!, Rus.]." This sentence is as famous as the sentence "*Sa
Rodinu, sa Stalina!*" ["For the motherland, for Stalin!"] recalled by many soldiers before
dying. Remembering both was reconfirmed and encouraged through repetition in
different Soviet films.
196 It is important to note that the Russian word *Rodina* is based on the root, *rod* [lit. native,
inborn] and *rodnoi* [closed, soul mate, familial].

Slavic-Christian revival, and employed as a mechanism for solidifying the entire CIS's collective.[197]

Other topics connected with the war and victory, previously taboo, have started to be articulated, albeit in a limited, hesitant manner and only during certain crises. These topics include the Holocaust; the so called *"strafnye bataliony"* [vengeance battalions, Rus.] who were composed of condemned prisoners sent to fight without weapons and used as a human shield; the murder of Polish officers in Katyn after the Soviet and German occupation of Poland; the occupation of Eastern Europe by the SU after the war; the fate of so-called "missing war victims;" and the difficulty distinguishing between victims of the war and victims of Stalin's terror, when Soviet prisoners of war, who returned to the SU after the capitulation of Germany, were stigmatized as "traitors of the motherland" and sent to the Gulag.

On the whole, as part of the Soviet propaganda machine, the post-Soviet victory rhetoric remains strong, generally unreflected upon and rarely questioned. President Putin's official pronunciation of the myth was formulated as follows: "Our people brought liberty and rescued the Europeans from slavery."[198]

Normalization of this central myth imbues all aspects of everyday life in the SU/CIS. One very interesting expression of popular attachment to this myth can be found in commercial commemorations of the victory found in the wrapping of food products sold in the CIS and in Russian food stores in Israel and Germany. For example, Doktorskaya [doctoral, Rus.] is a traditional Russian sausage with the following statement imprinted on its skin: "Doctoral victory sausage"[199] (G) (picture 7:1). This statement is accompanied by a map of Europe indicating areas liberated by the Soviet army from the Nazis. The sausage was produced especially by the Dimov firm on the occasion of the 60th anniversary of the victory, but was so

---

197 Some scientific Russian books reflect the process of Slavic-national revival. For example, *The Psychology of Holiday* in which the authors, Volovikova, Tichomirova, and Borisova, mystify the Victory Day by pointing out the "amazing coincidence…[that] May 9, 1945 fell in the middle of the Orthodox Easter week." No further comment or analysis is offered [Rus.] (Volovikova, Tichomirova and Borisova 2003: 122). See also Lerner's (2006) study of the "mysterious Russian 'ethnicity' " in post-Soviet Russia.

198 Wolf Oschlies "Der große Sieg und sein hoher Preis," "Eurasisches Magazin," http://www.eurasischesmagazin.de/artikel/?artikelID=20050507, 21.06.2010

199 Original—*Doktorskaya kolbasa Pobedy*; Note: henceforth a capital "V" is used to indicate victory in WWII.

«Докторская»
колбаса...
ПОБЕДЫ
с картой освобождения Европы

К омпания «Дымов» в канун 60-летия Победы
решила преподнести нестандартный подарок
— праздничный выпуск колбасы. Приготов-
ленная по классическому рецепту в соответствии с
ГОСТом, колбаса вареная «докторская» будет про-
даваться в предпраздничные и праздничные дни в
необычной оболочке, на которой изображена карта
освобождения Европы от фашистской армии. Цель дан-

Pic. 7:1 "Doktorskaya Sausage[doctoral, Rus.] accompanied by a map of Europe indicating areas liberated by the Soviet Army from Nazis with the: "Doctoral victory sausage" (G)

Pic. 7:2 Vodka "Pobeda" [Victory, Rus.] (G)

Pic. 7:3 "Gvardeiskaya Slava" [lit. Guard Glory Chocolates, Rus.] (G)

Pic. 7:4 "Pobeda" chocolates [Victory chocolates, Rus.] with the statement "VICTORY of the taste" (I)

popular that it remained in the shops, continued to be advertised, and was sold in Russian food stores in Germany, at least through the end of the field research in 2008.

This commercial message combined three concepts—food, a medical doctor, and victory—in what for a non-Russian may seem to be an unlikely, even contradictory, manner. First, everyday knowledge is politicized in design of a food commodity through the combination of a historic, military event and a sausage. Second, non-Russians may think that there is a contradiction between Western ideas about healthy food, as a significant consumption criterion, and the image of a cheap, fatty sausage with a name alluding to its capacity for healing (commercial name, "Doctoral"). Yet, for ex-Soviet, CIS citizens, this food product has a significantly different, ironic meaning that evokes nostalgic feelings for a powerful but lost empire and national pride connected to *Pobeda* [The victory, Rus.], one of the most meaningful events in Soviet history.

Such examples demonstrate that given strong emotional attachments, the Victory Day was sacrosanct for Soviet citizens, as it stressed "sentimental aspects of collective reality."[200] Similarly, in her discussion of the commercialization of the concept "motherland" in the Russian language's "minor canon," Samdomirskaya pointed out that it was a form of post-Soviet *patriotic lyricism* that in her view is the

"compensation for the moral and social loss experienced by most of the 'former Soviet people,' déclassé and marginalized in the new capitalist conditions" (Sandomirskaya 2004, 131).

Given the longstanding, ongoing Soviet tradition of politicized commodities,[201] seeing victory on a regular sausage was not disturbing or irritating for persons with a CIS background, but rather familiar, intimate, easily recognizable and memorable. Given the search for new, positive forms of the motherland following the collapse of the SU, there was an increase in the use of different patriotic expressions in advertising whose goal was to attract consumer attention to certain goods (Sandomirskaya 2004). Indeed, after the Perestroika, former Soviet companies employed political symbols similar in design to well-known Soviet food commodities, as a trend to preserve, even extend, old patriotic images mixed with new ones.[202] In

---

200 Handler (1988, 7); Golden (2002, 13) discussed constructing of the nation.
201 See Chapter Four.
202 Discussed in Chapter Four.

analyzing transformations of the motherland since the end of the 80s, Sandomirskaya described a similar tendency:

"In its new quality of a commercialized fetish motherland does not offer itself to its subject through a repressive ideological machine anymore; it is rather seductive than repressive" (Sandomirskaya 2004, 131).

In regard to the reference to health, it should be recalled that in a society characterized by economic difficulties and food shortages the health criterion in the consumption process is not as central as it is in societies enjoying abundance. Indeed, in the SU, obtaining such food products demanded initiative and effort.[203] For example, the Doktorskaya brand of sausage has been familiar to most persons since their childhood and its advertising messages are taken for granted, positive, and unquestioned. Further, it evoked associations with a desired, reliable quality food product imbued with memories of the Soviet past, including waiting in seemingly endless lines to obtain a small portion of the product. Combining such associations with the positive, indisputable concept of Soviet victory was an extraordinary winning combination for nearly all Soviet citizens.

Another advertisement promoted on the German TV channel SuperRTL by the time of completing this book (2010) concerned the Russian vodka *Pobeda* [victory, Rus.]: on the label it shows a Soviet monument dedicated to the "unknown soldier" depicted with a sword and holding a small rescued child (picture 7:2). Interestingly the name of the vodka was not translated for German consumers, for whom the exotic Russian name "Pobeda" should indicate "Russianness" (in this case as positive stereotype for goodness) of vodka as a Russian drink.

Other examples of commercialization of the victory myth include *Gvardeiskaya Slava* [lit. Guard Glory Chocolates, Rus.] (G) (picture 7:3); a souvenir designed bottle of Red Army Vodka (I) (picture 4:74) shaped as an ammunition shell and packed in a wooden ammunition like case; and wrapping paper of *Pobeda* [lit. Victory Chocolate, Rus.] (I) (picture 7:4) displayed the statement: "The *victory* of taste" in which the word "victory" is written in a large, bold font common from the 1950's against a red background, topped by a gold flag, in contrast to the word "taste" that is so small that one needs a magnifying glass to read it. "The victory of

---

203 As discussed in the Chapter Four.

taste" is easily associated with the colossal patriotic victory of WWII. Further, such a name is a tease to play with a reversed version; that is, it can be easily be associated with *the taste of the victory*.

In part, such commercialization practices reproduce historic Soviet images developed in the immediate postwar period of the 1950's when ideas promising the soon-to-arrive communist paradise infused politicized books, such as Stalin's *On the Tasty and Healthy Food Book*. For example, the exact design printed on the wrapper of the chocolate bar *Slava* [lit. Glory, Rus.], sold in 2008 in a Russian food store in Israel (picture 4:34), can be found in Stalin's book. Indeed, all of the examples previously mentioned use nationalist, militaristic terms that appeal to having pride in the epic political mythic narrative of the strong empire of the Soviet (now post-Soviet) motherland.[204]

Participants who experienced WWII as children, as well as those of the postwar generation deeply internalized the Soviet war rhetoric repeated yearly in different contexts and public events. As Roman (Germany) put it: "These sentences reside here in me [points to his head]. They were driven strongly into our heads."

The previous description of the Jewish community's 8th of May celebration indicates that participants wanted to celebrate this day under the Soviet identity "umbrella" of active ex-fighters and winners, not necessarily as Jews. However, this does not mean that this contradicts or involves rejection of their Jewish identity (as is often presumed to be the case in Israel and Germany). On the contrary, the participants prefer the selective knowledge practiced in the SU that acknowledges that Soviet Jews, along with other nationalities, made significant contributions to the victory. Their recognition of the death of many Soviet Jews, as well as the display of medals, orders, and military ranks stressed their steadfast sense of belonging to and identity with the victorious Soviet nation. And, there are undisputed facts that support this allegiance: Of the entire Jewish population of approximately five million persons who lived in the SU in 1941,[205] approximately 500,000 Jews served in the Red Army as active solders (Adar 2004; Kandel 2005; Sleskin 2004). Altogether, it is estimated that 1,300,000 Jews

---

204 Other new military motifs found on the wrapping paper of commercial products, reproduced from various Russian war efforts, are presented in Chapter Five.

205 The exact number is 5,200,000.

worldwide fought against Nazis during the WWII.[206] About 500 Russian Jews were awarded the highest Soviet decoration—the *"Geroi Sovetskogo Sojusa"* [hero of the Soviet Union, Rus.]. Per capita this was far greater than their percentage among the entire Soviet population.

While these facts are well-known, indeed taken for granted, among Soviet citizens, they are hardly known in the West and rarely mentioned in the dominant Western discourse about the Holocaust and the six million exterminated Jews. Soviet knowledge, for its part, excludes the very important fact that out of 2,700,000 SU Jews killed during the war (amounting to c-50 percent of the entire Jewish population in 1941), "only" 200,000 (about 7 percent) were killed in active duty; the rest, 93 percent, were victims of Nazi extermination.

As noted at the beginning of this chapter, reluctance to see themselves as part of the collective of victims is one of the central ways in which Soviet Jews differ from all other European Jews, as well as, from the Western perception of Jewish historical destiny. Several factors need to be taken into consideration when explaining their view: First, few Jews had access to a complete, true description of the facts of the Holocaust while living in the SU. Consequently, few internalized this narrative. Rather, due to strong censorship imposed on this and other subjects during the totalitarian regime, only fragmented bits of information were exchanged, in most cases in secret discussions that took place in the private sphere [as Katia (Germany) related: "In the kitchen, we whispered, because the walls have ears as well."[207] People exchanged and compared different versions of new information learned from others in this closed private sphere. Thus, in discussions with young family members [the generation investigated in this study], the older generation was only able to relate short fragments of information retained from their familial and personal biographies about the extermination of Jewish relatives by the Nazis or during Stalin's regime.

Second, the Holocaust theme was never a topic of public discussion during the Soviet period. Then, the primary political interest was to stress

---

206 Approximately 2,700,000 Soviet Jews were exterminated by the Nazis (c-50 percent of the entire Soviet Jewish population in 1941). Among them, 200,000 Jews died in combat as active solders (Adar 2004; Kandel 2005).

207 She refers to secret bugging by KGB devices mounted on the walls of flats used to monitor private discussions as evidence to persecute violators later on. Katia recalled "secret talks" in her family kitchen when people raised the radio volume and talked quietly about forbidden topics in hope the radio would block the bugging device.

the common Soviet, multi-national[208] struggle against fascism. In doing so, it sought to present itself as a victorious people rather than designate one special group as a victim, who suffered more than others from the "German plague" [Soviet media term]. Ksenia Polouektova mentions additional important reasons in withholding this topic, namely „the need to counter the Nazi propaganda claims about special closeness between Jews and Bolsheviks ("Judeo-Bolshevism") which suggested that Hitler waged the war against the Soviet Union with the sole purpose of destroying the Jews" (Polouektova 2009, 2) and

"the attempt to downplay the scale of local collaboration in the destruction of the Jews that undermined the myth of inner-ethic 'brotherhood and unity' paraded by Soviets" (ibid).

Furthermore, the Holocaust was neither presented as a unique phenomenon,[209] which according to the Western narrative must remain as a separate human sphere, nor as an incomprehensible event (Gitelman 1994; Kandel 2006; Lustiger 1998).

Given the centrality of the Holocaust in the Western narrative, the fact that the word "Holocaust" was unknown to the participants during their lives in the SU until the 1990's and that Jews had limited knowledge about the *Shoah* [Holocaust, Heb., referring to the Jewish view that this was THE sole such occurrence of genocide] sounds almost implausible, requires an explanation, and even habituation. Indeed, the *Shoah*, or equivalent forms, were never used in the public sphere, in Soviet literature, or books.[210] The theme of the Holocaust was never mentioned in Soviet WWII museums (Slezkine 2004, 337). All copies of *The Black Book of Soviet Jewry* by Erenburg and Grossman, an authoritative book about the destiny of the Jews during the WWII, were confiscated and destroyed in 1948 and the book blacklisted. Although this book was reissued in 1993, most participants had not read it in 2010. Only after the *Perestroika* the term "katastrofa" (extermination of the European Jews)—started to be applied to the Jewish victims (Gitelman 1994, 1997), less often the term Holocaust. The first official Holocaust Memorial Day in St. Petersburg was organized in 1990 and a year later there was the first big national event to commemorate the 50th

---

208 In Soviet terminology, "international" refers to different Soviet nationalities.
209 Diner (2006, 1) claimed that Western societies present it as a unique phenomenon, even dissociated from the WWII.
210 After the Perestroika, words like "catastrophe," "Holocaust,"or "extermination" were used in discussion of the history of Jewish people (Gitelman 1994, 117).

anniversary of the mass extermination of Jews in Babi Yar in Kiev (Gitelman 1994; Kandel 2006).

After the Perestroika and Glasnost' the process of desacralisation did
not influence the cultivation of the Great Patriotic War as well as it

"did not alter the peripheral place of the Holocaust within the matrix of official
Soviet/Russian memory of the war" (Polouektova 2009, 3) "….since the public
attention of the time focused largely on the legacy of communism and its crimes"
(ibid., 2).

Although, officially, the Holocaust was allowed to be discussed following
Perestroika, the discussion has been limited and certainly not as extensive
as in the Western discourse. Particularly, in her research about the role of
the Holocaust in the post-Soviet Russian history textbooks, Ksenia Polouektova mentions that not one of the analysed books had a separate
chapter or subchapter dedicated to the theme of the Holocaust (Polouektova 2009, 13). Some authors (as for example of the history book of Aruti-
une Ulunyan and Yevgeny Sergeev, 2005 for the 11th grade, recommended
by the ministry of education) succeed in discussing the Nazi extermination
politics without mentioning the word "Holocaust" even once (ibid.)

As another example of the way the theme of the "Holocaust" appears
in the post-Soviet public discourse I would like to introduce the new film
"12" by one of the most prominent Russian producers, Nikita Mikhalkov.
His film is an adaption of Sidney Lumet's Hollywood film "12 angry men",
which was produced in 1957. Two characteristic scenes are worth to be
mentioned.

In one scene an anti-Semitic protagonist tries to identify, or more precisely to unmask someone as a "Jew" [in the film context the word Jew
equals a "national traitor"]. "I am a half Jewish"—is the justification of the
latter. The following reaction of the first can be considered to be the pathetic key sentence of the producer: "There are no half Jews!" [in the Soviet cultural habitus it means: Only one drop of Jewish blood makes the
entire person Jewish.] Later, there is another scene, during which another
protagonist, cast according to all stereotypes about darkhaired Jews with a
hooked nose, starts to talk about his father in the concentration camp. The
same anti-Semitic actor (a patriotic and simple character with a common
touch) interrupts him immediately, when he hears the word "camp" and
asks pathetically: "Do you want to tell us again (in the meaning of enlight-
ening us] about the Holocaust?" The last scene is particularly interesting,
because the word "Holocaust" is used, which happens rarely in Russian

conversations and has never been heard in Russian-speaking feature films in particular. Here we see that the theme of the Holocaust, which had scarcely been spread in the Russian-speaking post-Soviet public sphere and had barely a chance to be internalised as an important topic, is ascribed a stale and uninteresting character.

On the basis of my research, even though most participants in Germany claim that they knew about the Nazi policy of Jewish extermination as well as names of sites of mass massacres (e.g., Babi Yar in Kiev or Drobezkii Yar in Kharkov), they assert that it was not until the 1990s that they learned the full extent of the Holocaust (e.g., it was not clear to them that six million Jews were exterminated). This claim was reaffirmed by participants in Israel who, I submit, have no particular reason to deny this knowledge. For example, Mila (Israel) stated:

Mila: "Of course I knew about Babi Yar and that the Nazis had especially murdered Jews. But I had never read that it was genocide primarily against Jews and that there were six million! It was always said that all people suffered from this war. For me it was always a war, above all else a war, and not only genocide…"

JB: "And the word Holocaust?"

Mila: "No, no one knew it; that is for sure." [211]

Throughout the fieldwork period in Germany, the word *Holocaust* was mentioned by participants on very few occasions [often using the wrong pronunciation as *Galakost* or *Halakosta*; suggesting that they had not used this word previously or extensively].[212] The Hebrew word *Shoah* was foreign and not used by many participants in Germany.[213] Most participants

---

211 All of the Israeli participants confirmed that prior to the 1990s they did not know the exact number of Jews exterminated in the Holocaust. However, many claimed that one could understand the dimensions of this terrible event while living in the SU, and for other reasons decided not to immigrate to Germany. My overall impression is that the participants' knowledge about Jews in the SU was filtered through the local perspective of their current location—Israel or Germany. This explains the interest of some participants in their attachment to the Israeli collective from which they are often excluded as Russians."

212 This finding corresponds with those in other studies; for example, Schoeps's study of Russian-speaking Jewish migrants in Germany found that 9.3 percent of all interviewees claimed that memory of the Holocaust embittered their relation to Germany and Germans (Schoeps 1996, 151).

213 This is not the only concept absent in Soviet as well as in the post-Soviet public discourse. The concept of "collective guilt," which became an inseparable part of German collective identity, is unknown in the Russian language [*kollektivnaya vina*]. There

did not know the date of Holocaust Day; some thought that it was same commemoration date of the *Kristallnacht* when they attend synagogue services.

Paradoxically, as a result of the totalitarian Soviet policy that withheld information, Russian-speaking Jews were "protected" from having to cope with the topic of the Holocaust as a separate, unprecedented historical phenomenon throughout their life in the SU.

As Tamara formulated it: "They [probably, Germans] don't understand that all our roots were taken away from us. I walk on the street [in Germany] and see a building from 1341, and I don't even know the name of my grandmother."

Furthermore, parents did not share their own traumatic experiences and the biographies of exterminated family members, nor did they discuss the subject in public. Rather, they preferred to protect their children from having to confront it. As a result, most of the Israeli as well as the German participants knew very little about it. German participants tended to dissociate such personal references with the general subject of the Holocaust and facts about millions of exterminated Jews. This explains their behavior during the victory celebrations described above: Personal biographical references to relatives who were killed and stories about suffering during the wartime (i.e., emotional affiliations) were transferred to the ideological, patriotic construction of the victorious Soviet motherland, which remained the focus of the celebration. This created an invisible link between "common places" of private life and state dreams that blurred the borders between these two spheres (Boym 2002, 39). Or, as Sandomirskaya put it in her analysis of different canons of the motherland:

"A private biography is inserted in this collective mega-project [in which]… identity turn[s] into simulacra of the state" (Sandomirskaya 2004, 131).

---

is no similar concept that is applied to Nazis or to participants in the Stalinist repressions. Indeed, it is also difficult to translate adequately to Russian speaking migrants in Germany several other concepts, deeply rooted in the German language, that are an inseparable part of the war rhetoric (e.g., *Auseinandersetzung, Be- und Verarbeitung* ["process of coping with and working up", Ger.]), *Mitläufer* [passive collaborators, Ger.; also the concept often applied to Jewish co-citizens in Germany *Mitbürger* [fellow citizens, Ger.], *Tradierung* [passing on, Ger.] or "*Tätergeneration*" [generation of perpetrators, Ger.]. The only understandable word for ex-Soviet citizens that belongs to the German war rhetoric chain as well as to the Soviet totalitarian regime is "*Schweigen*" or "*Verschweigen*" [extended silence, Ger.].

The fact that during their lives in the SU most participants did not share the Jewish collective memory about the Holocaust in the same form as have other European Jews since 1945 is often scorned in both German as well as Jewish German discourses. Stated in a simplified manner, this fact is used as evidence of their lack of Jewishness or in questioning the authenticity of Jewishness. Furthermore, it is not only the case that participants lack knowledge about personal family biographies; they have not internalized the Holocaust narrative. Indeed, as Belkin noted, accurately, they are "missing [a] language for the debate about the Holocaust."[214] Today they are slowly developing such awareness due to exposure to a diversity of Russian-speaking discourses in the CIS, as well as, in Israel and Germany.

We know that language plays a central role in the process of the perception and construction of reality. However, the case in point leads us to ask, more specifically, under what conditions do persons learn the appropriate terms used in these new discourses? I would claim that, whereas in Israel these conditions are provided through the common collective national history, learning this narrative language in Germany involves additional inner conflicts and contradictions. Not only are they living amidst persons who have internalized their presence in the Holocaust narrative, they are forced, continuously, to legitimize their emigration and decision to live in Germany, as land of the persons who permitted and committed the Holocaust.

7.4 Transnational praxis of the everyday knowledge after migration to Germany

The discourse about the Soviet victory that epitomized the motherland myth was accepted as unquestionable and absolute (in comparison to the Holocaust, which was strong relativized). And, the Soviet rhetoric immigrated with the migrants and was articulated when relating to their initial difficulties upon arrival and sharing their excitement, indeed rapture, with capitalist abundance. Interestingly, their statements evoked different asso-

---

214 *"eine fehlende Sprache* für die Auseinandersetzung mit dem Holocaust" Belkin (2006, 30—31).

ciations—most of which were stereotypic about the Nazi period, as demonstrated in the following two examples:

Sveta (65 years old): "When we arrived, my God, weapons, Hitler, as if we arrived to a concentration camp. There were Germans all around. We fell into the arms of every Russian we met."

Born before WWII, Katia (former Russian language and history teacher, 70 years old) has strong memories of the war period and the Nazis. She recalled an incident from their arrival in Germany in which she saw a German shepherd being held by what she described as a "young thug in uniform with sleeves rolled up"[215] on the German border. Her son, who accompanied her could not confirm this incident, as he did not remember seeing any dogs at the border and made no connection between border guards and Nazis.

During the fieldwork in Germany, it became clear that, even many years after migration, the participants continued to use the collective "victor/enemy" as opposed to the local German "victim/perpetrators" rhetoric. Some people like Leonia, for whom Soviet version of the victory and the Soviet liberation of the world from the Nazis remains an absolutely objective fact, wondered why Victory Day was not "specially marked" and officially commemorated in Germany. He speculated that the normative Soviet victory narrative, the "elementary history" they brought with them to Germany, was not known to the Germans.

Leonia: "Sometimes they [Germans] don't know elementary history. [For instance] today is the 9th of May and they just don't know it. For us [in the CIS], we enjoyed it. Every year there were films about the war, books."

Internally, within the Russian-speaking enclave, émigrés share and reproduce these well-known communication terms. However, outside the enclave, many participants are easily irritated when they come upon symbols that remind them of the German Nazi past during the few contacts they have with Germans. The limited number of personal contacts and absence of knowledge about the "other sides'" biographies make it easier for them to use gross, stereotypic categories. As a result, for some participants, the seemingly unbridgeable gap between their different historical affiliations widens even more when the category Germans is reduced to "ex-Nazis" or "former enemies."

---

215 A strong Nazi image found also in Soviet films about the war.

Varia (68 years old): "We are often asked [by friends in the CIS], "How is it in Germany?" But, actually, we only know Russian Germany [the enclave]. I have never been in a German house. No, I did once. A German lady wanted to learn Russian and I wanted to learn German from her. She showed me their family album with pictures of her brother in Hitler's uniform. I just felt bad."

From the Western perspective, the coexistence of Soviet and Jewish identities contradicts one another. The migrants did experience difficulties putting aside their identification with the struggle of the Soviet collective and were not entirely prepared to accept the role of only being Holocaust victims.[216]

In my discussion with Pavel Lovsky (82 year old organizer of the 8th of May celebration, former physics professor, WWII veteran and resident of Germany for 15 years), I attempted to engage him in the topic of the war and Holocaust:

JB: "In local [German] discussions, one speaks about Jews in the context of the war referring to victims, however [...]"

Mr. Lovsky interrupts: Where did you hear *that*? Well, [speaking about] the victims is unknown to me ... Jews [meaning Russian-speakers] speak about themselves as Holocaust victims when they want to get something from the state, otherwise they don't. [pause, and then hesitating, as if thinking aloud he says] I don't sense this attitude. And they [Jews] know *exactly* that we all struggled for the victory."

Well [in an offensive, angry tone] I don't know where you heard *such* attitudes. That Jews are the victims! You should look at our video cassette about the last celebration. [pause and then a little defensively without any sign or question from me] This is a *normal European* state, with a well-developed social welfare system and organized society. Order here is better than in Israel or Russia! On 9th of May [for the celebration] several police cars came to the synagogue, they protected and took care of us..."

---

216 One could also hear statements such as "we struggled against the Nazis, while you studied Torah;" or "they went as sheep to the slaughter, whereas we struggled" when Russian-speaking Jews compare their attitudes about the war with those of "other" European Jews. Such formulations (also mentioned by other researchers, e.g., Elias 2005) are not an individual construction, but rather should be considered in the Soviet as well as in the Israeli context as repeating a widespread, conventional claim about the "wrong" passive behavior of the victims. In this case, one can recognise a typical, often repeated Soviet (as well as Israeli) construction of the image of an active, self-assertive group determining its destiny in juxtaposition to the actions of passive, religious, weak Diaspora Jews. Moreover, through such expressions, which apply reductive dichotomies, the anti-religious position of ex-Soviet Jews becomes especially visible. This is the result of decades of the atheistic Soviet politics.

This citation demonstrates the reproduction/preservation of the victory discourse as well as a kind of amazing vehemence [from an outsider's view] with which the one-dimensionality of the *victim* perspective is rejected. The offensive tone, in which he [without any question from my side] turned to justification of his decision to immigrate to Germany, characterizing it as a "normal" European state, points, in my opinion, to his awareness of the loaded, double morality involved in discussion of Jews emigrating to THE former enemy state.

Many of the participants interviewed admitted that it was only post-migration that they realized, seemingly for the first time, that the theme of the Holocaust plays a central role in the German discourse, felt forced to justify themselves, and acted in a defensive manner.[217]

There are different strategies of coping with Jewish attachment, stigmatized in the SU and brought to Germany with its Holocaust history. Pavel presented Jews as above all strong Soviet victors, which supports or even justifies and dignified Jewish attachment. In contrast, here Naum pointed out that being Jewish in Germany is reserved exclusively for the safe private sphere:

"Nobody shouts aloud here: 'I am a Jew.' Everyone tries to present themselves as Russian Germans or Russians. Many try to hide. As a Jew you feel depressed everywhere. *This Germany* [strong stressed] is a *kleimo* [strong Russian word for yoke or stigma branded on the body] of the Holocaust [uses German for Holocaust]."

For Alex, the *kleimo* (stigma) of the Holocaust is both alienating and unbearable in the context of his life in Germany, one with which he is forced to cope, but for which he was unprepared. It may be that for this reason he claimed that an exaggerated Holocaust narrative existed in Germany, of which he was unaware upon arrival:

"If I had known which story did they [Germans] made out of the Holocaust before I came here, I am not sure I would have come. For us it seemed to be different, you know. We did not immigrate to the land of the Holocaust, but to a well-developed Western country, which changed long ago, and is not a Nazi land any more…"

---

217 This finding emanates from the fieldwork. The local Holocaust discourse remains unknown for some of the older migrants, even after ten years of residence in Germany. This demonstrates the impenetrability of the established Soviet myth, as well as, the absence of knowledge about and involvement in local German discourse.

Generally, discussions about the Holocaust are perceived by Russian-speaking Jews in Germany to be foreign and comparisons are usually limited, though consistent with continuation of the Soviet political tradition. Indeed, throughout my fieldwork in Germany, claims regarding the unprecedented dimensions of the Holocaust were attacked aggressively whenever I attempted to discuss the Holocaust with participants. They applied a variety of techniques in these discussions that in many cases reproduced the Soviet official line and forms of speech. For example, they included the history of the extermination of Jews along with other Nazis atrocities, such as burning villages in Belarus, Russian forced laborers in Germany, extermination of handicapped and other persons (e.g., Sinti and Roma). Others compared Hitler's repressions with those ordered by Stalin, thereby personifying and reducing such orders to the actions of only two persons, claiming, very emotionally, that Stalin's final atrocities were even worse, because altogether Stalin's regime exterminated more people than the Nazis and these acts were committed against his own people (against the peoples of the SU and not "only" Other Jews).

Interestingly, the participants did not use Jewish categories (e.g., extermination of Jews by Stalin and Holocaust). Rather, they compared dimensions of the Holocaust with suffering by Jews and the general Soviet population during the repressions. This kind of claim represented a general consensus of many participants. It seems they felt alienated from the phenomenon of the Holocaust and, thus, they related to it, briefly, and then quickly diverted discussion to the dual repression suffered at the hands of Stalin (i.e., to their group as Jews and as differently thinking Soviets), which they felt were more painful and with which they were more involved.

In my opinion, in contrast to the discussion of aspects of the Holocaust in which they seemed to feel insecure and were easily disoriented, the participants were more comfortable discussing acts committed by Stalin and sufferings imposed by different Soviet regimes, as if to say "here I know my way around." That is, participants possessed expansive knowledge of historical facts, used different but relevant terms, and argued comfortably. The more they described the difficulties of their life under Stalin's regime, the more foreign sounded the theme of Holocaust. Even if mentioned, the Holocaust narrative supported the participants' claims about other Jewish oppressions. This narrative strengthened the general claim about the difficulties of the collective Jewish destiny. Overall, the Holocaust narrative was separate from the Soviet discourse. Thus, on the basis of the fieldwork, I would claim that the theme of the Holocaust had not become part of everyday consciousness or a frame of reference of Russian Jews living in Germany who participated in the study.

Some participants, for example Tamara (Ph.D in Chemistry, 62 years old), argued that the Holocaust was a Western phenomenon; one of no concern or consequence for her or other Soviet Jews. Her presentation of her position ignored historical facts. Further, she was vehement in her unwillingness to be considered as part of a victim collective:

> "Our state [SU] also had its camps and the same fascists. And we said nothing. We continued to live there and were normal people, as we are here. It is already another generation. A long time has passed. For me, to live there, also meant to live with fascists. We came to a modern European country. I don't like it when *nashi* ["ours", Rus., meaning here, Russian-speaking Jews] only make demands. They think that because of the Holocaust somebody owes them something. It did not concern them at all! The Holocaust is a Western phenomenon. They speculate about others' suffering from *soplemenniki* view [literally co-tribes, Rus.] but many were born only after all that [...]"

Tamara's rationale for her decision to come to the "modern European country" of Germany is not the sole argument she shares with other participants. In criticizing Russian-speaking Jews, who identify themselves as victims, Tamara, Pavel,[218] and others cited above also attempted to demonstrate their loyalty to the German state. Their critique is directed at those whose self-identification is instrumentalized in order to obtain goods and services from the German state.

In this regard, one of the more amazing findings of the fieldwork in Germany was that there was no third alternative to the dichotomy of "Soviet victors" and "Jewish victims who exploit the German state," instrumentally, exploiting Germans' guilty feelings about the Holocaust. This phenomenon recalls Walser's anti-Semitic claim of the instrumentalization of Auschwitz as *Moralkeule* [a moral cudgel, Ger.]).[219]

Scrutinizing Walser-like statements about migrants reveals a transnational biographic split between victims and victors that must be contextu-

---

218 An organizer of the celebration on the 8th of May 2005 in the city investigated.

219 I find it amazing that "loyalty" statements of some Jewish participants in Germany reproduce, in effect, Walser's image of *Moralkeule* in his 1998 anti-Semitic speech in the Paulus Church. There he spoke about the Holocaust as an instrumentalization of Auschwitz, affecting Germans as a moralistic cudgel (or "moral battering-ram of Auschwitz") with which they feel they cannot object or argue, due to guilty feelings for the Holocaust.

alized in the German migration context. In the following citation Rita combined all three controversial narratives together:

"My father fought [as a soldier against the Nazis], and he wrote his name on the Reichstag [Rita refers to the well-known event when Soviet soldiers who liberated the Reichtag wrote their names on its outside walls as a sign of the victory]. But this catastrophe affected almost all people. Most of our relatives fell in a small Jewish sthetl. [pause] But we did not have any doubts about coming [to Germany], because here they [Germans] suffered even more [probably means at the end of the war and after the surrender]. The war became a tragedy for Germans, as well. Here they were bombed by the Americans and the British. And, now, if one thinks that they have to answer for their grandparents, then we have to answer for ours; for the repressions, for the revolution [of 1917, referring to the fact that many Jews participated in it]. [pause, then concluding] For Jews the most important thing is to survive, no matter where."

Rita chose to use the word "fell," not "exterminated" or "killed" when she spoke about her relatives who were Holocaust victims. This choice corresponds with her general attempt to bridge significantly different narratives, in fact to span huge gaps and to relativize this event in relation to other groups affected by the war (e.g., Soviet soldiers who fought hard for the victory, but also Germans who suffered). She argued that there is a common pain and tragic suffering as a result of which all people have been changed significantly and presumably learned. The logic of this rationale requires that she tries to understand the Germans, against whom her father fought, as Others. It also legitimates her right to live in the current German state as an ex-Soviet Jew. Moreover, in explaining attempts to adapt to having relations with "Germans," she repeated a common argument used by Germans that recalls their suffering from the bombings and deprivations (n. b., there has been increased use of this argument since 2005). According to this construction, her father was a Soviet soldier who won the war, whereas "other" Americans and British (but not the Soviets) bombed the Germans, with whom she sympathized. This construction corresponds completely with the Soviet rhetoric of the absolutely *right* winners, presented at the beginning of this chapter.

Rita also noted in her statement that—"For Jews, the most important thing is to survive, no matter where." This is another important aspect characteristic of the investigation group; namely their depoliticized disappointment, as Jews and as ex-Soviet citizens, with the collapse of the Soviet state in which they lived and worked for most of their lives, and that failed to provide them with a secure and dignified pension.

It became clear throughout the interviews that the weight of the Holocaust and the WWII did not play a central role in the participants' decision-making in regard to immigrating to Germany. Rather, most did so due to personal considerations and different difficulties they were facing.[220] However, this does not mean that various recollections, connected primarily with the war, disappeared upon their arrival in Germany or only surfaced during Victory Day celebrations on the 8th of May.

Lida: "I did not think about the Holocaust [she pronounced the word in German, not Russian], but all of us had recollections of Germany and the fascists. But, we did not have a choice. Our material needs were not being met. I had nothing to put in my child's school sandwich."

Lida, one of the few participants who spoke directly about the connection between Germany's past and her decision to immigrate, stressed her "heteronymous action" (Schütze 2007); that is, a pre-determined situation with given macro-conditions that leaves no latitude for agency and consequently individual responsibility (e.g., structural conditions such as economical difficulties "decided for her" immigration to Germany).

As we will see, the association with Germany and fascists mentioned by Lida remained in the background, as taken for granted, and unarticulated upon meeting "Germans."

7.5 Proud of the Soviet victory, offended by the Soviet state or marginalized winners

The status of the Soviet victors, as molded in the past through state politics, supposedly strengthened the entire national collective and nourished the concept of the Soviet motherland. However, residing now in the context of the new Germany, such status takes on new meanings, some of which have the potential to engage the migrant in conflicts. For ex-citizens living abroad in Germany, the role of the Soviet motherland as *total signifier* is ruptured. Indeed, only after migration does the necessity for reflection on familiar parts of diverse identities emerge. In this process, some participants remained proud of the former victorious motherland and their belonging to the collective of victors. Others problematized this sense of the

---

220 See discussion in Chapter Two.

attachment and were unable to continue to identify with the familiar collective of winners, especially while living in the former enemy's land.

This position explains the following example of different reactions by two women to the Victory Day announcement posted in a Russian food store:

Ira: "Ja, right, let's celebrate the 9th of May! We still won the war!"

Ludmila: "Shhh, you shouldn't say that here. We are still in Germany."

Ira: "You mean still Nazi Germany?"

Ludmila: "Leave me alone. I don't want to speak about it here."

For some migrants, actualization of the victory myth and affiliation with the winner's collective played a symbolic, supportive role in the context of a difficult migration process and labor conditions. This role was often instrumentalized as a compensation mechanism, as we see in this statement by Lisa (a nurse in a home for the elderly, 40 years old[221]):

Lisa: "At the beginning I felt totally unsure and I worried a lot at work. I found a sentence that calms me down and even empowers me, strongly! [pause, looks at me as if she is waiting for me to continue questioning her]."

JB: "Really? What is the sentence?"

Lisa: "When it is especially hard at work, I think: Still, we won the *war*. Just as it was not easy then, so I will succeed in my work in Germany, opposed to what they [Germans] think: The *Ausländer* [lit. foreigners; used negatively to refer to immigrants; German word used by Lisa in Russian statement] aren't capable of doing as good a job as the Germans."

Lisa drew strength for her work, which is difficult for her both psychologically and physically (detailed in the interview), from the familiar collective victor narrative known to her since childhood. This seems to serve a defensive function for her. Despite the fact that she was born 22 years after the end of the war and her father did not serve at the front as an active solder, she stated: "Still, *we* won the war." The reference to the Soviet collective seems to be an act of symbolic affiliation, as well as, a historic archetype and ideal referring to the collective's superhuman effort, persistence, and valor under unbearable war conditions [mentioned above as part of the official political Soviet narrative]. According to her description and

---

221 Lisa is the youngest participant in the German study. She is married to a 57 year old man.

way of thinking, Lisa seems to transfer the conflict between the dominant powerful group—the Germans—and the dominated minority group of migrants deprived of many rights—the Russians—to a different historical context when relations between Germans and Russians were reversed (i.e., when Germans were defeated by Russians[222]). This incident demonstrates especially well how the compensation mechanism functions. The "victory" in her statement, stated in a manner similar to advertising statements printed on product wrappers (e.g., for products such as Victory, Glory or Glory Guard, mentioned above), is an expression of symbolic resistance against the low social status ascribed migrants in Germany. Or, as Roberman formulated it precisely in her work about Russian-speaking veterans in Israel, it is a "struggle against marginalization, humiliation, and ethnic hostility" as well as "revitalization of agency (Roberman 2005, 2)."

In my opinion, in both her work and statements, Lisa not only tries to preserve her dignity, but also copes with presumed hostile attitudes of Germans towards foreigners. She also attempts to dispel contradictory images about "diligent and hard working Germans" as juxtaposed to "lazy foreigners" derived and generalized from her everyday interactions and conflicts with the German chief nurse at the old-age-home where she works.[223]

The *victory* narrative also functions as a compensation mechanism in other difficult situations; for example, when people feel particularly powerless, deprived of their rights, and/or simply do not know their way around. Thus, even ordinary everyday situations, when no obvious connection is made between the action of a German person in the present and during the war, can result in an actualization and instrumentalization of the symbolic power of the Great Victory narrative exhumed from the past. For example, Sveta (48 year old music teacher who lives on social welfare) related this incident in an angry tone:

"Yesterday, my son [9 years old] and I went to the bus station. We had to run as the bus was leaving. The driver saw us, but didn't wait. He closed the doors in our face just as we arrived and left. Then I told my son *all* about the war and Holocaust."

---

222 In presenting Russian speaking rhetoric, I purposively used the word Russians instead Soviets as was usually the practice in Soviet public discourse.
223 Related in the full interview.

Sveta's reaction might seem to be overly reactive and a misinterpretation. However, following Schäffter (1991), this may be Sveta's way of coping with the strangeness of being in a new foreign situation. Here it appears that Sveta did not know the local regulation that bus drivers in Germany must follow their schedule very strictly and usually do not wait for people who might delay them. Sveta is dismayed by what she perceived to be the driver's inhuman, lack of respectful behavior. She interpreted this as a hostile act aimed at immigrants; an act that humiliated her in the eyes of her son. As consequence, she used a kind of practical solution that applied strong cultural ascriptions. In fact, she generalized the driver's behavior to the macro-category "Germans," whom she stigmatized by connecting this situation to their historical guilt, followed by relating to her the terrible acts committed by the Nazis during the war and the Holocaust. This, in spite of the fact, that the driver in this particular situation might have been a fellow immigrant from Turkey.

7.6 Challenging the victory narrative and *burdensome identities*

The war theme is a central, public, political narrative employed in constructing the myth of the victorious Soviet nation in the SU. However, in Germany, use of this narrative was restricted to the private sphere, expressed only behind closed doors. The narrative's only "public performance" is celebration of the 8th of May, which takes place in a space inaccessible to the wider German community. In general, despite its compensative role, the Soviet victory narrative appears to be insufficiently resistant, as it seems incapable of providing an exclusive, positively loaded, collective affiliation. That is, the local German context inevitably penetrates through this narrative limiting and challenging its symbolic power, and as significantly, creating inner conflicts for migrants.

According to evidence found among former Soviet citizens, the extensive success of Soviet socialization in infusing the politically constructed victory narrative means that it accompanies migrants' lives for many years after immigration to Germany. Thus, while the victory rhetoric and its well-known images are only actualized publicly, on occasion, when it does happen in everyday situations in the new German context old patterns and categorizations lead to the development of attendant complexities. For example, certain situations or symbols arouse immediate associations with THE war, when fireworks are lit in a neighborhood. While for non-Russian speakers (i. e., for outsiders who do not share the Soviet victory narrative and its symbolic associations), such occasions may appear disconnected with the war, former Soviet citizens recall how the 9th of May victory celebrations are conducted.

Ira (60 years old) expressed in a much more dramatic manner how Germans sometimes remind her of Nazis and the war time:

"Here, everything is good: life, the standard of living, leisure time, money. But, you look out the window and there are *nemzy* [Germans, Rus., meaning enemies]."

Thus, the pastwar rhetoric leads to associations with potentially conflictual recollections that introduce stimuli into the current reality. It also reveals an inner conflict in Ira who is content with the quality of her life, but not with living amidst Germans. In a sense, we could say she is trapped: On the one hand, she cannot disassociate Germans she sees in everyday life from Nazis. Nor, on the other hand, can she rid herself of the Soviet victory rhetoric.

Roman's victory recollections take a very different path as sometimes they placed him in the role of a Soviet secret agent portrayed in WWII war films:

"When I go out to the street after the weekend [i.e. leaves his flat after viewing Russian satellite cable TV] and suddenly hear German, I feel like Shtirliz [the name of a Soviet secret agent in of one of the most famous Soviet TV series about the WWII called 17 Moments of Spring, whose protagonist, Isaev, was a secret agent]."

Both war films and the Pobeda/victory celebration on the 8th of May in Germany returned the immigrants, albeit momentarily, to the war and in doing so revived the socialized Russian war rhetoric and their historical identity in their consciousness. Such associations with Germans who they met in their everyday lives stimulated and perpetuated perceptions of them within the generalized category of *Germans as Nazi enemies*. It seems that this thinking structure arouses inner conflicts related to the legitimacy of their residing in Germany.

Gaps between competing and complex narratives were revealed and reinforced when migrants, who are for the most part dependent on receiving social welfare from the German state [necessary for the most of the persons in the investigated group], participated in the re-actualization of the victory liberation narrative at 8th of May celebrations. Yet, in noting the presence of this gap, we should not ignore the problematic, critical view that produces the fragmented nature of this narrative. That is, we should not conclude that the celebration of the 8th/9th of May and re-construction of the victory–liberation narrative infers complete acceptance and blind identification with all policies of the Soviet motherland, especially as presently defined and implemented. Indeed, quite the opposite is true: Many participants in these celebrations were critical of the Soviet state and disillusioned with the policies implemented over the years. For many persons this gap involves an extended process of wrestling with the problem of accepting the fact that the once omnipotent Soviet empire no longer exists, that its power was limited, and not absolute.

Leon (computer programmer on social welfare, 55 years old) stated: "I have to admit, when we arrived, the Germans helped us. They brought us clothing. I had to cry: The *nemzy!* [Germans, Rus., he means enemies] [pause] helped us! Throughout our whole life they have been seen as our enemies and *we* were the victors! And now they support us with social welfare and we get nothing from our Russia, our motherland, [stated with irony], from the victorious empire!"

In general, during the fieldwork in Germany, I found that participants had difficulty recognizing as well as accepting the collapse of the victorious empire and certain confusion about current affiliations with collective images from the past. Indeed, confusion about current multiple affiliations have to be contextualized within the general inner uncertainty that can be attributed to the act of migration and the entire migration process. Such a feeling is a common characteristic of this process and has different forms of expression.

Particularly conspicuous are rhetorical components that have the potential to cause conflicts in the new reality. For example according to the Soviet motherland canon, migration is perceived to be an act of individual ingratitude, a "betrayal of the most treasured of all we have—the motherland (Sandomirskaya 2004, 131);" choosing "his home is everywhere [when] it is comfortable" (ibid). Consequently, the use of this rhetoric creates a strong conflict with via individual agency and the personal biographies of migrants. Clear examples of the presence of such conflict occurred in two interviews when participants used the word "betrayers" to refer to themselves. One can trace in their descriptions of these incidents the inner dialogue taking place between two different reference groups or Anderson's (1991)"imagined communities:" On the one hand, a community comprised of dead relatives who fell in the war and those exterminated in the Holocaust; and, a second community of contemporary friends who did not emigrate, but stayed in the CIS and still live through the abstract generic concept of "victorious Soviet motherland" and participate in its actualization.

Tamara: "Recently I gave my seat to an elderly man on crutches. He said: 'You are a very kind woman.' And, I thought to myself: 'I am sure you were injured at the front. How many *nashich* [lit. of ours, Rus., meaning Soviet people] did you kill?' [...] I just could not speak with him. [pause] All of us, who left [the SU] are *betrayers* and will always have nowhere to belong..."

The second manifestation of their inner conflict is finding that most participants hide their Jewish identity in interactions with Germans. The following example reveals how different self-identities coexist (as Jews, as Soviet victors, and their recently acquired identity as ex-Soviet, Jewish migrants in Germany).

Katia (11 year resident in Germany) mentioned suffering from occasional nighttime panic attacks: She awakens suddenly to hear the German language. Before realizing where she is, she associates it with the war, when as a young girl she and her family were evacuated due to the bombing. In one of our conversations she also described an incidental interaction with an elderly German man, in a bus similar to the previous account, in which her deep identity conflict surfaced:

"I gave up my place to an elderly German man. We started to talk and he asked me what do I am doing here? I told him that I am a pensioner. And he looked at me and asked if I worked in Germany and if not where I was actually from? I said that I was from Russia. 'And with which program?'

I just could not tell him that I am Jewish and that I get social welfare here. I just could not, so I lied. I told him that I am a German from Kazakhstan and my work experience was recognized here. That was okay for him, but for me it was horror."

Here a chance situation reproduced the hierarchy present in local social power relationships. On the one hand, any German person can presume to be a representative of the local order and feel he has the right to request that a migrant explains her residence in the country. On the other hand, because of her uncertainty and insecurity, Katia accepts his functioning in this role and acts in accordance with a perceived inferior role in this situation, and later feels depressed, gloomy, and guilty. What is also clear in accounts of many similar incidents shared by participants is how unimportant is the fact that she celebrates the 8th of May and feels she belongs to the victorious Soviet collective. In comparison to daily confrontations in which migrants must reveal themselves and conform to existing social hierarchies between the dominant group and subordinate migrants, celebration of the victory seems to represent an important, but very limited defense and compensation mechanism.

Thus, whereas in the present Russian state, the victory narrative strengthens national stature and "envisage[s] a desired future" (Maier 1987, 151—2; Golden 2002, 8), in the transfer to the German context, its revival and preservation leads migrants to conflicted self-positioning as well as revives strong negative emotions connected with the past. This entire situation is difficult in the settling in process in Germany, in particular for elderly ex-Soviet people.

Generally, we may assume that these *fragmental affiliations* of migrants change according to the group constellation and special situations at particular moments. This explains how migrants can criticize the Soviet state harshly and at the same time be proud of certain events in the country's history. One gains a relative perspective of the limited power of the Soviet victory rhetoric, as a main signifier of the concept of Soviet motherland, when participants raised such criticisms as suffering from anti-Semitism in the SU; repressions and the totalitarianism of the Soviet regime; the poor quality of life and other economic deficiencies in the SU; negative Soviet policies in regard to Israel; or the previously noted theme of their pensions after so many years of work in the SU. This means that pride in the Soviet victor's narrative coexists alongside other different signifiers of the Soviet empire, some of which are no longer sources of pride.

Thus, critiques of the Soviet state are comprehensible and well received by compatriots in Germany as well as welcomed by many people from the dominant local (German) groups as a sign of their loyalty and gratitude to the receiving society and its policies. However, certain components of the national Soviet terminology are still kept alive and revived in the migrants' everyday life. Whereas these Soviet national narratives[224] might seem strange to the non-Russian in Germany, for the migrant they reflect the presence of deep inner conflict that only surface once a year during the 8th of May celebrations, but accompany some throughout the year.

---

224 Such as those from Soviet war songs: "*Rodina*" [motherland, Rus.], "fatherland," "true [Soviet] patriotism," "Russian winners and collective victory," or "betrayers of the fatherland."

Thus, in general, the Soviet victory narrative appears to be insufficiently resistant despite its compensative role, as it seems incapable of providing an exclusive, positively loaded collective affiliation. That is, the local German context inevitably penetrates through this narrative, limiting and challenging its symbolic power, and its significance creates inner conflicts for migrants.

7.7 The Outsider perspective

The highly politicized decision to accept Russian-speaking Jews in Germany assumed that they belonged to the same survival group of Holocaust victims. As such, they were granted the right to migrate to Germany,[225] and consequently were presumed to be symbolic representatives of the victim group by local communities. This decision was part of the German policy of reconciliation or retribution for moral guilt [*Wiedergutmachung*, making amends, Ger.] (Becker and Körber 2001; Dietz 2003; Joppke 1998; Schütze and Rapoport 2000). However, the Soviet victor attitude has quite a different perspective from the Germans' collective view about the role of Jews during WWII.

Overall, it does not seem that in the debate in Germany that anyone had a clear appreciation of the Russian-speaking Jews' perceptions of their identity, their role during WWII, or their own understandings of Jewishness. Rather, it was assumed that they would become part of and expand the local Jewish communities, defined as a *Kultusgemeinde* [lit. cultural community, Ger.]; more specifically, above all else, a religious community in accordance with the German idea of Jewishness as religious affiliation.[226]

Anatolii (Germany): "You are wanted here only as a victim […] They like you as a memory, as a part of history. But, different people come, not all necessarily pleasant or nice ones, and they spoil the ideal picture of Holocaust victims presented in the cruel black and white pictures in the museum. This reality is for them already

---

225 Becker and Körber (2001) quote a representative of the SPD party.
226 The German language makes no distinction between Judaism and Jewishness; both are expressed through the word *Judentum* as an exclusively religious affiliation. This one-sided view of Jewish identity stands in contradiction to and in strong rejection to the Nazi, bio-anthropological notion of race and ideology of ethnicity connected to "Blut und Boden" [blood and earth, Ger.] (Calloni 1999) employed in legitimization of the extermination of the Jews.

black and white, a history, and then suddenly you come to them with your problems and visions."

Most of the migrants interviewed did not become religious after migration. And, most were—and many still are—unprepared to accept the role of victims, nor ready to be taught by settled Jews how to become "real" Jews by learning the Jewish religion and tradition.[227] Furthermore, through interactions with Germans as well as with non-Russian-speaking Diaspora Jews, Russian-speaking Jews learned that their victory narrative significantly contradicts the local narrative about the place of the Jews in the history of WWII. In fact, complex perceptions are often reduced to dichotomous, conflicting images: strong, powerful victorious Soviet Jews as a part of triumphant empire and the discriminated minority of persecuted Diaspora Jews who, as defenseless victims, were exterminated in the Holocaust or who escaped and were spared from the disaster.

The Soviet victory narrative and migrants' attitude to the Western perception of the Holocaust narrative emerged as problematic in the perception of settled Jews in Germany as well as in general German parlance. Furthermore, the Russian-speaking Jews neither shared the "right" version of WWII events (as not only Soviet victory) nor were they prepared to provide the "proper" response to the question "What does it mean to be Jewish?"

For members of the Jewish community, Russian-speaking Jews had insufficient knowledge of Jewish traditions and rituals. And, their insistence on retaining the status of victors was interpreted as suspicious and damaging to their association with and belonging to the Jewish collective. This notwithstanding, 13 years after the beginning of the mass immigration of Russian speakers to Germany, Victory Day is now celebrated in most of the Jewish communities in Germany that have Russian-speaking members. Indeed, it is celebrated even in those communities where Russian-speaking Jews are in the minority (e.g., Frankfurt am Main). This development demonstrates the potential influence of different self-perceptions held by the Russian-speaking group on the general character and the collective identity of Jews in Germany in the future.

---

227 A similar form of resistance emerged in response to attempts by the Jewish religious establishment in Israel who attempt to impose Jewish religious traditions and "appropriate" Jewish Israeli national consciousness on Russian-speaking Jews in order for them to become "real" Jews. See Golden (2001).

If in interactions between participants and non-Jewish Germans the issue of Jews and WWII was problematic, this was even more so the case
with the settled Jewish community. Participants usually preferred, in most
contacts with this group, to avoid discussing the war and many presented
themselves as Russians, not as Jews. This tactic seems to have been
adopted so as not to revive victor/enemy images, to avoid dealing with
questions related to the Holocaust, to limit explanations about their decision to emigrate, and/or due to fear of anti-Semitism.[228]

Nevertheless, it is important to note that the participants' Russian self-
identification (by which they mean Russified-Soviets) is not chosen as a
defense mechanism for public presentation to Others, but is an expression
of multiple self-identities. Presuming active involvement in the war as
soldiers, the Russified Soviet self-identification of participants does not
contradict but rather co-exists with their Jewish Soviet identity, including
the history of their active involvement in the war as Jewish soldiers, who
also contributed, significantly, to the common victory.

7.8 Principally Others: Media discourse about the topic

Jews are seen primarily as victims and nearly all topics related to Jews are
discussed through the historical prism of the Holocaust in the dominant
German discourse and the media. However, the victory narrative as well as
the Jewish contribution to the victory may well have caused a certain conceptual confusion. Analyzing German press media between the years
1991—2007, I was able to identify and to trace the existence of a strategy
to reproduce and to spread historically developed, negative labels of "Russians" and "Soviets". This strategy devalues victory celebrations of the
Soviet liberation of Europe from the Nazis through use of negative
stereotypical ascriptions applied to the veterans. This implies hostility,
rejection, and exclusion of this group and stresses the presence of un-

---

228 It is important to note that self-presentation as Russians may have had misleading
consequences, especially when immigrants are interviewed by non-Russian German
speaking researchers whom they may not trust. Thus, Russian speaking migrants have a
tendency to present themselves in the public sphere with their Russian identity as the
main and most important one. However, this may not necessarily reflect their self-
perception.

bridgeable cultural gaps. Such derision presented this group as corrupt, criminal, "actually not Jewish," and undesired.[229]

Authors of newspaper articles invoke presumed local knowledge about how the past should be interpreted and in doing so reproduce this knowledge as legitimate or "true." For example, according to local German norms, war veterans should refrain from display of military honors, medals, or national decorations in public. Yet, the media present ex-Soviet soldiers displaying their medals and decorations during the 8th of May celebrations. Here the press conveys the message that these ex-Soviet veterans, now residents of Germany clearly transgress cultural limits and norms. Thus, the media take a stand regarding this implied assumption as well as the impossibility of their being national military heroes or victors in contemporary German rhetoric. Doing so supposes historical reflection rather than praise and admiration for national German symbols.

Stern: "Ilja Riaboi is no victim. He displays his decorations. He pricked a finger attaching them to his jacket." The sub-headline reads: "In full glory—former Red Army soldier, Ilja Riaboi, at a home for the elderly in Hanover" [Ger].[230]

Zeit: "Now he paces around here with his decorations" [Ger.]. [231]

The following two provocative examples are concerned with what is considered to be inappropriate ways of celebrating the victory in Germany. Also included is the expectation that Soviet victors leave rhetoric behind:

Berliner Zeitung: "Russian-speaking immigrants don't know English, as if they still want to live in the former Soviet Union. Veterans of the Red Army meet regularly" [Ger.].[232]

Deutsche Allgemeine Zeitung: "Most immigrants from the former Soviet Union are secular, don't keep Shabbat, eat pork, and celebrate Christmas and *even* the 8th of May—"Victory Day over fascist Germany" [Ger.].[233]

---

229 Becker and Körber 2001; Elias and Bernstein 2006; Ostow 2003.
230 Von Stefan Braun, "Juden in Deutschland. Jetzt reden sie Tacheles," Stern http://www.stern.de/politik/deutschland/587598.html?nv=ct_cb, 21.06.2010.
231 Jan Ross cited Judith Kessler, editor of *Jüdisches Berlin* in his article: "Eine Reise durch die jüdischen Gemeinden Deutschlands im Schatten des Nahostkonflikts," *Die Zeit* (2002, 21).
232 Marlies Emmerlich, "Deutschland ist das Paradies geworden," *Berliner Zeitung* (December 21, 2004). (http://www.berlinonline.de/berliner-zeitung/archiv/.bin/dump.fcgi/2004/1221/politik/0009/index.html, 21.06.2010.
233 Veronika Wengert, "Russischer Wodka und unkoscheres Schweinefleisch," *Deutsche Allgemeine Zeitung* (June 2, 2006).

Here one can see how listing transgressions refers to commonly assumed key symbols of the German discourse about Jewish affiliation; namely statements that Jews should be religious, eat no pork, be victims, and do not celebrate Jewish holidays. Later, the claim is reinforced by revealing supposed contradictions: Jewishness in Germany is presumed to be primarily a religious affiliation and, consequently, Jews are not expected to celebrate Christian holidays. Yet, the newspapers report that they actually do celebrate Christmas. In fact, ex-Soviet migrants only celebrate "*Novyi god*" [New Year celebration on 31 December—1 January, Rus.], observed as an atheistic holiday in the SU. The fact that most settled Jews are secular and consume pork is not mentioned. In fact, a double transgression of the symbolic borders of the normative past is argued: Not only is their authenticity as Jews doubted, but they are also presented as disloyal to German norms. This can be seen in use of "even;" that is, they are so bold as to even celebrate victory over Germans in WWII while living in Germany.

7.9 Shifting of the collective "we:" Media presentation of Germans and settled Jews as the symbolical "we" compared to "Russians"

The Holocaust is an inseparable part of the personal identity of settled Jews and is taken for granted as part of the common Jewish historical fate. Migrant Jews resistance to adopting this view is conflictual. The German media have picked up this conflict and the Holocaust is often cited as a kind of confirmation of the normative German discourse:

Zeit: "What does he want here? He struts around with his decorations. He celebrates the 8th of May, but doesn't come to the commemoration ceremony on the 9th of November" [Ger.]. [234]

Zeit: "It is painful for many of them [Jews living in Germany] when only a few Russian immigrants come to the synagogue on the 9th of November. In contrast, Russian Jews celebrate the 9th of May, the Peace Day. Many served in the Red Army against Germans as soldiers" [Ger.]. [235]

234See note 70.
235 Busse (2005). "Die Opferrolle wollen wir nicht," *Die Zeit* (May 11, 2005, 20).

Stern: "'I was victorious against Hitler.' This is an unthinkable sentence for Jews in postwar Germany [...] Nothing has influenced them as strongly as the awareness to the fact that we are living in the land of the *perpetrators*. Now here come the Jewish victors and their children" [Ger.].[236]

Journal Frankfurt: "Suddenly there were Jews taking up German citizenship without any hesitation, without reference to the years between 1933—1945. In the tradition of the Red Army, they come out of the blue as proud victors. The hegemonic commemoration culture of the community is confused. While some group members commemorate the victims of Kristallnacht on the 9th of November, others celebrate the 9th of May, the date they defeated Nazi Germany" [Ger.]. [237]

Aside from being an insulting way to present this group, in general, and the victory celebration, in particular, what is characteristic of these citations is the authors' use of double terms of foreignness and exclusion: These people neither fit the accepted images of the Jewish collective of victims nor do they share the "right" cultural codes concerning the interpretation of the past. In either case, they cannot belong to the German collective, for whom it seems to be unthinkable to celebrate defeat when there is even no consensus about whether or not to view the 8th of May as a liberation day.[238] Editors choose such provocative titles for articles as "We don't want the victim's role."[239] In doing so, the image of *principally Others* is fashioned so as to reinforce evidence demonstrating significant Otherness and insufficient Jewishness of *homo soveticus*. Symbolically, then, through the mechanism of *principally Others,* a general consensus is produced about coherence between settled Jewish and dominant German groups, a consensus that otherwise would be missing and could hardly be achieved through other means.

In order to compare different meanings associated with the celebration of the Victory Day in Israel and Germany, the following summary of research studies is intended to highlight several comparative tendencies developing in Israel. During my fieldwork in Israel, I found that the

236 Braun (2007), "Juden in Deutschland. Jetzt reden sie Tacheles," *Stern* http://www.stern. de/politik/deutschland/587598.html?nv=ct_cb, 16.06.2010.

237 Sälzer and Schröder (pictures) *Journal Frankfurt* (June 12, 2005).

238 After many years of discussing the topic, the German majority reluctantly and hesitantly recognized the 8th of May as a day of liberation. See Botsch (2007) in "Der Holocaust-Gedenktag am 27 Januar und die deutschen Juden: Vergangenheit, Gegenwart und Zukunft jüdischen Lebens in Berlin," 5. http://www.touroberlin.de/TOURO_PDF/Holo caust-Gedenktag.pdf, 21.06.2010.

239 Busse "Die Opferrolle wollen wir nicht," *Die Zeit* (May 11, 2005, 20).

Victory Day and its celebration was the preserve essentially of WWII veterans and that it remained inconspicuous among the postwar generation of the investigation group. Whereas only war veterans marched in parades on the streets of Jerusalem on the 9th of May, we have seen that it is a significant social event in Germany: It is celebrated within the framework of the entire Jewish community and participants include many Jews from three postwar generations. Moreover, in Germany, I found the war and Holocaust to be especially meaningful and delicate issues. Thus, the empirical materials reveal an asymmetric situation between the German and the Israeli situations.

7.10 "Without us Israel would not have come into existence. We won the war and put an end to the Holocaust..."

Many former WWII veterans who are Russian-speaking immigrants living in Israel have struggled for recognition by Israeli authorities as well as for public support for having made an essential contribution to the establishment of the State of Israel through their struggle as active Soviet solders during WWII (Zilberg 2002). As a result, parades, memorial plaques, and obelisks now honor Jewish soldiers who struggled against fascism. In 1996, the Victory Day was recognized as an official national celebration. And, in 2000, the Knesset [parliament] enacted a law that related to all WWII veterans (ibid).

The huge size of the Russian-speaking population in Israel,[240] as well as, the presence of three Russian political parties in the Knesset in 2000 succeeded in advancing significant changes in the Israelis' historical perceptions of the role of the Jewish collective during WWII. As a result, a symbolic connection has been created between the heroism of Soviet Jewish soldiers and the history of Israel (Roberman 2005, 2007; Zilberg 2002).

In my opinion, the introduction of veteran parades in Israel demonstrates the success of the struggle by Russian-speaking migrants there against the receptor society's conservative perception of their status (Golden 2002) and understanding of these historical events. The self-perception of Soviet Jews as active soldiers who sacrificed their lives "for the

---

240 Now one million out of six million of the total Israeli population.

sake of the emergent Israeli state" (Roberman 2005) played a growing role in their absorption process and contributed to the significant status they have achieved in the Israeli society and its history. Indeed, the relationship between the crucial role of the Soviets during the war and the establishment of the State of Israel has been an essential part of the socialization of children who grew up during or immediately after the war who reside now in Israel and Germany.

Mila (Israel, born 1950): "Without us Israel would not have come into existence. We won the war and put an end to the Holocaust."

The symbolic historical continuity as well as the significant number of Russian speakers in the Israeli society contributes to their demand for participation in adoption of historical narratives and their demand for social influence in the Israeli society. Both active social participation and positioning distinguishes them significantly from their compatriots in Germany, where the latter suffer from the image of being a weak minority immigrant group living on the edge, the margins, of the receiving society. Thus, in Israel, as opposed to the usual identification of Diaspora Jews as weak victims of the Holocaust, the image of the Soviet Jewish victors has been nationalized as a part of the Jewish Israeli self-image as a strong, self-confident collective. Interesting, the original view that it was a citizen's duty to fight on behalf of the Soviet Union was instrumentalized 50 years later in Israel to be a *Jewish* battle that contributed to the establishment of the state.

As imported to Israel, the meaning of the Soviet political narrative changed. This modification contributed to establishing a positive immigrant image, symbolized their historical affiliation with the Jewish-Israeli collective, and enriched the local version of the collective political narrative of the history of Jewish people.

7.11 Comparative conclusions of different modifications of the original narratives in Israel and Germany

In the case of Germany, the meanings attached to the same narrative changed in quite different ways. At first glance it seemed that the Jewish victory narrative contributed, symbolically, to the development of a new image of the local German Jewish community as well as of the German nation through liberation of Germany from the Nazis.[241] However, this narrative also contributes to the evolving identities of Russian-speaking Jews in Germany and, as well, has the potential to lead to conflicts between those who do and do not share this narrative—be they Jewish or German. An example of the latter point is the frequent number of occasions in which Russian-speaking Jews in Germany revert to the Soviet war rhetoric. In such cases, words associated with "German" are exchanged with "Nazi." This rarely happens in Israel. And, again, different from Israel, use of the original meanings of the Soviet victory narrative results in *double alienation* of the investigated group from the local German as well as local settled Jewish collectives, that already have negotiated historical relationships with one another.

Historically, Soviet, Polish, and German Jews were all Holocaust victims (Adar 2004; Gitelman 1994; Kandel 2006; Lustiger 1998). The Soviet victory narrative that accompanied the Russian-speaking Jews to Germany served a central role in establishing a conflictual relationship between the groups. Three tendencies emerged in the fieldwork in this regard: confusion, separation, and partial change. Conceptual confusion was created for both non-Jewish and settled Germans as it stressed the image of strong Diaspora Jews who were exterminated, but also struggled. This transgression of borders might well have led to questioning previously held understandings about what was an "appropriate" and accepted discourse. Second, while the Soviet victory narrative could lead to separation between groups, it also raised new questions that could have developed into multiple senses of attachment and identity.

A Jewish German woman who was an audience member during a presentation of a paper related to this research demonstrated this confusion:

"Well, they liberated us as Jews, but they defeated us as Germans. What should I think now? Why didn't we [Germans] accept the victory until now? We and our children [as Jews] missed it, this participation. We don't have any heroes, just victims."

I submit that both of these cases involve use of compensation mechanisms involving the victory narrative in new contexts; or, in the terms of Robermann (2005, 2007), these are cases of agency and self-positioning amidst the situation of weakness, marginalization, and humiliation. However, in

---

241 According to Elias (2005) in her investigation of the Jewish community in Cologne.

the German case, this mechanism also causes further inner identity conflicts, as it renews previous antagonistic relationships that existed between
Jewish, Soviet, and German narratives and consequently forces people to
cope with a nearly impossible task of combining them. Thus, references to
the collective "we" are created in very different ways in both cases.

In Israel, the Soviet victory narrative attains a new status as a Jewish
Soviet act by joining the Jewish-Israeli collective image of the collective
"we." Moreover, Russian-speaking migrants in Israel who are linked to the
official, local Israeli commemoration dates relate to the discrimination or
extermination of Jews in the Diaspora, such as the *Kristallnacht* and Holocaust day. These commemorative events along with documentary media
accounts about Jewish life in the Diaspora function as an integral part of
the evolving Jewish Israeli collective narrative; providing permanent support for the seemingly recurrent need for Israel to legitimatize the very
existence of the Jewish national state.

In contrast, in Germany, the history of Jewish discrimination and extermination in the Diaspora, in general, and in Germany, in particular,
function as a determinative context in which their current controversial
position is often perceived as forced and conflictual. Their unwillingness to
internalize the Holocaust narrative as part of their identities can be explained as an intuitive attempt not "to be entrapped" in a local discourse
that requires them to justify and to legitimate, continually, their decision to
immigrate and to live in Germany.[242] Actually, such a decision cannot be
legitimated through the Holocaust or the German national narrative, and
consequently lends a sense of amorality. Such a position disconnects the
Russian-speaking group both from being an integral part of the settled
Jewish community which has its own affiliation with the Holocaust narrative as well as with German historical interpretations that serve to legitimate their life in Germany. The latter can only be supported if they are
seen as children and grandchildren of Holocaust victims. In this case, the
Soviet victor's narrative—the "we" reference—is directed neither to the
settled Jewish collective nor to the German dominant collective.

Thus, by playing a similar role as a "means of transportation," Jewish
affiliation by emigration from the CIS to two destination countries attained
significantly different meanings for migrants in Israel and Germany. The
migrants' Jewish affiliation in Israel is functioning over the long term as a

---

242 See Chapter Eight.

source of support; first, the "we" refers to the entire dominant collective; and, second, it is a resource for the potential sociopolitical participation. For example, answering questions about their decision or their rights in Israel is redundant. In contrast, the Jewish affiliation of migrants in Germany is the basis on which they were formally accepted into the state. But, it is a burden because it reduces their identities to what is considered by the dominant group to be the most significant category in the national terms, namely, to be identified as Jews. This may possibly exclude them over the long term from attaining association with the "we" reference group associated with the "German" national collective. This means that they are granted limited sociopolitical participation—through the Jewish community—which, in turn, has its own established ideas about Jewishness, which is rejected by most of the migrants investigated.

8 "Will you prepare gefillte fish for Christmas?" Paradoxes of living in simultaneously contested *social worlds*[243]

The social context of every receiving society influences how migrants articulate their decision to go there. The local sociocultural and political discourse into which emigrants arrive and about which they are often unaware plays an important role in the settling-in and affiliation processes that follow, as well as, how migrants articulate them.

This study applied the classic principles of anthropological research, as well as, the fundamental principles developed by Anselm Strauss and Barney Glazer in their Grounded Theory[244] Approach. The research field of Russian-speaking Jewish migrants in Germany and Israel dictated, in quite different ways, the relevant topics for analysis of statements articulated by participants and their projection of self-positioning in each new land. Whereas in the German context the topics of World War II, the Holocaust, and capitalism emerged as primary topics of concern, the central issue contested in Israel was the question "Who has a right to define what it means to be Jewish?" This having been noted, the participants in both contexts were forced to cope, frequently, with contested affiliations that required compromises and creative solutions. The participants' ways of self-positioning in both contexts were found to be tied inextricably to diverse individual strategies of coping with multiple controversies and contradictions.

---

243 Schütze (2002, 57).
244 Further developed by Strauss and Corbin (1990).

8.1 Reconsidering identities, reproducing stereotypes, coping with hierarchies

Two of the key problems identified in this study required that migrants develop strategies to cope with contradictions that exist in the different cultural and political narratives related to collective affiliations in Israel and Germany. First, participants had to develop coping strategies for their multiple affiliations, that is, about being Russian, Jewish, ex-Soviet, European, or an educated person who belonged to the intelligentsia stratum pre-emigration. Each of these affiliations came to be interpreted, modified, and had been assigned a different status post-immigration as participants adjusted to life in their new context. Second, participants were forced to cope with clashes and discrepancies between their subjective ideas about personal affiliations and collective narratives versus those of different resident groups in both societies.

Both sets of problems are inextricably linked together and interact constantly with one another. In addition, the destabilizing challenges encountered in the migration process caused migrants to feel obligations and pressures in many spheres of their everyday life and praxis. For example, Tamara (Germany) reported that nine years after immigration she remains anxious when her telephone rings because "perhaps someone is calling in German." She elaborated on her memories in the present tense, as if they were still relevant at the time of the interview:

"In the beginning you are like a person without skin. You are afraid to open your mouth. Somebody says something and for you it is already a tragedy. You worry because the expression on everyone's face, everywhere, looks [like they are trying] to "catch" you. You feel that the environment is hostile to you. You are afraid that people look at you and think you are an idiot because you do not react as expected and have nothing to say…"

Objectively, there were many new aspects of life for participants who emigrated from the SU/CIS to Israel or Germany; for example, the abundance of material objects, market economies, self-marketing, diversity of political parties, democracy and freedom, as well as, exposure to the Jewish religion, history, and culture. All had to be perceived, interpreted, and responded to by each individual participant.

As in other studies, this process and accompanying transformations proved to be far from being easy, indeed quite often problematic.[245] Additionally, the migrants linguistic insecurity often becomes noticeable as *existential insecurity* in the self-perception and behavioural patterns of migrants (Ehlich 1992 by Reitemeier 2005). In a manner similar to the statement by Misha that we recall from Chapter Two—"our Soviet residues are everything," Kolya (Israel) referred to this process through another strong metaphor—"Soviet nails." In his view, these iron nails, deeply driven by Soviet socialization, were disturbing and hard to discard:

"We all still have the long nails of the Soviet system in us [displays the length of 10 cm on his fingers of the proverbial nails]. They grew so deeply in our bodies and brain that they became almost an inseparable part of us. It is often easier for people to neglect them than to try to get rid of these nails."

In this process, many of the assumptions about collective identities to which they had been socialized were taken for granted (i.e., Schütz's "thinking as usually"[246]). And, those that supported and reaffirmed their pre-emigration lives were revealed to be precarious, controversial or even negatively laden in the receiving society. Furthermore, being highly educated turned out to be especially painful and frustrating, because many years after arrival nearly none of the participants had succeeded in realizing themselves professionally or had even obtained employment in their profession. As a result, they remained either unemployed (in Germany) or employed in jobs that did not require professional qualifications (in Israel) (Becker 2003; Cohen and Kogen 2005; Grüber and Rüßler 2000; Kessler 1996).

Pre-migration association with the stratum of Soviet intelligentsia, for example, held no status or was of little or no interest to members of resident groups in post-migration host societies. Yet, as an essential part of their pre-migration lives, their possession of and capabilities for expression through a refined Russian language reflected their previous social position, was also an object of pride, and a supportive resource. However, in their new home, the migrants' difficulties in expressing themselves in their new language became one of their main sources of anxiety and insecurity, even after ten years in Israel or Germany. And, indeed, many did experience

---

245 For complexities involved in transformations in post-socialist European societies, see Galligan, Clavero and Calloni (2007); Humphrey (2002); Shevchenko (2002).
246 "Denken wie üblich," Schütz (1972, 54).

sustained difficulties expressing themselves in Hebrew or German in a manner that reflected their self-perception as educated persons. Also, their pride in possessing the European cultural *habitus* was not reciprocal and even highly questioned, especially in Germany where they are often seen as "half Asian" (Stolting 2000, 34). The host's view was due to the long history of juxtaposing of Eastern and Western European affiliations (ibid) as well as socialization to negative perceptions of the totalitarian regime of Soviet European republics, such as Russia and Ukraine. Once a source of great national pride and a highly desired dream in the SU,[247] having "Russian" or "Soviet" affiliations turned out to be a source of stigmatization in the new, receiving society. Furthermore, idealized ideas about Israel and Germany that participants learned from literature written in or translated into Russian (e.g., about Christian Jerusalem in Bulgakov's *Master and Margerita* or depictions of Germany in books by Böll, Hesse, or Remarque) proved to be far different from realities encountered upon arrival. Indeed, certain Russian cultural elements grounded in Christianity and atheistic socialization considered to be progressive turned out to be an evidence of Jewishness that was challenged and questioned in the host society.

In addition, affiliation and identification with the collective winners of WWII shifted significantly from being a source of pride and strong support to be another *narrative of Others*, and in their case to the role of victims reserved for Jews.

Finally, the migrants' identification as "being Jewish," which had involved so much pain and difficulties in the SU, was perceived to be a falsification by resident groups in both new contexts. Indeed, their Jewishness is often patronized by such statements as the "community must make them real Jews."[248] Migrants' difficulties in understanding host perceptions and what they perceived to be their own inadequate responses to host residents' claims were the result of decades of Soviet policies that prohibited learning about or observing the Jewish religion, traditions, and culture. Thus, Russian-speaking migrants not only lacked knowledge about but were even alienated from their Jewish heritage. The long term effects of such politics remain unclear and unpredictable for former Soviet Jewish

---

247 For example, as noted by Nikolai [Israel] in Chapter Six: "I always dreamed of being Russian or at least Ukrainian."

248 "Die Gemeinde muss sie vor allem zu echten Juden machen." As the journalist, Hans Riebsamen, wrote in "Kleine Jüdische Wunder" [small Jewish wonders, Ger.] in one of the leading German newspapers FAZ (November 11, 2006, 1).

migrants in Israel and Germany as well as for resident groups. Nor are the effects of having lived most of their lives within the totalitarian system with its strongly regulated and sanctioned forms of social action as well as cultivation and objectification of the social order as "absolute system."

Migration to both societies offered numerous possibilities as well as difficulties, many of which have continued to be an integral part of the post-emigration lives of migrants until today. Most participants in both contexts considered migration to be a result of "destiny; of having been born in the wrong place." It seems that for the cohort of the age group investigated in this study immigration was above all a result of deep and sincere dissatisfaction with the living conditions in the land of origin.

Sergei (Germany): "The best situation would have been to be born in *your normal* state, to live and die there, to bequeath a house to your daughter, and not have to immigrate anywhere."

Ella (Israel): "To immigrate and to live in Israel *is* difficult, *very* difficult. Of course, the best is to be born somewhere in Switzerland, to go out with your doggy and not to know the word *mashkanta* [mortgage, Heb.; meaning to have more economic resources from the very beginning of life]."

Many years after migration Russian-speaking Jews continued to engage in what Breckner referred to as "paradoxes in lived we-references"[249] that includes an inner dialogue as well as a dialogue with different non-Russian speaking resident groups in Israel and Germany. Among the key "topics" discussed were the validity of transported habits, the changes undergone, acclaimed affiliations, and controversial statuses. In questioning discontinuities in their different affiliations throughout their social transition, migrants struggled to be perceived in their own terms, even if these were deemed to be illegitimate by resident groups (e.g., to proclaim the feeling of "being Jewish" yet consume pork; to purchase food products with Slavophil images of nationalized Russia; or to celebrate the Soviet victory in WWII).

Power relations with host societies are a very important dimension of the existential migrant state of mind. Participants in both contexts were exposed to the *normative dominant thinking* of the resident groups and to the receiving societies' integration policies, both of which embody power hierarchies. Whereas in Israel, the participants' alienation was twofold—as immigrants and as "Russians," it was fourfold in Germany—as immigrants,

---

249 "Paradoxien in den gelebten Wir-Bezügen," (Breckner 2005, 86).

as a minority, as Russians, and as Jews. According to the participants' interviews in both contexts, the *normative dominant thinking* as well as integration policies were grounded in several primary assumptions: Migrants were the only members of society expected *to adopt, to adjust, to change, to learn*; and in the most extreme form of expression, they were expected to be *grateful* to the receiving society and to its (self-) appointed representatives for granting them the right to immigrate to the "Western paradise."[250]

These key assumptions determined the prevailing atmosphere in both receiving societies that was perceived and felt by the participants as well as implied in interactions between migrants and members of resident groups—even if not explicitly articulated. That is, viewed sociologically, they remained a "second pair part." Schiffauer referred to frequently observable representations of normative dominant thinking regarding the local receiving societies' expectations from migrants as *"gereizte Grundstimmung"* [irritating prevailing atmosphere, Ger.] (Schiffauer 2003, 156). Previously mentioned examples of this phenomenon in other chapters include Misha's (Chapter Two) statement that it is hard to change and that nobody from the dominant group can "accuse him" of having been shaped in the SU. In a similar manner, Tamara (Germany) stated:

"When does integration happen? This is only a concept, because there is no day when I get up and think to myself: 'Well, today I am integrated!' [pauses] My son also [like "Germans"] keeps saying to me on the street: 'Mom, please don't speak Russian aloud!' [pauses] But I want to continue to be myself. To live as well as the Germans do, but to remain myself and to speak Russian. Is that too much to ask?"

Felix (Israel), too, shared the following: "It is not only language difficulties. You had assumed that one studies [as a student] until you are 25 years old and then no longer. But immigration is connected with an inner pressure and learning to live, again, as if you're still a pupil. This has to be overcome [the inner barrier or conflict]. And, you are also treated like that. This is a permanent status that is humiliating, undignified, and an insurmountable barrier, especially for men [hint towards their inflexibility]." [251]

---

250 For presentation of Germany as the Western paradise for Russian speakers, as represented in the media, see Elias and Bernstein (2007).
251 This opinion about the special difficulties encountered by men in adjusting and their being forced to change was noticed numerous times in both contexts. The topic of different gender difficulties in the migration process is also investigated in the sociological migration research; see for example Morokvasić (2007).

Also, the following advertisement in a Russian language newspaper in Israel demonstrates how the use of transported *habitus* and the Russian language in particular (n. b., where its practice is limited to the closed, private home sphere) is *justified* by presenting it as an exception to conducting their public life in Hebrew:

"I speak Hebrew. I think in Hebrew. I live in Hebrew. But, when I come home, I open the *Vesti*."

The expectations of the receiving society are not stated most of the time, rather they remain implicit or implied in everyday interactions, as well as, in the media. However, there are many occasions experienced by participants as unpleasant, e.g. direct initiatives by members of the resident groups who assumed that they should teach migrants the rules in the new society. In the following excerpt from the fieldwork in Germany, Katia admitted that she had not understood this aspect of the new reality and allowed herself to be taught, even if it was not pleasant for her:

Katia (Germany): "We do not understand anything here. We *have gotten used* to this situation [of not understanding]. I don't argue with anybody and am ready to learn. [pause] One neighbor of mine [an elderly German lady] came to me and said: 'It's your turn to clean the stairs and the entrance.' I [said]: 'I cleaned yesterday!' She [said]: '*Mmm, kommen Sie, ich zeige Ihnen, wie man putzen muss!*' [Come with me. I'll show you how one has to clean [Ger.; Katia used German in middle of speaking Russian]. She takes [Katia uses present tense] my hand, leads me to the entry, shows me a black carbon spot on the wall, and says: '*Das muss man auch putzen!*' [One has to clean it, too!, Ger.]. I say: 'It was not there, yesterday!' She [says]: '*Doch!*' ['It is ([still] there!', Ger.] And then goes to the windowsill and says: 'Das auch!' [This too!, Ger.] I: '*Ich habe das geputzt!*' [I cleaned it!, Ger.] She touches the windowsill with her hand, looks at her finger, and says: '*Ja, etwas*' [Yes, a little bit, Ger.]. She showed me everything and then we went upstairs and she said: '*Sind Sie böse auf mich?*' [Are you angry with me?, Ger.] I said: 'No, but I did not just fall out of the tree. I am a veteran teacher. I taught for 36 years!' And she replied: 'Yes, but you know, everything *in Germany* is different!' [speaks for German lady in Russian again] Now we meet each other and smile [Katia smiles an artificial smile] [pauses] I don't want to be angry with anyone. And, besides, we *do not understand anything* here. [pauses] Then [after this situation] I asked my friend, who cleans their [Germans'] houses. She told me one *does* clean differently here [in Germany]."

The descriptive structure of Katia's presentation of this incident is interesting. She begins and ends with the same general statements, using the plural in reference to migrants: "We" instead of "I" do not understand anything in the new reality. Therefore, it appears that statements repeated as a mantra indicate that there are matters that she has yet to internalize; that is, matters that she is not quite convinced of herself. Further, she stressed statements that were especially problematic for her by raising her voice, as in: "We have gotten used to this situation;" "everything is different;" and "we do not understand anything." These general, frozen-like statements about normativity in the new and different type of situation that migrants do not understand does not correspond with the middle portion of the vibrant description of a very unpleasant interaction that Katia remembered and reproduced in a very detailed manner. In describing an especially unpleasant experience, Katia used the present tense and scattered brief sentences in German (which she has yet to master). This seems to create an emotional distance from what happened, as well as, the impression that she re-experiences this situation each time she describes what happened. Overall, in my opinion, this statement points to difficulties Katia experiences in coping, psychologically, with her suffering from the position she has been forced to assume in these hierarchical relations. It is exactly the contradiction, on the one hand, between awareness of the necessity to learn and to change in the post-migration process; and, on the other hand, her self-perception as an educated, competent, mature person—rich with life experience—that cause the psychological difficulties involved in coping with the obvious humiliation that occurred when she was treated as an incompetent social actor, as migrant who had not learned the "appropriate" action and who—from the resident's point of view—should "not take it personally."

Such exchanges confirm the findings in Golden's (2001, 2002) research in Israel and Schiffauer's studies in Germany (2003): Participants in both field contexts complained that they are often treated as children, as mentally disabled persons, or people who come from the primitive lands.

Leonia (Germany): "They think if you don't speak German you are fully-fledged idiot, who does not understand anything in general about life, and has no education. You are an *empty* person and they speak to you as if to a child or a mentally disabled adult."

Tania (Germany): "It's not always pleasant for me to hear such sentences as— 'Where did you learn *German*?' 'You speak *goo-ood*!' 'How do you like being here in Germany?', 'Here, in Germany, it's so and so…' 'It's not Russia here…'

Ella (Israel): "They [Israelis] love to remind you—'*At lo berusiya*!' [You are no longer in Russia!, Heb.], especially when they [Israelis] disagree with you. This is ongoing, as if you understand nothing here [in Israel]. And that's why we have this and not *their* opinion."

Similarly, the statement—"it's not Russia here"—repeated in both contexts reaffirms what host-residents consider to be the inappropriate nature of migrant actions. And, that they perceive migrants according to one generalized "Russian" (or, speaking precisely, ascribed to be Russian) behavioral type—as if they were "still" in Russia (i.e. have yet to change their "attitudes" and behaviors in accordance with dominant—presumably homogeneous—ideas about the transformations necessary for "integration").

In fact, the analysis of the data collected suggests that "integration" is not actually the main or most important topic addressed in similar types of numerous interactions between participants and resident groups in both contexts, even if it seems to be so at first glance. Rather, I found that in such interactions residents are involved, principally, in defining their own collective affiliation through a mechanism that creates and excludes Others. Consequently, especially conspicuous differences frequently are interpreted as Others' deficiencies and generalized through the use of an abstract, cultural category that points to "different mentalities" (Schiffauer 2003) or stresses *unbridgeable differences*. For example, in the following citation, Tania described the reaction by a German person who heard her speak German:

"One [German] person said proudly: 'German is a beautiful but difficult language!' [in a pedagogic, moralistic tone]. He did not invent it! He has generally nothing to do with the fact that he was born here and he knows it [German language] and I don't. In [speaking] this way he showed that in contrast to him I don't belong here."

Similarly, Olga (Germany) elaborated about her general feeling being treated through significant Otherness:

"We all are aliens here. I saw an unemployment statistic that stated: 'Men, Women, *Ausländer*' [foreigners, Ger.]. Do you get it? There are—'men,' 'women,' and there are us—the aliens without a history—the *Ausländer*."

In such a schema of self re-definition (i.e., by means of comparing and contrasting oneself with Others), reductionist features ascribed to Others can be assigned negative characteristics and a primitive nature. Doing so in an implicit manner enables members of the host/receiving society to legitimize their own cultural, civilized, and "correct" ways of conducting interactions. Consequently, as reported by Schiffauer (ibid) the participants

reported being forced to assume predetermined interactional roles projected on them as *cultural representatives of the Others* who possess a *different
mentality*. This role limited expression of the migrants' own opinions and
attitudes. Yet, according to the participants, many Russian-speaking migrants refused to assume these roles and to act according to this *script*.

Tania (Germany): "If you are ready to admit that you came from a primitive land,
you find a lot of understanding and sympathy, and people [Germans] are ready to
help. Otherwise you are a competitor, [too] pragmatic a person, [seen as one who]
exploits their system."

Leonia (Germany): "Many people think that we came from a backward land where
all things were prohibited and all of us, of course, were drunk on vodka. When you
say you are an engineer, many [Germans] think—a primitive engineer."

Felix (Israel): "At the beginning I was shocked when I was asked if we had a
washing machine or TV in the SU? You know it came after the first sentence '*Eich
ha'ochel b'aretz, ta'im?*' [How is food in the land (meaning in OUR land; i.e. Israel), is
it good? Heb.]. But then I started to answer that there were some cities where
bears crossed the streets and that my dog loved vodka, too. And [then, I] watched
to see how people reacted. Some were perplexed, because they did not know what
to believe, what is going on in *this Russia?* And, then I said: 'Really! It was like that!'
but the clever ones laugh [present tense] and then do not bother me with their
nonsense anymore."

Tania, Leonia, and Felix articulate one of the central issues confronted by
migrants—the residents' perceptions of migrants in the new land. While
Felix responded through humor to the problematic view that he had emigrated from a primitive land, many other participants in both contexts—
but especially in Germany—were hurt by frequently received similar hints
or remarks, and found it difficult to cope with humiliating ascriptions.
Such incidents reinforced the vulnerability and insecurity typical of the
migrant experience. Indeed, such experiences contribute to the presentation of self and senses of belonging that are questioned, blurred, and/or
evolve in the migration process. Hence, even if a person has a clear idea
about how he/she wants to present themselves, resident group stereotyping can deprive a person of the possibility for expressing and presenting
her- or himself in her or his own preferred ways. Indeed, based on the
evidence gathered in both field contexts, it appears that interactions with
Others lead to a mutual reproduction of extant stereotypes and frozen
categorizations.

Leonia (Germany): "Germans always smile and then calmly refuse to help you. They are not ashamed to say 'no' to you. [pauses] The help you expect to receive from friends that you received in Russia is not present. [Here] everybody is their own individual, each person takes care of himself. The maximum you can count on here is that they [Germans] will keep their fingers crossed for you. You know, *Daumen drücken*' [repeats the same expression in German with emotion via a hand gesture] [pauses] [we all laugh] It's very difficult to find Germans who have a real interest in you, your past, your thoughts, and your real culture. It's difficult for me."

Boris (Israel): "Although I never drink vodka, when I have birthday I bring vodka to work because I know that is what they expect of me and think of who I am. I say to myself: 'Let them think like that all they want.' Why and to whom do I have to prove that I am not a camel?"

Fixed stereotypes and categories reproduced in superficial interactions often lead to mutual feelings of what Schiffauer referred to as "komlpementäre Desillusionierung" (Schiffauer 2003, 158) [complementary disillusioning, Ger.] and consequently reinforce mutual distrust. Subjective perceptions of interactions between participants of a given age and resident groups revealed "Das Monolithische des Alltagswissensbestandes"[252] [the monolithic nature of everyday common knowledge, Ger.] from both sides. Such a *monolithic nature of everyday common knowledge* combined with the assumption about Others, who are "empty" people without (appropriate) history, as reported by participants, matches Schütz's thematization of the "stranger" (Schütz 1972).

In such situations, people are often overwhelmed by the open, dynamic processes of crossing cultural borders and searching for mutualities rather than for differences. Under the general category of "different Russians," all rich individual biographical experiences and thoughts were assigned a one-dimensional, 'boring' perspective that served the goal of exclusion. Of course, the stereotyping process took place on both sides, but was especially painful for those located at the bottom of the social pyramid.

Practically, everyday contacts with non-Russian speakers most frequently took place in routine interactions with agents of the official state institutions upon which participants were dependent. This was especially the case in the German context where most of the participants receive social welfare. Accordingly, these were the interactions that served as a basis for Russian speakers' generalizations about "the locals."

---

252 Schütze (2002, 58) based on the approach of Schütz (1972).

Marina (Germany): "Even if I would speak the language of Goethe, she would still not understand me—the social worker in the *Behörde* [civil authority/administration, uses German word, Ger.]. I am the next "*case*," the foreigner, and consequently don't speak German.

Sergei (Germany): "The *Beamtin* [female civil servant, Ger.] said to me immediately when she heard me: Please bring a translator with you! It took a lot of effort to find somebody who could come with me. We came together and, finally, all she wanted to know was my family name, date of birth, and address. I could have told here all of this on my own…"

In an especially interesting case, with which I became involved, Pasha's frequent trips to the welfare office produced no results—due to language problems. To assist, I phoned a civil servant in the welfare office and found out that his request still had not been addressed:

Pasha (Germany) in our meeting afterwards responded: "What exactly did she say?"

JB (in German): "*Die Unterlagen sind noch nicht bearbeitet worden*" [The documents have not yet been prepared, Ger.]

Pasha: "Did she say it like *that*?"

JB: "Yes."

Pasha: "Bastard!"

JB: "Why?"

Pasha: "You see, they are hostile to you in official institutions and speak extra so you cannot understand them. Instead of saying, simply '*Es ist nicht fertig*' [they are not yet ready,' Ger.], they [public servants] say—'*Die Unterlagen sind noch nicht* mmm this…[means '*bearbeitet*,' forgets the word] *worden*' ["The papers have not yet been attended to." This passage was especially difficult for Pasha due to the grammatical construction that uses passive and past-perfect, a tense which does not exist in the Russian language].

In similar situations, routine sentences would not likely arouse questions and in all probability would be responded to pragmatically by native speakers. Hence, Pasha's strong reaction may appear at first glance to be not only inadequate but also irrational. However, upon reflection, several levels of Pasha's alienation are revealed and as such this is an example of what Schäffter referred to as "everyday strangeness" (Schäffter 1991, 14). In a situation of emotional *foreignness*, a small detail or a couple of words can spark a feeling of helplessness or create the impression that a humiliating act has been committed out of spite. This reaction may be evoked irrespective of whether the public servant was or was not being cooperative. Here, a colloquial German grammatical construction involving use of the past perfect tense was interpreted by Pasha as a crisis experience.[253] Communication in the public sphere, especially in bureaucratic institutions that require use of the German language, remained foreign and an "impenetrable" (Schütze 2002, 58) challenge given his limited capabilities in German. Based on the work of Berger and Luckmann, Schütze observed that what becomes especially visible in such moments is the system of theories related to symbolic areas and in particular societal structures; what he referred to as the "Typisierungs-Wissensschicht [...] einer Alltagssprache" [typified stratum of ...everyday knowledge," Ger.] (Berger and Luckmann 1969 by Schütze 2002, 57). Consequently, it is difficult for Pasha to perceive and trust everyday local knowledge in such an environment. And, accordingly, Pasha experienced difficulties living amidst, settling into, and developing the comfortable feeling necessary for active social agency, as reflected in his statements.

This having been noted, it would be false to claim that Pasha's reaction is unrelated to the actual treatment migrants receive in official institutions and organizations. Participants in both cases reported experiencing— frequently—hostile treatment, presumably because they are Russian speakers. As a result, many concluded that, generally, they are not wanted in the new land.

In some cases preserving the low status of the migrants was assessed, accurately, as the normal state of affairs in the receiving society:

Sveta (Germany): "When I said to the social worker that I wanted my daughter to attend the gymnasium [considered the best and highest level of German secondary school], he suddenly freaked out and said me: 'You come here not knowing either German nor English. You don't know anything [about life] here and you all want your children to go directly to the *gymnasium*.'

They [Germans] see you as zero. Treat you like stupid migrants who should go to the *Hauptschule* [extended elementary school which does not enable a pupil to earn a high school diploma]."

Furthermore, I could follow quite easily how existing ideas and fixed stereotypes held by both sides were reactivated in both field settings. This made existing communication difficulties more difficult. In extreme cases,

253 In terms of Schütz (1972).

prejudices and fixed ideas about Others led to misunderstandings and reconfirmations of unbridgeable differences. For example, following complaints about the inhuman treatment they received in Germany, participants often made a connection between "Germans" and "Nazis."[254] The following are but two of many such examples noted during participant observation in the field: First, Naum reported the following scene as evidence of German anti-Semitism. This exchange took place when he came to see the principal of the gymnasium where he wanted his son to study:

Naum: "I came in and he asked me: 'Do you speak German?' I [said]: 'Yes, and do *you* speak Russian?'

He totally freaked out and lectured me at length about the inappropriate behavior of migrants in Germany. He explained that he doesn't have to learn Russian, because he is here, in Germany. And, he wondered how some migrants came up with idea [pauses]. In short, he did not accept Valerii [the son] into the school."

Naum spontaneously interpreted the principal's question—"Do you speak German?"—as a hostile attack as well as questioning the social competencies required in Germany. In trying to defend his dignity, Naum's reaction was based on having learned from previous encounters that Germans' assume that "migrants are primitive and can be treated inhumanly." In his response, he tried to accomplish the impossible by shifting the hierarchical relationship assumed by the principal to social equality by means of his question—"and do you speak Russian?" Implicit in this exchange, from Naum's point of view, is the assumption that while migrants currently are deficient in German, they are fluent not only in another language—Russian, but bring with them to this new land knowledge of one of the most meaningful and rich cultures. Obviously misunderstood by the principal, who was shocked by the migrant's flippant response, Naum also misunderstood the principal's reaction when he claimed that the principal's response was representative of an anti-Semitic attitude. In this fatal communication clash, Naum also assumed that the principal was aware of their Jewish affiliation (through his belief that there is a Jewish look, described in the Chapter Six). The charge of anti-Semitism was the only reasonable explanation Naum could find for the principal's unwillingness to value his (as well as his son's) cultural baggage.

    The second example of the clash of expectations and conflicted statuses happened in Israel. Faina gave an account of one of her first inter-

---

254 See discussion in Chapter Seven.

actions with non-Russian speakers soon after her arrival in Israel. To the best of my knowledge, this situation continues to be quite characteristic in contemporary Israel:

"There was nothing in our flat when we first arrived. The neighbor from across the hall knocked on the door and told us she had brought us a chair. But it only had three legs [laughs]."

JB: "mmmm?"

Faina: "Yes, only three legs. Well, actually, it would have been easier for her to take it to the garbage bin downstairs. But she wanted us to take it. She said: 'I am sure your husband can fix it quickly and then you can use it for a long time' [Entire sentence stated in Hebrew]. I said: 'Thanks, but we don't need anything [signs 'no' with her right hand]. We sent a container from Russia. It will arrive soon and we have everything there.' But she insisted that we take it [and said]: 'I don't have bad intentions, *ze mikol halev*!' [It is (a gift) from the heart!, Heb.]. Imagine this old chair with three legs as a heartfelt gift [we all laugh].'

Then it started snowing and I started to wear my fur coat [actually] it was the only over garment I had, but it was a good one, made from natural fur and a fine, hand knitted, white scarf from the Orenburg network [known in Russia as a very good quality, expensive scarf].

Once, just as I came out of my apartment, the same neighbor woman [who offered the broken chair] entered the hallway at the same time wearing a black knitted hat and hand gloves [that cost] 10 shekels [very inexpensive]. She started to say hello but saw me and did not say anything. Since then she has never greeted me. [pauses] She was shocked. It was too rich for an *olimchiki* [newcomers, uses Hebrew word but with Russian diminutive]. This was many years ago and I threw this coat away quite some time ago. Now I dress differently. Well, still elegant, but not so [rich][pauses] Now I realize how rich my appearance was for her, then, but even now they [Israelis] want to see us just like *olimchiki*."

Faina's report reveals clashes between different images and expectations that lead to misunderstandings and even conflict. Without discussing the absurdity of the idea of giving an old chair that is missing a leg as a present to "poor immigrants," it is apparent that the two sides held very different positions and perceptions of the situation. For Faina, her fur coat and white afghan coat were the only expensive objects she had at that moment. She brought them with her from the "old reality." And, even if it was absolutely useless and perceived to be Russian kitsch in Israel, she still valued it as a symbol of her struggle against her actual low economic status as a new migrant. It also reminded her of her respectable social position in the

SU, where she could afford to purchase such a fur coat and where one's economic status had to be (and usually was) reflected in one's clothing..

In contrast, the expensive fur coat was perceived by the neighbor as exaggerated and unbefitting her status as *"olah hadashah m'rusiya"* [new immigrant from Russia, Heb.]. This perceived status implied, first, that Russian speakers were encumbered with economic difficulties; and, second, that a certain hierarchical relationship exists between immigrants and residents. In such a relationship, residents were those who helped the new migrants by sharing old clothing and furniture as well as by explaining the rules. And, immigrants were those who should learn and gratefully accept these presents.

Both Naum and Faina were unwilling to accept the hierarchical relationships imposed on them by residents in everyday situations. The reconfirmation of their factual position at the bottom of economic and social pyramid in the new society through such everyday situations had effects that obviously were painful, especially since this situation did not correspond with their own inner self-perception as qualified people who considered themselves able to contribute to the new society, but unsuccessful in fulfilling themselves as they expected.

These and many other examples demonstrate that it was not only language difficulties that made communication problematic. Existent prejudices, as well as, ideas about imagined communications between migrants and resident groups were imposed on these interactions. It seems that participants were particularly misunderstood when they reacted in a manner different from expectations; when imagined interactions were not realized; and when stereotypical mechanisms were applied. In such situations, local residents did not receive confirmation from migrants that their higher position in the interactional hierarchy was recognized. This encumbered and made this situation even more difficult. One can surmise that such interactions led to alienation and biased further interactions. In general, the study found in both fieldwork settings that even after many years following their immigration, informal friendships and contacts between the participants and residents of the same age cohort were nearly non-existent, except for a few cases.[255]

---

255 Two participants in Germany had German spouses; the daughter of one participant family in Israel was married to native born Israeli.

8.2 Alienation, home, and homeland: "Why not Israel?" Self-positioning of Russian-speaking Jews in Germany and Israel

> "You think a thousand times before coming to Germany, and then you need a thousand reasons to explain why you did it."
>
> *Elianora (Germany)*

Though there were multiple alienating aspects of the participants' lives in Israel and Germany, one very central set of pressures was the need to prove and re-prove their "appropriate" Jewishness as the necessary condition that legitimized their immigration to each of these societies. The Jewishness of participants, in both contexts, was often doubted by different resident groups and they were accused frequently of instrumentalizing their Jewish affiliation as a means to immigrate to Israel or Germany. This was especially the case in Germany, as from their arrival and onwards participants had to cope, nearly incessantly, with the necessity of having to explain their decision to immigrate.

Fundamentally, post-Holocaust Jewish immigration to Germany continues to involve an unavoidable question, which often alluded to a moral issue: Why do immigrants prefer Germany as destination over Israel? This question arose in different situations, first, in direct everyday interactions between participants and non-Russian residents—both Jewish and non-Jewish Germans. However, it was also discussed in the media discourse in the public sphere in Germany, in the resident Jewish community, as well as, in research about Russian-speaking Jews conducted in Germany.[256] Given the moral framing assumed in this context, migration for economic reasons that would usually be perceived as legitimate in other receiving societies, such as in the USA, and therefore remain unquestioned, were often interpreted as being (too) "pragmatic" or insensitive to the terrible historic events of the previous generation.[257]

---

256 For further research about Russian-speaking Jews in Germany that touch upon this topic, see Becker and Körber (2001); Elias (2004); Elias and Bernstein (2007); Kessler (1996); Oswald and Voronkov (2000); Rapoport and Schütze (2000); Remmenick (2005).
257 There are traces of implied judgments in sociological research; for example, when choosing such provocative titles for an article as Remennick: "Idealists Headed to Israel,

The participants were conscious of the ideological background of immigrating to Israel as well as of the fact that there was frequent judging of
pragmatic economic immigration to Germany. Given this situation, some
interviewees felt obliged to justify themselves. In doing so, some claimed
that they had the right to decide this on an individual basis, instead of in
the name of the collective. Furthermore, they felt justified to opt for a
convenient way of life should they choose to do so:

Dima (Germany): "I don't want to hear anything ideological anymore in my life.
It's [Israel's] patriotism. We've had enough "isms" in our lives in the SU. One
should have the right *to live for oneself.*"

This and many similar quotes (see selection below) reveal two matters that
require further consideration: First, in contrast to the implied assumption
that collective history and political consciousness played (or had to play) a
crucial role in the decision process of choosing a land for immigration
(both for Israel and Germany), the data collected in both contexts suggest
that, ultimately, this decision was made as part of a search for a practical
solution to composite individual difficulties.

Second, in the German case, the participants had a variety of differing
identities—as Jewish, Russian cultural, Soviet, intellectual, European, gender, age group identity and certainly others. However, I concluded that
ultimately and perhaps involuntarily their Jewish identity was the most
stressed, definitive, central, and important for local perceptions, even
though in the German context it seems to be the most contradictory and
painful one of all. In addition, the evidence suggests that independent of
whether or not their Jewish identity was *in their own view* the most essential
and pervasive in the process of deciding to immigrate to Germany and
their actions after arrival, I submit that, involuntarily, this became the most
essential and pervasive identity the moment they crossed Germany's border. In
turn, this situation forced migrants to reconsider and to explain their immigration from a particular perspective—now as one chosen for them, by
their hosts in the receiving society.

Similar questions were addressed, on occasion, to participants in Israel;
for example, "*Lama batem?*" [Why did you come here?, Heb.] The person
asking has doubts about the migrant's Jewishness. However, such questions were rare and always replied to deliberately and self–consciously by

Pragmatics Chose Europe:' Identity Dilemmas and Social Incorporation among Former
Soviet Jews Who Migrated to Germany", (Remennick 2005).

the migrant with a statement such as: "I have as much a right to be here as you do." This response was plausible due to the general Israeli Zionist narrative that holds among its foundations the right of every Jew in the world to immigrate [in national language "to return"] to Israel. In Germany, in contrast, such a question represents—exactly—an unresolved conflict, multiple contradictions, and is a cause for misunderstandings and confrontations. Pasha elaborated on this situation in a language class that occurred soon after his arrival:

"Our language teacher told us—'You know I think it is very good that Jews are coming to Germany once again [after the Holocaust]. It is a real addition to our country. But to be honest, I try to imagine myself in your situation and *I* [in your place] would never come here after all that happened. Don't you sympathize with your relatives who were killed?'

There was silence in the class. I saw in her eyes that she wasn't interested in challenging us. She really does *not* understand how we could come here. I just could not find anything to answer her, no one did. [pause] How can I explain all that happened *in Russia* and *who* we actually are and *our whole life* [very loud] [pause and then with a sad tone] It is better for them to think of us as Russians."

In keeping with the central purpose of this investigation—to understand and to reflect on the question "Who are they really?"—presented and analyzed in previous chapters, here I will try to summarize and contextualize the reasons why Germany was a destination preferred over Israel, as articulated by the participants themselves in different situations during my fieldwork.

Overall, this issue was revealed to be delicate, especially during my interviews with migrants in Germany, as they felt forced to legitimize their choice, though I never initiated or pressed this topic. I did sense that interviewees retained moral ambivalence and reticence regarding this issue, perhaps for fear of being judged or criticized for their decision. This reticence was particularly obvious in the beginning of the fieldwork, when participants seem to "read" me, initially, as an Israeli or as a representative of the Israeli side; that is, as one who might not support or be trusted to understand their decision.

An example of one such encounter with a couple was presented in the first chapter (in the part on methodology) when Fira called out to me immediately upon entry "Well, we made a mistake!" [meaning, when we came to Germany]; and her husband added, "But we are proud of you!" [meaning, me, the researcher, as a person who made a right decision to immigrate to Israel rather than to Germany].

This defensive act of providing a pre-emptive excuse is not only indicative of an initial mistrust projected onto me as a researcher by some migrants, but it also signifies pre-existing ideas, *imaginary relationships*, or an inner dialog between personal migration stories and migrants' stance in regard to a presumed question—what should we tell different Others (i.e. Germans, local Jews in Germany, Israelis, Russian-speaking Israelis)?

This having been noted, it is also the fact that throughout the later stages of interviewing and participant observation in the field, self-justifications were replaced by addressing, implicitly, a second key question addressed to me: "Have you decided to remain in Germany?" This I submit is a certain sign that rapport had been established and that I had gained acceptance by the group. Through development of mutual respect and establishment of a sensitive "work alliance" between researcher and participant,[258] our discussions became a kind of productive dialogue in which life in Israel and Germany was constantly being compared. Consequently, the typical answer at the beginning of the fieldwork—such as "we are here by chance," a direct but superficial response, was enriched amidst an evolving sense of mutual trust and rapport when it started to change and to reveal complexity of multiple *real* reasons which were meaningful for participants.

Most participants were very curious about details of life in Israel and current events there, referring to it (by reapplying a Russian cliché) as "our historical motherland." As discussed in Chapter Six, this is by no means a new interest, rather a continuation of the participants' previous emotional affiliation with Israel from the period when they lived in the SU that continued post-migration in Germany. Their speech and interest reflected a significant emotional involvement in all topics connected with Israel and especially in the ways in which events there are discussed in German public and private spheres. This discourse was often interpreted by them as an indicator of the degree to which the potential for public anti-Semitism was realized. That is, it related to their suspicion that insipid forms of anti-Semitism were eternally present in Germany. Thus, throughout the fieldwork in Germany, it was evident that participants were preoccupied with

---

258 Inowlocki and Bernstein (2006) is based on Resch and Steinert (2003).

the topic of Israel, their affiliation with Israel, and the problematic nature of Jews living in Germany.

The data analyses revealed that some participants applied rather standard, sometimes formal reasons or arguments that in some cases applied superficial slogans in support of choices they made. In contrast, others presented deep, reflective narrations about the period prior to immigration that set the context for their immigration decision. These narratives were insightful in that they revealed more information about their situations and aspirations. Characteristically, the participants combined in one speech very different and sometimes contradictory arguments. Schütze referred to this phenomenon as "biographic refractions" (Schütze 2007). Such a form of speech includes different presentations of their decision to immigrate to Germany highlighted by inclusion of various "corners" of the long, complex process of reflection about the past. Schütze referred to this process as "biographic work" (ibid).

Enumerating different, contradictory points about "coming to and then living in Germany" revealed that some participants were involved in an inner search for a satisfying and reasonable argument, primarily in order to satisfy themselves. As will be seen in the examples that follow, the use of multiple and contradictory arguments revealed different aspects of a very complex situation with expectations and the inability of some participants to describe difficult stages of their own biography (ibid). Some participants repeated reductive metaphors and generalized sentences that may have been attempts to shield themselves from revealing personal contradictions and doubts. One could recognize in other statements a desire to be open in articulating and being actively engaged with the issues. However, in all cases, there seemed to be a permanent search for an appropriate and suitable explanation for their decision that was satisfying to them, as well as, to different reference groups who were keen on asking and judging them.

Before emigrating to Germany, most of the interview partners had followed with great interest reports by close relatives and friends about the settling-in process they experienced in moving to Israel (earliest account was from 1989). This information played an important role in their decision-making process and differentiated them from people who emigrated to Israel during a previous wave of immigration, from the end of the 1980's and into the beginning of the 1990's. This previous wave began immediately after the fall of the Iron Curtain and was characterized by migrants having abstract, even fuzzy ideas about what awaited them in the new country. Similarly, when Russian-speaking Jews started to immigrate to Germany in the middle of the 1990's, they were well-informed about the situation in Israel (n. b., Germany was the only officially sanctioned alternative to Israel as an emigration site). The exchange of letters and telephone calls as well as visits by friends and relatives from the Russian-speaking enclave in Israel informed them about current economic, social, and security difficulties there. As reported by interview partners, this information and discussions served as a permanent reminder of arguments not to emigrate there.[259]

Similar to findings by Cohen and Kogen (2004), many relatives and friends of participants in Germany who came to Israel could not find jobs in their original professions and were left with no alternative except to accept work in unqualified, low-payed jobs. Thus, many participants in Germany knew about this situation. Since they were searching for a better quality of life, they realized that it was unlikely that they would find employment in their original profession in Israel. Furthermore, they were also unwilling to allow fate to determine what unqualified as well as what they perceived to be humiliating, jobs would be available to them, if they immigrated to Israel. For example, letters received in the CIS from relatives and friends in Israel related stories of people over fifty years of age having to accept janitorial jobs and caretaker positions in order to supplement their minimal old age pension or grants from Israel's National Insurance Institute. And, consequently, they also had to live in poor neighborhoods.

In contrast, social conditions offered to immigrants in Germany seemed to be more attractive and, consequently, played one of the most important roles in their decision to immigrate to Germany.

Marina (Germany) elaborated on this point: "We knew that we were not going to share a flat with strangers here [Germany], because to rent an entire apartment is too expensive in Israel [in comparison to Germany where rent is completely subsided by the state] or to have to clean floors for two years in order to be able to fix our teeth, as my friends in Israel did [both engineers, 70 and 65 years old, who worked as janitors at the Technion University]."

Varia (Germany) provided the following reductive, laconic summary of Israel as an immigration option: "It's economically poor and permanently in a state of war."

---

259 Since the largest wave of immigration started in 1995, people had about five years to receive information about life in Israel from relatives and friends there.

Of course, in some cases, it was impossible to separate, on the one hand, the opinion based on personal experience and interaction; and, on the other hand, the internalization of the strong Soviet anti-Israel propaganda that had socialized and been absorbed by Russian speakers (Oswald and Voronkov 2000, 344). Additionally, German participants reported that their relatives and friends in Israel complained frequently about the local military situation, social confrontations with non-European groups, their stigmatization as Russians, and the less extensive medical services provided in Israel.

Aside from these very important reasons, participants in Germany offered various additional, rational explanations for their decision not to immigrate to Israel. These reasons, too, are pieces of the "puzzle" that I am trying to construct in order to understand the complex, multisided nature of their decision. Some interview partners offered as an explanation that they immigrated to Germany in loyalty to their spouses who were not Jewish and who might have experienced discrimination in Israel as a Jewish state.

Naum (Germany): "It's too far from visiting the graves of our relatives in Russia and my wife is not Jewish. So I did not want her to come to the Jewish state and feel uncomfortable there."

Naum formulated his decision to come to Germany in the form of a compromise, chosen due to concern for his wife who as a non-Jew might have experienced additional integration difficulties in Israel, which as a nationalist, primarily Jewish society has a history of allocating secondary status to non-Jews. Additionally, as demonstrated in this example, the physical distance from the land of origin, with which they would like to remain in contact, was an important consideration mentioned in many cases, for varying reasons (e.g., to visit relatives' graves, to visit their social network of friends and keeping their flats in the land of origin).

However, different from the detailed knowledge about life in Israel, participants knew relatively little about migrants' lives in Germany. What they related consisted of a spotty knowledge and imaginary projections such as economic prosperity, stability and being a safe European society. There was an element of adventure in their explanations about the project of family migration to the new foreign country that was supported by knowledge that they could at any time continue on to Israel should their project not succeed.

Coping with the two common sets of meanings and morally loaded images—an emotional, irrational choosing of Israel or rationalized, pragmatic/cold choice of Germany, Katia (Germany) like many other interviewees tried to rationalize her decision, in the best way she could, as follows:

Katia: "We wanted to try something else and then decided, because we knew that we could immigrate anytime to Israel if we didn't like it here. I went to the OVIR [local migration service authority] and asked a representative where she would recommend that we emigrate. She told me: 'It's your decision, but since I've been working here, I have seen many people who came back from Israel and nobody from Germany.' It was quite a convincing argument, and besides I did not want my son to come here alone."

Different from Naum's explanation in the previous citation, Katia shifted the nature and weight of very different arguments in her rationale for the decision to immigrate to Germany. Interestingly, Katia's initial argument gave strong weight to an argument offered by an absolute stranger, the migration service representative. This was followed by the use of a more illusive argument that hints at the need she felt to "save" her son from the Soviet army, widely known for its brutality (an argument that she articulated explicitly earlier in the interview and referred to here). Presumably this was intended to be an even more convincing and personal argument. During other fieldwork encounters, Katia returned to the issue several times on her own initiative and on each occasion she brought different arguments: "Not being able to stand the climate;" "not wanting to clean" [to work as a janitor]; "not being able to live in the Orient;" that she would be unable to survive on the small social welfare allocation awarded in Israel; and finally since her son did not want to immigrate to Israel, she wanted to immigrate with him to one country. Once she even claimed that "in Germany you need a really convincing argument why you immigrated here."

Irrespective of the rationale behind each of these arguments, the fact that she continued to raise the issue suggests that choosing to live in Germany was unsettling and continued to preoccupy her. This conclusion is reinforced when recalling her strong views about Germany, WWII, and the Holocaust cited in the previous chapter. Furthermore, near the end of the fieldwork, she heard about the activities of extreme right-wing movements and their regular demonstrations, permitted by authorities in Standstadt, and she stated: "You see, there is a high price that we pay here [in Germany], constantly, for a comfortable life and their social welfare [assistance]."

Interestingly, the phrase "you see" was an initiation not prompted by any previous reference that day about her immigration to Germany. This suggests that this issue remains among the most important and problematic ones in Katia's life.

Israel remained an unattractive but important destination for participants in the sense of sharing an imagined collective affiliation. Yet, for many who had lived in the big cities of the Soviet empire, Israel seemed to be a small peripheral state tangled in military problems for many potential emigrants. Their most popular description of Israel was as "a ticking bomb" and "a barrel of gunpowder." Therefore, emigrating there seemed to be irrational. Sveta (Germany), who never removes her *Magen David* necklace (Star of David symbol, similar to the crucifix worn by Christians), and who believes that most Germans are anti-Semites, presented her decision as follows:

"We were astonished when people emigrated from gigantic the USSR to the small Israel. We had so many doubts, including questioning coming to Israel after the story of Afghanistan? I had dreams about coming to Israel when I was younger and I played [games] with children against Germany [...]. We deliberated and deliberated [pause] for a very long time, eight years [1990—1998], and even studied Hebrew. And then I met Petya [a friend], who asked: 'Why do you need Israel, when everyone is going to Germany?'"

This statement also demonstrates Sveta's long period of doubt, vacillation, and hesitation until "suddenly" she became quickly and surprisingly convinced by one short and simple sentence issued by a friend she met by chance: "everyone is going to Germany." This sentence is similar to the argument used by Katia when she presented the statement by the representative of a local (St. Petersburg) migration service authority. A similar type of reference was offered by Olesia (Germany), mentioned in the Chapter Two, who stated: "We flopped down and found ourselves amidst advanced capitalism." All three migrants seemed to have made an arbitrary, even absurd choice. However, I submit that such arguments function to transfer direct personal responsibility for this decision to the massive collective phenomenon.

Similar to Sveta, who compared the military situation in Israel to Afghanistan [a reference to horrific scenarios of Soviet soldiers fighting a long and meaningless war], other participants who are parents cited that their decision saved their sons not only from the negative experiences of the Soviet army, but also from Israel's obligatory military service. Tamara included this point in her mix of arguments:

"Germans are close to us *culturally* [...] [while] Israel is completely foreign to us and their Oriental traditions seem wild or exotic to us. [It is] great for a vacation, but not for living there. And, besides, I saved my son from the Russian army, and for what? To let him be taken, again, into the Israeli army?"

Since the argument of escaping military service was stressed, it seemed to be especially important. Presumably, this suggests another legitimate argument: "to immigrate for the sake of one's children." Indeed, this argument is offered on numerous occasions as a main reason for immigration by participants in Israel. Similar to the other interviews in terms of speech construction, this argument is characterized by use of an additional argument symbolized through use of "and then" or "besides" phrases. Thus, whereas one feels that the argument about their son's military service is personal, alive, and emotional (Tamara speaks as if somebody is about to attack her: "and then what? To let him be taken again into the Israeli army"), the first part of her presentation is detached, abstract, and based on generalized dichotomies.

The perception of Israel as a foreign, Oriental, exotic land was shared by most of the other participants in the German case study. In doing so, interviewees stressed repeatedly their close affiliation to "cultural and civilized" Europe while juxtaposing and contrasting it with the "distant, peripheral, and strange" Israel with its written language that moves from right to left. In some presentations Israel was seen to be "a small, peripheral Oriental fighting country," as opposed to an argument often used by Israelis and Westerners that it is "the only Western, technologically developed island in the Middle East."

Also interesting in this regard is that like Tamara, many interviewees used the concept "culture" in a particularly Soviet manner; as affiliation with the elite European culture of literature, poetry, classic music, theatre, ballet and art. That is, such use does not refer to an open market culture, the work culture, or that of a trade union; not the culture of left-wing political movements; nor a democratic or global, open, cross-border culture. Rather, this use of culture is usually contextualized by the migrants (both in Israel and in Germany) as a continuation of their affiliation—in the previous context—with the group of Soviet intelligentsia as well as upper class European culture. Though presented in a similar manner in Israel and

Germany, these arguments receive significantly different emphases, messages, and meanings in the two contexts. While participants in Israel often expressed pride in "bringing European culture to the Orient," interview partners in Germany framed their argument as distancing themselves from "Oriental Israel." Such an affiliation was very important in presenting themselves as an integral part of the European and the German culture, as it was the only argument offered for belonging to the receiving society. Yet, it is this very claim that belongs to the most questioned in the media and in their everyday interactions with non-Russian speakers in Germany.

Leonia (Germany) [seems to be using a somewhat perplexed tone, even mimicry]: "You know, we arrrre *Europeans*. There [in Israel] was no future for us, and it is [on the] periphery, a big village, a province without future for you. There is a war and no feeling of security. And I would never be able to learn *this* [seeming to stress its strangeness] language."

Sasha (Germany) applies a dichotomy between Western and Oriental as follows: "There is an incessant state of war, religiosity, the Orient, although there are many Western people. I prefer to feel this state, which is pleasant and close to me, from a distance… [means 'I prefer to empathize with this state, which is pleasant and for which I have fond feelings, but to do so from a distance']."

What I find especially interesting in Sasha's statement is the unusual combination of "feel…from a distance" which demonstrates very well the inner conflict and mixed feelings Sasha had for Israel. On the one hand, there is a sense of self-distancing and foreignness (through "*war, religiosity Orient*") and, on the other hand, strong emotional affiliation and positive feelings for Israel (through "*feel* this state, which is pleasant and for which I have fond feelings").

An additional argument to explain why they chose not to immigrate to Israel used by all interview partners in Germany was that the hot Israeli climate would be difficult for them. This argument was based on complaints received from participants' friends or relatives living in Israel. In the German case (as well as in Russia or Ukraine, where they emigrated from), the hot Israeli climate epitomized a foreign Oriental land to which the participants anticipated having adjustment difficulties. Participants, compared it to hot sites in the SU they had visited, as Boris and Inna explained:

Boris (Germany): "Once I was in Baku [capital of Azerbaizhan]. I couldn't *sleep* there, I couldn't *breathe* there. [It was] so steamy, like in a sauna. The air is so thick [pause]. And [to live there] without work, with two old women [his wife and his mother-in-law]. We would had have more close friends there, than here. That's true. [pause] There are a lot of difficulties, [but] they bring people together. And even now, in Germany, I am interested to know about all that is happening there. For sure it doesn't leave me cold.

Luba (Germany): "It's almost Africa with its dusty southern cities. It's *not an understandable* state for us [presumably Europeans]. When you see this Wall [referring to the Western Wall] and people praying in black coats with *payos* [long side curls; pause, breathes deeply]. *Nevertheless,* I sympathize with it [presumably with Israel/Jewish culture] and I am on the Israeli side.

Articulating their sense of feeling foreign to Israel, due to its hot climate and the religious aspects of communal life there, Boris and Luba also stressed their affiliation with the Israeli collective. They seem to feel and want to be seen affiliated with it. While like Boris and Luba most participants remarked that it would be probably difficult to live and to realize themselves in Israel, they expressed simultaneously—and in very different ways—rapture, bewilderment, and pride in Israel. These latter expressions romanticized and even mystified Israel, as we see in the following selection of statements. Bella and Misha expressed their excitement and wonderful memories from of a vacation trip to Israel. Bella, for example, began to believe in God after her visit to Israel; Misha romanticized the fact that Israel was built so quickly in the desert and is still connected to its long history.

Bella: "I visited Israel before coming here [to Germany]. My face was sunburned the first day. It's just too hot and too military a state, but it is *beautiful* [pause]. I was astonished. I started to believe there is something [there... pause... maybe] to believe in God; because two mystical events happened to me there [long descriptions of two situations when she suddenly met one and then a second friend from school that she had not seen for 40 years]. But I am not sure I could realize myself there."

Misha: "It is a deeply moving country, an endless conglomerate. I did not build anything nor did I plant a tree, but I glowed with pride when I walked there. It is unbelievable what people have done there in 50 years: gardens, cities, and highways [pause] When I was there I thought, that, actually, if you are honest with yourself, you understand that you should be there and not here [in Germany]. Because the state survives and there is a lot that should be done there and this is a hard time for Israel. [pause]

Yes, and you know the colors there! We arrived late, in the middle of the night, and I saw the sun rising early in the morning and then everyday after that. [pause] I bought a cap [that said] 'Don't worry, be Jewish!' [pause]

Elke [his non-Jewish German wife] was very anxious, felt threatened by this trip and how Israelis would see her there [as a German]. 'And then, people were so open and kind to her. Suddenly and unexpectedly a bus driver spoke German with her. She was touched. [pause]'

You know, I am a person who likes to be impressed. I had very strong impressions from seeing Massada and the burial marker of Pontius Pilatus.[260] I see [uses present tense] how old the stones are [pause] and this is the only country where there is competition to be accepted into the medical school, psychology, and archaeology! I like it, incredibly! [excited, smiles]"

Misha's mixed, manifold, and mostly ambivalent position toward Israel is especially obvious. On the one hand, he shares romantic ideas about his Jewish affiliation with Israel; and, on the other hand, an account mixed with images from Russian literature from the Christian view of the Holy Land and Jerusalem. Although Misha admitted that he "[...] did not build anything [there] nor did I plant a tree," both he and Bella described Israel as a "beautiful land" and a "deeply moving country," of which both are proud. Misha's Zionist views are also of interest. He "likes, incredibly" the fact that studying medicine and psychology is as prestigious as being accepted to study archaeology in Israeli universities. Archaeology is of interest because it is the main scientific discipline that provides evidence of the Jewish right to live in Israel, simultaneously delivering continuation with the Jewish settling in the far past through research of Jewish material culture. Misha also uses the politically laden, key Jewish Israeli cultural metaphor of "planting a tree" used to epitomize the transformation of the desert into a flowering land, one in which every new born child is honored by planting a new tree.[261] Thus, the planting of a tree is the symbolic act of joining the Jewish Israeli collective to which Misha feels he belongs.

On the other hand, Misha's idealized presentation is interwoven with a "strand" of bad conscience about affiliation from abroad. Through visits to Israel and sympathizing with current events there, his personal affiliation is articulated explicitly and in doing so sharpens his inner conflict: The gap between making the ideally "right" decision by emigrating to Israel (Misha: "you should be there and not here") along with the feeling of "homeless-

---

260 The reference to Pontius Pilatus is not happenstance. Christian Jerusalem is a theme in Russian literature and especially Michael Bulgakov's *Master and Margarita*. Forbidden by the Soviet regime, this book was hidden and read extensively, in secret, by the Soviet intelligentsia community.

261 Reference to a *Keren Kayemet LeIsrael* project, an organization responsible for reforestation.

ness" while living in Germany becomes visible and seem to grow. The tension of coping with this contradiction is released, symbolically, through the use of humor in the form of the statement printed on his cap— "Don't worry, be Jewish." Misha seems to be proud of the "national home" to which he can only partially belong because he does not live there.

Indeed, most participants mentioned—directly or indirectly—their strong connection to Israel and feeling of belonging to the Jewish collective. I saw different Israeli symbols in many migrants' houses in Germany, such as a small Israeli flag on the TV in the guest room or on a magnet attached to the refrigerator door; postcards showing falafel (thought to be the symbol of Israeli national food); and pictures of participants taken against the background of the Western Wall, Negev mountains, or Massada during visits in Israel.

Finally, there were also some participants who seem to repress having a connection to being Jewish. For example, they presented this connection as being "just formal" and articulated their distance from Jews by stigmatizing them with various different negative characteristics. Surprisingly, one member in at least five families offered, as a reason that they did not emigrate to Israel, the anti-Semitic claim that they could not stand being with so many Jews gathered in one place.[262] This was combined with a direct or indirect statement of superiority about it being too noisy an Oriental place for Europeans. For example, this is how Olga formulated this sentiment:

"You know, there are so many Jews there, one could go crazy! Have you ever been in Tiflis? In the beginning it was great, but after three days it was too much. It's noisy, crowded, and busy. Everyone is hustling and bustling [idiomatic usage to relate to one who acts quickly or is always busy because he is continuously worried about something; here she means it to be very negative]. Everyone who has gone to Israel said they found themselves in Asia."

This provocative statement is very deceptive; as such a statement may be a self-defensive act of reaction to raising the issue of Jewish identity. Internalizing the anti-Semitic rhetoric of dominant groups in their previous society does not necessarily mean that there is an absence of affiliation to Jewishness, but rather that it is painful. Even in the cases when any connection with Jewishness was denied (perhaps repressed), interview partners expressed concern about anti-Semitism in different Diaspora countries

---

262 This sentence recalls another idiom repeated by participants cited in Chapter Six: "When Jews are distributed throughout in the world they have an effect on the local landscape as fertilizer. And, when they are concentrated in one place it starts to smell."

and, as well, expressed—often in emotional terms—their interest in political events developing in Israel.

Perhaps one could argue that while the participants tried to convince
themselves that they do "not have anything in common with Jewishness,"
many of the thoughts and attitudes shared in interviews revealed that being
Jewish actually did play an important role in their personal identities.[263] I
suspect, that in many cases participants did not realize the anti-Semitic
nature of the sentences with which they related to their Jewishness. On the
one hand, there was a mixture of denied or repressed Jewishness that was
undesired but inevitable, an essential sense of belonging or matter of the
bad destiny and "misfortune" (Shternshis 2006, 185) into which they were
born.[264] On the other hand, there were multiple emotional expressions of
strong affiliation with the Jewish collective and Israel. Taken together, in
the context of the history of their pre-migration life, both sets of views
present the complexity of being Jewish given their background as a minority in the Soviet context with its anti-Semitic history, as well as, being Jewish in the context of the Holocaust, in Germany in particular.

In summary, in coping with the pervasive and essential character of
being Jewish in the German context, the participants seem to be split between different connotations of being Jewish—some positive and others
negative, and their different personal collective affiliations with which they
try to compensate their stigmatized Jewishness.

While all participants referred in one way or another (through implicit-
ness or hints) to the problematic nature of deciding to prefer living in
Germany to Israel, only a few participants articulated, openly, their inner
conflict about this issue. For example, in her initial statement during her
interview, Elianora established that she had actually nothing in common
with being Jewish. Yet, she dealt with this complex aspect of her identity
throughout her entire interview.[265] For example, in the following citation
she presented the nature of her connection to Israel:

"I am pro-Israeli and pro-American from head to toe. I would come to live in
Israel if my husband [not Jewish] would have agreed to, but he didn't. Well, today
[she is divorced], I know he was really anti-Semitic. [pause; gives numerous examples of evidence of ex-husband's anti-Semitism and finally returns to the topic
Israel] I still haven't ruled out the possibility that I will move there [to Israel]. I

---

263 See discussion in Chapter Six.
264 See presentation in Chapter Six.
265 Ibid.

pray for Israel, suffer with it. You live there with people like yourself. You think a thousand times before coming to the Germany and then you need a thousand reasons to explain why you did it …"

Tamara (Germany, has a German-born spouse) was quoted earlier making the claim that she has always been proud that "she is Jewish," and in the following quote relates to Germany versus Israel issue:

"With Israel it was clear. I visited it and received letters. Everything seems to be upside down there [in contrast to what she knows and has become accustomed to]: climate, they hate immigrants, no European culture, and terrible numbers of Jews. No one has gotten used to it. And, I was all alone with my son [she lived alone with her son in St. Petersburg]. It would be difficult there in every sense. What [immigrant receiving country] was left? Only Germany. Although it is amoral for Jews to come to Germany for the social welfare [looks at me and confirms once again]. Yes, I do think it is amoral. I don't blame or reproach myself, but rather I was being realistic and sober in assessing it [my decision]. I think Germans just 'destroy' themselves with this question [pause], even more than Jews do. They don't even have any national patriotism."

Tamara's difficulty being around "*terrible numbers of Jews*" stands in contrast to her prior claim of being proud that she is Jewish. An additional *controversial conjunction* occurs between Jewish history and the collective image of "Germans" whom she mentions as an additional imagined reference group and to whom she tries to show her loyalty while living in Germany (with a German spouse). Her claim that "Germans" suffer because of the Holocaust and are destroying their own collective positive identity—a claim with which many persons living in Germany would disagree—can be explained as an outcome of her socialization in the SU; namely that national patriotism has to be an inevitable part of collective consciousness, seen by her as a normative societal characteristic.

Using an altogether different approach, some interview partners referred to an imagined opinion "offered" by dead relatives, many of whom were witnesses to important historical events. In doing so, they related to contemporary issues in their lives as migrants, as we see in another citation from the interview with Katia. The following citation demonstrates the problems involved in reviving these voices while living in Germany.

Katia (Germany) emerged from several moments of reflection to say: "I have often thought and continue to think about what I would have said to my mother about that [her decision to live in Germany and her current life there], if she was still alive. It was during the Perestroika that my brother [who later immigrated to Israel] told her that there were some who were leaving for Germany. She said: 'How could you think about it? We are still Jews! Have you forgotten that we lost your father there [fell as a soldier] and that they killed your paralyzed grandmother in the courtyard of the house.' [pause] We did not discuss this issue as long as she was alive."

Such imaginary inner dialogues frequently referred to both topics: Germany as a previously enemy state and Nazi policies to exterminate Jews. In immigrating to a very different, changed, no-longer Nazi country, a few of the participants mentioned that this decision was not easy. As well as giving rise to many difficult inner dialogues, there were confrontations with relatives and friends who remained in Russia or the Ukraine, along with those who immigrated to Israel. Some participants discussed the moral judgment employed in these confrontations, while others claimed that such judgments were the result of envy for the better economic life they were enjoying.

Roman (Germany) remembers: "Co-workers and our relatives in Israel asked us: 'How can you go to a fascist country?'"

His wife Toma nods sitting next to him: "Yes, and even now, especially Israelis [Russian speakers] still [keep asking]: 'How can you live there?' And, I answer: 'Normally, as do all others.'"

As these and other quotes presented from this study demonstrate, it is very difficult for the participants to construct the normalcy claimed by Toma. Many self-accounts demonstrate how participants cope with obvious contradictions, such as attempts to be loyal to multiple collectives and their narratives. The transnational networks composed of compatriots in Israel and the CIS can make coping even more difficult. For example, a claim of betraying the Soviet intergenerational collective identity through immigration was articulated in some interviews. Tamara put this quite dramatically, feeling herself betrayed by other families and the collective memories of parents and grandparents who struggled as Soviet soldiers against the country in which they now reside. In making reference to the Russian culture, she compared herself with the Russian poet Anna Achmatova, whose son Lev Gumilev was imprisoned during the repressions before WWII. Achmatova wrote that she suffered together with her people as they underwent difficult repressions. In recalling this poetess, Tamara stressed her disassociation from the Soviet collective in favor of seeking an economically better life in the West.

In doing so, Tamara elaborated on the same issue: "I did not reveal that we were going to Germany, because I knew they would not accept it very well. While our fathers and grandfathers fought and fell there, we 'sell' [uses present tense] ourselves for a piece of sausage. For a long time I had pangs of conscience. Yes, a feeling that we betrayed them. Here, there are so many things and so much prosperity, while there [in Russia] they live very poorly. So I could not enjoy all these things [abundance] here. You know, as Anna Achmatova has written [quotes passages from Achmatova's famous poem *Requiem* about living in difficult periods of Soviet repression]: 'I was at that time with *my people* there, where my people [Soviet folk] unfortunately were…' And *I*, I just *was not THERE!*"

Tamara's statement recalls Soviet patriotic terminology in which "identity turns into simulacra of the state" (Sandomirskaya 2004, 131). Hence, Tamara refers to her immigration as a betrayal of a motherland that gave all to its ex-citizens, who in return

"paid back with ingratitude. He put his own interests above the motherland's, above public interests….his home is everywhere, wherever he is comfortable" (ibid., 130).

However, it would be a mistake to reduce the claim of betrayal only to Soviet patriotic terminology. The multiple nature of the feeling of betrayal becomes even clearer by the statement of Katia (Germany):

"First, we betrayed our state [Soviet state to which she still feels she belongs]; then Israel [to which she feels she belongs as well]; then our friends and relatives in both [CIS and Israel] and above all our all dead relatives who died in this war [referring to those who fell as soldiers or were exterminated as Jews]. All this can hardly be combined with the personal interests and material wealth. It is as if you had no right or that there is no place for comfortable good life."

This quote reveals contradictions between multiple imagined referential groups (or entire collectives) that can, would, or have judged the decision of Katia to emigrate to Germany and her personal desire to attain a good quality of life, a need that seems to be legitimate to her.

In addition, as members of the Soviet *intelligentsia* stratum socialized to live through spiritual ideals positioned in opposition to the material goods of a "decaying" capitalist world [as stated by the Soviet propaganda],[266] participants had been confronted with the necessity to articulate their decision to immigrate to Germany in a legitimate (i.e. non-materialistic) manner. This proved to be a very difficult task for many participants. In this

---

266 See presentation in Chapter Two.

case, the process of even developing an appropriate language that enables persons to speak about their lives in such a situation develops more slowly than the changes in the behavioral patterns of people in the post-Perestroika era. Consider, for example, Katia's claim that there is "no right [and] place for a comfortable good life" or Tamara's overstatement—"we 'sell' ourselves for a piece of sausage." Both are expressions of the difficulty these members of the intelligentsia stratum of immigrants have in admitting that economic immigration is legitimate, even if their everyday economic wealth does function as an important value.

Overall, it seems that immigrants seem to be confused as they attempt to preserve the dualistic Soviet style of thinking that juxtaposes "spiritual" versus "material,"[267] and in which the Russian word *potrebitel'* [consumer] is still highly negatively laden. Spiritually directed decision-making does not seem to be compatible with material values in one's descriptive biographic narrative. That is, it takes time for the participants to develop an "available" rhetoric that is familiar and can be used regularly.

Thus, we can conclude that there are several contradictory narratives and referential groups that both pose a burden and challenge migrants' capabilities for normative living in Germany. One narrative set includes the materialistic rhetoric of ex-Soviet educated people to which they were socialized which is perceived to be partially illegitimate and also foreign, and which does not always correspond to their actions and desires. A second narrative includes difficult to reconcile feelings of loyalty to the Soviet collective of winners; Jewish history including the Holocaust; relatives and friends who died as soldiers; and Jews living in the CIS or Israel. In addition, there is constant pressure to explain their decision and its legitimacy to resident members of German and Jewish groups. Exposure to these conflicting challenges can be a cause for alienation and feelings of inferiority among many participants.

Many participants in Israel also mentioned and complained about these same challenges and difficulties, and included them among their considerations in deciding whether or not to immigrate to Israel; namely, the military situation, low quality of life in comparison with their compatriots in Germany, the "Oriental mentality," and the hot climate. However, especially during visits to Germany or in meetings with visitors from Germany in Israel these elements were more frequently stressed and always symboli-

---

267 See elaboration in Chapter Two.

cally compensated, as we see in Ella's (Israel) formulation in a conversation with her friend living in Germany:

"Sure *it is difficult* to live here, but compared to them [Russian speakers in Germany] *we are at home*! [Ella's emphases bolded]."

In fact, it was in these meetings as well as, in their everyday lives, that narratives about participating in the nation building process in Israel along with a corollary argument requiring "subordinating the private present for the collective future" (Maier 1987, 161; Golden 2002, 16) were articulated, instrumentalized, and proven to be counterresistant.[268]

Thus, given the discrimination (as "Russians") and alienation they experienced everyday in Israel, it appears on the basis of this study, that the Israeli participants' aspiration for *home* could be realized only though comparison with compatriots in Germany. That is to say, through interactions with compatriots in Germany they presented themselves within the constructed category of collective affiliation—*nashi*—as Israelis. And, in comparison, immigrants to Germany lacked such a group for self-realization and the topic of home and homeland remains among the most problematic challenges they faced in rationalizing their decision to choose to live in Germany.

8.3 Conclusion

In conclusion, the study has documented and illuminated the multilayered and dynamic process of coping with different forms of contested affiliations—such as *doing being nashi* or *nashi-zation*—as fluid key-symbol category in the investigated group. Every chapter of this work has demonstrated how participants referred to the category of imagined collective as "our people" or "people of our kind." On each occasion the concept of *nashi* was given a different meaning that stressed a particular affiliation. "Shifting" other affiliations to the background was dependent on certain situations and the immediate/concrete group constellation.

In the second chapter, *nashi* was understood by participants as people involved in coping with the complexities of capitalism in everyday practice in the new society through their socialist socialization. The reflections they

---

268 The findings of this research project confirm those of Golden (2002).

shared made evident their difficulties in remaining loyal to other affiliated *nashi,* namely educated ex-Soviet intellectuals, while simultaneously becoming a part of *nashi* as people who *live and practice capitalism.*

In the third chapter, *nashi* were people socialized in coping with the realities of the deficit Soviet economy. They depended upon their mastery of certain consumption skills that were applied in post-migration to realize their visions as participants in the new consumer culture in Israel and Germany. Additionally, *nashi* were not only people who economized and manage to lived on limited economic resources which is the fate of most migrants, but also those who revived Soviet consumption patterns and artificially created scarcities.

In the fourth chapter, *nashi* were those who aspired to find and achieved a new *home* within the framework of Russian food stores in Israel and Germany, albeit in different ways (e.g., through manifestation of *nashi* affiliation with those who participate, symbolically, in the realization of the Soviet paradise abroad; as those who cultivate Russian elite culture but simultaneously purchase proletarian food). The identity category of *nashi* was often purchased along with food products, imported from the CIS. In doing so, it was strongly influenced by the politics of nationalization and *nashi-ization* processes in current Russia, where recently this key symbol of collective national affiliation has become even stronger. The discussion also explained how the current national Russian meaning of *nashi-zation* attained through food products abroad contradicts Jews' affiliation with *nashi*; especially when directed to the historic category and destiny of Jews living in Russia and the Ukraine over the last centuries.

The fifth chapter presented the case of *nashi* who are Russian-speaking migrants in Israel who claim to be Jewish while consuming pork and developing non-kosher Israeli food stores. In this category, *nashi* influence is involved in developing the emerging character of the *nashi* [Our] national Jewish Israeli cuisine. An additional category of *nashi* analyzed in this chapter related to transnational Russian-speaking actors whose practice relates to the globalized world. This disproves an outsider's (non-Russian speaker in Israel or Germany) first impression, since the use of the Russian language seems to exist as a "closed" Russian *world of meaning.*

The sixth chapter presented an analysis of participants' understanding of *nashi* as Jews in the Diaspora and in Israel, and in the particular meaning to Jews whose background is in Soviet-Russian cultural intelligentsia who were an oppressed and discriminated minority. Whereas emigration to

Israel imbued this category with positive connotations when participants became part of the dominant Jewish *nashi* collective, emigration to Germany made this affiliation even more contested and painful. Moreover, in the German context *being Jewish nashi* was an affiliation determined by the Holocaust discourse and in an involuntary manner becomes a pervasive and essential identity stressed by dominant groups.

The seventh chapter demonstrated the category of *nashi* as above all else Soviet winners, who are confronted with being quite a different form of *nashi* (for example as German residents and as Jews) who quite often are not ready to assume and internalize "only" the role of Jewish victims in the Holocaust forced upon them by the dominant group in Germany. Thus, in the German context, the meaning of *nashi* as winners was hardly perceived, recognized, or legitimated by non-Russian speakers (both Jewish and non Jewish). Hence, this affiliation did not have a supportive and compensatory function. Furthermore, it remained highly controversial as it revived dichotomized collective categories of Germans as Nazis that made the everyday interactions of participants even more painful and complicated.

Finally, in this last chapter, we discussed how the category of *nashi* as immigrants and/or as Russian-speaking Jews abroad was perceived according to dominant local knowledge forms and expectations from migrants in Israel and Germany. It both contexts, this identification as *nashi* meant that participants were not ready to accept an imposed process of becoming "appropriately Jewish," according to the local perspectives nor act within frozen, dichotomous, hierarchical categories: those who teach versus those who have to learn to grow, to become mature social agents, and to be content as migrants with their current position at the bottom of the social pyramid.

8.4 Contributions of this research

Viewed through the transnational perspectives of migrants as active, creative social agents, this interdisciplinary study investigated contested concepts and everyday conflicts connected with settling processes, lives and affiliations of Russian-speaking Jewish immigrants in Israel and Germany, as reflected in different areas of the migrants' everyday life. Conducted by means of extensive periods of participant observation and open interviews, this cultural anthropological, ethnographic work sought to reveal key issues, concepts, and multiple affiliations as perceived, interpreted, performed by participants as central research actors in their everyday practice, verbal expressions, and food consumption in Russian food stores. The conjunctions of different affiliations, narratives, ideas, and imagined referential groups were the particular foci of the study. This enabled us to scrutinize different aspects of the migrants' self-definitions and identities in both contexts. Collectively, the study investigated the rich, complex, contested, and contradictory world that lies behind the excessively used, one-dimensional, stereotypic outsider view of migrants as "Russians." The findings of this fertile investigation were made possible through partnership with participants whose "voices" and insights were documented, preserved, and placed in the foreground of this scientific "end product."

Multiple aspects of the migration phenomena of ex-Soviet Jews in Israel and Germany have been investigated in previous studies. In building on these previous efforts, this study contributed the following new directions, i.e. ex-Soviet migrants perceptions of capitalism and their coping with abundance; changes in consumption patterns as reflections of social competence acquired in the SU; affiliation images obtained by purchasing food products at Russian food stores and the consumption of food products within the enclave as transnational practice; the continuation of the politicized character of food product design within the Russian enclave; the clash of different national cuisines, key symbols, and narratives of national foods in the praxis of Russian-speaking Jews abroad, transport and changes in aspects of *being Jewish* pre- and post-migration to Israel and Germany, the meaning of WWII and the Holocaust in everyday transnational practice of Jewish migrants in Germany, and finally the determinative role of receiving societies on personal collective identities. Again, none of these topics have been investigated to date.

Further, by applying a comparative perspective to investigate the significantly different nature of the receiving contexts, the current research illuminated the following central questions:

– How do people interact in a situation in which different bodies of knowledge, different political narratives, and different constructions of *social worlds*, usually taken for granted, meet and clash in the inner phenomenological domain, as well as, in the transnational biographic experiences of migrants?

- What happens, when through migration and intercultural interactions, the same events are remembered, understood, and interpreted in a completely different manner not only by different groups in the CIS, Israel, and Germany, but also by different Jewish groups in these countries?

- How do migrants cope with the unique situation in Germany when as ex-Soviet Jews there is pressure to demonstrate loyalty to narratives that contradict one another in many significant ways?

- What individual strategies do migrants in Israel and Germany develop in order to cope with different contested affiliations?

The analyses of the empirical fieldwork revealed numerous collisions. One such major collision occurs between the ways in which ideas were transported with the migrants about each new society and prevailing ideas in receiving host societies about the positions of migrants. Another collision occurs as the cultural habitus of Russian-speaking Jews (because of their persistent nature) is revealed in real interactions. Often this leads to misunderstandings, confrontations, and migrants' alienation. In Israel, such alienation is two-fold—as immigrants and as "Russians;" in Germany, it is four-fold, as immigrants, as a minority, as "Russians," and as Jews. Furthermore, the research findings help us understand how transnational networks and participation in the Russian-speaking enclave help migrants in both contexts to feel comfortable in the new society. Such social support and recognition are necessary in migration, and also serve as an antidote to the various forms of alienation. An associated finding illuminates how everyday transnational practice and consumption of products in Russian food stores in both contexts enable migrants in two distinct ways: First, to seek and to create evolving perceptions of *home* and *homeland*. And, second, to redefine, modify, and perform their multiple identities, as "new participants in the capitalist world," as "Europeans," as "ex-Soviet intellectuals," as "cultivators of the Russian culture," as "winners in the WWII," and as "Jews."

Yet, while frequenting Russian food stores as well as performing transnational practice are very popular and form important parts of the migrants' lives in both contexts, they do not always prove to be supportive and may actually be challenging, if not contested, in the complex process of creation, re-confirmation, and performance of collective and personal affiliations. Thus, it is exactly such practices that reveal significantly different or even unbridgeable narratives that are reactivated in one framework.

In such cases migrants tended to cope with different *social worlds* by stressing one narrative and repressing or neglecting others. In this sense, the fragmentary, situated nature of re-defining and performing identities in certain social constellations affirms the arguments of other researchers.[269] Moreover, on the basis of numerous examples, the presentation of the findings demonstrated the fragmentary character of different inner *nashi* constellations or *doing nashi* processes that are dependent on momentary situations and concrete interactions. In this situated *nashi-zation* process of (re)creating affiliation categories—namely "we" and "Our kind of" as juxtaposed to "they" and alien(ated)/foreign "Others"—*Nashi* was often constructed and performed in very different ways—as educated people, as new Israelis, as Europeans, as Jews, as ex-Soviet citizens, as migrants, as transmigrants, as cosmopolitans or those who share the Russian culture.

8.5 Further development

Findings of the current research suggest several useful and interesting directions that could be pursued in future investigations:

- The nature and strategies with which Russian-speaking Jews in Israel and Germany live with multiple contradictions could be compared with third groups, such as compatriots who immigrated at the end of 1980's and beginning of 1990's to the USA where they have established a large community.
- Given that pre-migration Russian-speaking Jews grew up and lived through the period in which the study and practice of Jewish history, culture, and religion were prohibited, it would be fascinating to investigate the understandings and changes in praxis related to Jewish history, religion, and culture that emerged post-migration in these three new countries.
- Post-migration Russian-speaking Jews experience long term unemployment and/or employment in non-qualified jobs. Such a situation has significant consequences for them as well as the host society, but is not

---

269 For example, Schütze's (2003,74) concept of "biographical collages" is based on Berger, Berger, and Kellner (1975) and Piotrowski, Czyzéwski, and Rukuszewska-Pawelek (1994).

unique to this population group. Further studies might investigate the migrants' psychological state of mind, in general, and the specific needs and conditions of Russian-speaking migrants in Germany, Israel, and USA; as well as the psycho-social and medical care afforded them. Such studies would not only be interesting but could be developed as an action research project with important practical applications.

– The current research revealed the contradictions and difficulties (including the extended length) of settling into life in capitalist societies, after socialization to and life in a socialist society. Future studies might investigate other aspects and examples of multiple transformation processes, collective affiliations, and behavioral patterns that change and develop in pre- and post-Perestroika societies, as well as, the effects of their entrance into the EU. For example, since this study demonstrated that the study of material culture, in general, and food procurement-consumption practices, in particular, is a very useful domain, future studies might continue to pursue such an investigation.

– As documented in this research, the migrants' transnational practices and development of cultural enclaves can be a supportive resource, as well as, sources of conflict and contradictions. Future studies might investigate the nature of different *home* and *homeland* constructions as they coexist in one or multiple multicultural receiving societies. Especially challenging would be an investigation of *national food* and *food nationalism* that are emerged, are shaped, and performed in contested transnational practices in multicultural societies.

– Finally, in my view the most important area for further research is the dynamic interrelationship of integration policies and the transnational nature of migration. Such a study could be informed by following the development and adaptations of insights, views, and *habitus* of migrants in Israel or Germany.

Bibliography

Al-Haj, Majid and Leshem, Elazar (2000). *Immigrants from the Former Soviet Union in Israel: Ten Years Later. A Research Report.* Haifa, Israel: University of Haifa with support of Zeit Stiftung Ebelin und Gerd Bucerius.

Allison, James (1997). "How British is British Food?" In Pat Caplan (ed.). *Food, Health and Identity,* pp.: 71—86. London and New York: Routledge.

Althanns, Luise (2006). "Zarenzigaretten und Verbrecherautos: Konsumenten und ihre Produkte im Übergang vom Plan zum Markt in Moskau." In *Osteuropaforschung—15 Jahre "danach." Beiträge für die 14. Tagung junger Osteuropa-Experten,* Arbeitspapiere und Materialien von der Forschungsstelle Osteuropa, Bremen, n.77, (Online) http://www.forschungsstelle-osteuropa.de: 166—175, 21.06.2010.

Altshuler, Mordechai (1987). *Soviet Jewry since the Second World War. Population and Social Structure.* New York: Greenwood Press.

Amon, Denise and Menasche, Renata (2008). "Comida como narrativa da memória social." *Sociedade e Cultura, Goiânia,* 11(1): 13—21.

Anderson, Bendict (1991). *Imagined Communities: Reflections on the Origin and Spread of Nationalism.* London and New York: Verso.

Appadurai, Arjun (1988). "How to Make a National Cuisine: Cookbooks in Contemporary India." *Comparative Studies in Society and History.* 30(1): 3—24.

Appadurai, Arjun (1991). "Global Ethnoscapes: Notes and Queries for a Transnational Anthropology." In Richard G. Fox (ed.) *Recapturing Anthropology.* Santa Fe, NM: School of American Research Press.

Appadurai, Arjun (1996). *Modernity at Large: Cultural Dimensions of Globalization.* Minneapolis: University of Minnesota Press.

Arad, Itzhak (2004). *History of the Holocaust, Soviet Union and Annexed territories,* 2: 1010—1014. Jerusalem: Yad Vashem.

Avraham, Eli, First, Anat, Elephant-Leffler, N. and Leor, N. (2004). *The Absent and the Present during Prime Time: Cultural Variety in Commercial Television Channels Broadcasts in Israel.* Research Report. The Second Authority for Television and Radio.

Becker, Franziska (2003). "Migration and Recognition: Russian Jews in Germany." *East European Jewish Affairs.* 33(2): 20—34.

Bade, Klaus J. and Troen, Ilan (eds.) (1993). *Zuwanderung und Eingliederung von Deutschen und Juden aus der früheren Sowjetunion in Deutschland und Israel.* Bonn, Bundesverband der Arbeitwohlfahrt, Bundesministerium des Innern.

Balcerowicz, Leszek (1995). *Social, Capitalism, Transformation.* Budapest, London, New York: Central European University Press.

Barthes, Roland ([1957] 1984). *Mythologies.* New York: Hill and Wang.

— ([1964] 1967). *Elements of Semiology.* (Translated by Annette Lavers and Colin Smith). London: Jonathan Cape.

— (1989). "Toward a Psycho-Sociology of Contemporary Food Consumption." In Forster, Robert and Ramun, Orest (eds.) *Food and Drink in History*, pp.: 83—97. Baltimore: The Johns Hopkins University Press.

Basch, Linda, Glick Schiller, Nina and Blanc-Szanton, Cristina (1994). *Nations Unbound: Transnational Projects, Post-Colonial Predicaments, and De-Territorialized Nation States.* Langhorne, PA: Gordon and Breach.

Beagan, Brenda, Chapman, Gwen E., D'Sylva, Andrea and Bassett B.Raewyn (2008). "'It's Just Easier for Me to Do It:' Rationalizing the Family Division of Foodwork." *Sociology.* 42(4): 653—671.

Beardsworth, Alan and Keil, Theresa (1997). *Sociology of the Menu: An Invitation to the Study of Food and Society.* London: Routledge.

Beck, Stefan und Welz, Gisela (1997). „Naturalisierung von Natur—Kulturalisierung von Natur. Zur Logik ästhetischer Produktion am Beispiel einer agrotouristischen Region Zyperns." *Tourismus Journal.* 1(3/4): 431-448.

Becker, Franziska und Körber, Karen (2001). "'Juden, Russen, Flüchtlinge'. Die jüdisch-russische Einwanderung nach Deutschland und ihre Repräsentation in den Medien." In Freddy Raphael (eds.) „...*das Flüstern eines leisen Wehens...*" *Beiträge zu Kultur und Lebenswelt europäischer Juden.* UVK Verlagsgesellschaft mbH: 425—450.

Becker, Franziska (2003). "Migration and Recognition: Russian Jews in Germany." *East European Jewish Affairs.* 33(2): 20—34.

Belkin, Dmitrij (2006). "Sieger oder Opfer? Das Erinnern an den Zweiten Weltkrieg und den Holocaust in der ehemaligen Sowjetunion." *Jüdische Gemeindezeitung Frankfurt.* 39 (2): 30—31.

Bell, Daviv and Valentine, Gill (1997). *Consuming Geographies. We are Where We Eat.* London and New York: Routledge.

Ben Porath, Gie (forthcoming). *Sir HaBasar. Kal'kalat HaShuk Vetahalichei Hachilun Beisrael,* [Crock pot, market economy and secularization processes in Israel].

Berdahl, Daphne (2002). „Ostalgie und ostdeutsche Sehnsüchte nach einer erinnerten Vergangenheit", in Thomas Hausschild und Bernd Jürgen Warneken (eds.). *Inspecting Germany. Internationale Deutschland—Ethnographie der Gegenwart,* Münster: LIT, S.:476—496.

Bernstein, Julia (2000). *Food for Thought: Identity Contructions of ex-Soviet Immigrants in Israel through Material Culture, Namely through Food Practices.* Unpublished MA Thesis, Faculty of Sociology and Anthropology, University of Haifa.

Bernstein, Julia and Carmeli, Yoram (2004). "Food for Thought: The Dining Table and Identity Construction among Jewish Immigrants from the Former Soviet Union in Israel." In Carmali Yoram S. and Applbaum K. (eds.), *Consumption and Market Society in Israel*, pp.: 95—123. Oxford and New York: Berg.

Bertaux, Daniel (1981). *Biography and Society*. Beverly Hills: Sage.

Blaxter, Mildred and Paterson, Elisabeth (1983). "The Goodness is Out of It: The Meaning of Food to Two Generations." In Murcott, A. (ed.) *The Sociology of Food and Eating*. pp.: 95—106. Gateshead: Paradigm Presss.

Bloch, Ernst (1963). *Tübinger Einleitung in Die Philosophie*. Suhrkamp Verlag, Frankfurt am Main. (Russian translation, Ceu Press, 1997).

Bodnar, John (1985). *The Transplanted: A History of Immigrants in Urban America*. Bloomington & Indianapolis: Indiana University Press.

Bojadzíjev, Manuela (1998). "Fremde Töpfe. Kulinarische Vorstellungen von Multi-culturalismus." In Mayer, Ruth und Terkessidis, Mark (Hgs.) *Globalkolorit. Multikulturalismus und Populärkultur*. pp.: 303—312. St. Andrä/Wördern: Hannibal.

Borrero, Mauricio (1997). "Communal Dining and State Cafeterias in Moscow and Petrograd, 1917—20." In Glants, Musya and Tommre Joyce (eds.) *Food in Russian History and Culture*, pp.: 162—176. Bloomington and Indianapolis: Indiana University Press.

Bourdieu, Pierre (1977). *Outline of a Theory of Practice,* Cambridge: Cambridge University Press.

— (1984). *Distinction: A Social Critique of the Judgment of Taste*. Cambridge, Mass: Harvard University Press.

Boyarin, Jonathan (ed.) (1994). Remapping *Memory: The Politics of Time Space*. Minneapolis, London: University of Minnesota Press.

Boym, Svetlana (2001). *The Future of Nostalgia*. New York: Basic Books.

— (2002). *Common places: Mythologies of everyday life in Russia*. Moscow: Novoe literaturnoe obosrennie. (Russian version. Cambridge, MA: Harvard University Press, 1997. Translated and extended by the author).

Breckner, Roswitha (2000)."Processes of Reconstructing Migration Biographies: The Experience of 'Return' from the West to the East of Europe after 1989." In Biko Agozino (Ed.) *Theoretical and Methodological Issues in Migration Research: Interdisciplinary, Intergenerational and International Perspectives*. pp.: 91–106. Aldershot, Brookfield, USA, Singapore, Sydney: Ashgate.

— (2005)."Ambivalente Wir-Bezüge in ost-west-europäischen Migrationsbiographien. Konstruktionen kollektiver Zugehörigkeit in gesellschaftlichen Polarisierungsprozessen." *Sozialer Sinn*. 1(6): 71–92.

Brednikova, Olga and Patchenkov, Oleg (1999). "Ethnicity of 'Ethnic Economy:' Economic Immigrants to St. Petersburg." *CISR. Working Papers*. 4: 3. St. Petersburg, (Online) http://www.indepsocres.spb.ru, 21.06.2010.

Brednikova, Olga, Chikadze, Elena and Voronkov, Viktor (eds.) (2000). *Ethnic Economy in Post-Socialist Space.* CISR. Working Papers, №8. St.Petersburg, 128, (Online) http://www.indepsocres.spb.ru, 21.06.2010.

Brewster, Scott (2002). "Das Unheimliche [The Uncanny]." *The Literary Encyclopedia,* http://www.litencyc.com/php/sworks.php?rec=true&UID=5735, 21.06.2010.

Brunnek, N. Gavrilova N., Ivanikova E, Kolesnikova, A. Milukova V, Okovolok J, Pankova A, Slashre L., Ivanov, L. (1955 [2002]) *Kulinariya* [Culinary], Moscow: Voskresenie.

Brunner, Karl, Michael (2008). "Essenskulturen im Sozialen Wandel." Engel, Gisela and Scholz, Susanne (Hg.) *Essenskulturen. Beiträge zur Rechts-, Gesellschafts- und Kulturkritik.* S. 11—24. Berlin: Trafo Verlag.

Çaglarm, Ayse, S.. (1999). "McKebap: Döner Kebap and the Social Positioning Struggle of German Turks." In Carola Lentz (ed.). *Changing Food Habits. Case Studies from Africa, South America and Europe,* pp.: 263—285. Newark, NJ: Harwood Academic Publishers.

Caldwell Melissa L. (2002). "The Taste of Nationalism: Food Politics in Postsocialist Moscow." *Ethos.* 67(3): 295—319.

— (2003). "Race and Social Relations: Crossing Borders in a Moscow Food Aid Program." In Davide Torsello and Melinda Pappová (eds.) *Social Networks in Movement. Time, interaction and interethnic spaces in Central Eastern Eurasia* pp.: 255—273. Lilium Aurum: Dunajská Streda (SK).

— (2005). "Domesticating the French Fry: McDonald's and Consumerism in Moscow." In Watson, James L. and Caldwell, Melissa I (eds.). *The Cultural Politics of Food and Eating: A Reader.* Malden and Oxford: Blackwell.

Calloni, Marina (1999). "Culture, Territory, and Ethnisation. Use and Abuse of the Construct „Ethnicity" in public discourse." In Ursula Apizsch (ed.) *Migration und Traditionsbildung,* pp.: 116—130. Opladen/Wiesbaden: Westdeutscher Verlag.

Carmon, Naomi (ed.) (1996). *Immigration and Integration in Post Industrial Society.* Houndmills Basingstoke: Macmillan Press Ltd.

Cavalli-Sforzam, Luigi Luca and Francesco (1994). *Verschieden und doch gleich.* München: Knaur.

Chervyakov, Valeriy, Gitelman, Zvi and Shapiro, Vladimir (1997). "Religion and Ethnicity: Judaism in the Ethnic Consciousness of Contemporary Russian Jews." *Ethnic and Racial Studies.* 20(2): 280—305.

Ching, Lin Pang (2003). "Beyond 'Authenticity:' Reinterpreting Chinese Immigrant Food in Belgium." In Döring Tobias, Heide, Markus and Mühleisen, Susanne (eds.) *Eating Culture. The Poetics and Politics of Food,* pp.: 53—70. Universität Verlag Winter, Heidelberg.

Clavero, Sara and Calloni, Marina (2007). *Gender Politics and Democracy in Post-socialist Europe.* Opladen and Farmington Hills: Barbara Budrich Publishers.

Clifford, James (1986). "Introduction: Partial Truths." Clifford James and Marcus, George E. (eds.) *Writing Culture: The Poetics and Politics of Ethnography*, pp.: 1—16. Berkeley: University of California Press.

Cohen, Yinon and Kogan, Irena (2005). "Jewish Immigration from the Former Soviet Union to Germany and Israel in the 1990s." In Grenville, J.A.S. and Gross, Raphael (eds.,) *Leo Baeck Institute Year Book,* pp.: 249—265.

Cohen, Steven M. (1991). "Sociological Analysis of Jewish Identity." Gordis Davide, Ben-Horin Yoav The Susan and David Wikstei (eds.) *Jewish Identitiy in America*. pp.: 27—29. Los Angeles: Institute of Jewish Policy Studies. University of Judaism.

Corrigan, Philip and Sayer, Derek (1985). *The Great Arch: English State Formation as Cultural Revolution*. Oxford: Blackwell.

Darieva, Tsypylma (2000). "Managing Identity: Some Insights into Post-Soviet Russian Language Media in Berlin." *Center of the Independent Sociological Research,* 8, (Online) http://www.indepsocres.spb.ru 21.06.2010.

— (2003). "Von anderen Deutschen und anderen Juden. Zur kulturellen Integration Russischsprechender Zuwanderer in Berlin." In Warneken, Bernd/ Hausschild, Thomas (eds.). *Inspecting Germany. Internationale Deutschland—Ethnographie der Gegenwart*, pp.: 405—20. Münster: LIT Verlag.

— (2004). *Russkii Berlin: Migrants* and *Media in Berlin and London*. Münster: Lit Verlag.

Demirović, Alex (2004). "Gouvernementalität und kognitiver Kapitalismus. Gesellschafts-theoretische Bemerkungen zur Immanenz des Wissens." In Thomas Ernst, Bettina Bock von Wülfingen, Stephan Borrman, Christian P. Gudehus (eds.) *Wissenschaft und Macht*, S. 250—263. Münster: Westfälisches Dampfboot.

Diemling, Maria (forthcoming). "The Ethnographer and the Jewish Body: Johann Jacob Schudt on the Civilization Process of the Jews of Frankfurt." *Jewish Culture and History*.

— (2005). "Daß man unter so viel tausend Menschen so fort einen Juden erkennen kan:" Johann Jacob Schudt und der jüdische Körorper, Fritz Backhaus, Gisela Engel, Robert Liberles, Margarete Schlüter (eds.), *Die Frankfurter Judengasse. Jüdisches Leben in der frühen Neuzeit*, S. 77—89. Frankfurt: Societätsverlag.

Dietz, Barbara (2000). "German and Jewish Migration from the Soviet Union in Germany: Background, Trend, and Implications." In *Journal of Ethnic and Migration Studies*. 26(4): 635—53.

— (2003). Jewish Immigration from the Former Soviet Union in Germany: History, Politics, and Social Integration. *East European Jewish Affairs*. 33(2): 7—19.

Diner, Hasia R. (2001). *Hungering for America: Italian, Irish, and Jewish Foodways in the Age of Migration*. Cambridge, Mass.: Harvard University Press.

Diner, Dan (2006). Director of Simon-Dubnow-Institute for Jewish History and Culture at the University of Leipzig in his Interview in the Program "Diskussion mit Professor Peter Voß und Gästen." Broadcast 3SAT, Germany, 22 May, 2006 Montag, 21:35—23:05.

— (2006). Public presentation to the Jewish community of Frankfurt am Main.

Diner, Dan (2007). *Gegenläufige Gedächtnisse: über Geltung und Wirkung des Holocaust*, Göttingen: Vandenhoeck und Ruprecht.

Dolve-Gandelman, Tsili (1990). "Ethiopia as a Lost Imaginary Space: The Role of Ethiopian Jewish Women in Producing the Ethnic Identity of their Immigrant Group in Israel." In Jerry MacCannell (ed.) *The Other Perspective in Gender and Culture,* pp.: 242—257. New York: Columbia University Press.

Doomernik, Jeroen (1997). *Going West: Soviet Jewish Immigrants in Berlin since 1990.* Avebury, Aldeshot, Brookfield USA , Hong Kong, Singapore Sydney.

Döring Tobias, Heide, Markus and Mühleisen, Susanne (eds.) (2003). *Eating Culture. The Poetics and Politics of Food.* Heidelberg: Universitätsverlag Winter.

Douglas, Mary (1966). *Purity and Danger: An Analysis of the Concepts of Pollution and Taboo,* London: Routledge and Kegan Paul.

— (1975). "Deciphering a Meal." *Daedalus.* 101(1): 61—81.

— (ed.) (1984). *Food in the Social Order: Studies of Food and Festivities in Three American Communities.* New York: Russell Stage Foundation.

— (1984). "Standard Social Uses of Food: Introduction." In Douglas, Mary (ed.) *Food in the Social Order: Studies of Food and Festivities in Three American Communities.* New York: Russell Stage Foundation.

— (1987). *Constructive Drinking: Perspectives of Drinking from Anthropology.* Cambridge: Cambridge University Press.

Dovlatov, Sergei (1995, [1993]). *Sobranie prozy v trekh tomakh.* Sankt-Peterburg: Limbus Press.

Elias, Nelly (2005). "Living in Germany, Longing for Israel: Elderly Jewish Immigrants from the Former Soviet Union in Germany." *East European Jewish Affairs.* 35(2): 167—187.

— (2007). "The Honey, the Bear, and the Violin: The Russian Voices of Israeli Advertising." *Journal of Advertising Research.* 47(1): 113—123.

— (2008). *Coming Home: Media and Returning Diaspora in Israel and Germany.* Albany, NY: SUNY Press.

Elias, Nelly and Greenspan, Leah (2007). "The Honey, the Bear and the Violin: The Russian Voices of Israeli Advertising." *Journal of Advertising Research.* 47(1): 113—123.

Elias, Nelly and Bernstein, Julia (2007). "Wandering Jews, Wandering Stereotypes: Media Representation of the Russian-speaking Jews in Russia, Israel and Germany." In *Relation: Communication Research in Comparative Perspective.* n.s.(2): 15—38.

Elias, Nelly and Lemish, Dafna (2008). "Media Uses in Immigrant Families: Torn between "Inward" and "Outward" Paths of Integration." *International Communication Gazette.* 70(1): 23—42.

— (2008a). "Internet and Immigrant Youth Hybrid Identities: The Case of Former Soviet Union Immigrant Adolescents in Israel." In Ingegerd Rydin and Ulrika Sjöberg (eds.), *Mediated Crossroads: Identity, Youth Culture and Ethnicity—Theoretical and Methodological Challenges*, pp.: 173—192. Nordic Information Centre for Media and Communication Research: Göteborg University.

Erdreich, Lauren, Lerner, Julia and Rapoport, Tamar (2005). "Reproducing Nation, Redesigning Positioning: Russian and Palestinian Students Interpret University Knowledge." *Identities: Global Studies in Culture and Power*. 12: 539—562.

Falk, Pasi (1991). "Homo culinarius: Towards a Historical Anthropology of Taste." *Social Science Information*. 30(4): 757—90.

— (1991). "The Sweetness of Forbidden Fruit: Toward an Anthropology of Taste." In Fürst, Elisabeth L. (ed.) *Palatable Worlds: Sociocultural Food Studies*. Oslo: Solum Forlay.

Feingold, Henry (1991). "The American components of Jewish Identity." In Gordis, Davide, Ben-Horin, Yoav, Susan and David Wilstein (eds.) *Jewish Identity in America*, pp.: 69—81. Los Angeles: Institute of Jewish Policy Studies, University of Judaism.

Fialkova, Larisa and Yelenevskaya, Maria (2003). "How to find the West in the Middle East: Perceptions of East and West amongst 'Russian' Jews in Israel." In Attila Paládi-Kovács (ed.), *Times, Places, Passages: Ethnological Approaches in the New Millennium*. Budapest: Publishing House of the Hungarian Academy of Sciences.

Fischler, Claude (1980). "Food Habits, Social Change and the Nature/Culture Dilemma." *Social Science Information*. 19 (6): 937—53.

— (1988). "Food, Self and Identity", *Social Science Information*. 27 (2): 275—92.

Galligan, Yvonne and Fiedman, Mordechai (1995). "*Klitatam hatarbutit-Jehudit shel olei chever hamadinot.*" [Cultural Jewish Absorption of repatriates from the CIS] *Arachot*. 44: 64—68. (Hebrew)

Geerz, Clifford (1993, [1973]). *Interpretation of Culture*. New York: Basic Books.

Genis, Alexander and Vail, Peter (2003 [1983]). *Poteryannyi rai. Emigraziya: popytka avtoportreta*. (Lost Paradise) Ekaterinburg: U-Faktoria.

Gilman, Sander, L. (1986). *Jewish Self-Hatred: Anti-Semitism and the Hidden Language of the Jews*. Baltimore and Londone: Johns Hopkins University Press.

— (1994). "The Jewish Nose: Are Jews White? Or, the History of the Nose Job." In Silberstein Laurence J. and Cohn, Robert, L. (eds.). *The Other in Jewish Thought and History. Construction of Jewish Culture and Identity*, pp.: 364—401. New York and London: New York University Press.

Gitelman, Zvi (1994). The Reconstruction of Community and Jewish Identity in Russia." *European Jewish Affairs*. 24(2): 35—56.

— (1995). *Immigration and Identity. The Resettlement and Impact of Soviet Immigrants on Israeli Politics and Society*. The Susan and David Wilstein Institute of Jewish Policy Study. Los Angeles: Wilstein Institute.

— (1994). "Sowjetische Holocaust-Politik." James E. Young (ed.): *Motive, Rituale und Stätten des Gedenkens*, München auch Zvi Gitelman: Die sowjetische Holo-caust-Politik, a.a.O.:115—123.

— (1997). "Politics and the Historiography of the Holocaust in the Soviet Union", in Zvi Gitelman (ed.) *Bitter Legacy: Confronting the Holocaust in the USSR*, Bloom-ington and Indianapolis: Indiana University Press, 1997), 15—42.

—(1997). *Bitter Legacy. Confronting the Holocaust in the USSR*, Bloomington/ Indianapolis: Indiana University Press.

— (1997). "From a Northern Country: Russian and Soviet Jewish Immigrants to America and Israel in Historical Perspective." In Lewin-Epstein, Noah, Roi, Yaacov and Ritterband, Paul (eds.) *Russian Jews on Three Continents. Migration and Resettlement*, pp.: 21—45. London: Frank Cass.

Gitelman Zvi, Chervyakov Valery and Shapiro Vladimir (2000). "Nationalnoe samososnanie rossiiskich yevreev [National Identity of Russian Jews] Materials of sociological research 1997—1998." *Diasporas*. 3: 52—86

— (2001). "Nationalnoe samososnanie rossiiskich yevreev" [National Identity of Russian Jews Materials of sociological research 1997—1998] *Diasporas*. 1: 210—244.

Glants, Musia (1997). "Food as Art: Painting in Late Soviet Russia." In Musia Glants and Jerald Toomre (eds.). *Food in Russian History and Culture*, pp.: 216—237. Bloomington and Indianapolis: Indiana University Press.

Glants, Musia and Toomre, Jerald (1997). (eds.) *Food in Russian History and Culture*. Bloomington and Indianapolis: Indiana University Press.

Glick Schiller, Nina, Linda and Cristina Blanc-Szanton (eds.) (1997). *Towards a Transnational Perspective on Migration: Race, Class, Ethnicity and Nationalism*. New York: New York Academy of Sciences.

Goffman, Erving (1963). *Behavior in Public Places. Notes on the Social Organization of Gatherings*. New York: Free Press.

Gofton, L. (1995). "Convenience and the Moral Status of Consumer Practices." In David W. Marshall (ed.) *Food Choice and the Consumer*, pp: 152—182. Glasgow: Blackie.

Golbert, Rebecca Leah (1997). "The Problem of Studying Post-Soviet Jewish Identity." Working paper [Online] http://www.jewish-heritage.org/jr1a6r.htm, 21.06.2010.

Golbert, Rebecca (2001). "Transnational Orientation from Home: Constructions of Israel and Transnational Space among Ukrainian Jewish Youth." *Journal of Ethnic and Migration Studies*. 27(4): 713—731.

Gold, Steven J. (1996). *From the Worker's State to the Golden State: Jews from the Former Soviet Union in California*. Boston: Allyn and Bacon.

— (1997). "Community Formation among Jews from the Former Soviet Union in the United States." In Lewin-Epstein, Noah, Roi, Yaacov and Ritterband, Paul (eds.) *Russian Jews on Three Continents—Migration and Resettlement*, pp.: 261—284. London: Frank Cass.

— (2001). "Gender Class, and Network: Social Structure and Migration Patterns among Transnational Israelis." *Global Networks: A Journal of Transnational Affairs.* 1(1): 57—78.

Golden, Deborah (1996). *Belonging Through Time: Israelis, Immigrants, and the Task of Nation-Building.* Doctoral Dissertation. University of London: University College.

— (2001). "Storytelling the Future: Israelis, Immigrants and the Imaging of Community." *Anthropological Quarterly.* 75(1): 7—35.

— (2001a). "Now, Like Real Israelis, Let's Stand Up and Sing: Teaching the National Language to Russian Newcomers in Israel." *Anthropology and Education Quarterly.* 32(1): 52—79.

— (2002). "Belonging Through Time. Nurturing National Identity among Newcomers to Israel from the Former Soviet Union." *Time and Society.* 11(1): 5—24.

Grasseni, Cristina (2005). "Slow Food, Fast Genes: Timescapes of Authenticity and Innovation in the Anthropology of Food." *Cambridge Anthropology.* 25(2): 79—94.

Grossman, Vasilij Semenovič and Ėrenburg, Il'ja Grigor'evič (1980). (eds.) *Černaja kniga. O zlodejskom povsemestnom ubijstve yevreev nemecko-fašistskimi zachvatčikami vo vremenno-okkupirovannykh rayonach Sovetskogo Soyuza i v lageryakh uničtoženija Pol'šej vo vremja vojny 1941—1945 gg.* Jerusalem 1980. First Soviet publ. Sowjetische Erstausg.: Kiev 1991. [Grossman, Wassili and Ehrenburg Ilja (eds.): *Das Schwarzbuch. Der Genozid an den sowjetischen Juden.* Reinbek Rowohlt Verlag GmbH 1994.]

Grüber, Sabine and Rüßler, Harald (2000). *Hochqualifiziert und arbeitslos*, Leske-Budrich Verlag.

Guarnizo, Luis Eduardo (2003). "The Economics of Transnational Living." *International Migration Review.* 37(3): 666—699.

Guarnizo, Luis Eduardo, Portes, Alejandro and Haller, William (2003). "Assimilation and Transnationalism: Determinants of Transnational Political Action among Contemporary Migrants." *American Journal of Sociology.* 108(6): 121—148.

Gudeman, Stephen and Rivera, Alberto (1990). *Conversation in Colombia: The Domestic Economy in Life and Text.* Cambridge: Cambridge University Press.

Gustafson, Thane (1999). *Capitalism Russian-Style.* Cambridge UK: Cambridge.

Haney Lopez, Ian F. (1994). "The Social Construction of Race: Some Observations on Illusion, Fabrication, and Choice, 29 Harvard Civil Rights-Civil Liberties." *Law Review:* 1—62, 6—7, 11—17.

Hannerz, Ulf (1998). "Transnational Research." In Russell Bernard (ed.), *Handbook of Methods in Cultural Anthropology.* London: Sage.

— (1990)."Cosmopolitans and Locals in World Culture." In Featherstone, Michael (ed.). *Global Culture. Nationalism, Globalization, and Modernity*, pp.: 237—251. London: Sage Publications.

Harbottle, Lynn (1997). "Taste and Embodiment: The Food Preferences of Iranians in Britain." In Macbeth, Helen (ed.) *Food Preferences and Taste—Continuity and Change,* pp. 175—186. Province and Oxford: Berghahn.

Heckmann, Friedrich (1997). "Ethos—eine imaginierte oder reale Gruppe? Über Ethnizität als soziologischer Kategorie." In Robert Hettlage, Petra Deger, Susanne Wagner (ed.), *Kollektive Identität in Krisen. Ethnizität in Religion, Nation, Europa,* S. 46—56. Opladen: Westdeutscher Verlag.

Hegner, Victoria (2008). *Gelebte Selbstbilder. Gemeinden russischer Juden in Chicago and Berlin.* Campus Verlag.

Heller, Mikhail and Nekrich, Alexandr (1986). *Utopia in Power History of the Soviet Union from 1917 to the Present.* New York: Summit Books.

Herzfeld, Michael (2001). *Anthropology. Theoretical Practice in Culture and Society.* Malden MA and Oxford UK: Blackwell.

Hobsbawm, Eric and Ranger, Terence (eds.) (1983). The Invention of Tradition, Cambridge: Cambridge University Press.

Horkheimer, Max und Adorno, Theodor W. (1987). "Dialektik der Aufklärung. Philosophische Fragmente." In Max Horkheimer, *Gesammelte Schriften* Bd. 5, Fischer, new ed.: 11—290.

Horowiz, Tamar (1998). "Von Zuwanderten zu Mitgliedern der Gemeinschaft: Juden aus der ehemaligen Sowjetunion in Israel." In Klaus J.Bade und Hans H. Reich (eds.) *Migration—und Integrationspolitik gegenüber gleichstämmigen Zuwander.* Osnabrück: Universitätsverlag: 50—73.

Hubert, Annie (1997). "Choices of Food and Cuisine in the Concept of Social Space among the Yao of Thailand." In Helen Macbeth (ed.), *Food Preferences and Taste. Continuity and Change,* pp.: 167—174. Providence & Oxford: Berghahn Books.

Humphrey, Caroline (2002). *The Unmaking of Soviet Life. Everyday Economies after Socialism.* Ithaca and London: Cornell University Press.

Inowlocki, Lena (2000). "Doing Being Jewish:" Constitution of 'Normality' in Families of Jewish Displaced Persons in Germany." In Roswitha Breckner, Deborah Kalekin-Fishman and Ingrid Miethe (eds.): *Biographies and the Division of Europe. Experience, Action, and Change on the "Eastern Side,"* pp.159—178. Opladen: Verlag Leske und Budrich.

— (2003). "Kritische Theoriebildung zu Antisemitismus, Rassismus und Reaktionen auf Einwanderung." Demirović Alex (ed.), *Modelle kritischer Gesellschaftstheorie. Traditionen, Perspektiven der Kritischen Theorie,* S. 225—246. Stuttgart. Weiner: J.B. Metzler.

— (2007). Podium discussion at round table with Prof. Inowlocki, Prof. Schneider, Prof. Lustiger and Ms. Bernstein to the theme "Chances of the New Jewish Life in Germany?" Jewish Dialog Days 2007, Active Museum Spiegelgasse for German-Jewish Contemporary History, Wiesbaden, Germany.

Inowlocki, Lena and Bernstein, Julia (2006). "Perhaps You Could Tell me more about the Fact that you are a Quiet Man:" Communicating Disease and

Strangeness in a Family Interview. *Biography and Society. Research Committee 38 of the ISA. International Newsletter.* Common Publication on the basis of the paper in the Session 6, RC 38, *Three-generation families of ethnic Germans from the Soviet Union. Different ways of analyzing biographical case studies,* UK, XVI ISA World Congress of Sociology, Durban, South Africa. http://www.ucm.es/info/isa/pdfs/rc38newsletter.pdf, 21.06.2010.

Jackson, Peter and Holbrook, Beverley (1995). "Multiple Meanings: Shopping and the Cultural Politics of Identity." *Environment and Planning.* 27: 1913—1930.

Jochnowitz, Eve (2008). "Foodscapes the Culinary Landscapes of Russian-Jewish New York." In Julia Brauch, Anna Lipphardt, and Alexandra Nocke (eds.) *Jewish Topographies—Visions of Space, Traditions,* pp.: 293—308. Aldershot, England: Ashgate Publishing Co.

Joppke, Christian (1998). *Immigration and the Nation State.* New York and Oxford: Oxford University Press.

Kandel, Felix (2002). *Kniga vremen I sobytii. 1 istoriya rossiiskich evreev* [The book of the times and events I. The history of Russian Jews], Moscow and Jerusalem: Mosty Kultury and Gesharim.

Kapphan, Andreas (2000). "Russian Entrepreneurs in Berlin: The Role of Ethnicity and Opportunity Structures." *Center of the Independent Sociological Research.* 8, (Online) http://www.indepsocres.spb.ru/sbornik8/8e_kapph.htm, 21.06.2010.

Kattmann, Ulrich (1982). "Biologische Unterwanderung? Genetik als Rechtfertigung völkischer Ideologie." *Unterricht Biologie.* 6 (72/73): 35—42.

— (2003). "Sind wir alle Neger? Biologische Rassenkonzepte sind wissenschaftlich nicht haltbar." *Geschichte lernen.* 16 (93): 4—6.

Kaufmann, Jean-Claude (2005). *Kochende Leidenschaft. Soziologie vom Kochen und Essen.* Konstanz: UVK Verlagsgesellschaft mbH.

Kaupen-Haas, Heidrun (ed.) (1999). Wissenschaftlicher Rassismus. Analysen einer Kontinuität in den Human- und Naturwissenschaften. Campus Verlag.

Kehrer, Michaela (2005). "Transnationale Konsumgüterunternehmen in Ägypten. Eroberung des Massenmarktes zwischen „ruralem Marketing" und „Konsumentenintifada." *Prokla. Zeitschrift für kritische Sozialwissenschaft.* 138(35/1): 73-90.

Keller, Margit and Vihalemm, Triin (2005). "Coping with Consumer Culture: Elderly Urban Consumers in Post-Soviet Estonia." *Trames.* 1: 69—91.

Kershen, Anne J. (2002). "Introduction: Food in the Migrant Experience." in Anne J. Kershen (ed.) *Food in the Migrant Experience,* pp. 1—13. Aldershot, England: Ashgate Publishing Company.

Kessler, Judith (1996). *Jüdische Migration aus der ehemaligen Sowjetunion seit 1990. Beispiel Berlin,* gekürzte Fassung einer Magisterarbeit an der Fernuniversität Hagen/Fachbereich Soziologie.

Kimerling, Baruch (2004). *Mehagrim, Mityashvim, Elidim* [Immigrants, Settlers, Natives: Israel Between Plurality of Cultures and Cultural Wars]. Tel Aviv: Am Oved.

Kivisto, Peter (1990). "The Transplanted Then and Now: the Reorientation of Immigration Studies from the Chicago School to the New Social History." In *Ethnic and Racial Studies*, 13 (4): 455—485.

Kloosterman, Robert und Rath, Jan (2003). "Mixed Embededness: Markets and Immigration Enterpreneurs." In Usrula Apitzsch (ed.) *Immigrant Business*, pp.: 6—27. London: Macmillan Press.

Klumbyté, Neringa (2010). "The Soviet Sausage Renaissance", *American Anthropologist,* 112(1): 22—37.

Kneafsey, Moya and Cox, Rosie (2002). "Food, Gender, and Irishness: How Irish Women in Coventry Make Home." *Irish Geography.* 35(1): 6—15.

Kopytoff, Igor (1986). "The Cultural Biography of Things: Commodization as Process." In Arjun Appadurai (ed.) *The Social Life of Things: Commodities in Cultural Perspective,* pp.: 64—91. Cambridge: Cambridge University Press.

Körber, Karen (2005). *Juden, Russen, Emigranten. Identitätskonflikte jüdischer Einwanderer in einer ostdeutschen Stadt.* Frankfurt/New York: Campus Verlag.

Krupnik, Igor (1994). "Constructing New Identities in the Former Soviet Union: The Challenge for the Jews." In Jonathan Webber (ed.) *Jewish Identities in the New Europe.* London: Littman Library of Jewish Civilization.

Kunow, Rüdiger (2003). "Eating Indian(s): Food, Representation, and the Indian Diaspora in the United States". In Döring Tobias, Markus Heide and Susanne Mühleisen (eds.). *Eating Culture. The Poetics and Politics of Food,* pp.: 151—177. Heidelberg: Universitätsverlag Winter.

Kyle, David (1999). "The Otavalo Trade Diaspora: Social Capital and Transnational Entrepreneurship." *Ethnic and Racial Studies.* 22: 422—446.

Leblanc, Ronald D. (1999). "Food, Orality, and Nostalgia for Childhood: Gastronomic Slavophilism in Midnineteenth-Century Russian Fiction." *Russian Review,* 58(2): 244—267.

Lenz, Carola (2007). "Constructing Ethnicity: Elite Biographies in Ghana." Paper presented at the International Conference on *Ethnicity, Belonging, Biography and Ethnography.* Georg August Universität, Göttingen, Sweden.

Lerner, Julia (2003). "Knowledge in Migration: Russian Migrants in Israeli University." In Rivka Eisikovitz (ed.). *On Cultural Boundaries and Between Them: Young Immigrants in Israel,* pp. 123—156. Tel Aviv: Ramot Press, Tel Aviv University.

— (2006). "'Ethnicity' contests 'Ethnos' and 'Nationalities': Recruiting a Global Category in Post-Soviet Russian Academic Discourse." Paper presented at 11th Annual World Convention of ASN—"Nationalism in an Age of Globalization."

Lerner, Julia, Rapoport, Tamar, and Lomsky-Feder, Edna (2007). "The 'Ethnic Script in Action: The Re-grounding of Russian-Jewish Immigrants in Israel." *Ethos.* 35 (2): 168—195.

Lévi-Strauss, Claude (1965). *Das Ende des Totemismus.* Frankfurt am Main: Campus.

— (1970). *The Raw and the Cooked.* London: Jonathan and Cape.

Levinson, Alexej (1997). "Attitudes of Russians towards Jews and their Emigration 1989—1994." In Lewin-Epstein, Noah, Roi, Yaacov and Ritterband, Paul (eds.) *Russian Jews on Three Continents Migration and Resettlement*, pp.: 222—233. London: Frank Cass.

Levitt, Peggy and Glick Schiller, Nina (2004). "Conceptualizing Simultaneity: A Transnational Social Field Perspective on Society." *International Migration Review*. Fall, 38(3): 1002—1040.

Levitt, Peggy and Sorensen, Nyberg, Ninna (2004). "The Transnational Turn in Migration Studies." *Global Migration Perspectives*, Vol. 6, Global Commission on International Migration (GCIM). www.gcim.org, 21.06.2010.

Levontin, Richard C., Rose, Steven and Kamin, Leon (1984). *Not on our Genes: Biology, Ideology and Human Nature*. London: Penguin Notes.

Lewin-Epstein, Noah, Roi, Yaacov and Ritterband, Paul (eds.) (1997). *Russian Jews on Three Continents Migration and Resettlement*. London: Frank Cass.

Lissak, Moshe and Leshem, Elazar (1995). "The Russian Intelligentsia in Israel: Between Ghettorgation and Integration." *Israel Affairs*, 2(1): 342—51.

Lomsky-Feder, Ednah, Rapoport, Tamar and Lerner, Julia (2005). "Orientalism and the Challenge of Migration: Russian Students Read Israeli Ethnicity." *Theory and Criticism*. 26: 119—147.

Lomsky-Feder, Edna and Rapoport, Tamar (2000). "Visit, Separation, and Deconstructing Nostalgia: Russian Students Travel to Their Old Home." *Journal of Contemporary Ethnography*. 29(1): 32—57.

Lomsky-Feder, Edna and Rapoport, Tamar (2001). "Homecoming, Immigration, and the National Ethos: Russian-Jewish Homecomers Reading Zionism." *Anthropological Quarterly*. 74(1): 1—14.

Lupton, Deborah (1996). *Food, the Body, and the Self*. London: Thousand Oaks and New Delhi: Sage Publications.

Lustiger, Arno (1998). *Rotbuch: Stalin und die Juden Die tragische Geschichte des Jüdischen Antifaschistischen Komitees und der sowjetischen Juden*. Berlin: Aufbau-Verlag.

Lynn, Harbottle (1997). "Fast Food/Spoiled Identity: Iranian Migrants in the British Catering Trade." In Pat Caplan (ed.). *Food, Health, and Identity*, pp.: 87—111. London and New York: Routledge.

Mahler, Sarah and Pessar, Patricia (2001). "Gendered Geographies of Power: Analyzing Gender across Transnational Space." *Identities: Global Studies in Culture and Power*. 7: 441—459.

Malachov, Vladimir (2001). "Skromnoe Obayanie Rasisma" [Discreet Charm of Racism], *Vremya Iskat'*. 5: 97—108.

Mankekar, Purnima (2005). "Indian Grocery Stores and Transnational Configuration of Belonging." In Watson, James L. and Caldwell, Melissa L: (eds.). *The Cultural Politics of Food and Eating. A Reader*, pp.: 197—214. Malden/Oxford: Blackwell.

Mannur, Anita (2005). "Culinary Fictions: Immigrant Foodways and Race in Indian

American Literature" in Kent A. Ono (ed.) *Asian American Studies After Critical Mass*, Blackwell, pp.: 56—70.

— (1995)."Ethnography in/of the World System. The Emergence of Multi-Sited Ethnography. " *Annual Review of Anthropology*. 24: 95—117.

Morawska, Ewy (2004). "Exploring Diversity in Immigration Assimilation and Transnationalism: Poles and Russian Jews in Philadelphia." *International Migration Review*. Fall, 38(4): 1372—1413.

Markowitz, Fran (1988). "Jewish in the USSR, Russian in the USA: Social Context and Ethnic Identity." In Walter Zenner (ed.) *Persistence and Flexibility: Anthropological Perspectives on the American Jewish Experience*, pp.: 79—95. Albany, New York: SUNY Press.

Markowitz, Fran (1993). *A Community in Spite of Itself: Soviet Jewish Émigrés in New York*. Washington, DC: Smithsonian Institution Press.

Mertens, Lothar (1993). *Alija. Die Emigration der Juden aus der UdSSR/GUS*. Bochum. 2. aktual. und erw. Aufl. Bochum: Brockmeyer.

Meyer, Michael A. (1990). *Jewish Identity in the Modern World*. University of Washington Press: Seattle.

Milesm, Robert (2002). "The Concept of Racism." In Karin Liebhart, Elisabeth Menasse, Heinz Steinert (eds.), *Fremdbilder Feinbilder Zerrbilder. Wir Wahrnehmung und diskursive Konstruktionen des Fremden*, pp.: 79—94. Klagenfurt/Celovec: Drava Verlag.

Miller, Daniel (1987, 1989). *Material Culture and Mass Consumption*. Oxford: Blackwell.

— (1995). "Consumption and Commodities." *Annual Review Anthropology*. 24: 141—61.

Mintz, Sidney W. (2003). "Eating Communities: the Mixed Appeals of Sodality." In Döring Tobias, Heide, Markus and Mühleisen, Susanne (eds.) *Eating Culture. The Poetics and Politics of Food*, pp.: 19-34. Heidelberg: Universitätsverlag Winter.

Min, Zhou (2004). "Transnational Entrepreneurship." *International Migration Review*. 38(3): 1040—1075.

Mittelberg, David and Borshevsky, Nikolay (2004). "National Minority, National Mentality, and Communal Ethnicity: Changes in Ethnic Identity of Former Soviet Union Jewish Emigrants on the Israeli Kibbutz." *International Migration*. 42(1): 89—114.

Möhring, Maren (2007). "Foreign Cuisine in West Germany." *GHI Bulletin*. 41: 79—88.

Morawska, Ewa (2003). "Disciplinary Agendas and Analytic Strategies of Research on Immigrant Transnationalism: Challenges of Interdisciplinary Knowledge." *International Migration Review*. 37(3): 611—640.

— (2003). "Immigrant Transnationalism and Assimilation: A Variety of Combinations and a Theoretical Model They Suggest." Joppke, Christian/Morawska, Ewa, (eds.) *Integrating Immigrant in Liberal Nation States*. London: Palgrave Press.

— (2004). "Exploring Diversity in Immigration Assimilation and Transnationalism: Poles and Russian Jews in Philadelphia." *International Migration Review*. 38(4): 1372—1413.

Morokvasic, Mirjana (2007). "Migration, Gender, Empowerment." In Lenz, Ilse, Ulrich, Charlotte and Fersch, Barbara (eds.). *Gender Orders Unbound. Globalization, Restructuring, and Reciprocity*. Opladen, pp.: 69—97. Farmington Hills: Barbara Budrich Publishers.

Murcott, Anne (1986). "'It's a pleasure to cook for him': Food, Meal times and Gender in some South Wales Households." In Gamarnikow, Eva Morgan, David H.J., Purvis, June, Taylorson, Daphne (eds.). *The Public and the Private*, pp.: 78—90. London: Gower.

— (1982). *The Sociology of Food. Essays on the Sociological Significance of Food*. Aldershot: Gower.

Nosenko, Elena (2004). *To be or to feel? Main patterns of Jewish self-identity among the offsprings of mixed marriages in today's Russia*. Moscow: IV RAN, Kraft.

Ohnuki-Tierney, Emiko (1993). *Rice as Self: Japanese Identities through Time*. Princeton: Princeton University Press.

Okun', Alexander and Guberman, Igor (2003). *Kniga o vkusnoi i sdorovoi zhisni* [The Tasty and Healthy Food Book]. Jerusalem: Gesharim—Mosty kultury and Tel Aviv: Sefer Israel.

Olwig, Fog Karen and Sorensen Nyberg, Ninna (2002). "Mobile Livelihoods: Making a Living in the World." In Olwig, Fog Karen and Sorensen Nyberg, Ninna (eds.) *Work and Migration: Life and Livelihood in a Globalizing World (Transnationalism)*, pp.: 1—19. London: Routledge.

Ortner, Sherry (1973). "Key Symbols." *American Anthropologist*. 75: 1338—1346.

Ostow, Robin (2003). "The Post-Soviet Immigrants and the Jüdische Allgemeine in the New Millennium: Post-Communism in Germany's Jewish Communities." *East European Jewish Affairs*. 33(2): 54—70.

Oswald, Ingrid (2000). *Die Nachfahren des "homo sovieticus." Ethnische Orientierung nach dem Zerfall der Sowjetunion*. Münster, New York, München, Berlin. (German)

Oswald, Ingrid and Voronkov, Viktor (2000). "Tricky Hermeneutics: Public and Private Viewpoints on Jewish Migration from Russia to Germany." In Breckner, Roswitha, Kalekin-Fishman, Deborah and Miethe, Ingrid (eds.). *Biographies and the Division of Europe. Experience, Action and Change on the "Eastern Side,"* pp.: 335—348. Opladen: Leske und Budrich.

Parkes, Stuart (2000). "German Society." In Allinson, M. (ed.). *Contemporary Germany: Essays and Texts on Politics, Economics, and Society*, pp.: 279—331. Great Britain: T. J. International Ltd., Padsow Comwall.

Pécoud, Antoine (2001). "*Weltoffenheit schafft Jobs: Turkish Entrepreneurship and Multiculturalism in Berlin*." Working Paper, Internet: WPTC-01-19, http://www.transcomm.ox.ac.uk, 21.06.2010.

Pessar, Patricia and Mahler, Sarah J. (2001). *Gender and Transnational Migration*. Working paper. http://www.transcomm.ox.ac.uk, 21.06.2010.

Polouektova, Ksenia (2009). "The Holocaust in Post-Soviet Russian History Text-books: Texts and Contexts, " paper held at the postgraduate conference *New Voices in Russian, East European and Eurasian Studies,* University Tel-Aviv, School of History, Kimmerling Institute for Russian and East European studies, 18-19.11.2009.

Portes, Alejandro, Haller, William and Guanizo, Luis E. (2002). "Transnational Entrepreneurs: The Emergence and Determinants of an Alternative Form of Immigrant Economic Adaptation." *American Sociological Review.* 67: 278—298.

Pries, Ludger (ed.) (1997). *Transnational Migration. Soziale Welten.* Sonderband 12. Baden-Baden.

Rapoport, Tamar, Lomsky-Feder, Edna and Heider, Angelika (2006). "Recollection and Relocation in Immigration: Russian-Jewish Immigrants 'Normalize' their Anti-Semitic Experience." In Gloeckner Oolaf, Garbolevsky Evgenija and von Mering Sabine (eds.) *Russian-Jewish Emigrants after the Cold War: Perspectives from Germany, Israel, Canada and the United States,* pp.: 76—102. Brandeis University: The Center for German and European Studies.

Razin, Eran and Scheinberg, Dan (2001). "Immigrant entrepreneurs from the former USSR in Israel: not the traditional enclave economy." *Journal of Ethnic and Migration Studies.* 27(2): 259—276.

Ray, Krishnendu (2004). *The Migrant's Table: Meals and Memories in Bengali-American Households.* Philadelphia: Temple University Press.

— (2008). "Nation and Cuisine: The Evidence from American Newspapers ca.1830—2003." *Food and Foodways.* 16: 1—39.

Reitemeier, Ulrich (2005). "Gute Gründe für schlechte Gesprächsverläufe. Sozial-arbeiterInnen in der Kommunikation mit Migranten", in Chirly dos Santos-Stubbe (ed.) *Interkulturelle Soziale Arbeit in der Theorie und Praxis,* Aachen: Schaker Verlag, S.: 83—104.

Remennick, Larissa (2005). "Idealists Headed to Israel, Pragmatics Chose Europe:" Identity Dilemmas and Social Incorporation among Former Soviet Jews who immigrated to Germany. *Immigrants and Minorities.* 23(1): 30—58.

— (2007). "Soviet Jews in the New/Old Homeland: Between Integration and Separatism." *Russian-Jewish Emigrants after the Cold War: Perspectives from Germany, Israel, Canada and the United States,* pp.: 69—75. Waltham, MA: The Center for German and European Studies, Brandeis University.

Resch, Christine and Steinert, Heinz (2003). *Die Widerständigkeit der Kunst. Entwurf einer Interaktions-Ästhetik.* Münster: Westfälisches Dampfboot.

Ritterband, Paul (1997). "Jewish Identity among Russian Immigrants in the United States." In Lewin-Epstein, Noah, Roi, Yaacov and Ritterband, Paul (eds.) *Russian Jews on Three Continents Migration and Resettlement,* pp.: 325—344. London: Frank Cass.

Rivkina, Rosalina (1996). *Jews in Post Soviet Russia How are they? Sociological Analysis of Jewish Problems in Russia,* Moscow: A.R.S.S.

Roberman, Svetlana (2005). *Reconstructing Israeli National Narrative: Soviet WWII Veterans Struggle to Belong.* Paper presented at the Van Leer Conference—Russians in Israel and Beyond. Jerusalem: June 2005.

— (2007). "Fighting to Belong: Soviet WWII Veterans in Israel." *Ethos.* 35(4): 447—477.

Roesler, Jörg (2005). "Massenkonsum in der DDR: zwischen egalitärem Anspruch, Herrschaftslegitimation und 'exquisiter' Individualisierung." *Prokla.* 138 (1): 35—52.

Römhild, Regina (2002). "Practised Imagination. Tracing Transnational networks in Crete and Beyond." Ina-Maria Greverus, Sharon Macdonald, Regina Römhild, Gisela Welz, Helena Wulff (eds.), *Shifting Grounds. Experiments in Doing Fieldwork in Anthropological Journal on European Cultures.* 11: 153—190.

Röhmhild, Regina, Abresch, Christian, Nietert, Michaela, Schmidt, Gunvor (2008). *Fast Food, Slow Food. Ethnographische Studien zum Verhältnis von Globalisierung und Regionalisierung in der Ernährung.* Institut für Kulturanthropologie und Europäische Ethnologie, Fachbereich Sprach- und Kulturwissenschaften, Johann Wolfgang Goethe Universität, Frankfurt am Main: Kulturanthropologie Notizen.

Salein, Kirsten (2005). "Was heisst Russisch? Portraits und Erkundigungen, im Rhein-Main-Gebiet." *Anthropolitan.* Heft 12.

Sandomirskaya, Irina (2004). "The Motherland (Rodina) in Soviet and Post-Soviet Discursive Practices." *Inter.* 2—3: 123—132.

Schäffter, Ortfried (1991). "Modi des Fremderlebens. Deutungsmuster im Umgang mit Fremdheit." In Schäffter, Ortfried (ed.): *Das Fremde. Erfahrungsmöglichkeiten zwischen Faszination und Bedrohung,* S.11—42. Opladen: Westdeutscher Verlag.

Schegloff, Emmanuel and Harvey, Sacks (1973). "Opening up Closings." *Semiotica.* 7: 289—327.

Shevchenko, Olga (2002). "'Between the Holes:' Emerging Identities and Hybrid Patterns of Consumption in Post-socialist Russia." *Europe-Asia Studies.* 54(6): 841—866.

Schiffauer, Werner (2003). "Kulturelle Zuschreibungen und Fremdethnisierungen." Margrit Fröhlich, Astrid Messerschmidt und Jörg Walter (Hgs.), *Migration als biographische und expressive Ressource. Beiträge zur kulturellen Produktion in der Einwanderungsgesellschaft,* Frankfurt a. Main, Brandes and Apsel Verlag, S. 151—161.

Schoeps, H. Julius, Jasper, Willi and Vogt, Bernhard (eds.), (1996). *Russische Juden in Deutschland.* Weinheim: Beltz AthenäumVerlag.

Schoeps, H., Julius, Jasper, Willi and Vogt Bernhard, (1999). *Ein neues Judentum in Deutschland?* Impressum, Potsdam Verlag für Berlin-Brandenbug.

Schroer, Markus (2004). *Raumnahme—Über die Aneignung von Räumen im Globalisierungsprozess.* Paper presented at the Conference: "welt.r@um.körper: Globalisierung, Technisierung, Sexualisierung von Raum und Körper." 14—17 Juni, Bad Bevensen, Germany.

Schütz, Alfred (1972). "Das Fremde." *Studien zur soziologischen Theorie. Gesammelte Aufsätze*, Bd.2, S. 53—69. Den Haag.

Schütze, Yvonne (2000). "Ich bin nur ein Jude und dann ein Russe." *Soziale Welt.* 51 (4): 303—324.

Schütze, Yvonne and Rapoport, Tamar (2000). "We are similar in what we are different: Social Relationships of Young Russian Jewish Immigrants in Israel and Germany." In Breckner, Roswita, Kalekin-Fishman, Deborah and Miethe, Ingrid (eds.). *Biographies and the Division of Europe. Experience, Action, and Change on the "Eastern Side,"* pp.: 349—366. Opladen: Leske and Budrich.

Schütze, Fritz (2002). "Das Konzept der sozialen Welt im symbolischen Interaktionismus und die Wissensorganisation in modernen Komplexgesellschaften." In Inken Keim und Wilfried Schütte (eds.) *Soziale Welten und kommunikative Stile*, pp.: 57—85. Tübingen.

— (2007). Interpretationswerkstatt im Rahmen der Workshop-Reihe "Methodologie und Methodik zentraler Ansätze qualitativer Sozialforschung." Internationales Promotions-Centrum, Fb Gesellschaftswissenschaften, Johann Wolfgang Goethe-Universität Frankfurt am Main.

Schweid, Eliezer (1994). "Changing Jewish Identities in the new Europe and the Consequences for Israel." In Jonathan Webber (ed.) *Jewish Identities in the New Europe*, London: Littman Library of Jewish Civilization.

Sen, Amartya (1999). *Reason before Identity,* Oxford: Oxford University Press.

Shimron, Daphne (2002). "Israelisches Essen." In Gisela Dachs (ed.) *Vom Essen Jüdisches Almanach des Leo Baeck Instituts*, Jüdischer Verlag im Suhrkamp Verlag, S. 71—78.

Shternshis, Anna (2006). *Soviet and Kosher. Jewish Popular Culture in the Soviet Union 1923—1939,* Bloomington and Indianapolis: Indiana University Press.

Sivolap, Igor (1952). (ed.) *Kniga o Vkusnoi i Zdorovoi Pishche,* [The Tasty and Healthy Food Book] published by the USSR Ministry of Food Industry, approved by the Nutritional Committee of the USSR Academy of Medical Sciences, Moscow, Pishchepromizdat.

Slezkine, Yuri (1996). "The USSR as a Communal Apartment or How a Socialist State Promoted Ethnic Particularism." in Eley, Geoff and Suny Ronald G. (eds.) *Becoming National.* New York and Oxford: Oxford University Press.

— (2004). *The Jewish Century.* Princeton University Press, Princeton and Oxford.

Slezkine, Yuri (2005). *Era Merkuriya. Yevrei v sovremennom mire.* (Translation in Russian of *The Jewish Century*). Moscow: Novoe Literaturnoe Obozrenie.

Smedley, Andrey and Smedley, Brian D. (2005). "Race as Biology is Fiction, Racism as a Social Problem is Real. Anthropological and Historical Perspectives on the Social Construction of Race." *American Psychologist,* pp.: 16—25. http://www.apa.org/journals/releases/amp60116.pdf, 21.06.2010.

Smith, Michael Peter (2003). "Transnationalism, the State, and the Extraterritorial Citizen." *Politics* and *Society.* 31(4): 467—502.

Smith, Robert (2001). "Comparing Local-level Swedish and Mexican Transnational Life: An Essay in Historical Retrieval", Pries, Ludger. (ed.), *New Transnational Social Spaces: International Migration and Transnational Companies in the Early Twenty-First Century*, pp.: 55—74. London: Routledge.

— (1998). "Transnational Localities: Community, Technology and the Politics of Membership within the Context of Mexico and U.S. Migration." *Transnationalism from Below, Comparative Urban and Community Research*. 6: 196—238.

Starr Sered, Susan (1988). "Food and Holiness: Cooking as a Sacred Act among Middle-Eastern Jewish Women." *Anthropological Quarterly*. 61: 129—39.

— (1992). *Women as Ritual Experts: The Religious Lives of Elderly Jewish Women in Jerusalem*. Oxford: Oxford University Press.

Stender, Wolfram (2000). "Ethnische Erweckung. Zum Funktionswandel von Ethnizität in modernen Gesellschaften—Literaturbericht." *Mittelweg*. 36(4): 65—82.

Stöckel, Andrea (2001). "Rezension zu Nils Zurawski (2000) Virtuelle Ethnizität.Studien zu Identität, Kultur und Internet." *Forum: Qualitative Social Research*. (Online Journal), 2(2), http://www.qualitative-research.net/fqs-texte/2-01/2-01review-stoeck/-d.htm, 21.06.2010.

Stolping, E. (2000). "The East of Europe: A Historical Construction." In Breckner Roswitha, Kalekin-Fishman, Deborah and Miethe, Ingrid (eds.). *Biographies and the Division of Europe, Experiences, Action, and Change on the "Eastern Side,"* pp.: 139—158. Opladen: Leske and Budrich.

Stonequist, Everett V. (1935). "The Problem of the Marginal Man." *The American Journal of Sociology*. 41(1): 1—12.

— (1937). *The Marginal Man: A Study in Personality and Cultural Conflict*. New York: Charles Scribner's Sons.

Strauss, Anselm and Corbin, Juliet (1990). *Basics of Qualitative Research. Grounded Theory Procedures and Techniques*. New Bury Park, London, New Delphi: Sage Publications.

Strüver, Anke (2005). "Spheres of Transnationalism Within the European Union: On Open Doors, Thresholds, and Drawbridges Along the Dutch-German Border." *Journal of Ethnic and Migration Studies*. 31(2): 323—343.

Sutton, David (2001). *Remembrance of Repasts: An Anthropology of Food and Memory*. Oxford: Berg.

Tempest, Snehana (1997). "Stovelore in Russian Folklife." In Glants, Musya and Toomre, Joyce (eds.) *Food in Russian History and Culture*, pp.: 1—18. Bloomington and Indianapolis: Indiana University Press.

Tress, Madeleine (1995). "Soviet Jews in the Federal Republic of Germany: The Rebuilding of the Community." *Jewish Journal of Sociology*. 37(1): 39—54.

Turner, Victor (1986). "Betwixt and Between: The Liminal Period in *Rites de Passage*." In *The Forest of Symbols*, pp.: 93—111. Ithaca, NY: Cornell University Press.

Vallianatos, Helen and Raine, Kim. (2008). "Consuming Food and Constructing Identities among Arabic and South Asian Immigrant Women." *Food, Culture and Society: An International Journal of Multidisciplinary Research.* 11 (3): 355—373.

Van Gennep, Arnold (1909, 1960). *The Rites of Passage.* Chicago: University of Chicago Press.

Verdery, Katherine (1996). *What Was Socialism and What Comes Next?* Princeton, New Jersey: Princeton University Press.

Vertovec, Steven (2004). "Migrant Transnationalism and Modes of Transformation." *International Migration Review.* 38(3): 970—1002.

Volovikova, M., Tichomirova, S., and Borisova, (2003). *Psychologia i prasdnik: Prasdnik v zhisni cheloveka* [Psychology and holiday. The place of holiday in human lives], Moscow: Perse. Voronkov, Viktor (2000). "Is there such a Thing as Ethnic Economy?" In: Brednikova Olga, Voronkov Victor *Ethnic Economy in Post-Socialist Space.* Collection of Articles. CISR. Working Papers, №8. St. Petersburg, 128, (Online) http://www.indepsocres.spb.ru, 21.06.2010.

Wang, Lu and Lo, Lucia (2007). "Immigrant Grocery-Shopping Behavior: Ethnic Identity Versus Accessibility." *Environment and Planning.* 39: 584—699.

Webber, Jonathan (1994). "Modern Jewish Identities." In Webber Jonathan (ed.) *Jewish Identities in the New Europe,* pp.: 74—85. London: Littman Library for Jewish Civilization.

Weber, Max (1980)[1922]. "Ethnische Gemeinschaftsbeziehungen." In Max Weber *Wirtschaft und Gesellschaft. Grundriss einer verstehenden Soziologie,* S. 234—244. Tübingen: Verlag für Sozialwissenschaften.

Weinerman, Eli (1997). "Does the Country Gain or Lose from the Exodus of Jews? The Discussion in Russian Society." In Lewin-Epstein, Noah, Roi, Yaacov and Ritterband, Paul (eds.) *Russian Jews on Three Continents Migration and Resettlement,* pp: 194—222. London: Frank Cass.

Weingart, Peter, Kroll, Jürgen und Bayertz, Kurt (1992). *Rasse, Blut und Gene. Geschichte der Eugenik und Rassenhygiene in Deutschland.* Frankfurt am Main: Suhrkamp Taschenbuch.

Welz, Gisela (1994). "Die soziale Organisation kultureller Differenz. Zur Kritik des Ethnosbegriffs in der anglo-amerikanischen Kulturanthropologie." In Berding, Helmut (Hg.), *Nationales Bewusstsein und kollektive Identität. Studien zur Entwicklung des kollektiven Bewusstseins in der Neuzeit 2,* S. 66—81. Frankfurt am Main: Suhrkamp.

— (1996). *Inszenierungen kultureller Vielfalt.* Frankfurt am Main und New York, Berlin.

— (2000). "Wo sich neun sattessen, werden auch zehn besiegt. Das Mesedessyndrom: Mutationen einer nahrungskulturellen Praxis." In Institut für Europäische Ethnologie der Universität Wien (ed.): *Volkskultur und Moderne. Europäische Ethnologie zur Jahrtausendwende. Festschrift für Konrad Köstin zum 60. Geburstag am 8.Mai 2000,* S. 169—178. Wien.

Wilk, Richard, D. (1999). "Real Belizean Food: Building Local Identity in the Transnational Caribbean." *American Anthropologist.* 101(2): 244—255.

Williams, Brett (1985). "Why Migrant Women Feed Their Husband Tamales: Foodways as a Basis for a Revisionist View of Tejano Family Life." In Linda Keller Brown and Kay Mussell (eds.). *Ethnic and Regional Foodways in the United States. The Performance of Group Identity,* pp.: 113—127. Knoxville: University of Tennessee Press.

Wimmer, Andreas and Glick Schiller, Nina (2003). "Methodological Nationalism, the Social Sciences and Study of Migration: An Essay in historical Epistemology." *International Migration Review.* 37(3): 576—610.

Wolffsohn, Michael and Bokovoy, Douglas (2003). *Israel. Grundwissen—Länderkunde Geschichte, Politik, Gesellschaft, Wirtschaft (1882—2001).* Opladen: Leske und Budrich.

Yelenevskaya, Maria (2005). "A Cultural Diaspora in the Making: Former Soviets in Israel and in Germany." *Jews and Slavs. Judeo-Bulgarika, Judeo-Russica et Palaeoslavica. Jerusalem-Sofia.* 15: 265—279.

Yelenevskaya, Maria and Fialkova, Larisa (2004). "My poor cousin, my feared enemy: the image of Arabs in personal narratives of former Soviets in Israel." *Folklore.* 115(1): 77—98.

— (2005). *My Aliya: Personal Naratives of Soviet Jews in Israel.* Guest lecture presented at the University of Basel, January 26, http://www.jewishstudies.unibas.ch/dateien/Yelenevskaya%20Basel%20Jan05.pdf, 21.06.2010.

Yuval-Davis, Nira (2006). "Belonging and the Politics of Belonging." *Patterns of Prejudice* 40(3): 196—213.

Zaslavsky, Tatyana and Horowitz, Tamar (2007). "Young non-Jewish immigrants in Israel." Paper presented at the international conference *Ethnicity, Belonging, Biography and Ethnography.* Georg August Universität, Göttingen, Germany.

Zilberg, Narspi (2002). "Russikie yevrei v ierusalime: kulturnye kody i manifestatsiya etnichnosti." [Russian Jews in Jerusalem: cultural codes and manifestation of identity] *Vremya iskat,':* 141—162, (Online) http://www.teena.org.il/index.php?a=st&id=151, 21.06.2010.

Index

Social Science

Fritz W. Scharpf
Community and Autonomy
Institutions, Policies and Legitimacy in Multilevel Europe
2010, 391 pages, ISBN 978-3-593-39188-5

Debra Hopkins, Jochen Kleres,
Helena Flam, Helmut Kuzmics (eds.)
Theorizing Emotions
Sociological Explorations and Applications
2009, 343 pages, ISBN 978-3-593-38972-1

Walter R. Heinz, Johannes Huinink, Ansgar Weymann (eds.)
The Life Course Reader
Individuals and Societies Across Time
2009, 591 pages, ISBN 978-3-593-38805-2

Klaus Schlichte
In the Shadow of Violence
The Politics of Armed Groups
2009, 256 pages, ISBN 978-3-593-38817-5

Cornelia Bruell, Monika Mokre, Markus Pausch (eds.)
Democracy Needs Dispute
The Debate on the European Constitution
2009, 193 pages, ISBN 978-3-593-38820-5

Svea Luise Herrmann
Policy Debates on Reprogenetics
The Problematisation of New Research in Great Britain and Germany
2009, 240 pages, ISBN 978-3-593-38792-5

campus

Mehr Informationen unter
www.campus.de/wissenschaft

Frankfurt · New York